RAIDERS AND REBELS

DE FOE.

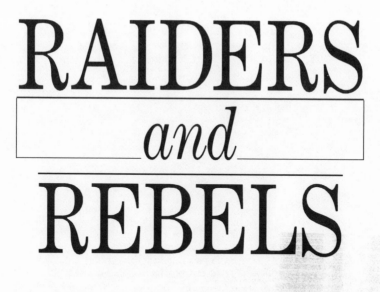

RAIDERS
and
REBELS

The Golden Age
of Piracy

Frank Sherry

HEARST MARINE BOOKS
New York

Library of Congress Cataloging-in-Publication Data

Sherry, Frank, 1934–
Raiders and rebels.

Bibliography: p.
Includes index.
1. Pirates.   I. Title.
G535.S53   1986   364.1'64   85-21943
ISBN 0-688-04684-3

Printed in the United States of America

First Edition

3 4 5 6 7 8 9 10

BOOK DESIGN BY RICHARD ORIOLO

*This book
is for
Su*

Author's Note

The era covered in this narrative—roughly from 1690 through the 1720s—has sometimes been called "The Golden Age of Piracy." This is because, during those decades, the world experienced the most intense outbreak of seaborne banditry ever recorded.

This book is an attempt to give an account of the main events of that enormous eruption of piracy—and to portray the often-outsized personalities who played the chief roles in it.

Although our present-day knowledge of the pirates of that era derives from relatively few original sources, there has been no dearth of scholarly books in the past on pirates and piracy. I have naturally relied upon many of them in assembling the *facts* of my own narrative—and they are acknowledged fully in the bibliography accompanying this book.

I have, however, made it my particular task in *this* account to try to lay bare the chain of cause and effect that created the piracy—and shaped the pirates—of that explosive epoch. I have also sought to relate the incidents of the great pirate outbreak to the vast historical movements that were taking place during the decades covered in these pages. In brief, I have tried to present the pirate outbreak—accurately, I believe—as a series of linked events, a coherent *story*, rather than as a jumble of outlandish characters who all just happened to be engaged in outrageous acts of piracy in the same period.

I have also endeavored to suggest in this account that there were often reasons other than mere lust for wealth that caused men and women to choose the pirate life.

Finally, I should point out that the reader need not possess any special knowledge of, or interest in, the sea or its lore in order to gain a full appreciation of the story told in this volume. For although this story is *incidentally* about ships and the sea, it is *primarily* about human beings in conflict with themselves, with each other, and with their times. It is also a tale made all the more fascinating because it really happened.

Contents

Illustrations

ILLUSTRATIONS

RAIDERS AND REBELS

Our Lady of the Cape

Approximately four hundred miles due east of Madagascar, the French-ruled island of Réunion lies like an emerald chip in the vastness of the Indian Ocean.

Here, on Sunday, April 26, 1721, a Portuguese merchant ship, *Nossa Senhora Do Cabo—Our Lady of the Cape*—rode at anchor under a blazing tropical sun.

The *Cabo*, a sturdy vessel of 700 tons—160 feet long and 34 feet at the beam—had taken shelter in the island's peaceful harbor after losing her mainmast in a storm.

The *Cabo*, armed with twenty-one cannon, and carrying a crew of 130 tough sailors and gunners, was normally a formidable craft and a swift sailer. Minus the spire of her mast, however, she seemed a clumsy cripple on the glittering, almost transparent, water of the harbor.

Before the storm had interrupted her journey, the *Cabo* had been bound from the Portuguese colony of Goa, on the southwest coast of India, to Lisbon, a voyage of more than a hundred days that would take her more than 12,500 miles, across the Indian Ocean, around the Cape of Good Hope, and then northward home.

While riding the ocean currents east of Madagascar, however, the *Cabo* had run into a fierce gale that had fractured her mast. She had limped into the nearest safe anchorage for repairs.

Now, even though it was the Sabbath, the ship's carpenters and crew labored urgently in the steamy heat to rig a new mast. Their haste stemmed from the fact that the *Cabo* was carrying a most eminent and powerful passenger who was extremely anxious for the *Cabo* to get under way again as soon as possible.

This passenger was His Excellency Dom Luis Carlos Ignacio Xavier de Meneses, Count of Ericeira and Marquis of Lourical, who was returning to Portugal after many years of service as viceroy of Goa.

The retiring viceroy had good reason for his anxiety, for the *Cabo* was not only carrying her own rich cargo of Oriental silks, textiles, spices, and porcelains, she was also carrying Dom Luis's personal fortune: chests brimming with diamonds, exotic Indian art, and precious illuminated manuscripts. Dom Luis calculated that the diamonds alone would command a worth of more than £500,000—an enormous sum in the purchasing power of the day. The art treasures and manuscripts were beyond price.

In addition to his own diamonds, Dom Luis carried a consignment of gems destined for the coffers of the Portuguese king, as well as a smaller number intended for a consortium of merchants in Lisbon.

For Dom Luis, who had obtained this wealth through a series of shrewd purchases made during his tenure as viceroy, the chests of diamonds were the keys that would unlock a future of glory and ease. The king, he anticipated, would delight in his treasures from India, and would subsequently bestow his warmest favor on Dom Luis and his family. With the royal patronage secured, Dom Luis planned to make his name great in Portugal. He would sell most of his own diamonds and with the proceeds rebuild his family's estates, which had fallen into disrepair. He would live the rest of his days surrounded by magnificence. The realization of this vision of the glorious future, however, depended upon the *Cabo*'s reaching home safely. Until he saw Lisbon again with his treasure intact, the former viceroy of Goa could not rest easy.

It was for this reason that Dom Luis himself—a proud slim figure in a scarlet waistcoat belted with a jeweled sword—watched fretfully from the quarterdeck as the repairs to the *Cabo* proceeded on that humid April Sunday.

It was for this reason, too, that Dom Luis felt an upsurge of anxiety when one of the *Cabo*'s crewmen suddenly called out that two strange sails had appeared on the horizon.

Nervously Dom Luis popped open his glass and examined the two strangers. Clearly they were making for the island. As the newcomers approached, Dom Luis could see that one of them was an East Indiaman—a merchant vessel like the *Cabo*—while the other was a mere brig.

Dom Luis sighed with relief when he made out the British flags flying from both the approaching vessels, and the plain, honest faces of their crewmen visible on deck. Satisfied that these were ships of the British East India Company, probably on their way to trade with the Great Mogul, the Portuguese viceroy prepared to fire a salute to the oncoming Englishmen, as courtesy required. Perhaps he would even invite their officers aboard the *Cabo* when they had anchored and refreshed themselves.

As Dom Luis continued to observe the British ships, however, uneasiness began to creep into the pit of his stomach. He saw now that the two strangers were not anchoring after all. Instead they were bearing down menacingly on the helpless *Cabo*.

Dom Luis watched with alarm as the larger ship slid smoothly into position alongside the *Cabo*'s port beam, while the brig ranged in close to starboard. Then alarm swelled to terror as the British ensigns that the strangers had been flying suddenly fluttered down—and black flags rose in their place, grim white skulls snapping in the wind.

Now pandemonium broke out aboard the *Cabo* as her officers and crewmen, all at once aware of their mortal danger, sprinted to defend their disabled ship.

But it was too late. A flash of orange fire, accompanied by a thunderous roar, erupted over the *Cabo* as the pirate vessels fired.

The *Cabo* shuddered under the impact. Wooden splinters flew through the air like lethal shards. Wounded men screamed. Dense black smoke billowed over the decks. Then, shouting oaths in barbaric English and French, two hundred wild-eyed cutthroats, like demons from Hell itself, swarmed onto the *Cabo's* deck from both pirate ships.

Firing muskets at point-blank range, and slashing at all who resisted, the pirates routed the *Cabo's* defenders in the first moments of the onslaught. Some of the *Cabo's* crewmen deserted to the pirates. The rest—including officers—realized they were overwhelmed, and threw up their hands in surrender. The *Cabo* belonged to the pirates.

But Dom Luis refused to surrender so easily. With his jeweled sword in hand, he launched himself recklessly into the midst of the outlaws, as if he no longer valued his life now that fate had demolished his dream of future splendor. With his gaudy scarlet coat flying, Dom Luis fought a desperate hand-to-hand combat against the astounded brigands who had taken his ship.

Roaring with anger, the surprised outlaws slashed furiously at Dom Luis, who expertly parried their thrusts until his ceremonial sword shattered and he could no longer defend himself.

Surrounded by a ring of cursing, sweating villains, Dom Luis must have expected cold steel in his heart. Instead, upon a gruff command in English, the circle of pirates around him parted, and Dom Luis came face to face with a burly, dark-visaged man who wore a tricornered hat and carried a brace of pistols in his wide belt—the pirate chieftain himself.

With a sardonic grin and a mock bow, the pirate captain returned Dom Luis's broken sword, making it clear to the Portuguese nobleman that his life had been spared—at least temporarily—in recognition of his gallant resistance.

Held captive on the *Cabo's* foredeck, Dom Luis could only look on in helpless anguish as the pirates began to loot their prize. Soon the decks were piled with chests of diamonds, bales of silks, barrels of spices, and mounds of Dom Luis's precious books and works of art.

The outlaws whooped with raucous joy at the enormous treasure they had found. Throughout the night they ransacked the *Cabo*, celebrating their great luck by drinking huge quantities of liquor and firing off their muskets. The captive Dom Luis must have writhed in fury when the pirates, seeing no value in his infidel manuscripts and artworks, used these priceless materials to provide a festive light for the *Cabo's* deck, and as wadding for their jubilant musketry.

Ashore in his residence overlooking the harbor, the French governor did nothing to stop the rape of the *Cabo*. The island, which was at best a French layover station for ships bound for India, possessed no forces sufficient to contend with the brazen pirates in the harbor. Moreover, the governor knew he had to tread carefully when it came to dealing with pirate raiders because many retired pirates lived under French pardons in his little colony and might revert to their old, dangerous ways if provoked. Finally, it was not altogether displeasing to the governor to see a Portuguese ship in these dire straits. Portugal was, after all, a rival of France in the struggle for commercial and political domination of the Indian Ocean.

And so the pirates who had seized the *Cabo* collected their spoil unhindered. When they had gathered all they thought valuable, they calculated that their take would exceed £800,000—an incredible haul.[1]

Impelled to generosity by good fortune, the pirate leader, a hitherto obscure English marauder named John Taylor, proposed to his crew that they grant the brave Dom Luis not only his life but his freedom by setting him ashore.

Some of Taylor's men objected to the proposal. They argued that in accordance with the usual pirate custom, Dom Luis, as a high-ranking noble, should be taken to the Portuguese colony of Mozambique and there be offered for a suitably high ransom. But others in Taylor's crew argued that they had gained more than enough wealth from the *Cabo*—and they should now prudently make for safe waters as soon as possible.

In the end Taylor's crew came to a compromise, agreeing to sell Dom Luis and their other prisoners to the French governor of the island for a nominal ransom of £400. They had concluded, according to one witness, that "t'were better to take a smaller sum than to be troubled further."

On the morning after the *Cabo*'s capture, therefore, the pirate captain, with derisive ceremony—including a viceregal twenty-one-gun salute from his ship, the *Cassandra*, and shouts of "*Vive le roi!*" from his crew—put Dom Luis ashore in a longboat decorated with the ex-viceroy's own banners.

Then Taylor and his men, with their prize, set sail for the open sea.

When it came time for a final tally and share-out of the spoils,

Taylor and his crew reckoned that the loot from the *Cabo*, together with plunder from prizes taken earlier, amounted to more than £1 million. Each of Taylor's men received more than £4,000, plus forty-two diamonds from Dom Luis's chests—gigantic wealth at a time when honest sailors earned only £1 or £2 per month.

Taylor and his crew were never caught.[2]

Dom Luis, on the other hand, despite his gallantry, paid a hard price for the *Cabo* debacle. The Portuguese monarch blamed him for the loss of the ship and the diamonds and refused to receive his ex-viceroy at the royal court. Only after ten years had passed was Dom Luis allowed into the presence of his king. He never regained his fortune or his king's favor, but he did gain an immortal place in the annals of the sea—as the victim of the largest single pirate strike ever recorded.

The *Cabo*'s ordeal, aside from the immensity of the booty involved, was characteristic of hundreds of such hostile encounters that took place yearly in that turbulent time of seaborne lawlessness. For the *Cabo* met with her fate during the longest and most intense outburst of piracy the world has ever experienced, when thousands of reckless, daring men—and a number of women as well—ranged the seas of the globe plundering the merchant fleets of the maritime countries.

For thirty-three years—roughly between 1692 and 1725—these pirate raiders, declared enemies of the whole world, terrorized the sea-lanes, disrupted commerce, and threatened the advance of a nascent western imperialism, while fighting off all efforts to exterminate them. In effect, the pirates of that era made war against the civilized world for a third of a century.

In the course of their war, fought over millions of square miles of ocean from Madagascar to the Bahamas to the steamy west coast of Africa, the pirate outlaws became fused into a loose-knit but powerful confederacy—a rough-and-ready republic of rebels, robbers, and rovers.

The pirates also evolved an original and lurid style of life that has become a familiar part of the lore of the western world.

Rum-soaked villains gripping cutlasses in their teeth as they board a helpless victim, swashbuckling captains engaged in flashing swordplay, captives forced to walk the plank, marooned traitors, swaggering earringed mates with a brace of pistols in their belts, chests of glittering gold, deserted tropic isles where fortunes in loot lie buried, the sinister Jolly Roger suddenly grinning from a mast as a swift black hull cuts through the ocean swell—all these images have become inextricably associated with the treasure-hunting pirates of the late seventeenth and early eighteenth centuries.

Yet many of these popular images are false. Few captains were swashbucklers. No pirate captives ever walked the plank. Real pirates *spent* their loot. They seldom buried it, even for a short time.

Further, while it is true that the pirates of that era sought to take the treasure of their foes, it was not for treasure alone that the pirate brotherhood waged its war on the world. Most pirates also fought to avenge themselves on an oppressive civilization that they hated and feared. But above all, the rebellious seafarers of that day turned outlaw in order to live as free men in an age that permitted liberty only to the wealthy and the well-born.

The story of the pirate war against the world begins in 1692 with a fateful voyage eastward.

1

The Opening Gun:
The Cruise of the *Amity*

Captain Thomas Tew, of Newport, Rhode Island, was an easygoing, sociable man in his fifties who doted on his loving wife and two charming daughters.[1]

Slim, clean-shaven, and of middle height, Captain Tew usually wore his longish hair in a beribboned queue—as many seafaring men did in the late seventeenth century—although in most other respects he dressed in the style of a prosperous merchant.

Born of a good Rhode Island family, Captain Tew was liked and respected by his Newport neighbors even though he did have the seaman's bad habit of bursting into salty language whenever the spirit moved him—which was often.

Affable and cordial of manner, Captain Tew relished nothing so much as a dinner of turkey and venison with friends at a tavern, followed by a long-stemmed pipe, a noggin of rum, and a convivial evening of storytelling before a comfortable fire.

But this fond father and jolly companion was also a tough and experienced "privateer" who, by the year 1692, had already enjoyed a long and profitable, if unspectacular, career in the service of England.

Generally speaking, privateers were "civilians"—privately owned vessels that governments commissioned in time of war, by special "letters of marque," to attack and capture the shipping of enemy nations.

Although theoretically privateers might, under some circumstances, serve as auxiliaries to regular naval forces, their chief role was to raid the commerce of the enemy. For the most part privateers avoided hostile naval vessels, preying instead on the more or less helpless merchant ships that fell under their guns.

Some maritime states, Spain most notably, regarded privateering as no more than a form of legalized piracy.

During her numerous long wars with England, Spain had suffered greatly at the hands of privateers. Well-armed raiders—based both in England and her American colonies—had found easy pickings among the rich and clumsy Spanish fleets that plied the West Indies. As a result, the Spanish usually refused to recognize privateering commissions—and claimed the right to hang privateers as *piratas* whenever and wherever they might capture one of these independent operators.

Despite the attitude of the Spanish and a few critics and lawyers, privateer captains—as well as those who outfitted and backed their enterprises—hotly defended privateering as legitimate warfare, not piracy. Pirates, they argued, sailed "on their own account," and against all flags, while privateers sailed in the service of their sovereign. If there was profit to be gained thereby, well, so much the better.

Captain Tew of Newport, amiable as he was on most subjects, certainly resented any suggestion that he was in any sense a pirate. He could point out, in his own defense, that in all his long career he had never fired on any but the king's enemies. Nor had he ever undertaken a mission without proper papers, or lacking the authorization of His Majesty's government.

For such as Captain Tew, privateering was a lawful pursuit, honored by custom, sustained by profit.

This assertion was heartily supported by the majority of the merchants, bankers, and governors of England's colonies in North America. For many of these gentry, in fact, privateering had become an almost essential enterprise, as well as a lucrative one. This was largely due to the policy of the English government with regard to trade with the American colonies.

Beginning in 1651, England had adopted a series of laws that became known as the Navigation Acts. In sum, these laws required English colonies to sell their goods only to England, and to import only English goods, at prices set by English merchants. Further, the Navigation Acts stipulated that all trade between England and her colonies be carried on in English or colonial ships manned by subjects of the Crown.

Because of the Navigation Acts, England was able to monopolize virtually all trade with her North American colonies. The effect of this enforced traffic on colonial merchants and consumers, however, was pernicious. The colonies could sell their tobacco, farm products, and other commodities only to London brokers at prices lower than they might command in other markets, while they had to buy English manufactured goods at higher-than-free-market prices. In addition, cargoes from England were subject to customs duties that added even more to their costs in the colonies, and non-English manufactures could not be imported except in English vessels and through English merchants. As a result, many items, especially luxuries such as silks, spices, perfumes, and the like, were vastly overpriced or simply not available in the colonies.

To compensate for this inequity, and to procure otherwise-unobtainable goods, colonial merchants, with the active cooperation of governors, port officials, and the general population, provided a "black market" for privateers—and a few admitted pirates as well—to dispose of their plunder. In colonial cities all along the Atlantic coast, privateer loot was "imported" in defiance of the Navigation Acts and resold openly. In almost every colonial port, privateers could be sure that they would not only find buyers for their booty but also obtain hospitality, provisions, protection, and crewmen for future enterprises. Very often the same merchants and officials who furnished the illegal market for privateer plunder also outfitted expeditions in exchange for guaranteed shares in a ship's loot. If the selling of privateer loot was against the king's law, it was not against the law of the sea, or the law of supply and demand. If the more righteous in colonial society regarded privateering with suspicion, they had no compunction about buying the luxuries that privateers made available.

To the dealers in privateer plunder, Captain Thomas Tew was a much-valued colleague. From Newport to Boston to New York, the trim and jaunty captain had, in the course of his professional pursuits, won a reputation as a fine seaman, a steady leader of men, a man you could rely upon to carry out a task—and, above all, a man of business, a man who would always bring home a rich cargo for sale.

But in 1692, privateers like Captain Tew, as well as his merchant partners, had fallen upon hard times. England, in a sudden reversal of her long-term policy, had concluded a peace with her old archenemy, Spain, and was now at war with France. Suddenly the days of the easy scores on the Spanish Main were gone. Profitable French cargoes were scarce in western waters, and French men-of-war were far more formidable than the Spanish had been.

Then, in the spring of 1692, a consortium of tradesmen and government officials in the Crown Colony of Bermuda hit on an idea that might restore their depleted fortunes: a very special, secret privateering venture. They offered the leadership of this clandestine enterprise, as well as a large share of the spoils, to Captain Thomas Tew of Newport.

After going to Bermuda, hearing the proposal of his backers in detail, and inspecting the 70-ton sloop *Amity* that the Bermudians proposed to arm and provision for the venture, Captain Tew accepted the proffered commission.

Over the succeeding weeks and months he oversaw preparations for the voyage. He personally recruited a crew of sixty veteran privateers—tough old dogs who had sailed with him in the past. Tew told his men that *Amity* had been chartered by the English Royal African Company to carry out a raid on a French trading post on the western coast of Africa. He assured them that at the end of the cruise, there would be "great spoils" to share out. This was a crucial point, since the only wage that privateer crews received was a share of the plunder, which might amount to a considerable sum on a successful cruise.

When *Amity* was ready to sail, Captain Tew, meticulous as ever in obtaining legal license for his enterprises, made sure that his backers purchased a commission from Governor Isaac Richier of Bermuda, authorizing *Amity* to act as a privateer against French shipping. Without such a warrant, he said, he would refuse to take *Amity* to sea.

In December 1692, duly commissioned as a privateer in English service, the *Amity*—with her eight cannon gleaming and all flags flying—set sail eastward.

At the outset of her cruise, *Amity* was joined by another privateer vessel under a Captain George Dew of Bermuda. Privateering ships often sailed together for mutual aid and greater firepower against an armed enemy. But *Amity*'s companion, damaged in a storm, soon returned to Bermuda. *Amity* continued on alone into the Atlantic.

Although he and his backers had given out that *Amity* was making for Africa, in reality Captain Tew had a different destination, and a much different mission, in mind. It was a venture, Tew recognized, that would require the consent by democratic vote of *Amity*'s crew in order to succeed. Accordingly, when *Amity* was far out to sea, Captain Tew assembled his entire crew on deck to explain to them the daring idea that he and his backers had conceived.

Raiding a French trading post in Africa was all very well, he told his grizzled crewmen, but it would be a difficult task. Furthermore, whatever profit it might bring, the greater part would go to the gentlemen of the Royal African Company who had, supposedly, chartered *Amity*. On the other hand, he said, he had heard tales that beyond Africa, in the Indian Ocean, the Muslim infidels transported wealth past measure in slow and clumsy vessels that resolute men might easily capture. If they possessed the will and daring, Captain Tew told his crew, he would lead them on a course to ease and plenty for the rest of their days. Further, he promised, they could accomplish their purpose in one bold stroke—and with only slight danger. They would return home, he promised, not only rich but famous.

Nor was it true piracy, he reassured his veterans, to take treasure from the infidel enemies of Christendom. Besides, they were protected by a license from the king's own governor.

The crew acclaimed Tew's proposition, crying out: "A gold chain, or a wooden leg, we'll stand by you."

At this, Captain Tew set a course for the East, beyond the Cape of Good Hope, where infidel ships carried cargoes of gold and gems for the taking.

In reality, the tale that Captain Tew had told his men about the fabled riches of India was not much exaggerated.

The Great Mogul—whose ships Captain Tew intended to

hunt—was the Muslim ruler of India. Claiming descent from Genghis Khan (hence the name Mogul, as a corruption of *Mongol*), the Mogul hordes had conquered Hindu India in the 1520s. By the middle of the sixteenth century, these Muslim invaders from the north had consolidated their power in India. The Mogul rule over the numerous divided peoples of India was a period of matchless splendor and opulence. It was also a time of magnificent artistic achievements—among them the Taj Mahal, built in memory of a favorite wife by the fifth Great Mogul, Shah Jahan.

No western monarch—not even Louis XIV—could begin to match the grandeur and wealth of the Mogul empire. The Great Mogul issued his decrees from the radiant Peacock Throne, a golden imperial seat studded with rubies, pearls, diamonds, and emeralds—and surmounted by a golden canopy dripping with jewels.

The sixth Great Mogul, Aurangzeb, who sat upon the Peacock Throne in the 1690s, was the owner of one of the most famous diamonds in history, the 280-carat Koh-i-noor, the "Mountain of Light." European travelers to Aurangzeb's court reported that the Great Mogul annually received as personal tribute from his subjects more than £3 million.

But the wealth of the Great Mogul did not derive solely from the tribute of his subjects. The Muslim Moguls of India carried on a lively and lucrative trade with the Arab world. Fleets of Mogul ships incessantly crossed the Indian Ocean to the Arab ports of the Persian Gulf and Red Sea with cargoes of spices, ivory, silks, drugs, perfumes, and precious stones, returning with chests of gold and silver, the fruit of their commerce.

These Mogul vessels were extremely vulnerable. Large and slow, their armament was scanty, and their cannoneers and soldier guards poorly trained by European standards. Because of their vulnerability, and the vast loot possible, the ships of the Great Mogul had long been targets of native Indian Ocean pirates, as well as occasional pirates from western nations. Although a plague and a costly vexation to the Mogul merchant fleets, the sea raiders who had preyed in eastern waters up till now had never seriously disrupted Mogul commerce.

But all that was about to be changed by a chain of events set off by the cruise of a little colonial privateer named *Amity*.

It was April 1693 when *Amity* entered the Indian Ocean and headed north toward the Red Sea. Aboard her hopes were high for a quick kill. But anticipation of a rapid score soon evaporated as *Amity* began to search these strange, warm seas for the rich prize pledged by her master.

Day after day, under a broiling sun, *Amity* scoured the sea routes between Arabia and India, seeking suitable prey. Through storms that threatened to tear the rigging to shreds, and through sultry calms, *Amity* searched. In all, she voyaged, by Captain Tew's own reckoning, more than 22,000 miles, crisscrossing the empty waters between the Gulf of Aden and the western coast of India, always hunting a victim.

From time to time *Amity* did sight what seemed a fitting quarry. But on each occasion, after chasing down and boarding the prize, the loot proved disappointing—and *Amity* resumed her quest.

Despite her discouraging run of ill luck, *Amity's* crew never lost faith in their captain. They knew that if and when a treasure ship did cross their path, Captain Tew was the man to find her and take her.

Then one brilliantly hot day, as *Amity* was cruising near the well-traveled mouth of the Red Sea, she sighted a magnificent merchant vessel flying the device of the Great Mogul, and apparently making for one of the nearby Arabian ports. The men of *Amity* had never sighted a Mogul ship of this size and type before.

Amity immediately gave chase.

Excitedly the crew of *Amity* watched as their swift little ship overtook the much larger Mogul vessel. As *Amity* drew alongside the clumsy merchant, her crewmen—with muskets primed and cutlasses at the ready—crowded to the rails, preparing to board the fat prize that now wallowed awkwardly to starboard. The hard-bitten men of *Amity* could see, as the two ships drew together, that there were at least five hundred turbaned soldiers on the deck of the huge Mogul ship, all apparently prepared to receive the onslaught of *Amity's* boarding party with muskets and wickedly disciplined spears and scimitars.

Captain Tew now cried out to his crew that the Mogul vessel "carried their fortune." Nor would she prove difficult to take, he shouted, for in spite of their guns and swords, the men of the infidel ship lacked what they needed most for victory: "courage and resolution."

When the time came, the men of *Amity* never hesitated.

Shouting oaths and firing off their muskets, *Amity*'s crewmen swung aboard the Mogul merchant. At this the Indian guards, instead of resisting, threw down their weapons and surrendered. Not a single one of Captain Tew's men received more than a minor scrape.

Now Captain Tew's voracious crew began to ransack their prize. They soon discovered a treasure that exceeded all their hopes. In her capacious holds, the Mogul ship carried chests of spices, bales of rich silks, a great quantity of elephant tusks—and more than £100,000 in gold and silver coin.

Quickly Captain Tew's men transferred this immense plunder to their own sturdy ship. Minutes after the last bale of silk had come aboard, *Amity* cast off from her quarry and set out southward.

Before heading for home Captain Tew took his agile little sloop to the safe haven of St. Mary's (now called Sainte-Marie), a tiny island off the northeast coast of Madagascar.

On the beach of this snug hideout, Captain Tew careened *Amity* for hull repair and refitting prior to taking her back across the Atlantic.[2] It was on St. Mary's, too, that the shrewd captain shared out the loot according to the agreed-upon split. After setting aside the backers' shares, Tew doled out one share for each ordinary seaman, two shares for the captain, and one and a half shares each for the quartermaster and surgeon. Each crewman's share came to £1,200. This was a splendid sum, more than any of them could make in a lifetime of toil at sea.

In December 1693 the cleaned and refitted *Amity*, with her happy crew and her hold bulging with booty, sailed for home. In April 1694, Captain Tew took *Amity*, with all flags flying, into Newport harbor. Her cruise had lasted sixteen months. The news of her success had already begun to spread, carried by European merchants in the eastern trade.

The people of Newport—from shopkeepers to leading citizens—hailed Captain Thomas Tew and those who had sailed with him as heroic adventurers. The tavern owners on the docks plied the *Amity*'s crew with copious amounts of rum that the men soaked up with a will after more than a year at sea. The merchants of the town marveled at the richness of the goods Captain

Tew had brought back. And they were only too happy to purchase those goods for profitable, if illegal, resale. Other captains and seamen were astonished at how easily the men of the *Amity* had made themselves wealthy—and they wondered if they might not do the same.

Captain Tew himself took great pleasure in his new celebrity. He and his wife and his two daughters were much in demand as dinner guests at the handsome homes of the Rhode Island aristocracy. With great relish, the jolly captain told and retold the story of his voyage, and basked in the adulation poured out upon him.

He and his little family even went down to New York at the invitation of his old friend Benjamin Fletcher, the royal governor, who had himself invested heavily, and often, in profitable privateering ventures.

Fletcher, a hearty, beefy man with a worldly, cynical turn of mind, had been appointed governor in 1682. In the twelve years since, he had earned a well-deserved reputation as a man who understood the special needs of privateers. In addition to making his own covert investments in privateering ventures, Fletcher made a business of selling privateering commissions to men such as Captain Tew, and of accepting bribes to allow plunder to be brought ashore for sale. In one notorious incident, a privateer captain, having disposed of his booty for a fortune to New York merchants, *gave* his ship to Governor Fletcher—who then sold it for the tidy sum of £800. It was a neat, and in this instance quite legal, bribe.

Over the years Fletcher had cultivated many privateer captains, encouraging them to utilize New York as their home port, and making sure they understood that—as long as he was the king's governor and they made the proper "gift" to him—they might flout with impunity the Navigation Acts he had sworn to uphold.

From such business contacts Fletcher had developed genuine friendships with a number of tough privateers. He had discovered that he liked their company and their gruff, straightforward ways—even though he was much criticized by ordinary citizens for his bribe taking and for his shameless association with men who lived by circumventing the law, Fletcher continued to consort openly with these adventurers and their backers.

The governor, therefore, did not hesitate to invite Captain Tew and his family to the gubernatorial home after the *Amity*'s return.

In fact, he entertained the captain royally, and the Tews reportedly enjoyed their visit immensely. Mrs. Tew and her daughters cut imperial figures in their glittering jewels and dresses of Oriental silk, all bounty from the captain's venture in the East—as the Tew ladies happily acknowledged.

The captain also relished his new prominence. He was seen on several occasions during his New York visit driving with Fletcher in the governor's coach, smiling and nodding to all who greeted him. (When told that such coach rides with a privateer captain were unseemly, Governor Fletcher replied, with the cynicism of the true politician, that he was merely attempting "to cure Captain Tew's vile habit of cursing in public.")

Tew's tales of his voyage also provided many hours of entertainment for his host. Wrote Fletcher later of the jolly captain: "A very pleasant man; so that at some times when the labours of my day were over, it was divertisement as well as information to me, to hear him talk."

As the Tews and the crew of the *Amity* enjoyed the afterglow of their success, other captains and crews—just as canny and tough as Tew and his men—reasoned that if Thomas Tew could make so successful a voyage to the East, so could they. Sparked by the stories told by Tew and his men, tales began to circulate of the fabulous wealth of the Muslims of India—wealth that resolute sailing men might, if they dared, appropriate for themselves at the point of a musket. Treasure, and with it adventure, lay beyond the Cape of Good Hope, where the infidels wallowed in gold.

Those who heard these tales knew that there had always been a few privateers operating in eastern waters, and that some of them had done well. But these eastern privateers had never excited many imitators before. Now, however, after Tew's success, and with privateering all but dead on the Spanish Main, throngs of enterprising merchants and officials not only in colonial North America but also in most of the ports of the western world, began to ready plundering voyages to the East.

Hundreds of privateer seamen, unemployed since the cessation of hostilities with Spain, as well as runaway slaves, indentured servants, debtors, drunks, ne'er-do-wells, and romantics, sought berths on these eastbound armed ships. Most of them believed that the infidel wealth would be theirs for the trying. Hadn't each of Tew's men earned £1,200? This was an amount double and triple the income of the richest bankers and merchants of London. It was a sum equal to the annual incomes of England's greatest lords. Suddenly it seemed that the wildest dreams were possible, if a man dared to challenge fortune.

Although the celebrated preacher Cotton Mather thundered from his Boston pulpit that "the privateering stroke so easily degenerates into the Piratical," no clerical admonition, nor any qualm of conscience, could stem the flood eastward. It was, after all, no sin for Christians to rob Muslims who denied Christ's divinity.

And so, within weeks of Captain Tew's triumphal return to Newport, seafarers from New York, Boston, Charleston, Bristol, London, and a dozen other port cities began to sail for the Indian Ocean, determined to equal Captain Tew's great score.

Captain Tew himself was soon among them.

After only seven months ashore Captain Tew ordered *Amity* prepared for a new voyage. Perhaps the adulation of colonial society had begun to wear thin. Perhaps he yearned for action. Perhaps he had, as sailors often do, simply grown restless for the sea. But more than likely the merchants and brokers of his acquaintance had prevailed upon him to lead a second, larger, expedition to Indian waters.

In any case Tew purchased a privateer's commission from his dear friend Governor Fletcher, paying £300 for the needed papers.

Then, in November 1694, Captain Thomas Tew and his veterans set sail in *Amity* for the Indian Ocean. This time they were accompanied by three other vessels, all under Tew's command. Two of these other ships, however, returned to port because of storm damage.

When *Amity* and her remaining consort reached the Indian Ocean, Tew found that a flotilla of marauders had already arrived in the Gulf of Aden, and were searching for a Mogul convoy to attack. Clearly the word had already spread about the opportunities in the East.

Tew now decided to join forces with these other sea raiders, reckoning that there would be sufficient loot for all. Together the raiders patroled the waters of the gulf, looking for prey.

Then, on a hot September day in 1695, after weeks spent fruitlessly scouring the sea-lanes between India and the mouth of the Red Sea, *Amity* finally spotted a likely Mogul prize and struck off after her.

With all sails unfurled, *Amity* bore down on her prey, finally coming alongside and grappling with the Mogul vessel. But this ship, unlike Tew's first victim, offered fierce resistance. As the crew of *Amity* was preparing to board the merchantman, the Indian soldiers aboard her discharged their muskets in a fusillade. Cannon aboard the Mogul ship also roared a salvo. When the clouds of smoke cleared a little, the *Amity*'s crew beheld Captain Thomas Tew staggering on his quarterdeck. His face was ashen. He was holding his guts with his hands to keep them from falling out of his shot-away belly.

Captain Tew fell to the quarterdeck. Within minutes he died in a puddle of his own blood. He spoke no word before dying. *Amity* broke off the engagement with the Mogul ship.

The disheartened men of *Amity* buried their captain at sea.[3]

But the news of Captain Tew's bloody death did not deter the many other seafarers now intent on hunting the Great Mogul's treasure ships.

In fact, even before Tew's demise, fleets were already following his wake to the Indian Ocean and the Red Sea. Many of those who sought the Mogul's wealth insisted—like Captain Tew himself—on the fiction that they were privateers in service to Christianity. But many others now openly scorned the euphemism "privateer." Most of these were ordinary seamen who had seized the ships of their masters in mutiny, and who had set out defiantly for the eastern seas "on their own account."

By the mid-1690s, dozens of such ships—self-proclaimed pirates commanded by elected captains and manned by admitted outlaws—were plying the vast watery triangle between the Cape of Good Hope, the Red Sea, and the western coast of India in search of plunder.

The pirate war on the world had begun.

But even these early pirate captains and crews were only the vanguard of the brigand armadas still to come as—year by year— legions of rebellious sailors fled from a civilization they had come to hate, and declared themselves enemies of the world.

What was that world, that civilized society that the pirate outlaws detested and fought, really like?

It was, above all, a world of stunning contrasts.

2

A Brilliant Time, a Brutal Time

In the spring of 1697, twenty-five-year-old Czar Peter I of Russia—later to be called "The Great"—embarked on a bizarre mission.

The Russian autocrat, who had been on his throne for eight years at the time, set out to visit the chief cities of western Europe in order to absorb as much as he could of the culture of the age.

Although, with his six feet seven inches of height, and his trailing entourage of courtiers, aides, and guards, the imposing Russian czar was recognized everywhere he went, Peter, throughout his long journey, denied his true identity, insisting that he was merely a private citizen on a private excursion.

Descending like a whirlwind on the capital cities of the West, Peter visited factories, met with scientists, conversed with artisans, mechanics, and shipwrights, and even labored for a time in a Dutch shipyard—all to learn, firsthand, as much as he could of the new science and technology then emerging in Europe. The czar's ultimate object was to import the new technology and learning to Russia so that, using the tools of western science and the skilled hands of western workers, he could remake his backward, conservative nation in the image of the "civilized" West.

After months of observing the achievements of European civilization, Peter was reportedly astonished by the advances that he had seen. Nor was Peter alone in his assessment. To most educated Europeans of the time, it seemed that humanity had entered upon a Golden Age when the mind of man, using the new tools of science, would at last prevail over Nature, if not over God.

It was the first true Age of Science, a time of splendid intellectual departures from a past in which religious dogma had forbidden inquiry beyond the "truths" already revealed in the teachings of the Church. As Bertrand Russell has written: "The modern world, so far as mental outlook is concerned, began in the seventeenth century."

By the time that century had reached its last decade, scholars all over Europe, utilizing the new "scientific method" of discovering truth from an objective examination of reality, had developed the microscope, the telescope, the compass, the first reliable clocks, the calculus, and the barometer. Physicists were investigating the properties of gases, writing treatises on optics and the composition of the stars, and hazarding intelligent guesses about the basic nature of matter. Isaac Newton, by describing the laws of gravity, had already changed humankind's view of the universe.

It was a scintillating age in the arts as well. Rembrandt and Rubens, Velásquez, Van Dyke, and Vermeer all produced their masterworks in this century. Every literate man and woman read Milton, the greatest poet of the time. Most also knew Dryden and Marvell. Montaigne's wise essays, the fables of La Fontaine, and the cynical brilliance of La Rochefoucauld, delighted readers not only in France but wherever thoughtful men and women gathered. The immortal plays of Molière, Corneille, and Racine amused, disturbed, and outraged the court of the Sun King at Versailles, and won audiences all over the Continent and the world.

Master musicians like Corelli and Purcell were heard in the

houses of the rich. Vivaldi, Handel, Bach, and Scarlatti would each begin creating his own glorious music within a few years.

If science and art sparkled as never before, so did social life—at least among the nobility.

In the ballrooms of the great houses, silk-clad ladies, rouged, powdered, and dazzling in jewels and the latest fashion, danced with bewigged gentlemen in embroidered waistcoats and silk stockings, while orchestras played the stately music of the day.

The salons of the wealthy also served as stages for masques, plays, musicales, and poetry recitals. But witty conversation and gossip were the favorite social pastimes in the houses of the rich, and gala evenings were usually accompanied by sumptuous repasts that often included champagne, tea, chocolate and coffee—luxurious beverages that first came into use at this time. Many evenings concluded with the smoking of a pipe or two of tobacco—another innovative luxury. Over the munificence of this new age shone the glittering light of wax candles, then newly invented, which lent an unheard-of luster to the pleasures of the night.

Perhaps the brilliance of the age was best personified by King Louis XIV of France, who gloried in his appellation "The Sun King," a title conferred upon him both for the magnificence of his court and for the power he wielded as the ruler of a France that dominated Europe, and most of the civilized world.

Standing only five feet four inches tall, and with a face badly scarred by childhood smallpox, Louis was not impressive physically. But as a monarch, he was a colossus. As the last decade of the seventeenth century began to unroll, he had governed France for more than thirty years—and he had stamped his personality on the age.

Louis ruled France as an absolute monarch. The glorification of his reign, and of France, was his chief occupation. Toward that end he had imposed crushing taxes on his subjects in order to build his unmatched armies—so far undefeated—and to erect that splendid monument to himself and to *la gloire*: Versailles.

Although as a matter of historical fact, Louis never uttered the haughty words attributed to him by a later imaginative historian—"*L'etat, c'est moi*"—the quote, nevertheless, expresses not only the absolutism with which the French monarch ruled his

own nation but also the arrogance, born of power, with which he confronted the rest of the world.

France, under Louis, stood at the apex of her strength. She possessed the most formidable army in all the world, and an armed fleet that appeared to have no equal. She also controlled a vast empire in the New World, extending from Canada southward along the Mississippi Valley to the Gulf of Mexico.

Louis—and France—appeared even more formidable because much of the rest of Europe seemed politically disorganized or militarily weak.

Catholic Spain still ruled vast territories in the New World, and her yearly treasure fleets still carried immense amounts of gold and silver from her overseas possessions to the coffers of His Most Catholic Majesty. But Spain had in fact lost her ability to control events in the world. The Spanish had depended too much on captured treasure, failing to understand that a nation's true wealth lies in the production of goods and services, not in the possession of stolen gold. As treasure flowed to Spain, and from Spain into the rest of Europe, it degenerated in value, buying less and less until, inevitably, Spain's economic and military power had begun to fade.

In the brilliant seventeenth century, religious differences usually determined *political* enmities as well. With occasional expedient exceptions, nations with a preponderance of Protestant population were generally in conflict with the Catholic powers.

In the 1690s, Holland, despite her small size, was the foremost of the Protestant powers. She was at the height of her commercial success, a center of the arts and sciences, and a refuge for the dispossessed victims of Catholic persecution (including the philosopher Spinoza). Amsterdam was one of the largest cities of Europe and the financial center of the world. In government, Holland was an oligarchic republic under the control of a limited number of men who represented the various commercial and political interests in the country. The executive leadership of the country was in the hands of a "stadtholder," who led the armies and in general ran the nation with the consent of his councillors. In this era, Holland's stadtholder was the gifted William of Orange, an implacable enemy of Louis XIV, who had spent his life fighting the Sun King and who was intent on forming a coalition of European states to put an end to the ambitions of Royal France.

Fragmented by religious strife, Germany was a collection of principalities, ecclesiastical states, and "free cities," a geographic patchwork that was essentially the political debris from the breakup of the Holy Roman Empire.[1]

One Germanic state, however, wielded considerable political influence in Europe. This was Hapsburg Austria. Once the main component of the defunct Holy Roman Empire, Austria in this era found herself confronting the expansionist Turkish Empire which was pushing its way into Europe, even threatening Vienna itself.

In the north, Protestant Sweden, under a series of competent and successful kings, had turned the Baltic into a Swedish lake, dominating the northern fringe of Europe from Denmark to Poland and into the so-called Baltic States. Within a few years, however, Sweden would find herself challenged by the Russia of Peter the Great.

Far to the south, in the Mediterranean, the petty states of Italy continued to squabble and intrigue among themselves, as they had since before the Renaissance.

The Turkish Ottoman Empire, conqueror of Constantinople, dominated the eastern Mediterranean and virtually all the Middle East.

None of these states, however, could compare with the France of Louis XIV in wealth or military strength.

Yet, as the 1690s dawned, the Sun King found himself confronting what would be the most perilous challenge of his long reign. It came from a rising new power: England.

No longer the feisty little island kingdom of Elizabeth, England had begun to achieve considerable place in the European order. But she had arrived at her new eminence only after enduring a turbulent century of religious strife, bloody revolution, political repression, and painful economic and military growth.

When Elizabeth had died in 1603, the Tudor dynasty had died with her. Elizabeth was succeeded by the Stuarts, who believed implicitly in the Divine Right of Kings and who ignited civil war in England over the issue. After Charles I—the second Stuart to occupy the English throne—was beheaded on a January morning in 1649, England was ruled by the harsh hand of Oliver Cromwell, the Puritan Lord Protector, who had begun his career as a parliamentary firebrand.

Under Cromwell the Parliamentary forces crushed the Royalist cavaliers, suppressed an Irish insurrection with great cruelty, and won great victories at sea.

When Cromwell died in 1658, a reaction against his hard reign set in.

The Stuart dynasty was restored in 1660. The pleasure-loving Charles II, a professed if lighthearted Protestant, was given the throne of his forebears. Religious tensions, however, remained acute because of the continuing divisions between Catholics and Protestants, and between the Anglican Church and the Puritans and other dissenters.

But despite doctrinal divisions, England's power, especially at sea, continued to grow. Seaborne trade was encouraged. English seamen and merchants competed militarily and commercially with Holland and were rapidly wresting domination of the world's trade routes away from the Dutch. At the same time, England under Charles II avoided confrontation with Royal France.

After the death of Charles II, however, English policy toward both France and Holland began to change radically. Charles's brother, James II, a professed and devout Catholic, succeeded to the throne in 1685. James openly supported Louis XIV's policies, including the Sun King's brutal treatment of French Huguenots, and he seemed to support a religious reunion with the Church of Rome.

In a rapid series of events, later known as the "bloodless revolution," the Protestant Parliament in 1688 invited William of Orange, Protestant ruler of Holland and a resolute enemy of Louis XIV, to become England's sovereign. James fled to Ireland where he fomented an unsuccessful revolution against English rule. Eventually James took refuge in the court of Louis XIV. The Stuart dynasty was finished forever, and Holland and England were united under William.

The reign of William was one of the most significant periods in the history of England because it fixed forever the ascendancy of Parliament. William, a dour little man obsessed with destroying the power of France, agreed to grant Parliament virtually any power it requested in order to keep England part of a European league against Louis XIV. In effect, Parliament made a deal

with William. Parliament would permit England to participate with William in his struggle against France. In return, William would accept Parliament's supremacy in domestic and fiscal affairs.

War with France would henceforth dominate England's national life.

But despite the domestic and foreign strife that England had endured during the seventeenth century, the era had also been a period of splendor in the arts and sciences as well as a time of remarkable growth in commerce and wealth.

Nowhere was this reality more manifest than in the City of London.

London's population had grown from about 150,000 in 1560 to approximately 750,000 in 1690—a fivefold increase that had made London a close second to Paris as the most populous city in Europe.

In the 1690s the city pulsated with life, brimmed with enthusiasm for the future, and basked in its own renewed beauty. For it was during this period that the great architect Sir Christopher Wren had reconstructed London as a city of grace and beauty, building more than fifty new churches to take the place of buildings destroyed in the Great Fire of 1664.

The intellectual life of the city revolved around numerous public coffee houses where brilliant men conversed freely on all topics under the sun, from religion to poetry to the latest court gossip, while sitting by the fire and sipping that exotic new brew, coffee. Some of the coffee houses even specialized. Lloyd's, for example, attracted ship owners and eventually became the center for the new notion of maritime insurance. Will's Coffee House, on the other hand, became fashionable among literary men. Addison and Steele were frequent visitors, along with lesser literary lions.

The theater flourished, as Restoration comedy and drama flowed from the pens of Dryden, Congreve, Wycherly and others.

In this era, the first newspapers began to appear—and the biting satire of Swift and Pope was soon to burst on the scene. It was also during this time that meetings and discussions at London clubs gave birth to the political parties that would dominate English political life far into the future: the Whigs and the Tories.

London buzzed with new ideas, hatched in an atmosphere of intellectual liberty not seen in the world for centuries. Dryden himself expressed the era's attitude toward liberty of thought in these words: "Of all the tyrannies on human kind/The worst is that which persecutes the mind."

But for all her intellectual ferment, London was preeminently a city of the sea. This fact was most plainly visible in the forest of masts that crowded the London quays. It was said that as many as two thousand ships might lie at anchor along the Thames on any given day.

A great mass of Londoners depended on the physical handling of seaborne trade: seamen and warehousemen, all those concerned with the supplying and repairing of ships, dock workers, and on top of these, the thousands more who were employed in supplying the needs of sea-trade workers and their families. It has been estimated that in the 1690s, more than a quarter of the city's total population was, in one way or another, dependent upon the port of London.

In pursuit of the fortunes that astute dealers might accumulate by trading in goods brought in English ships from foreign shores, the merchants of London were rapidly establishing dozens of banking houses, exchanges, markets, and warehouses along the Thames docks. Before the end of the decade, London would surpass even Amsterdam in commercial activity.

England's new eminence in the world was also reflected in her colonies, especially those across the Atlantic in North America.

Initiated in the reign of Elizabeth I with the settlement of Virginia, England's empire—which now included the colonies of New York and New Jersey, seized from Holland—hugged the Atlantic Coast from Massachusetts to Spanish Florida. Other colonial outposts dotted the West Indies and the western coast of far-off India.

In the 1690s Boston, New York, and Philadelphia were already significant cities and brisk centers of trade.

In the process of creating, protecting, supplying, and exploiting this busy empire, England and her colonies had fashioned an oceangoing fleet second to none—and had trained the skilled sailors to man it.

It is estimated that in the six decades between 1630 and 1690 English shipping tripled from 115,000 tons to 340,000 tons. Much of this growth in sea power can be attributed to the fact that in her wars with the Dutch and Spanish, England had captured approximately three thousand enemy ships, while losing no more than two thousand vessels of her own—for a net gain of one thousand ships. Contemporary records indicate that more than half the ships in the English merchant fleet in the 1690s were Dutch prizes.

In addition, the Royal Navy—established under Elizabeth I and given its name by Charles II—was also in a period of expansion, although official naval forces were sparse in comparison to the merchant fleet. The armed navy, still in its formative years, was expensive to maintain however—and for this reason England regularly employed armed merchant ships—privateers—to supplement the growing power of her navy. All the maritime states of that era did the same. Because the merchant vessels of the day were constructed much along the lines of men-of-war, carried cannon, and were manned by crews trained to fight, merchant privateers were effective instruments for expanding sea power, especially in their role as raiders of enemy commerce and onshore installations.

With her large number of well-armed trading ships, added to her smaller but very effective Royal Navy, England, by the last decade of the seventeenth century, disposed of sea power at least equal to that of Royal France.

As the seventeenth century entered its final decade, then, an aggressive, thriving England, with her compact new empire sustained by matchless sea power, and governed by a Parliament and king implacably hostile to Louis XIV, confronted a seemingly omnipotent France.

The stage was set for a titanic conflict. Two brilliant powers faced each other in a brilliant age. That they would clash was inevitable.

For the ordinary people of those times, however, such lofty concepts were incomprehensible. For men, women, and children who had to work in order to eat, the splendor of the age did not exist.

The vast majority of humankind lived much as they had always lived: in misery and in toil. Most men and women throughout the world still worked the land, laboring from dawn to dusk to produce a meager crop that they hoped would see them through the long, dark winter, which they usually spent huddled around inadequate fires in rude shelters.

London merchants might gather at Lloyd's to share a meal of roast beef and claret before a roaring fire, and colonial masters

might enjoy a repast of venison and turkey in a Boston tavern—
but the poor of most western nations still subsisted on a diet of
coarse bread, turnips, beans, soup, occasional cheese, ale, or,
more often, plain water. The poor ate meat as a rule only when
the rich gave a feast, or when they dared to risk cruel punishment
to poach game from the great estates.

In rural areas, famine was not unknown. In France desperate
peasants, not allowed by the tax gatherers to retain enough of
their own produce to live on, rose in arms against their masters
several times during the century—only to be put down by the
well-armed and well-fed soldiers of the regime.

In Spain, it was said, "the rich ate, and ate to excess, watched
by a thousand hungry eyes as they consumed their gargantuan
meals. The rest of the population starved."

The ladies of Versailles might dance the night away by the light
of a thousand candles, but for the wretched majority the fall of
darkness meant only that the time had come to sleep in preparation for the next day's labor.

Explorers and geographers might discover and map new con-
tinents across boundless oceans, but for the vast numbers yoked
to the earth, the world consisted only of the immediate neighborhood—the village, the church, the estate of the lord of the
land. Few among the working classes, whether they labored in
the countryside or in the great cities, knew or cared what might
lie beyond their own vicinity.

For all except the rich, life was not only miserable, but brief.
Peasants, artisans, laborers, farm women—all usually wore out in
their forties, ground down by toil, disease, and inadequate diet.

Women customarily bore a dozen or more children. But only
half the infants born in this era lived past their first year—and
only half of those who *did* survive could expect to reach
adulthood. In this era, even the children of the wealthy were devastated by disease, although the life expectancy of the rich—unlike that of the poor—increased dramatically after they reached
puberty.[2]

Periodically plague ravaged the cities of Europe. In the summer of 1665 the plague swept through London, killing 100,000
people and leaving the city desolate. Wrote Samuel Pepys in that
bleak summer: "But Lord how everybody's looks and discourse in
the street is of death and nothing else; and few people going up

and down, that the town is like a place distressed and forsaken."

Yet as terrifying and destructive as such outbreaks were, starvation, as well as such diseases as cholera, typhus, and smallpox—which were endemic given the poor sanitation of the times—carried off more people over the years than did the periodic eruptions of plague. In fact, because of the perennial exactions of endemic diseases, coupled with the malnutrition of chronic hunger, the population of Europe actually *declined* over the last half of the seventeenth century from an estimated 118 million in 1650 to approximately 104 million by the century's end.

Nor were hunger, disease, hard labor, and lack of shelter the only miseries that the majority of mankind had to endure in that glorious age.

Nauseating filth, casual violence, economic exploitation, and judicial cruelty were also rampant.

Nowhere did the filth, violence, cruelty, and exploitation of daily life weigh more heavily on the impoverished multitude than in England, for if England often exemplified the best that the age offered, it also furnished graphic examples of the worst—especially in London itself.

For most of those who had to labor to exist, the London of the 1690s was not a place of scintillating coffee-house conversation and graceful architecture, but a dirty and dangerous city.

The narrow streets, mere alleys between tall buildings, ran like open sewers, with human and animal feces churned into a putrid morass underfoot. Smoke poured from thousands of fires and chimneys, mixing with the mists from the Thames to form poisonous fogs. Violence was everywhere in the great metropolis. Murder was common. Press gangs attacked unwary sailors, knocking them senseless in order to kidnap them for service aboard His Majesty's ships or aboard shorthanded merchants.

Even sports were violent. A favorite pastime was cockfighting, and gamblers often wagered large sums on contests between birds trained to fight to the death. Baiting bulls, bears, and even tigers with savage trained dogs was also a popular sport for gamblers and idlers, as was bloody, bareknuckle boxing.

It was also an age of murderous state violence not only in England but throughout the world, when incredible cruelty was a routine part of ordinary civic life.

Torture was legal not only as punishment but also as a judicially condoned method for extracting information. The use of the thumbscrew to tear fingers from their sockets, branding on the face with a red-hot iron, nailing by the ears to a post, or whipping through the streets—these were "mild chastisements," reserved for petty thieves and minor criminals. The law of the day reserved the direst punishments for those who dared oppose the will of the State or the Sovereign. In England, if a man was convicted of treason, he was strung up by the neck until nearly choked to death. Then, still alive, he was cut down, and the executioner cut off his penis and testicles, sliced open his belly, and tore out his entrails. Finally, the convicted man was beheaded—after which his body was cut into quarters.

Female traitors escaped this horrible punishment because, according to the law of the day, "the decency due to their sex forbids the exposing and publicly mangling their bodies." Female traitors were therefore burnt at the stake.

Such horrendous executions—performed in public—drew great crowds, including perfumed ladies and fine gentlemen, who often watched from their coaches or from wooden stands especially built for their convenience. The working people and shopkeepers of London often made a holiday of such grisly events, picnicking and laughing with their children, while the condemned screamed forth their last agony. The largest crowd ever to witness such an execution was estimated at 200,000.

Samuel Pepys—always a marvellous witness—gives the flavor of one such celebrated event in his diary: "Went out to Charing Cross to see Major-General Harrison hanged, drawn, and quartered, which was done there, he looking as cheerfully as any man could do in that condition. He was presently cut down and his head and heart shown to the people at which there were great shouts of joy."

Treason was not, by any means, the only capital crime. Witches died in flames at the stake after long agonies of broken bones and torn joints during interrogation. Poor men—and women, too—desperate for bread, often went to the gallows for stealing a few pence.

The executions of such criminals—carried out in a place called Tyburn, almost in the center of present-day London—were also occasions for public enjoyment. So popular did they become that Londoners referred to the public hangings as "Tyburn Fair."

In the remorseless struggle to stay alive, the desperate poor often surrendered themselves to vicious exploitation. Girls of twelve could legally become prostitutes—and thousands of young girls wore themselves out with gin and venereal disease in London's black, stinking lanes. The pale children of debtors were made to sweat in the choking dust of mills, or to shiver in the cold dampness of workhouses, in order to satisfy the obligations of their parents.

For relief many turned to alcohol—and drunkenness was pervasive. London's poor might not have enough money to feed themselves, but drink was cheaper than bread, and there was always enough money to get drunk. On Gin Lane, where poor sailors, prostitutes, and chimney sweeps drank themselves to death, sly pawnbrokers doled out farthings for drink in exchange for stolen goods—and the saying was: "Drunk for a ha'penny, *dead drunk* for a penny."

In the New World, too, life could be bitter. Although, in America's vastness, they were often invisible, the black slaves, displaced Indians, transported convicts, and indentured servants who performed the noisome labor in the colonies led lives every bit as wretched as those endured by the far more numerous poor of Europe. America—in the 1690s—was not yet the labor-hungry land of opportunity it was to become. At this time it offered no refuge to the "huddled masses yearning to breathe free." For the most part it mirrored Europe, bestowing its wealth only on landed aristocrats, the burghers of the new cities, and aggressive merchants.

Nor did the colonies lag behind their mother countries in the use of public cruelty against the helpless. The Spanish enslaved Indians to work their mines. French slave traders in New Orleans had no compunction about ruthlessly tearing slave mothers from their children to make a sale. British colonists freely employed the whipping post, stocks, ducking stool, and gallows to enforce the laws. And witches were hanged publicly in Puritan Massachusetts to protect the common weal.

Yet despite the horrors they had to bear, the helpless majority of people suffered in silent resignation for the most part because they could envision no alternative to their painful lot. Only occasionally did they become desperate enough to rebel—and such rebellions were cruelly and swiftly suppressed.

While most of the laboring poor endured in silence and hoped

for God's justice in the world to come, some sought to escape their wretchedness by running away from it. A few turned to criminal activity. Many more joined the army, or ran away to sea. In England, because of her maritime tradition, thousands of boys and young men fled the hard life of the impoverished in order to follow the sea. Virtually all of them managed to find employment because—during most of this era—England's rapidly expanding fleet stood in need of sailors.

From the perspective of the untutored poor, a sailor's lot must have seemed superior to a life of toil on land. At least the sailor labored in the fresh air, under the sky, sustained by the rough camaraderie of shipmates. These were conditions far better than the foul atmosphere of a mill or a mine or a prison. Furthermore, if the work a sailor did was hard, it was no harder than a farmer's daily toil. If the food aboard ship was often putrid with maggots and mold, at least a sailor could always fill his gut with some sort of fare. If the sailor was often cold and wet at his work, so were the miner and the coachman. In addition, sailors usually earned more than landlubbers. English and colonial seamen, at any rate, ordinarily earned twice what a laborer earned.

Life at sea certainly seemed to many to offer a better existence than life ashore.

But this was only a cruel illusion.

3

A Seaman's Lot

A mariner named William Richardson, who served as an ordinary seaman on a slave ship in the early 1700s, wrote in his diary that the captain of his vessel "would flog a man as soon as look at him."

Richardson was unusual—a sailor who could read and write at a time of almost universal illiteracy among ordinary seaman. In his diary he also recounts how the brutal captain of his ship "flogged a good seaman for only losing an oar out of the boat, and the poor fellow soon after died."

Such was the "discipline" that obtained aboard most merchant ships in the seventeenth and eighteenth centuries. If anything, discipline in the Royal Navy was even more capricious and harsh than that of the merchant service.

The sailor of this age, with his wage of a pound or more per month, and with his food and shelter provided by his employer, might *appear* to be better off than those who labored ashore, but in several crucial respects he was much *worse* off. The vicious attitude of the times that granted to the privileged and powerful a cruel license over the poor and weak not only pervaded life at sea (just as it did ashore), it was exacerbated in the enclosed world of a ship where long-term proximity, under miserable conditions, often inflamed tensions and incited passions.

Captains possessed the power of life and death over their crews, and savage mistreatment of helpless sailors formed an integral part of life aboard ship, whatever flag it might fly. All ordinary seamen, whatever their nationality, knew and feared the brutal discipline that called for whipping a man to death for losing an oar. Sadistic and psychopathic officers could—and did—indulge with impunity in the most atrocious mistreatment of sailors under their command. Richardson's account of the slave-ship master who would "flog a man as soon as look at him" is far from unique. For example, a Captain Staines of the English ship *Rochester* became so angry at an infraction of his ship's rules that he had a young seaman beaten with six hundred lashes from an inch-thick tarred rope. Although the ship's log did not record it, the chances are that the man died under such punishment.

While flogging was the most common form of punishment, it was by no means the only barbarity practiced aboard ship. The punishment for drawing a weapon in a quarrel, for example, was the loss of a hand. Other punishments an unlucky mariner might have to endure included keelhauling (being scraped across the barnacled hull of the ship), being ducked at the end of a rope from the yardarm, being strung up from the yardarm, and being towed, often with hands tied, from the stern. Some punishments, besides being barbarous, were also bizarre. One particularly sadistic mate forced his men to eat cockroaches as a punishment. Another delighted in cracking off the teeth of miscreants with an iron bolt.

The food supplied to seamen was usually abominable. Most sailors had to subsist on salt beef or pork crawling with worms or maggots, bread blue with mold, and water that stank from the barrel. Most sailors learned to swallow these disgusting provisions without looking at what they were eating or chewing more than was necessary. And when even these wretched provisions ran out, as they often did, the sailor ate shipboard rats, or whatever he could fish from the sea.

Nor were the sailors' accommodations in any way superior to the shelters of the poor on shore. The sailor had to sleep, when he was allowed to do so, in a crowded fo'c'sle, jammed in with other men, inhaling the fumes of unwashed bodies, sweating when it was hot, shivering when it was cold, and almost always wet through from weather or leaks. Sickness, especially scurvy, was a constant hazard.

Moreover, a sailor's life was dangerous. Fire aboard a wooden ship was a special hazard. Sailors often fell from the rigging, or were washed overboard during storms, or were maimed by equipment falling from the shrouds, or were tossed from a rolling deck into hatches or against bulkheads. The chances of being hurt in the course of his duties were very high for the ordinary seaman. At the same time, if he was disabled, he had no recourse. He was now unemployable at his trade. Nor was he eligible for compensation of any kind. There were no pensions or even medical care for an ordinary seaman.

The mariner of this period faced still another danger: He might be killed or wounded in battle. Merchant vessels of the day were almost always armed with cannon, and crewmen were expected to man them when ordered to do so. On many occasions during wartime, such armed merchants would capture enemy ships, often worth considerable prize money. Yet ordinary sailors never received a fair share in the prize, even though they might have been exposed to great danger, or even wounded, in its taking. While this inequity did not obtain aboard privateers (where special agreements divided booty in a relatively fair manner among officers, crew members, and backers), it was a serious grievance among the seamen who served on regular merchant vessels or on the men-of-war of the Royal Navy.[1]

Further, with all the inequities, dangers, discomforts, and cruelties he had to endure aboard ship, the sailor also lived with the dismal knowledge that under the all-encompassing class system of the day, he could seldom escape his role or better himself. Only under the most extraordinary circumstances could a seaman in "honest service" rise in the ranks. To become a ship's officer and buy a share of a cargo was extremely rare in the merchant service, although it did happen. In the Royal Navy, however, such an eventuality was not only impossible, it was unthinkable, since to qualify as an officer in the Royal Navy, a man had to be certifiably a "gentleman."

The ordinary sailor, therefore, could seldom expect to share to

any important extent in the wealth that his labor—or his bravery—made possible for his employers. (Of course, this rule did
not apply to those relatively few seamen who were fortunate
enough to land berths aboard successful privateers. Although ordinary sailors seldom rose in the ranks even as members of a privateering crew, they did at least realize a fair share of whatever
prizes their ship took. But privateers were always few in number
compared to the fleets of merchant ships that plied the sea lanes
in this era. The majority of sailors, therefore, were fated to spend
their entire careers aboard merchant vessels, or men-of-war.)

In one way the average seaman aboard a merchant ship or a
warship was far *worse* off than the poor man who labored for his
daily bread on shore: The sailor, once at sea, could not escape.
He could find no refuge, even for a brief time, from the wretched
conditions under which he lived and worked. Day or night, he
was always under orders, never sure when the lash or the rattan
cane might whip across his back. He had to eat what they gave
him, no matter how vile, and he had to take whatever rest he
could get, whenever and wherever his overseers permitted.
Aboard ship the ordinary sailor had no respite, no appeal, no
sanctuary. He was, except in name, no better than a slave.

Because of the cruelty and the injustices they had to bear, most
ordinary seamen eventually came to hate not only their own officers but *all* who wielded authority. Under the lash, even loyalty
to king and country eroded, until by the late seventeenth century
thousands of resentful and rebellious sailors manned the ships of
the seagoing nations. But life at sea did offer one escape route: If
they became bitter enough, or rebellious enough, they could
seize their ship and turn pirate.

By the 1690s piracy was already a time-honored, if censured,
occupation for seafaring men willing to risk their lives for fortune,
or for escape—or both. In one form or another piracy had existed
for centuries in every corner of the world washed by the sea.

Ancient Assyrian kings had complained of corsairs in the Persian Gulf who plundered goods en route from Arabia and Africa.
In the fourth century B.C., the sailors of Alexander the Great,
plying those same waters, encountered the descendants of those
earlier pirates. For almost ten centuries the Romans of both the
Republic and the Empire contended with the clever, oared pirates of the Mediterranean. These were usually local cutthroats

who employed the numerous islands and sheltered bays of the Middle Sea as bases. So much did the orderly, legalistic Romans despise these seaborne outlaws that they labeled them—in Cicero's words—*hostes humani generi,* "enemies of the human race." Before he entered upon his career as conqueror, the youthful Julius Caesar was captured by a flotilla of these pirates and held for more than six weeks until his noble family purchased his liberty.

After the fall of Rome, the Barbary corsairs of the north coast of Africa became the scourge of the Mediterranean. They remained a thorn in the side of European commerce well into the nineteenth century. The Vikings, too, were consummate pirates, plundering on both land and sea.

In medieval times, among the English, German, and French mariners who sailed the European Atlantic Coast, piracy as a way of life became almost commonplace as seaborne trade increased in the English Channel and the North Sea.

One of the most celebrated of these medieval pirates was a one-time monk from Flanders, who was believed to have sold his soul to the Devil in exchange for magical powers that enhanced his ability to capture victims.

Known as Eustace the Monk, this brigand—who operated around the year 1216—specialized in plundering French shipping in the English Channel, using Dover as his base. He was tolerated, and even occasionally employed, by England's King John as long as he confined his depredations to French shipping. But eventually, impelled by greed or wrath, he began to take English ships and the furious king outlawed him in England.

Eustace the Monk then made a deal with his former victims. He would guide the French in an invasion of England. But the effort misfired when the English blinded their enemies by flinging lime aboard their ships—and then destroyed the sightless French with a lethal hail of arrows. The traitorous Eustace, taken in the battle, had his head struck off.

Another infamous medieval pirate was the German Klein Henszlein who preyed on shipping in the North Sea. Captured by a fleet sent by German merchants, Henszlein and thirty-three of his crew were beheaded publicly in the city of Hamburg and their heads were jammed onto stakes as a warning to others.

In the early sixteenth century the sporadic piracy of the Middle

Ages became an organized affair in England, especially in the Scilly Isles, the south of Ireland, and the Cinque Ports of England's southeast coast. Pirate syndicates were especially brazen in the Cinque Ports (Hastings, Hythe, Dover, Sandwich, and Romney). These towns, originally established to provide men and ships to protect the coast and coastal trade in time of war, became the headquarters for corsairs known as the King's Pirates, a title conferred upon them because of their custom of forwarding 20 percent of their take to the monarch.

Protected by important noblemen, the pirates would sail out of the Cinque Ports to attack any merchant that happened into range. Returning to port, the plunderers, with the connivance of their protectors, would openly display their booty for sale on the decks of their ships. At one point during this era the Cinque Ports became a virtual pirate kingdom, where outlaw captains boldly swaggered in the streets. Yet despite its widespread practice, piracy—even when it was most popular—was never considered a minor crime. It was always, and everywhere, punished by death, provided the miscreants could be caught and convicted, which was usually no easy task.

By the time Elizabeth came to the throne of England in 1558, it was estimated that some four hundred pirate ships prowled the Channel with near impunity, thanks in no small measure to the connivance of officials ashore. Yet, for all their numbers, the Channel pirates had never seriously dislocated the trade of their day. In Elizabethan times, however, privateering began to dominate the fine art of attacking and appropriating the commerce of other nations.

Although there is evidence that the practice of commissioning privately owned ships to attack enemy merchants dated back to at least the thirteenth century, privateering became widespread only from the second half of the sixteenth century onward.

Privateering attracted many of the finest seamen of the age because it was a legally sanctioned activity, fundamentally different from illegal piracy in that pirates preyed on *all* shipping, while privateers took only enemy ships. Unlike pirates, privateers could be heroic, winning fame and their country's thanks, as well as high fortune, for their efforts. Privateering became especially popular among the English sea dogs of Elizabeth's reign.

The Spanish Main—primarily the coastal regions of Spanish

America in the Caribbean—became the chief theater of operations for the Elizabethan privateers. Spain claimed most of the Americas for herself, based on the fact that Columbus had planted the Spanish flag in the Caribbean in 1492. To back up her claim—which was supported by the pope—Spain treated all foreigners who entered the waters of the New World without her permission as illegal intruders in her domain. Because of this attitude, all foreign seamen on the Spanish Main were regarded as pirates by the Spanish colonial authorities, and were dealt with ruthlessly.

But neither Spanish threats, nor Spanish force, could deter the English privateers from Spanish waters. Captains such as Hawkins, Drake, Frobisher, and Raleigh swooped down like hawks on the Spanish fleets, capturing treasure and tearing great holes in the myth of Spanish invincibility. The English privateers also raided and pillaged Spanish shore installations. Many of the English privateers, denounced as *piratas* in Madrid, received knighthoods in London for their depredations. Many of them also played major roles in the defeat of the Spanish Armada.

Elizabeth herself not only derived considerable revenue from the sale of privateering licenses to her sea hawks, she is also said to have used the Crown's treasure to finance Drake and other likely privateers—and to have profited immensely by their pillaging.

By the seventeenth century privateering had become both a popular way of life for seamen who managed to obtain employment in such ventures and a lucrative, if risky, business for merchants willing to gamble a ship to win a fortune. At the same time outright piracy, though still in existence, had shrunk to negligible proportions—a refuge for only the most desperate of those who followed the sea.

For ordinary sailors in the seventeenth century, life aboard a privateer was, generally speaking, more attractive than life aboard a merchant vessel or a man-of-war. While food and accommodation were no better than merchant and naval vessels offered, a privateering berth provided an opportunity for a seaman to achieve some worldly prosperity. Furthermore, the cruel discipline aboard other ships was virtually absent on privateers. Enterprising sailors, therefore, were usually more than willing when offered a chance to join a privateering venture, even though the rule aboard privateers was always "no prey, no pay," and even though privateering seamen had to face the danger of combat at sea.

Privateering, however, was far less popular among traders than it was among sailors. Because of the high costs of mounting and maintaining a privateer, and because of the hazardous combat a privateer had to engage in, most businessmen preferred to invest in merchant vessels and their cargoes. For this reason there were always more sailors willing to go privateering than there were berths available.

Nevertheless, throughout the seventeenth century, merchants and other backers, especially in the English colonies, did finance privateering ventures in significant numbers. In fact, English and American privateers had played an important role in England's almost incessant naval wars with Holland and Spain in those years. During these wars, which had as their objective the establishment of England as a power in the New World, English and colonial adventurers had been especially active in the Caribbean, harrying the shipping and the ports of the Spanish Main—as Drake and Raleigh had in an earlier century.

Many of the privateers who fought the Spanish in this period became known as "buccaneers," from the French word *boucaniers*—"smokers of meat." The term was originally applied to English and French refugees who had settled on the large Caribbean island of Hispaniola—illegally according to the Spanish law that claimed all the New World for Spain. These settlers, herdsmen for the most part, had supported themselves by selling hides and meat that they smoked over a wooden frame known as a *boucan* in the language of the Carib Indians. Eventually the Spanish authorities had ousted the *boucaniers* from their settlements, and these one-time butchers and smokers of meat became sea raiders against the Spanish, switching their base to the uninhabited island of Tortuga.

These buccaneers—as the English came to call them—were full of hatred for the Spaniards who had driven them from their homes. Most of them were also Protestants and fired with religious zeal against the Catholic Spaniards, who treated all such "heretics" with great cruelty. Before long the buccaneers attracted recruits that included French Huguenots and English adventurers—many of them freebooters, all of them enemies of Spain. By degrees these motley groups became a formal confederacy known as the Brotherhood of the Coast. Tortuga became a fortified base for their operations against the hated Spanish.

By the middle of the seventeenth century, as adventurers of many nationalities began to drift into Tortuga, both French and English colonial governors started issuing privateering commissions that authorized levies of buccaneers to prey on Spanish shipping and ports. Tortuga became a thriving town, where freebooters, privateers, and refugees, of varying degrees of honesty and legitimacy, but united in their common hatred of Spain, came together under the generic name buccaneers.

Although the Spanish tried more than once to oust the buccaneers from Tortuga, they never succeeded. Many of those who operated from the island became infamous for the atrocities they inflicted upon their victims. There was, for example, the diabolical François L'Olonnois who sacked the city of Maracaibo on the coast of Venezuela, and who stated proudly that he had never permitted his men to spare a prisoner's life. There was also the Englishman Lewis Scott, who raided the town of Campeche on the Yucatán Peninsula. Other famed buccaneers on the Spanish Main were Roche Brasiliano, Bartholomew the Portuguese, Pierre François, and Montbars the Exterminator—names that testify to the international character of the brotherhood.

But the most famous and successful of all the buccaneers was a Welshman, Henry Morgan.

In 1671 Morgan, like an independent contractor in service to England, led a devastating raid on Panama, Spain's richest possession in the Caribbean. In the course of their invasion, Morgan and his men destroyed forts, desecrated churches, killed nuns, raped captive women, and tortured children as well as adults of both sexes in an attempt to force their victims to disclose hidden gold. The infuriated Spanish labeled Morgan an outright pirate and put a price on his head. But the English agreed with Morgan that he and his buccaneers were legal privateers. Subsequently the English even knighted Morgan—and Sir Henry Morgan, buccaneer, even became lieutenant governor of the island of Jamaica, which the English had seized from Spain in 1655 and which served thereafter as a base for English and American colonial privateers operating against Spanish America.[2]

In the 1680s—as England's sea power began to outstrip that of the Spanish empire—her own privateers, commissioned directly

Sʳ HEN: M O R G A N

Part. 2. Page: 60.

from her North American colonies and from England herself, began to outdo the buccaneers in the amount of damage they inflicted on the Spanish. Like sea wolves, these privateers
plundered the rich Spanish fleets with regularity and near impunity, even though the Spanish patrolled their coasts with armed
guard vessels and traveled the seas in bristling convoys.

Then, in the spring of 1689, the English and American privateers who had made the Spanish Main their hunting ground
suffered a blow that struck them like a cannon shot.

England's new king, William III—William of Orange—the inexorable enemy of Louis XIV, made peace with England's perennial enemy, Spain. Further, he brought England into the League of Augsburg—an alliance of Holland, Sweden, a number of German states, and Spain, against Louis XIV.

Suddenly—and incredibly—England was allied to her historical antagonist, Spain, and at war with France.

Known as King William's War among the English and Americans, the conflict that now ensued shattered the old buccaneering brotherhood in the Caribbean. English and French buccaneers found themselves on opposite sides of the conflict.[3]

In addition, several thousand English and American seamen who had made their careers in privateering against Spain now found themselves without employment.

Some of these tough seafarers turned to privateering against the new enemy, France. But French cargoes were by no means as rich as Spain's, and the French carried on far less commerce in the New World than Spain had. Moreover, French ships were far more difficult to capture than fat Spanish galleons and treasure convoys. Privateers thought twice before attacking French shipping in European waters since Louis XIV possessed a large and excellent battle fleet that made such actions extremely risky.

Within a year after the peace with Spain, privateering as a profitable enterprise for English and colonial seafarers had been greatly diminished. The merchants and bankers who had previously financed privateering ventures against the Spanish were no longer willing to put capital into much riskier, and far less profitable, ventures against French shipping.

(Ironically, as English privateering *decreased*, French privateering against English and allied shipping in the waters around England, Holland, and Spain became a serious threat to allied commerce. Operating from the relative safety of such Channel ports as Dunkirk, French privateers harried and captured allied merchantmen in coastal waters, while French men-of-war kept the Royal Navy at bay.)

Deprived of their livelihoods, the thousands of English and American ex-privateers who now found themselves on the beach had only a few options open to them. They could return to merchant service. They could join the expanding Royal Navy. They could turn to piracy. Or they could find alternative employment ashore.

Many, unhappily but out of necessity, *did* return to the merchant service, rejoining the sullen ranks of discontented seamen who endured the cruel existence that was the common lot of the merchant sailor. But a good number of these ex-privateers, accustomed to the free and easy life of their former employment, found it virtually impossible to tolerate the harsh conditions aboard a trading vessel. They often became insurgent spirits, preaching rebellion and anarchy aboard their vessels.

For the Royal Navy, King William's War ushered in a period of rapid growth. As a result, ordinary sailors were needed desperately aboard the new English men-of-war that were sailing forth to confront Louis. But few men volunteered. For ordinary seamen, service in the Royal Navy simply meant extraordinarily harsh discipline, little pay, an inequable share of any prize money—and great danger.

Unable to attract recruits to its ranks, the Royal Navy had to resort to the hated practice of impressment. This was, essentially, the physical abduction of men for service aboard His Majesty's ships. Impressment was bitterly hated by seamen, and at times the crews of merchant ships would resist violently when boarded by a naval press gang. Ordinary seamen feared forced recruitment not only because impressed men aboard a man-of-war were cruelly treated and often exposed to the most danger but also because forced recruitment into the navy usually meant that the families of impressed sailors would starve, since pay aboard a warship was low and, at best, intermittent.

As a consequence of the Royal Navy's impressment policy, desertions from men-of-war became epidemic—until the navy began to employ such barbarous methods as shackling and maiming crewmen to keep them from jumping ship.

A few former privateers, beached by King William's War and refusing to serve in the navy or the merchant fleet, turned to open piracy. But these were, for the most part, only the most desperate and reckless. For, despite the long history of piracy among English and colonial seamen, it was still a momentous decision to turn pirate. Privateering might not have been the most respectable of professions, but at least it carried a *veneer* of legality. But *pirates* were simply *outlaws*. Most ordinary seamen, resentful as they might be of cruel authority, angry as they might be over inequities in pay and treatment, and fearful as they might be of the cruel press gangs, still regarded open piracy as a game that was not worth the candle. The potential rewards of piracy, to most ordinary seamen, just did not seem equal to the risk involved.

Many seamen, both ex-privateers and merchant sailors, at the outbreak of King William's War, simply chose to give up the sea and to go into hiding rather than risk the press gangs of the Royal Navy. One contemporary writer, Henry Maydman, noted the phenomenon in these words: "Many men, when war is, do betake themselves to live with their friends in the inlands, and follow their occupations, and at the end of the wars, do return to their maritime lives, or wait to make slips into merchantmen."

As the brilliant seventeenth century entered its last decade then, it seemed that while King William's War with France had severely curtailed the business of privateering, it was *not* likely to trigger an increase in outright piracy. In fact, in 1690 piracy was no more than a sporadic hazard of sea trading, an occasional crime to be punished severely, but hardly a threat to the maritime commerce of great nations. There was absolutely no sign that before the decade was half over, the world would see the start of the greatest outburst of piracy in history, a virtual pirate war against the world.

But in fact, although few realized it, a series of singular events, political and economic realities, and social factors peculiar to the times were converging to make this explosion of piracy inevitable.

Expansion of world commerce and colonial empires, as well as the formation of trading companies such as the British East India Company, had created huge merchant fleets. Thousands of seamen toiled aboard these ships—and virtually all these men, victims of the cruel conditions of the times, bore a smoldering hatred for their masters.

For most of these ordinary seamen, who knew they would probably never earn a decent place in the society they enriched with their labor, the idea of loyalty to the nation had come to seem an absurdity comparable to the suggestion that the slave should love his overseer. Furthermore, as a result of their history and past employment, many ordinary seamen—especially those English and American privateers left unemployed by England's peace with Spain and war with France—had few scruples about the *concept* of piracy, even though they usually had paralyzing qualms about the great risks involved.

The merchant ships of the seventeenth century, generally ply-ing the sea-lanes singly, were extremely vulnerable to attack. At the same time, the fledgling naval forces of the day, while power-ful enough to deal with outlaw vessels if and when they caught up with them, were insufficient to protect trading vessels on the open seas. Communications were slow and cumbersome. It could often take weeks for news of an attack on a merchant ship to be-come known, and by that time the attackers could have journeyed halfway around the world. It was therefore extremely difficult for naval forces to track down a pirate ship, provided that ship was handled by skilled seafarers.

Furthermore, throughout this period there was a rough parity in armament and maritime technology between merchants and naval vessels on the one hand and sea raiders on the other. If there was mortal danger for a sailor in turning pirate, there was also a good chance that determined and capable men could gain the victory in any fight with warships or armed merchantmen.

Finally, there was a powerful, irrepressible tide flowing among the seamen of the day, a force that would greatly abet the pirate outbreak: the craving to live in freedom. Denied, this universal hunger for freedom inevitably breaks out in some form of re-bellion—as history has demonstrated again and again. And the thousands of disaffected, ordinary seamen who worked the ships of the world's maritime and naval fleets had the capacity to turn their craving into action.

In the last ten years of the century then, an array of circum-stances had combined to create an explosive environment for those who followed the sea, as well as for those who employed them. It required only a spark to turn the widespread unrest among seafarers into an epidemic of piracy.

The spark came in the form of electrifying news from the East: the 70-ton sloop *Amity*—a colonial marauder under Captain Thomas Tew of Newport, Rhode Island, mounting a mere eight guns—had voyaged through the Indian Ocean and had taken a huge haul of gold, silver, ivory, and precious goods from a ship of the Great Mogul of India.

The story of *Amity*'s enterprise spread like a shipboard fire.

For many years sailors had been hearing vague tales of the riches of the East. A few of them had even seen evidence of those riches in the cargoes of the ships of the East India Company. Now

Captain Tew's voyage in the *Amity* not only confirmed the existence of those riches but indicated the ease with which resolute mariners might obtain a share of that wealth. Suddenly there seemed an alternative to the merchant service, or to impressment into the navy, or to hiding out in some shore berth: A man might go east.

All at once it seemed to many a resentful seafaring man that the outlaw life—piracy—might be worth the risk after all. If a defenseless sailor could have the skin flayed from his body for stealing a biscuit at sea, or hang for pinching a shilling ashore, why not hazard as much for a treasure? And why not—in pursuit of that treasure—live merrily and free in a ship that belonged only to those who sailed her? And why not, as free men under sail, take vengeance on the hated lords and masters of a cruel and disdainful civilization?

As word of *Amity*'s Indian Ocean exploit spread, canny merchants and captains began to outfit ships for the east. Sailors from every port sought berths on these eastbound vessels—as did deserters from the Royal Navy and ex-buccaneers. Many sailors now made the decision to turn to outright piracy, and mutinies at sea increased dramatically as crews seized their ships and set sail for the Indian Ocean.

Before the century turned, thousands of seamen had declared themselves sea outlaws—and the sporadic piracy of past ages had become a worldwide eruption.

The pirate captain Bartholomew Roberts, writing almost thirty years later, used these words to describe the motives that lured men to piracy at this time: "In an honest service there is thin rations, low wages, and hard labor; in this, plenty, satiety, pleasure and ease, liberty and power; and who would not balance creditor on this side, when all the hazard that is run for it, at worst, is only a sour look or two at choking? No, a merry life and a short one shall be my motto."

One of those who joined the eastward invasion was to become the most famous, and one of the most successful, of all the captains who ever flew a pirate flag. He was an Englishman named Henry Every, alias John Avery, alias "Long Ben" Avery, called in his time "the Arch-Pirate."

If it was Captain Thomas Tew, the Newport privateer, who fired the opening shots in the pirate war, it was Henry Every, the Arch-Pirate, who touched off the first full broadside.

4

The Very Model
of a Pirate Villain

In May 1694, when King William's War against Louis XIV was in its fifth indecisive year, the English privateer *Charles II* lay at anchor in the port of La Coruña, in Spain.

A swift-sailing, well-armed fighting ship, the *Charles II* carried forty-six cannon and a crew of 120 tough veterans of privateering campaigns in the Caribbean. She had been chartered in Bristol by the Spanish government, England's new ally against the French.[1] Her mission was to intercept French smugglers operating in Spain's Caribbean colonies.

It was not much of a charter, for there was little chance that French smugglers, even if they could be caught, would yield much plunder. Prize money, therefore, would be meager. On the other hand, privateering ventures had become scarcer than sober sailors since the war with France had commenced. For that reason any seafarer who wanted to avoid service in the navy or aboard a merchant ship was glad to take whatever privateering berth presented itself, even if it was only a punitive expedition

against smugglers. Recruiters, therefore, had had no trouble signing men aboard the *Charles II*.

The *Charles II*, however, was not a happy ship.

Although her crewmen—as employees of the Spanish government—had been promised regular pay (in addition to shares in
any booty they might capture from French smugglers), they had
received no salary since signing aboard and they were grumbling
openly.

But despite the complaints of the crew, the commander of the
Charles II, a certain Captain Gibson, did nothing to improve the
situation. According to that omniscient chronicler Daniel Defoe,
Captain Gibson was a man "mightily addicted to Punch," and
usually drank himself into a stupor each night. It is likely that
Gibson was too drunk or hung over most of the time to know, or
care, about the plummeting morale of his crew.

Further aggravating the unhappiness aboard the *Charles II* was
the fact that neither Captain Gibson nor the Spanish government
seemed in any hurry to speed her on her mission to the Caribbean where her disaffected crew would at least get a chance to
obtain some plunder. Although it was months since Spanish officials had chartered her, the *Charles II* had still gotten no farther
than the port of La Coruña where, as the month of May waned,
she was delayed again, waiting this time to take on additional passengers and stores for the long voyage across the Atlantic, while
her crew seethed with resentment.

If Captain Gibson was unaware of—or unconcerned with—the
tension aboard his ship, there was one officer of the *Charles II*
who was very much aware of it. This was the ship's forty-year-old
sailing master, or first officer, Henry Every, who was soon to become the most celebrated pirate of his time.

According to contemporaries, Every was a man of middle
height, stocky, with a tendency to run to fat. Clean-shaven, as the
fashion was, he had a florid complexion—one that would redden,
rather than tan, in the sun—and cold eyes that looked out upon
the world with unswerving directness from under heavy lids. In
dress he was far from a dandy, usually favoring a rather plain cos-
tume by the standards of the time: a tricorn hat, breeches and
buckled shoes, and a plain, longish waistcoat that did not flatter
his somewhat corpulent figure.

Every more than compensated for his physical shortcomings,
however, with an intimidating personality, a cunning intelligence,

and a frigid and ruthless competence that caused other men to defer to him. Although Every's associates acknowledged his courage and his daring in action, all recognized that it was his capacity to contrive clever plans and then to execute them with cold, undeviating purposefulness, that truly set Every apart from the simple men who sailed with him.

The incidents of Every's career reveal him as one of that rarest of human creatures: a completely selfish man. He seems to have known at all times exactly what he wanted, and exactly what to do to obtain what he wanted. Nor did he scruple at any wrongdoing to achieve his ends. He was a man who always maintained control of himself. He did not drink, for example, although he operated in an environment in which drunkenness was a way of life. He seldom betrayed anger either, although he would occasionally feign it for effect. Self-disciplined himself, Every overflowed with contempt for the weak-minded and ignorant men around him. Yet he managed to hide his disdain behind a mask of good nature in order to get these simpler souls to do his will.

(At least one contemporary source says that Every was often "insolent" and that he gave himself the airs of a monarch. As if to underscore this judgment, he is depicted in some old woodcuts wearing fancy clothing and accompanied by a black slave who holds a parasol over his head to shield him from the sun. Given the character of Every that comes through in his career, however, it seems highly unlikely that he ever really adopted such royal airs. It is far more probable that, if he ever did behave in this manner, it was a pose he employed to achieve some devious purpose of his own. Other contemporary illustrations show a rather portly, heavy-lidded Every with a cynical half smile on his face. These portraits seem much more characteristic of the man. It is easy to imagine the smile of this Every turning into a snarl. It is also easy to imagine the man depicted in these illustrations speaking soothing, convincing words in a soft, velvety voice—and then cocking his pistols and coolly blowing his hearer's brains out.)

While it is necessary to infer much of Every's character from contemporary accounts and from events in his career, a few solid facts *do* exist about his early life.

He was born near Plymouth, England, about 1653, the son of poverty-stricken parents. He went to sea as a boy some time around 1665 and is supposed to have served in the Royal Navy in the Mediterranean. Bright and willing, he learned to read and write, a rare accomplishment among ordinary sailors of the time. He also had a predilection for mathematics, and became a first-class navigator. While still a young man—despite the pervasive prejudices of the day—he became a ship's officer, serving aboard a series of merchant vessels. At one point he served aboard a slave ship that worked the west coast of Africa in the service of the royal governor of Bermuda. He apparently employed his native ruthlessness and persuasiveness to good effect in filling the holds of his ships with human cargo, for he soon gained a reputation along the coast as a most successful practitioner of the gruesome trade in "black ivory." He must have remained in the slave trade for a number of years, because as late as 1693, a Royal African Company officer wrote: "I have no where upon the coast met the negroes so shy as here, which makes me fancy they have had tricks play'd them by such blades as Long Ben, alias Every, who have seiz'd and carry'd them away."

Probably it was while employed in the vile slave trade that Henry Every gained both his knowledge of command and the deep streak of contempt for humanity that was so evident in his piratical career.

In any event, Every had long since made himself into a master mariner and a practiced manipulator of men when, in May 1694, he found himself serving aboard the privateer *Charles II*.

Although nominally second-in-command under the drunken Captain Gibson, there is little doubt that Every was, in fact, the real leader of the discontented crew of the *Charles II*. He had helped recruit many of the ship's crew off the docks of Bristol. Many of them, no doubt, had sailed with him on slaving voyages in the past. They would have had no hesitancy about disclosing to Henry Every their dissatisfaction about the *Charles II*'s cruise— and he would have had no scruple about manipulating the crew's ire for his purposes.

The men aboard the *Charles II* must have already heard the first reports of the voyage of Captain Thomas Tew in the *Amity*, and the rich score that he had made. There must have been many nights, as the *Charles II* lay at La Coruña and Captain Gibson lay drunk in his cabin, when Henry Every whispered to his shipmates that they too might become rich. They had only to seize the *Charles II* and take her to the East.

Doubtless Every, using such blandishments, had little trouble recruiting a full complement of mutineers.

(It is not beyond the realm of possibility, as some suggest, that Every had planned to seize the *Charles II* from the very outset of her cruise. Given his devious nature, he might very well have recruited some of his old Bristol shipmates from slaving days specifically for purposes of mutiny.)

Having made sure of sufficient support among the crew, Every set forth a simple straightforward plan for taking the *Charles II*.

Every's plan revolved around the fact that it was captain Gibson's habit to go ashore almost every night and get blind drunk in a favorite tavern. He suggested that the mutineers simply wait for a night when the tide would be running out to sea and the moon obscured. While Captain Gibson was ashore getting drunk, they would take control of the ship and set adrift any dissenters to their enterprise. Then, after riding the tide far enough offshore, they would set sail and be away to gain their fortune. All agreed with Every's scheme.

But on the designated night, Captain Gibson did not go ashore. Instead he got drunk in his cabin.

The cool Every merely altered his plan.

He waited until the captain had drunk himself into his usual stupor. Then Every and his mutineers weighed anchor—so stealthily that they neither woke the drunken captain nor disturbed other members of the crew asleep below.

They headed the *Charles II* out to sea on the tide. Defoe tells the story from this point on in crisp detail.

The *Charles II* was far offshore when at last the motion of the ship and the sound of the sails being worked finally roused Captain Gibson.

The befuddled captain rang the bell in his cabin, signaling for his second-in-command. Every, who had been expecting the summons, entered the captain's cabin accompanied by two of his mutineers. (It is easy to imagine the portly Every, with a cocked pistol in his belt, smiling down on the confused, disheveled Gibson sprawled out in his nightshirt on his bunk.)

"What is the matter?" asked Captain Gibson, sitting up and

pointing to the lamp in his cabin, swinging with the movement of the ship. "What is the matter?"

"Nothing is the matter," Every replied smoothly.

"Something's the matter with this ship," insisted Gibson, emerging now a little further out of his alcoholic fog. "What weather is it?"

"No, no," soothed Every. "We're at sea with a fair wind and good weather."

"At sea!" the captain cried. "How can that be?"

"Come," Every murmured, the smile remaining on his face. "Don't be in a fright. Put on your clothes, and I'll let you into a secret."

Now, as the astounded Captain Gibson listened wide-eyed and struggled into his clothes, Every matter-of-factly spelled out the new status of the *Charles II* and those who sailed in her.

Said Every: "You must know that I am captain of this ship now, and this is my cabin; therefore you must walk out. I am bound to Madagascar, with a design of making my own fortune, and that of all the brave fellows joined with me."

Every, maintaining his tone of sweet reason, then went on to explain that Captain Gibson had only two choices open to him. He could join the mutiny as Every's second-in-command (provided he was willing to give up drinking), or Every would give him a ship's boat and let him find his way to shore.

Captain Gibson recognized that he no longer commanded his ship. He chose to be set ashore. Every agreed. The mutiny was over.

Now, with his purpose accomplished, Every and his mutineers called together the rest of the crew. Every explained what had happened, and the mission he now proposed for the *Charles II*. The great majority of the crew overwhelmingly approved Every's enterprise and enthusiastically elected him captain.

Six crewmen who did not endorse Every or his program were then put into an open boat along with the deposed Captain Gibson and allowed to row back to La Coruña. (By the time they reached the safety of the port, and told their story, Every was far out of reach.)

Every now renamed the ship the *Fancy*—a name soon to become famous. He then ran up the flag of St. George—a banner flown by many English ships—and his own personal flag: four silver chevrons on a red field, a flag soon to become infamous. He then set a course that would take *Fancy* around the Cape of Good Hope to the East, where Tew had won his fortune.

It was not long before *Fancy* took her first victims. In the vicinity of the Cape Verde Islands, located off the northwest coast of Africa, Every halted three English ships and helped himself to supplies from their larders. Although minor in scope, this offense against English ships was, in fact, an unpardonable act of piracy, one that put Every and his men irrevocably outside the law. Perhaps the devious Every deliberately chose to plunder these English ships in order to commit his men to him and to their mission. In any event, *Fancy* continued on her voyage southward along the African coast. Along the way she took two Danish ships, which yielded only a few ounces of gold for each man in Every's crew. But it was a taste of what was to come.

After rounding the Cape of Good Hope, Every fetched up at Johanna Island, a pleasant, well-watered island just off the northwest corner of Madagascar. Johanna was a popular place for mariners to victual, water, and clean their hulls. Here Every careened the *Fancy* and scraped her hull of marine growth so that she would slide more smoothly through the water. He also took this opportunity to remove much of *Fancy's* "upperwork" such as her deck cabins, forecastle bulwarks, and hatches. The idea was to achieve a "flush" deck that would give her more speed—a crucial requirement, Every felt, for success in the mission ahead.

While at Johanna an incident occurred that further illustrates Every's capacity to make swift, unsentimental judgments for the benefit of himself and his enterprise.

A French pirate ship, loaded with loot taken from Mogul ships, came into Johanna for water.

Every quickly assembled his men and pointed out that England and France were at war. He then suggested that it was their duty to their king to seize the French pirate. To the ordinary sailors who heard Every, the proposition seemed plausible, not to mention attractive. Without hesitation Every's men piled aboard the French pirate, and soon took control of the ship and her contents.

Every then invited the defeated French crew to join the crew of *Fancy*. Most of them, along with a dozen other Frenchmen, who had previously been shipwrecked at Johanna, did so with alacrity, obviously impressed with Every. They no doubt saw clearly that service with a captain who knew what he wanted and how to get it would bring considerable profit.

While at Johanna, Every also composed a cunning letter that he gave to a native chief to pass on to the first English ship that arrived in the harbor after he had departed. It is classical Every:

To All English Commanders:

Let this satisfy that I was riding here at this instant in the ship *Fancy*, man-of-war, formerly the *Charles* of the Spanish Expedition who departed from La Coruña 7th May 1694, being then and now a ship of 46 guns, 150 men and bound to seek our fortunes. I have never as yet wronged any English or Dutch or ever intend whilst I am Commander. Wherefore as I commonly speak with all ships, I desire whoever comes to the perusal of this to take this signal, that if you or any whom you may inform are desirous to know what we are at a distance, then make your ancient [ship's flag] up in a ball or bundle and hoist him at the mizzen peak, the mizzen being furled. I shall answer with the same, and never molest you, for my men are hungry, stout, and resolute, and should they exceed my desire I cannot help myself. As yet, an Englishman's friend,

At Johanna 18th February 1695
Henry Every

P.S. Here is 160 odd French armed men at Mohilla who waits for opportunity for getting any ship, take care of yourselves.

This mixture of threats and assurances was received by the English captain of an East Indiaman only a few days after Every sailed north from Johanna. It was eventually forwarded to London with a request for stronger measures against the growing pirate menace in the Indian Ocean.

Every's purpose in writing this cleverly contrived letter was to confuse the authorities regarding his purpose. He had hoped, also, to give the impression that if his men committed crimes, it was beyond *his* power to stop them, and *he* should not be held accountable. Always thinking of himself above all, Every appears to be trying to disassociate himself personally, in advance, from the crimes that he knew he and his men would soon be committing. By adding the postscript about the French threat at Mohilla (Mohéli), he was probably attempting to convince the ultimate readers of the letter, the authorities in London, that despite all appearances to the contrary, he remained a loyal Englishman in service to the king.

But Every's ploy, which he had probably regarded as a long shot in any case, failed to achieve its purpose. The authorities in

London set Henry Every down in their books as an outright pirate.

Meanwhile, *Fancy* was on her way northward, bound for the mouth of the Red Sea. Every's plan was to patrol the narrow Gulf of Aden where he hoped to seize a rich, Moorish ship on her way to or from India. (English-speaking sailors began around this time to call all Muslim vessels "Moorish.")

On the voyage from Johanna to the Red Sea, *Fancy* was joined by two smaller pirate ships from America. It was agreed the two Americans would operate jointly with *Fancy*, and that Every would serve as overall commander of the little fleet.

In August 1695, Every and his companion ships arrived at their destination and began their predatory patrol. Every soon learned from Muslim fisherman he had captured that the annual convoy of the Great Mogul's treasure ships was due to leave soon from the Red Sea port of Mocha for the return trip to India. The Arab prisoners said that in addition to precious cargoes of gold, jewels, and silks, the Mogul fleet would also be carrying wealthy pilgrims, returning home to India after visiting the Holy City of Mecca. Every ordered a round-the-clock watch for the Moorish convoy.

Now, as *Fancy* and her consorts waited for their Mogul prey to appear, two more American ships came into the area. One of them turned out to be the famed *Amity*, under the celebrated Captain Tew. The newcomers also agreed to join the pirate flotilla under Henry Every's command.

Day after day the pirate ships cruised, scouring the area for their victims. Although each ship patrolled independently, each kept within range of the flagship, the *Fancy*.

Then, on a moonless night, the Mogul convoy sailed. Despite the sharp vigil being kept aboard the pirate ships, the Mogul fleet, twenty-five ships in all, slipped past the pirate lookouts unseen.

When the sun rose the next morning the enraged pirates discovered that most of the long-awaited convoy had gotten too far beyond their picket lines to be caught. Every, however, refused to allow disappointment or anger to cloud his judgment. Examining the retreating convoy through his glass, he decided that two of the Mogul ships might still be within range. The nearest of these possible victims was a small vessel, while the other, farther off, was an enormous ship, clearly so powerfully armed that she would outgun any of the pirate fleet—including *Fancy*—by a wide margin. Nevertheless, Every ordered his ship to pursue the fleeing Moors.

Aboard *Amity*, which was closer to the two Mogul ships than *Fancy* was, Captain Tew also decided to pursue. Crowding on all sail, Tew chased after the smaller of the two Moors. *Fancy* followed.'

After a time *Amity* caught up with her quarry, whose Arabic name was *Fateh Mohamed*. There was an exchange of fire. Both ships recoiled from the shock. Men screamed oaths. Muskets cracked. Then, suddenly, *Amity* disengaged. A cannon shot from *Fateh Mohamed* had killed Captain Tew. The men of *Amity*, shocked by the death of their captain, turned away.

Fateh Mohamed sailed on. But she did not escape.

Every's speedy *Fancy* overtook her. His tough crew swarmed aboard her. The *Fateh Mohamed*'s crew, outnumbered and outgunned, this time decided not to fight. Every's men quickly ransacked the Mogul vessel, bellowing with joy when they discovered that the *Fateh Mohamed* carried some £50,000 in gold and silver, which they quickly transferred to *Fancy*.

Now Every exhibited the daring and steely resolve that was also part of his character. He saw that the other Moorish ship— much larger than the *Fateh Mohamed*—was still within range. It seemed to him that this great ship now lumbering toward the horizon might be carrying a cargo even more valuable than the treasure they had just taken from the *Fateh Mohamed*, for surely a ship so large and so heavily armed must be transporting the dearest treasures of the Great Mogul himself. As formidable as this Moorish giant might be, Every told himself, she was also the sort of prize that freebooters could hope to encounter only once. He sensed the chance of a lifetime—and he seized it without hesitation.

He broke out every scrap of sail. *Fancy* began the chase.

In fact, the ship Every was pursuing was the *Gang-I-Sawai*.

She was, in the words of Indian historian Khafi Khan, "the greatest ship in all the Mogul dominions." She carried sixty-two guns and five hundred soldiers. She also carried six hundred passengers among whom were a number of high-ranking officials of the Great Mogul's court who were returning from their pilgrimage to Mecca. She was also carrying, in her capacious holds,

500,000 gold and silver pieces. Her destination was the port of Surat on India's west coast.

Inexorably *Fancy* closed the gap between herself and the giant Mogul ship. Before long the men aboard the *Fancy* could make out the gaping muzzles of the *Gang-I-Sawai's* cannon and the heavily armed, turbaned soldiers crowding her decks. But despite being outgunned and outnumbered better than four to one, the crew of *Fancy* prepared for action, confident of their ability to overcome their Moorish enemy.

As her ponderous quarry came into range of *Fancy's* cannon, Every broke out his flag of silver chevrons as a sign that he was willing to give quarter if the Moors surrendered. There was no response to his signal. Every then ran up a plain red flag, the "bloody flag" as his men called it, signifying that the offer of quarter was withdrawn.

The battle was on.

Fancy fired a broadside. The Muslim guns replied. But as the Moorish broadside was fired, one of the *Gang-I-Sawai's* cannon suddenly exploded, killing a number of her well-trained gun crews and sending lethal fragments of metal scything across her decks, compelling her soldiers to take cover in confusion and terror. *Fancy* fired again. A lucky shot crashed into the Mogul ship's mainmast, disrupting her rigging and slowing her even more. With her rigging badly damaged, the *Gang-I-Sawai* soon became almost unmaneuverable.

Fancy now broke off firing and swung in alongside her much larger quarry whose gunports towered over her. As soon as the two ships touched, Every's crew, cutlasses and pistols at the ready, scrambled up the sides of the *Gang-I-Sawai* and hurled themselves against the Muslim soldiers who awaited them.

The pirates' ferocity made up for their lack of numbers. With cutlasses ringing on steel scimitars, the pirates fought for the ship for two hours.

Smoke, explosions, and the screams of dying and wounded men filled the air. The decks of the *Gang-I-Sawai* ran with blood as the Indian soldiers fiercely resisted the pirate onslaught. At one point in the confusion of battle, the *Gang-I-Sawai's* captain, Ibrahim Khan, fled below to a cabin where he had secreted a number of Turkish girls whom he had bought in Mecca to add to his harem. Apparently intending to safeguard his property from the marauding pirates who were still battling his troops on the decks above, the Mogul captain wrapped turbans around the girls' heads, hoping thereby to fool the infidel outlaws into believing they were boys. But the pirates, who burst into the cabin in the wake of the captain, were not fooled by the ruse. They dragged the girls up on deck where the pirates were now gaining the upper hand in the bloody battle.

By degrees the fighting diminished as more and more of the Muslim soldiers and sailors threw up their hands in surrender. Finally, the fighting ceased altogether.

In the wake of the noise of combat, an eerie silence now descended over the *Gang-I-Sawai*. The dead lay everywhere. Wreckage littered the decks. The *Gang-I-Sawai* creaked in the sudden quiet. Every's men had gained the victory but at the cost of fifteen to twenty dead comrades—a fact that so infuriated them that they began a vengeful orgy of murder, rape, and torture as they ransacked their prize.

Every's men had little compunction about meting out brutal treatment to their captives. Muslims, in their view, were only "black heathen," sinners who denied Christ and therefore deserved the harsh treatment they got.

Every's men stripped their captives, both men and women, of all their clothing and possessions. They tortured any captive they suspected of withholding valuables. In some cases the infuriated pirates simply killed their victims after taking their money. A number of the women, however, were dragged off to be gang-raped. One of those treated in this manner was the elderly wife of a high-ranking Mogul official who also happened to be a relative of the Great Mogul himself. Some of the women died under their savage treatment. Some threw themselves overboard rather than submit to ravishment. Some, feeling themselves shamed forever, later stabbed themselves to death with daggers.

Throughout the butchery, Every himself remained aboard the *Fancy*. He knew better than to take part personally in these brutalities. In any case, he was not temperamentally given to such outbursts of vengeance-seeking, although he had participated in the thick of the battle for the *Gang-I-Sawai*.

As the rage of the pirates spent itself, and as cooler heads began to restore order, it became clear that—as Every had anticipated—the *Gang-I-Sawai* was a mother lode of booty. The loot that was now piling up on her bloody decks included gold, silver, ivory, jewels, damasks, and even a saddle set with rubies, which had been intended for the Great Mogul himself.

Now Every, taking command again in the aftermath of his crew's explosion of violence, ordered all this wealth—and the surviving women as well—transferred to the *Fancy*.

When this was accomplished, Every ordered the *Gang-I-Sawai* cut loose to join its consort, the previously pillaged *Fateh Mohamed*, for the long, lugubrious voyage home.

Eventually both ships put in at Surat, the Great Mogul's chief port and the East India Company's main trading station in India. The tale of the pirate terror that the two ships' survivors told outraged the Great Mogul. The Mogul's fury, in turn, sent a chill of fear through the men of the East India Company who depended upon his goodwill for their continued prosperity.

Although the Muslim Indians were sympathetic toward the civilian victims of the pirate terror, they wasted little sympathy on the soldiers and sailors who had lost the *Gang-I-Sawai*.

Mogul historian Khafi Khan viewed the pirate victory as a disgrace for Mogul arms and he blamed the ship's captain for not putting up a better fight. "The English are not bold in the use of the sword," he wrote, "and there were so many weapons aboard that, if any determined resistance had been made, they had been defeated."

Meanwhile, *Fancy*, after rejoining the other ships of Every's fleet, set off southward for safe waters where Every planned to share out the loot and plan his next move.

Fancy and her consorts eventually made landfall at the island of Bourbon (later to be renamed Réunion) almost 2,500 miles away from the scene of the battle. At this time Bourbon, although claimed by France, was virtually devoid of French presence, let alone French law.

Here Every and his men divided the plunder from the *Gang-I-Sawai* and the *Fateh Mohamed*. The East India Company later estimated Every's loot at some £325,000—a truly imperial haul.

Each man in Every's company received more than £1,000, plus a number of jewels. The apprenticed seamen who sailed in the fleet, most of them boys between twelve and fifteen years of age, received £500 each. Every himself was awarded the pirate captain's usual double share. There is no record of the fate of the women taken from the *Gang-I-Sawai*. More than likely they were left stranded at Bourbon.

Now, with the loot divided, Every's fleet broke up, with each ship going its own way. Every himself wanted to take *Fancy* to the Bahamas. He knew of a local governor there, he said, who would help them sell their stolen goods for cash. But members of Every's crew wanted to go to Brazil instead. As usual Every finally won the argument, although about fifty of his men elected to remain in Bourbon rather than voyage farther. To fill their places Every took aboard a consignment of black slaves. Then, in April 1696, he set off for the Bahamas.

As the news of the capture of the *Gang-I-Sawai* reached Europe, tall tales began to circulate about Henry Every, tales that would make him a legend. At this time he was given the appellation of Arch-Pirate. It was said that he had captured and married one of the Great Mogul's beautiful daughters. Other stories had him settling down in Madagascar with one or more exotic beauties, and living in great state and luxury surrounded by adoring subjects. It was said in the drawing rooms of London that he had offered to pay off the national debt of England in order to obtain the king's pardon for his crimes. A popular play was written about him, its title *The Successful Pirate*. Defoe says that many contemporaries believed that Every had founded a new monarchy in far off Madagascar. (Every was clearly the inspiration for a novel Defoe himself wrote in 1720, *The Life, Adventures and Piracies of the Famous Captain Singleton*.)

It was even reported that Every had been one of Henry Morgan's buccaneers in his younger days.

Every had become in the public mind, the personification of all pirate captains: dashing, daring, cruel, and cool—the very model of a pirate villain.

Meanwhile, the subject of all these fictions had arrived with his ship *Fancy* at the Caribbean island of St. Thomas, then under Danish control. Here Every and his men sold some of their booty for ready cash to an appreciative populace who quickly snapped up whatever the pirates offered.

Every and *Fancy* then went on to the Bahamas where Governor Nicholas Trott received him and his men warmly after the pirates presented the governor with £7,000 worth of their booty as a mark of their high regard for him. Trott, in return, opened up his home for the entertainment of Every and his men.

Although Every no doubt enjoyed the hospitality that his new wealth bought in the Bahamas, he realized, far better than his men did, that he would never really be free to enjoy his good fortune as long as he remained a fugitive from the law. To deal with this difficulty, Every now sought some legal absolution from his friend Governor Trott—a document of pardon that would enable him to return to England and the full enjoyment of his ill-gotten gains. But even the obliging Governor Trott was unable to provide what Every wanted. He had, he explained, no power to issue pardons. Only the king and Parliament could do that.

Every apparently remained unconvinced. He sailed on to Jamaica where he sought out the local governor—one William Beeston—and offered him a considerable sum (Beeston said it was £24,000) for a pardon absolving Every and his crew of their crimes. But Beeston, like Trott, could do nothing for the Arch-Pirate.

Back in the Bahamas once again, Every and his crew suffered a serious loss: The *Fancy*, caught in a storm when her crew was too drunk to handle her properly, was driven up on a reef where she broke up. She was a total loss except for her guns, which Governor Trott salvaged for his own use.

Now some of Every's crew, growing weary of their captain's seemingly incessant search for an illusory pardon, began to leave him. Some found their way northward into the colonies of America. One of these even married the daughter of Governor William Markham of Pennsylvania. Others drifted away to one port or another. One, it was reported, went insane when he gambled away all his hard-won loot.

For all the romantic tales that the Arch-Pirate and his crew of desperadoes had inspired by their exploits, the truth was that many months after their victory over the *Gang-I-Sawai*, most of them were in serious trouble: stranded in the Bahamas and unable to find a place of refuge to enjoy their wealth. But Henry Every, always resourceful and always looking out for his own best interests, now came up with a daring plan to return to Britain secretly. In reality, it was a plan intended to benefit him alone.

Every suggested that he and his men buy two or three small sloops, vessels that could land unobserved in the numerous small bays of Ireland or the west coast of England. They would then, he continued, divide into several small groups, each group to man one of the sloops. Each sloop would then sail to a different destination on the Irish or English coast, after which each small crew would simply abandon its sloop and go ashore to blend in with the general population. The authorities, Every went on persuasively, would be searching for a large vessel in the Caribbean, or in the Indian Ocean. They would never expect pirates to be bold enough to return to England. Furthermore, Every suggested smoothly, the authorities would never be suspicious of an inoffensive little sloop entering an out-of-the-way harbor. The very audacity of the plan, Every assured his listeners, would guarantee its success.

About two dozen of his original crew agreed to Every's proposal. They now bought two sloops. Every and eleven men in one sloop, and the rest in the other, set sail for home, each sloop making for a different destination—according to plan. Every, who had furnished himself with papers and letters that identified him as "Captain Benjamin Bridgemen," now gave out different stories to his companions about his intentions once they reached their journey's end. His real plan he kept to himself.

In June 1696, Every's sloop landed at a small bay called Dunfanaghy in County Donegal, Ireland. Here Every deserted his companions and went off alone.

The other sloop had landed in Westport, County Mayo. She had immediately aroused local suspicion when the sailors who had brought her in began to unload cargo that seemed to consist only of chests of silver and gold. The county sheriff arrested a number of these careless sailors almost as soon as they had set foot ashore. A few, however, eluded immediate capture.

The men who had landed with Every in Donegal fared better. They got ashore all right, and they made their way to their various destinations. But they gave themselves away—as Every undoubtedly knew they would—by drunken boasting and by immodestly flashing the gold in their purses. One man, John Dann, was taken in Rochester when a maid at the inn where he was hiding out discovered that his jacket was too heavy to lift—not surprising since Dann had sewed £1,045 in gold into its lining. Other members of Every's crew were arrested when they tried to sell their foreign coin or jewels to goldsmiths.

In the end, all twenty-four of the men Every had talked into returning with him were arrested.

But Every himself eluded the net.

Questioned about their cunning captain's whereabouts, Every's men were unable to shed any light on the subject. One of his captured crew said Every had told him he planned to settle down in Scotland. Another said he had seen Every in Dublin. Still another said Every was making for Plymouth. Others thought Every was living in London where he had been joined by a Mrs. Adams, the wife of his former quartermaster on the *Fancy*.

Henry Every, the Arch-Pirate, had disappeared behind the smokescreen of false leads that he had fed his gullible men. He was never seen or heard from again.

If no one knows Henry Every's final fate, the record spells out clearly the destinies of the simple sailors he had used as decoys. These captured crewmen of Every's went on trial in October 1696. All were convicted. The court sentenced eighteen of them to be transported to Virginia as convict labor. It ordered that six of them suffer hanging for their crimes aboard the *Fancy*. On October 25, 1696, at Execution Dock, Wapping, the six condemned met the hangman.

One of those hanged was John Sparkes. A contemporary broadsheet described his end:

"This villain expressed his contrition for the horrid barbarities he had committed, though only on the bodies of heathens. The inhuman treatment and merciless tortures inflicted on the poor Indians and their women still afflicted his soul. He declared that he justly suffered death for such inhumanity even more than for his crime in running away with the *Charles*, which was the lesser concern."

Sparkes may have repented, but the other condemned men from Every's crew went to their deaths with bravado, and with contempt for the society that had condemned them. According to the broadsheet that described the execution, one of the unrepentant men, Dennis MacCarthy, took off his shoes, after which he "kicked them off the scaffold, saying he would prove those to be liars who had said he would die with his boots on."

As for the Arch-Pirate, his mysterious disappearance only added to his legend, giving rise to even more lurid tales about his career and speculations about his fate. One story that gained considerable credence held that Every had bought himself a royal pardon with his plunder—and, with a new identity, lived out his days in ease and comfort in a great house overlooking the sea. Other stories suggested that Every, repenting of his villainous past, spent the rest of his life doing penance. Some said it was Every himself who betrayed his returning crew members to the authorities in England—an act of perfidy that the Arch-Pirate was certainly capable of—and that he later went mad with remorse.

Even Defoe gives his tale of the Arch-Pirate a colorful ending. Defoe says that Every eventually ended up in the town of Bideford, in Devon, where he was cheated of his swag by local merchants who threatened to expose him to the authorities if he complained. Defoe says that in the end Every died "not being worth as much as would buy him a Coffin," and crying to all who would hear him that merchants were "as good Pyrates at land as he was at Sea."

Whatever Every's true fate may have been, it remains unrecorded. His exploits in eastern waters, however, were not only recorded, they were discussed avidly in the fo'c'sles of a thousand ships where sailors dreamed of Arab gold, the bodies of dusky women, and the liberty to do as they pleased.

If Thomas Tew and *Amity* had exposed the wealth of the East, Henry Every and *Fancy* had confirmed its amplitude—and had shown that resolute fighting men could take it for themselves.

As the 1690s ran out, the pirate war burned in full conflagration. In the wake of Every, English and colonial pirates infested the Indian Ocean. The Red Sea became a pirate lake. Ships with names like *Resolution, John and Rebecca,* (which belonged to the New York City merchant prince Frederick Philipse), *Portsmouth Adventure, The Charming Mary, Pelican,* and a dozen others, all manned by tough ex-privateers and mutineers from both the merchant fleets and the Royal Navy, cruised the Indian Ocean like the armed fleet of a country at war.

As with any combat fleet, the pirate men-of-war needed places to resupply, to rest and repair—in brief, a secure base of their own.

Luckily for them, such a base already existed, a ready-made fortress that would soon become the unruly "homeland" of a ragtag "nation" of rebels and raiders: Madagascar.

The Outlaw Nation

The world's fourth largest island—after Greenland, New Guinea, and Borneo—Madagascar lies approximately eight hundred miles below the equator, off the southeast coast of Africa. It is separated from the African coast by a five-hundred-mile stretch of water called the Mozambique Channel.

From north to south Madagascar is 980 miles long. It is 260 miles across at its widest point. In area Madagascar is about five times larger than England, and twice the size of Italy.

When approached from the Indian Ocean, the great island, green and jagged against the horizon, seems to emerge abruptly out of the ocean itself—as if a mountain range had suddenly heaved itself up from the sea. On this eastern side of Madagascar the land climbs sharply to a green plateau—geographically a long and narrow shelf of land thick with forests. Above this wooded shelf loom the mountains whose massive formation, like a huge rugged wall, runs the length of the island. Some of the peaks of this mountain chain rise more than 7,000 feet above sea level. One, Amboro, soars to 9,500 feet. Numerous short and violent rivers leap from the mountains, foam across the narrow, forested tableland, and hurl themselves in spectacular waterfalls over cliff faces into the sea below. Some of the mountain rivers, rather than ending in falls, have cut gorges for themselves down to the ocean.

In many places the wall of mountains is broken by deep, thickly forested, silent valleys, which afford passage from the precipitous Indian Ocean side of Madagascar to the gentler, western slope of the island.

The western plateau of Madagascar consists primarily of open grasslands, marked by occasional wooded areas. This side of the island slopes in a long, easy descent down to the Mozambique Channel. Here many rivers wind down to the sea through the open plains. These rivers are longer, deeper, and slower than are the streams on the eastern side of the island.

During the rainy season—which usually lasts in these latitudes from November to April—the forested eastern side of Madagascar receives more than one hundred inches of rain, while the grassy western slope receives less than half that amount. The extreme southwestern end of the island, however, receives almost no rain, and is virtually a desert.

Despite its proximity to Africa, Madagascar's people are not of African origin. They are rather of Malayo-Polynesian stock. It is thought that they migrated to Madagascar from Indonesia more than three thousand miles to the east across the Indian Ocean.

Because the great island offers numerous bays, coves, inlets, and harbors suitable as anchorages, seafarers have resorted to it from the very earliest times.

Madagascar was known to both Arab and Hindu traders in the Indian Ocean at least two centuries before Europeans "discovered" the island. Some time around the end of the fourteenth century small groups of Muslim traders, perhaps from Zanzibar, set up trading colonies in the north of Madagascar. Indian merchants also visited the northern part of the island during this period. It is likely that during this time Madagascar was part of a regular Indian Ocean trading route followed by both Arab and Indian merchants.

Although visited frequently by merchants, Madagascar remained a place of mystery and fable to eastern civilizations. It is, for example, described in early Arabic tales as the home of the giant bird called the roc, which was capable of carrying off elephants and which, in one tale, attacked Sinbad's ship.

Although Madagascar is mentioned in the writings of Marco Polo, the first European definitely known to have visited the island was Diogo Dias, a Portuguese navigator who touched on the island in 1500 on his way to India. The Portuguese, who called Madagascar the Isle of St. Lawrence, frequently raided the island during the sixteenth century in unsuccessful attempts to dislodge Muslim trading settlements there.

In the early years of the seventeenth century, as more and more European states initiated trade with the East, attempts were made to establish permanent European outposts on Madagascar.

In 1642 the French East India Company established settlements along the southern coast. The most important of these posts they named Port Dauphin. The French also attempted to lay claim to the entire island of Madagascar, but since France could not back up her claim with arms, other European powers active in the region ignored it.

In 1645 the English, not to be outdone by the French, also planted a colony in the southern sector of the island, in an area known as St. Augustine's Bay. The Dutch, too, attempted to establish a permanent settlement.

The English attempt at colonization failed miserably, primarily because of malaria and other tropical fevers. Of the original 140 colonists who had gone ashore at St. Augustine's Bay, only 23 survived the first year. This initial effort at colonization was abandoned. Twenty-three years later, the East India Company tried again, but this time hostile natives put an end to the effort.

The Dutch fared little better than the English, also abandoning their effort at colonization within a year or two. The French were more stubborn. They maintained their presence at Port Dauphin until 1674.

But though the European maritime nations failed in their attempts to colonize Madagascar, the great island and its environs played an important part in European trade with the East.

European and American merchant captains used the harbors and offshore islands on both sides of Madagascar as way stations on the long voyage to India. In addition to sheltered harbors, where mariners could clean and repair their hulls, Madagascar overflowed with fresh water, and meat was always available, as were limes and oranges—indispensable for preventing and curing scurvy.

Long before Europeans had attempted to settle there—and long after they had failed, too—the harbors of St. Augustine on the southwest, Port Dauphin on the southeast, and Ranter Bay on the northeast were all popular places for trading ships to put in.

The island of Johanna, just off the northwestern coast, and St. Mary's, off the northeastern coast, were also important ports of call. Less often visited but still frequently used by trading vessels were the farther islands in the Madagascar region: the Mascarenes to the east in the Indian Ocean, and the Comoro Islands to the west in the Mozambique Channel.

(It is important to keep in mind, however, that when these Madagascar islands are described as "popular" places, or "frequently visited," these are relative terms. Actual ship traffic in these harbors was extremely light when compared with the Great Mogul's ports, or Red Sea harbors. Even in the most frequently used Madagascar ports, weeks would often elapse between ships, and for more than one ship to be anchored in a roadstead at the same time was unusual.)

If Madagascar was an attractive stopping place for lawful trading vessels, it was equally attractive to—and as frequently visited by—ships engaged in less lawful, or less humane, traffic.

From the middle years of the seventeenth century onward, free-lance slave traders, most of them based in England's North American colonies, began to call at Madagascar, usually to refresh and repair before going on to their destinations across the Atlantic, but occasionally to obtain cargoes from local chieftains who dabbled in the slave trade.

Pirates also visited Madagascar's harbors even before the great outbreak of piracy after 1692. Although few in number, European freebooters had been present in the Indian Ocean as early as 1614 when French privateers, operating with Royal Commissions, preyed on shipping in the Red Sea.

In 1617 two London merchants, Sir Robert Rich and Philip Bernhardi, notwithstanding the fact that they were shareholders in the East India Company, fitted out two small ships, the *Francis* and the *Lion*, and sent them to attack "Moorish" shipping off the coast of India.

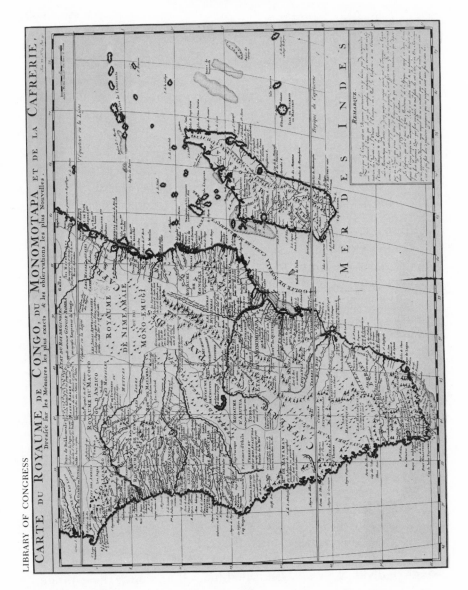

In 1630 Charles I himself financed a privateer called *Sea Horse* and sent her to attack Dutch shipping in the east.

Throughout the seventeenth century small-time piracies like these took place in the eastern waters as Danes, French, and of course, English pirates sought easy prey among the "heathen."

Although this handful of early eastern pirates made almost no impact on trade, they too discovered the attractions of

Madagascar. For pirates, however, Madagascar and its nearby islands offered even more than drinkable water, citrus fruit, and sheltered harbors. They also offered hidden coves where a pirate vessel could hide to careen or share out plunder. Even more important: Despite the legitimate cargo vessels that called there, Madagascar ship traffic was actually sparse when compared with the great number of vessels that crisscrossed the Indian Ocean or rounded the Cape for Europe or America, a fact that made it possible for pirates to frequent the area without much chance of discovery or interference. Moreover, warships seldom operated in Madagascar waters because the commercial and naval conflicts between the western trading powers usually took place far to the north in waters around India and Indonesia.

Another element that made Madagascar especially attractive to pirates was the fact that the native population was usually friendly, if not forced to conform to European laws or customs.

But by far the most important factor was its status as a political orphan. No European nation owned it. Despite hollow claims and pitiful attempts to colonize the island, there was no legitimate western presence on Madagascar. Furthermore, none of the numerous squabbling local tribes dominated more than a few square miles of the huge island.

Madagascar was unclaimed territory: pleasant, impregnable, and—above all—lawless.

It is little wonder that, few as they were, virtually all the pirates who operated in eastern waters before the 1690s regarded Madagascar and its nearby islands as a comfortable haven. Most of them had, at one time or another, visited the place.

Some pirates had even made more or less permanent homes in the area, establishing settlements of thirty to fifty "retired" pirates, plus their women and children.

Almost always these enclaves were under the command of a single individual, who often called himself a "king." These pirate settlements supported themselves by trade and by exploiting and dominating the natives of the neighborhood. Some of them remained in existence for many years. One pirate chieftain, a Captain John Rivers, set up his little "kingdom" some time around 1686 and continued to "reign" over it until he died in 1719.

There were perhaps half a dozen such small European enclaves, usually led by ex-pirates, on and around Madagascar by

1690. Although most of them traded with both the natives and the ships that called in their areas, none of them could be called thriving enterprises.

Then, early in 1691, a wily Scot named Adam Baldridge arrived at St. Mary's Island, just off Madagascar's northeastern coast. Here he set himself up as a trader—and soon began to prosper as no Madagascar trader ever had before, serving as the main supplier of the pirate ships that began pouring into the Indian Ocean and calling at St. Mary's in ever-increasing numbers starting about 1694.

A somewhat shadowy figure, Baldridge seems to have been an ex-pirate who had cruised extensively in the eastern seas and had come to know the Madagascar area well. It was after he killed a man in a tavern fight in Jamaica that Baldridge, seeking a refuge from authorities, had decided to settle down—as other ex-pirates had—in Madagascar.

He apparently chose the island of St. Mary's because it was often visited by both pirates and honest traders—and because its anchorage was almost landlocked and therefore easily defensible.

Arriving at the island with a full load of trade goods supplied to him by New York merchants, Baldridge built a stockade fort, with forty guns overlooking the harbor, strong enough to protect any ships that might anchor at St. Mary's from attack by other ships. In addition to the fort, Baldridge built himself a large and sturdy house on the top of a hill, which served both as a landmark for approaching ships and as a lookout from which to spot visitors.

Baldridge's little settlement eventually became the center of life for scores of ex-pirates, sailors, and retired seamen of the neighborhood who had chosen to live the rest of their days in the relative ease of Madagascar—where women, liquor, and other comforts were readily available to a white man for little money or effort. But it reached the zenith of its prosperity and influence when pirates from Europe and America poured into the Indian Ocean after Captain Tew's pathfinding voyage.

For these pirates, St. Mary's, where Adam Baldridge always extended a warm welcome, was the ideal port. But they used other harbors and anchorages as well.

(By the mid 1690s scores of pirate vessels were resorting to Madagascar and its satellite islands as bases from which to strike northward toward the Red Sea and toward the western coast of India, and as sanctuaries too remote, and too strong to attack.

With the influx of the pirate fleets, Madagascar bustled with activity. On any given day there might be as many as a dozen pirate ships anchored in Madagascar harbors, taking on stores, effecting repairs, bartering booty, or just lazing away a few days or weeks before resuming a plundering cruise, or returning home with holds stuffed with plunder.)

Baldridge, and other traders who followed him to Madagascar, made huge profits by exchanging such commodities as cattle, rum, guns, gunpowder, clothing, spices, wine, and tools for pirate plunder.

Baldridge also traded successfully with the natives, exchanging European manufactured goods and cloth for meat and produce that he later supplied to the pirates. Nor was he above an occasional deal in slaves.

A quintessential middleman, Baldridge filled his warehouses with luxury goods such as ivory and silks—all pirate plunder that would eventually be turned into cash through resale to "honest" merchants from New York, Boston, and other colonial cities, where the black market for such goods was booming as never before.

For the prosperity of Madagascar merchants like Baldridge, as well as the enormous success of the Madagascar pirates, depended not only on the unique attributes of their island bases and sanctuaries but also on the fervent economic support provided by American colonial merchants who dealt in pirate booty as a means of circumventing England's pernicious Navigation Acts.

American merchants who had once evaded the Navigation Acts by buying illegally the plunder that privateers "liberated" from the former Spanish enemy in the Caribbean, and who had often bankrolled such privateers, had now become the backers of pirates bound for the Indian Ocean. They had also become the brokers for goods plundered from the ships of eastern potentates.

The "Red Sea Men," as the eastern pirates were called in the colonies, not only had the financial backing of American merchants, they also had the sympathetic support of a public that tended to look upon them as almost-heroic figures, rather than as outright pirates. If they committed illegal acts, at least they committed them against "heathens."

The Red Sea Men and their merchant backers also had the help of corrupt colonial governors who were easily bribed to allow pirate ships to deliver their stolen goods to buyers ashore—without the bother of customs inspections. Some colonial governors, such as Captain Tew's good friend Benjamin Fletcher, not only took bribes from pirates but even invested in pirate expeditions to the East, and profited handsomely from their share of the plunder.

So great was the demand in the colonies for the luxury goods that the pirates provided that the Red Sea Men developed a regular sailing route and course of operation that they dubbed the "Pirate Round."

Following the Pirate Round, pirate ships would set out from any of several North American ports, cross the Atlantic, taking whatever merchants came into view, and then round the tip of Africa into the Mozambique Channel to Madagascar. Here they would rest, resupply, and clean their hulls before going on to savage the lumbering ships of the Great Mogul in the region of the Red Sea or along the sea-lanes to India. When they had sufficient booty, the pirate masters would then return to a Madagascar port, usually St. Mary's, where they would once again refresh and resupply themselves under the protective guns of Adam Baldridge's fort. Eventually they would retrace their route along the Pirate Round, returning to their starting point to dispose of their loot.

With the Pirate Round in full operation by the middle of the 1690s, ship builders in New England were hard-pressed to keep up with the demand for vessels suitable for the pirate trade in the Indian Ocean. Pirate booty was everywhere. In New York "Arab gold" even became common currency. So attractive was the trade that one syndicate of New York merchants decided to eliminate the middlemen in Madagascar by opening up their own depots there to resupply pirate ships (at a healthy markup) and to bid for pirate booty on the spot.

Yet the profits from piracy were so great that Madagascar merchants flourished in spite of competition.

In time Baldridge, as the key trader on St. Mary's, became in fact, as well as in name, the king of the island. He held court in his big house on the hill overlooking St. Mary's harbor, dispensing law for both the white and native populations. Warring tribes on the main island sought him as an ally, and he often participated in local wars, almost invariably deciding their outcome with his powerful arsenal of European weapons.

He not only acted like a king, he lived like one. He kept numerous slaves in his establishment. He enlarged and beautified his house, furnishing it with luxurious rugs, divans, hangings, and art all taken from bartered pirate loot. He kept a harem of Madagascar girls, and his entertainments were famous.

For Baldridge, and for the pirates who used Madagascar as a base, the "sweet trade," as they termed their calling, had never been so sweet.

For the first time in history, a large number of sea outlaws had come together to claim what was essentially their own piece of the globe, had achieved a phenomenal prosperity, and seemed capable of defying the power of any maritime state.

Unlike the buccaneers of Hispaniola and Jamaica, and the Channel pirates of earlier days, the Madagascar outlaws were more than a local nuisance, more than the desperate enterprise of a handful, more than a transitory phenomenon dependent upon conditions in the immediate environment. The Madagascar pirates were new in the experience of the world: international in scope, well financed, numerous, independent, and apparently powerful.

Furthermore, because the Madagascar pirates shared similar economic interests, similar personal backgrounds as authority-hating ordinary seamen, and a common geographic center in Madagascar, they began to experience a kind of "gravitational force" that, within a brief period, pulled them into a rough outlaw confederacy—out of which, many thought, an authentic state might emerge.

By 1696 the Madagascar freebooters were already using a generally recognized system of rules and laws to govern their relations with each other. All pirate ships, without exception, operated under "articles" that spelled out the rights and duties of all aboard, from captain to apprentice. These articles were remarkably uniform in both style and substance. Essentially they expressed the "laws" of what Defoe called a "roguish commonwealth." Because of the similarity of these ship's articles, pirates—like the citizens of any commonwealth—always shared a general understanding of what was acceptable and unacceptable behavior, no matter what port they might be visiting or what ship they might be serving on.

Another strong sign of an evolving nationalism was the loyalty pirates showed to their fellow outlaws. In fact, pirates were more loyal to each other than they were to their country of origin or to their religion or even to their own race. The evidence for this abounds. English, American, and French pirates sailed together and fought effectively together in Henry Every's crew, despite the fact that France was at war with England and her colonies. Irish Catholics and Protestant Scots worked alongside each other without friction aboard scores of pirate vessels, despite the religious antagonisms that divided their nonpirate countrymen. The ethnic and religious variation in the makeup of pirate crews was noted over and over again by Admiralty courts that tried pirates. For example, the court noted that of the twenty-four men of Captain John Quelch's crew tried in Boston in 1704, thirteen were English, four Irish, two Scottish, one Swiss, one Dutch, and three Americans.

Blacks were also welcomed in pirate crews. Black crewmen aboard pirate vessels were often runaway slaves, but many others were taken as captives from prize ships and offered their freedom if they would join the pirates. The famed Welsh pirate Bartholomew Roberts had more than twenty blacks serving in his crew. Blackbeard had a favorite officer who was a runaway slave. Every himself, despite his many years as a slave trader, freed some black slaves whom he had bought in Madagascar to help crew his ship on her voyage to the Bahamas.

The pirate captain Robert Culliford acknowledged this overriding loyalty in 1697 when, operating off the west coast of India, he demanded that English officials ashore pay him and his men £10,000 as ransom for three ships he had captured from the East India Company. Wrote Culliford in a letter to the English officials: "We acknowledge no country, having sold our own, and as we are sure to be hanged if taken, we shall have no scruple in murdering and destroying if our demands are not granted in full."

During this decade of the 1690s, the Madagascar pirates also developed many of their own peculiar styles, customs, and expressions—signs of their emergence as a separate community in the world. For example, "marooning" was initiated in these years as a specific pirate punishment reserved for traitors. The use of musicians beating loudly on drums and tooting mightily on horns as a pirate ship went into battle was also a peculiar pirate usage begun at this time. Pirates coined their own slang and code words. "On the account," for example, was the code for setting out to go pirating. "Pieces of eight," "peg leg," "rum," "punch," and dozens more were words and expressions initiated or given currency by pirates.

At this time, too, pirates developed a universally recognized password to make themselves known to each other at sea. When two pirate ships met at sea, one would ask where the other hailed from. A pirate ship had only to reply "from the sea" in order to identify itself to another pirate. Pirate vessels that met like this would then exchange news and information freely.

The pirates of Madagascar even developed a distinctive cuisine (which consisted primarily of red-hot spiced stews).

The Madagascar pirates, like any maritime state, formed fleets that sailed together and cooperated with each other against their merchant enemies—as Henry Every and Thomas Tew had cooperated to capture the Mogul's treasure ships.

As with the armed fleet of any authentic state, the pirates of Madagascar also flew the same or a similar flag. But this was not at first the famed black ensign with its grinning white skull and crossed bones.

In the beginning the Madagascar pirates used a red flag similar to the flags flown by the buccaneers and the privateer captains in the Caribbean. The red flag, symbolic of blood, had been used for many decades to signal a potential victim that if she offered resistance, she would receive no quarter when captured.

Henry Every had made a red flag with four silver chevrons his personal insignia, when he and his fellow mutineers had first set out for the East. He had run up an all-red standard before boarding the Mogul *Gang-I-Sawai*.

Although the red flag continued in use among many of the Madagascar pirates throughout the 1690s, the black flag began to replace it as the decade ran out.

According to some contemporary sources, even Henry Every switched from his original red flag after his battle with the Mogul ships—and began using a black ensign with a white skull in profile.

It is also said that Tew, on his final voyage, flew a black flag bearing the device, in white, of a muscular arm brandishing a cutlass.

But the first *authenticated* case of a pirate captain using a skull-

and-crossbones motif—the classic Jolly Roger[1]—occurred in 1700 when the French pirate Emanuel Wynne flew such a black flag during an indecisive action against a Royal Navy man-of-war off the west coast of Africa.

In any event, the black flag with a skull or skeleton theme had all but replaced the earlier red pennant as the symbol of the pirate confederacy by the end of the 1690s.

Pirate captains, however, usually personalized the pirate flag by utilizing their own peculiar variations of the skull-and-crossbones theme. For example, the black flag of Bartholomew Roberts showed a full-length skeleton holding an hourglass. Blackbeard also used a skeleton, but added a bleeding red heart.

The pirate captain Christopher Condent used three skulls side by side with crossbones. The variations were numerous, but the purpose was always the same: to identify pirates to their victims, and "to strike terror on all beholders," as Defoe put it.

If the Jolly Roger was the symbol of a loose pirate confederacy, it was also an indication of the impulse toward unity and authentic statehood among the pirates of Madagascar. Still another indication of this impulse was their propensity to form an attachment for the land itself and to settle there as permanent residents.

Most of those who chose to settle down used the riches of their booty to establish themselves in comfortable houses "with harems to rival the seraglio of the Turk," as Defoe put it. Some set themselves up as traders. Others became planters. Others simply enjoyed the luxury of uninterrupted ease. All of these new pirate settlers, however, lorded it over the natives because of their European firearms and their wealth.

A book published in 1729, *Madagascar; Or Robert Drury's Journal,* purports to be an eyewitness account of how these ex-pirate settlers lived on Madagascar. The author, who calls himself an honest sailor, "never a pirate," claimed he was wrecked on the island and held prisoner there for fifteen years. During this time, he says, he came to know many of the pirate settlers. Drury draws this picture of the life-style of a Dutch pirate named John Pro, who had taken up residence with a number of companions on the island: "John Pro lived in a very handsome manner. His house was furnished with pewter dishes, etc., a standing bed with curtains and other things of that nature except chairs, but a chest or two served for that purpose well enough. He had one house on purpose for his cook-room and cook-slave's lodging, storehouse, and summer house; all these were enclosed in a palisade, as the great men's houses are in this country, for he was rich and had many castles and slaves."

Contemporary sources estimated that in the ten years following Captain Tew's voyage to the Indian Ocean, as many as fifteen hundred pirates had made permanent homes for themselves on Madagascar and its nearby islands. Furthermore, these men had fathered any number of offspring whose primary loyalty was certainly not to the far-off Europe of their fathers or to the tribal hierarchy of their mothers.

It seemed to many observers of the day that there existed considerable potential for the ex-pirate settlers on Madagascar, together with their wives and children, to form a new nation, perpetually at war with the trading countries.

So likely did this scenario seem that a tale began to circulate in Europe about a pirate captain named Misson who had founded a socialist republic in Madagascar. According to the tale, the amazing Misson came from an old French family and had gone to sea as a boy, rising to become a keen ship's officer. According to the story, while visiting Rome, Misson became friends with a Dominican priest named Caraccioli who decided to throw off his habit and go to sea with his good friend Misson.

Misson and Caraccioli thereafter underwent a series of hair-raising adventures, culminating in Misson's becoming captain of his own ship, the *Victoire*, with Caraccioli serving as his first mate. These unusual pirates then set out to found a democracy where men could shake off "the yoak of Tyranny, and live in freedom." Instead of a black flag, Misson's ship flew a white flag on which was emblazoned the motto FOR GOD AND LIBERTY.

Although the tale says that Misson and his men took a number of prizes, it insists they never mistreated their captives, and in fact, took great delight in freeing the slaves aboard slave ships. The story tells how Misson and his liberty-loving crew arrived in Madagascar, where Captain Misson married the sister of a local queen, and Caraccioli her niece. Eventually they were supposed to have set up an ideal pirate colony on Madagascar, which they named, fittingly enough, Libertatia and which was run on socialistic principles with all property held in common under a democratic government. But Libertatia came to an end when Misson's ship foundered in a hurricane and he was drowned.

Although there is absolutely no evidence that a pirate named Misson ever existed, let alone his republic of Libertatia, the story does indicate that there was considerable contemporary disposition to believe that the pirates of Madagascar were, indeed, making themselves into a permanent force in the world. (The Misson story also makes it clear that whether people believed literally in Misson and Libertatia or not, they *did* grasp—however imperfectly and symbolically—that it was the freedom inherent in a pirate's life that attracted men to the outlaw nation.)

In addition to the Misson story, there is other evidence that contemporaries recognized the potential nationhood of the

Madagascar pirates. For example, throughout this period, Parliament received numerous appeals from merchants, investors in the East India Company, and owners and masters of cargo vessels, calling on the government to root out the Madagascar outlaws. One such petition, after noting that the Madagascar pirates are "a formidable Body" and have become "a manifest Obstruction to Trade and Scandal to our Nation and Religion, being most of them English, at least four-Fifths," goes on to warn that if the present generation of pirates on Madagascar should become extinct, "their Children will have the same Inclination to Madagascar, as these have to England, and will not have any such Affection for England." The petition goes on to say that it is therefore "a very desirable and necessary Thing," that the Madagascar pirates be "suppressed in Time," that is, before their children turn pirate too.

Defoe, although writing at a later date, also recognized that the pirates of this era had developed many of the hallmarks of a state. Noting that Rome itself was "no more at first than a Refuge for Thieves and Outlaws," Defoe wrote: "If the Progress of our Pyrates had been equal to their Beginning; had they all united, and settled in some of those Islands, they might, by this Time, have been honored with the Name of a Commonwealth, and no Power in those Parts of the World could have been able to dispute it with them."

To contemporaries who witnessed the enormous explosion of piracy in the 1690s, the seaborne outlaws of Madagascar must not only have seemed on the brink of establishing themselves as a nation, they must also have seemed invincible on their island.

In fact, the contemporary impression was not far off. From their Madagascar bastions, the pirates could scoff at both threats of punishment and promises of pardon. With the Royal Navy occupied with King William's War, the pirate flotillas feared no seaborne force. Financed by the merchants of colonial America, pirate captains lacked for nothing.

From the Mozambique Channel to the Red Sea to the western coast of India itself, the ships of an emerging outlaw nation roamed with near impunity, pursuing a relentless war with the trading nations.

The rich and powerful British East India Company soon found itself desperately engaged in this enormous combat—and fighting for its very life.

6

The Rage of
Rich Men Balked

On the last day of the year 1600, Queen Elizabeth I proclaimed
the formation of a new company of merchant adventurers.

Speaking from her throne in a quavering voice, the ailing old
queen, who had been monarch for forty-two years, granted her
"Royal Assent and License" to an association of merchants so that
they "of their own Adventures, costs and charges, as well as for
the honor of this our realm of England as for the increase of our
navigation and advancement of trade of merchandise . . . might
adventure and set forth one or more voyage, with convenient
number of Ships and Pinnances, by way of traffic and merchandise to the East Indies."

With Elizabeth's words was born the East India Company, a
most peculiar institution that would—over the ensuing 250
years—enrich its backers, fight private wars, represent British
prestige and power in much of Asia, and finally deliver India to
the British Empire.

The company to which Good Queen Bess granted her royal license that last day of the sixteenth century actually grew out of a series of events that began in 1587. In that year the great Sir Francis Drake, on one of the marauding voyages that the queen herself had helped to finance, captured a Portuguese ship homeward bound from Indian waters. Not only was the ship's hold stuffed full of treasure from her eastern trading, she also carried records of previous voyages that told of even richer cargoes.

Then, in 1591, an English merchant named Ralph Fitch wrote a report on an eight-year journey he had taken through India and the Malay Peninsula. His story confirmed the immense wealth of those nations. Finally, when an English sea captain, James Lancaster, returned home from an eastern voyage in 1594, bringing back further word of the profits that the Dutch and Portuguese were reaping in the East, London merchants, whose appetites had already been thoroughly whetted, resolved to obtain a share of the rich East India trade. A hundred merchants put up a total of £30,000 and formed the East India Company. They then sought royal permission for their endeavor. The charter they received from Elizabeth gave their company a monopoly of the "trade and traffic to the East Indies."

The company's first endeavor took place in 1601 when it sent a convoy of four vessels—*Red Dragon, Hector, Ascension*, and *Susan*—to Java and Sumatra. The convoy returned home more than two years later with an invaluable cargo of pepper and spices.

This initial success in the spice trade, however, was short-lived. English merchants soon encountered vicious opposition from the Dutch and Portuguese who were already firmly established in the East. English trading stations in Indonesia came under attack by the Dutch. By 1623 the Dutch had driven the English out of most of the Indonesian Archipelago, except for a single trading station in Java. Indonesia was to remain a Dutch stronghold thereafter.

In India, however, the East India Company fared much better. In 1612 company ships had defeated a Portuguese force in battle off the coast of India—and had won trading concessions from the Mogul Empire. Trading stations were established in Surat, Madras, and Bombay. The company was soon busily engaged in a lucrative trade in cotton and silk, indigo, saltpeter, and spices.

In the wake of Parliament's victory over the Royalists and the Stuarts in the civil strife of the mid-century, the East India Company, which had long received the favor of the Stuarts, seemed on the verge of losing the monopoly that had been granted to it by royal license. But Cromwell, who understood the value for England of the company's presence in the East, renewed its charter in 1657 despite the company's Royalist antecedents.

With the restoration of the Stuart dynasty in 1660, the company entered a new and prolonged period of prosperity.

By 1669 it employed some thirty vessels and more than three thousand sailors in its service, importing more than £180,000 worth of goods to England annually. A decade later the goods imported to England in the company's East Indiaman vessels, with their distinctive black-and-white hulls, amounted to more than £1 million per year. In the 1680s the company paid its shareholders annual dividends that ranged from a low of 30 percent to a high of 40 percent. During this decade, too, the value of company shares rose to £500 each—more than five times their original worth.

When the fateful decade of the 1690s opened therefore, the directors of the East India Company, discreetly ensconced in the company's London headquarters—an unpretentious four-story house in Leadenhall Street—could survey their company's condition with some satisfaction.

The company had succeeded in planting itself firmly in India. Its trading posts—many of them considerable establishments by now, with warehouses, loading docks, and living quarters for dozens of employees, including armed guards—dotted the western coast of India. Company ships, both those owned by the company and those under charter, plowed the Indian Ocean in ever-increasing numbers, making the company by far the most visible and influential European presence in those vast waters.

But the East India Company remained dependent upon toleration by Aurangzeb, the Great Mogul, whose distaste for and suspicion of European merchants and their crass culture was a very real hazard of trading in India.

Aurangzeb, whose own wealth and autocratic power dwarfed that of any contemporary European monarch, was openly contemptuous of the greedy European traders in his domain. At the same time he was skeptical of their motives, sensing that the company—as an independent force in his realm—harbored political ambitions that might one day threaten the throne. To remind the company who it was that ruled India, Aurangzeb would, from time to time, harass the company's representatives by restricting

their activities, or by imposing new taxes upon them, or even by threatening to expel the company entirely. (On some occasions in the past Aurangzeb's tactics had actually led to armed clashes between the Great Mogul's soldiers and the private troops of the company.)

For the most part the company regarded Aurangzeb's suspicious harassment as the price of doing business within the Mogul Empire. However, the company had recently concluded a new trade agreement with Aurangzeb in which the Great Mogul had renewed the company's trading privileges—and many of the company agents in India, aware of their dependence on the Great Mogul's tolerance, sincerely hoped that the new treaty would lead to better relations with Aurangzeb in the future.

But Aurangzeb in fact remained deeply distrustful of the Englishmen who worked so busily enriching themselves in the tiny commercial enclaves he had granted to them. Nor were the Great Mogul's misgivings entirely without foundation.

In 1685 the company had restructured its Indian operation, naming one of its prominent members, Sir John Child, as the first "Captain-General and Admiral" for India. (This very martial title must have grated sorely upon Aurangzeb's sense of his own majesty, even if he dismissed it as pretentious strutting.) The company had also granted Sir John extraordinary powers to decide company policy on the spot, without resorting to London for permission or confirmation of his actions. In addition, the company had begun to coin its own money in India, a haughty act that probably would have called forth suppression from Aurangzeb's government if the company money had been able to compete with the Great Mogul's own coin.

But the action of the company that did most to promote mistrust in Aurangzeb's heart was an internal declaration issued in 1689 that revised the stated purpose of the company to include political as well as commercial activities. Among other things, the declaration asserted that the company "must make us a nation in India. Without that, we are but a great number of interlopers, united by His Majesty's Royal Charter fit only to trade where nobody of power thinks it their interest to prevent us."

This remarkable statement clearly forecast the future of the East India Company as an ever more powerful state-within-a-state that finally became dominant on the subcontinent. There is no reason to think that Aurangzeb remained long ignorant of this company declaration. Even if, in view of the power of his own monarchy, he dismissed the document as the absurd scheming of an arrogant, but impotent, cabal of barbarians, Aurangzeb must have been extremely irritated by the presumptuous words and deeply suspicious of the authors. Certainly, as he was soon to demonstrate, Aurangzeb would not hesitate to crush the company if he became convinced that it constituted even the slightest danger to the Peacock Throne—or failed to exhibit proper respect for the Muslim religion.

As it entered the decade of the 1690s, however, the company seemed to believe that despite Aurangzeb's distrust and his continuing harassment, it had earned, and would continue to hold, a powerful commercial position in the Great Mogul's realm.

The most vexing problems facing the East India Company at that time, its directors thought, were not in India at all but in London—and derived not from the suspicions of the Great Mogul but from the jealousies of merchants, shippers, and political figures who had been excluded by the company's monopoly from the East India trade.

In the 1680s the company had begun to receive much criticism in London from powerful political and mercantile interests who pointed out that only five hundred shareholders made up the East India Company, and that this exclusive group derived its wealth-producing monopoly from the Crown rather than from Parliament, which was, after all, the nation's ruling body. The company had also come under considerable fire from merchants of Bristol, Liverpool, and Hull, who were outraged by the fact that the East India Company operated exclusively out of London, denying other ports any part of the trade.

In 1688, England's new king, William III, in response to the opprobrium directed toward the East India Company, had granted a second company the right to trade with India. Parliament, glad of this opportunity to chastise the East India Company of the Stuarts, confirmed King William's grant to the new company by a margin of ten votes. As Samuel Pepys put it: "The old East India Company lost their business against a new company by ten votes in Parliament, so many of their friends being absent going to see a tiger baited by dogs."

Although by 1690 the new company—which called itself the "English" East India Company to distinguish itself from the original—had been in business for less than two years, the directors of the East India Company in London were already noting a decrease in company profits.[1]

Nor was the challenge from the new trading company the only competition that worried the company's directors in London. Unauthorized merchants, to whom the company gave the name "interlopers," had begun to appear in increasing numbers in Indian waters. Many of these unlicensed merchants, whose ships brazenly defied the company's royal monopoly and traded independently with Indian businessmen, were from the American colonies—a fact that caused much ill will between the company and American merchants. This ill feeling was to worsen considerably in the years ahead.[2]

While the activities of the American interlopers in India did not constitute as serious an economic challenge as did the operations of the new English East India Company, the Americans certainly added to the anxieties of the company directors, who were well aware that even though the company stood at the apex of its profitability and power, it depended for its existence upon Parliamentary support as well as the continuing goodwill of the Great Mogul. Furthermore, the company directors knew better than anyone else that if the East India Company should go under because of ill-conceived competition from English rivals or American interlopers, then Dutch, Portuguese, and French merchant companies would fill both the commercial and political vacuums left by the company's demise—to the great detriment of England.

In the midst of these concerns, it is not surprising that company officials, both in London and in India, did not at first pay very much attention to reports of increasing piratical activity in Indian waters. Pirates, after all, had been an intermittent nuisance to eastern trade for decades, especially in the area near the mouth of the Red Sea. Moreover, company ships had not yet been attacked. Most of the pirates, according to company information, seemed to be from the English colonies of North America—and seemed to be intent upon taking "Moorish" ships.

When the first reports had been received in London that a Newport raider named *Amity* had pillaged a considerable amount of treasure from one of the Great Mogul's own ships, the company had regarded it merely as an isolated incident.

In fact, Aurangzeb himself seems to have considered this initial attack on one of his ships simply an unavoidable hazard of sea travel. After all, the Muslims of India's western coast were not unfamiliar with piracy, having long had to contend with their own local pirates.[3]

In any event Aurangzeb took no action in response to Tew's attack on his ship.

However, as English-speaking pirates began to flock into Indian waters in Tew's wake and began to prey in ever-increasing numbers on Mogul shipping, Aurangzeb's uneasy mistrust of the East India Company was aroused. Since the majority of the newly arrived pirates seemed to be English or Americans, it seemed to Aurangzeb that they might be acting in collusion with the English company. But he kept his mounting misgivings to himself.

Then came news that an English pirate, Henry Every, had captured and sacked the Mogul's own great ship, the *Gang-I-Sawai*.

Aurangzeb exploded in fury. Not only had Every dared to board one of the Great Mogul's own ships, he had also stolen goods and gifts meant for Aurangzeb's personal use. Further, the barbaric English pirates had murdered Aurangzeb's servants, and had committed an incredible sacrilege by attacking pilgrims bound home from Mecca. But even worse than these heinous crimes, Every had permitted his men to lay their infidel hands on Muslim women aboard the *Gang-I-Sawai*—some of whom were the wives of Aurangzeb's servants and relatives of the Great Mogul himself.

Never had Aurangzeb suffered so great an affront.

His wrath broke like a monsoon on the heads of the officials of the East India Company.

Accusing the company of being in league with the pirates, he seized the company's establishments at Surat, Agra, and other places. He jailed fifty of the company's English employees, including the company's manager. The Englishmen were kept shackled, three to a cell, in Aurangzeb's dark and primitive dungeon for up to six months. Some of the English prisoners were treated so severely by guards that they died.

Company officials tried to convince Aurangzeb that they had had nothing to do with Every, or with the other pirates now active in the Indian Ocean. They argued that, like the Great Mogul himself, they viewed all pirates as enemies, regardless of their national origins. They finally persuaded Aurangzeb of their innocence, and the imprisoned company employees were released. But the Great Mogul's anger against the European pirates was not appeased. Nor were his doubts about company complicity completely allayed. Aurangzeb informed company officials, and all other Europeans trading with India, that from now on he would hold them responsible for the safety of his ships.

Company officials, still quivering from their terrifying experiences in Aurangzeb's prison, realized that the Great Mogul's frustrated fury against the pirates threatened to tear down all that the East India Company had built up over the previous ninety years. They appealed to London for aid. The pirates, they warned the British government, could destroy the company and put an end to British influence in the East if their depredations were not stopped. The London government responded by offering a reward of £500 for Every and each member of his crew. The company added another £500 to the reward offer.

Regarding London's response as inadequate, the company then requested that the government permit the company itself to arrest and try pirates in special courts, rather than going through the long and expensive process of remanding captured pirates to London for trial. The request was denied without comment.

The company also beseeched London for help from the Royal Navy, even though company officials knew very well that London was not likely to provide such help since the war with France was still absorbing all the Royal Navy's energies. As expected, this request, too, was turned down.

Company officials then undertook to convoy Mogul ships with their own armed merchant vessels. It was the only strategy they could think of to comply with Aurangzeb's edict making the company responsible for Mogul ships.

But the company knew that this convoy strategy was at best a makeshift. Convoys could not protect all the Mogul vessels that plied between the Red Sea and the Malabar Coast of India. In any convoy under sail, company officials knew, there would always be stragglers who could be picked off. There would also be Mogul ships that for reasons of time could not wait for the formation of a convoy, but would risk sailing alone. Finally, company officials knew that their own armed ships were inadequate to ward off a really determined attack by pirates. Until now the company's "private navy" had been used primarily to frighten off the ships of interloping colonial merchants, who, more often than not, turned tail as soon as a shot was put across their bows.

In brief, the company's naval arm, crewed for the most part by inadequately trained Indian gunners and sailors, was no match for pirate vessels crewed by veteran English and American cutthroats.

Nevertheless, the company adopted a convoy strategy and hoped for the best.

Inevitably, from this time forward, pirates began to come into conflict with company ships sailing in convoy with Moorish vessels. Soon pirates who had previously avoided attacks on English vessels abandoned that policy, apparently deciding that if company ships were going to defend Moorish vessels, they were themselves fair game. Within months after commencing its convoy policy, East India Company ships were being attacked regularly by pirates, who almost always won any encounter.

Nor did the pirates treat company ships and personnel any more gently than they treated Moorish vessels—as an incident that occurred late in 1696 illustrates.

The incident began when two pirate ships, the *John and Rebecca* and the *Charming Mary*, cruising together off the coast of India, intercepted two East Indiamen, the *Ruparel* and the *Calicut Merchant*. Both merchants belonged to the East India Company and had English captains and officers.

The two pirate vessels, each heavily armed and each crewed by more than three hundred desperadoes, easily overtook the two merchants, boarding them without resistance from their native crews.

After ransacking both vessels and transferring valuable goods to their own ships, the pirates began to put the officers and men of the cargo ships in open boats and prepared to put both East Indiamen to the torch, intending to burn them to the waterline and leave them dead hulks. Suddenly the captain of the *Ruparel* suggested that rather than destroying the two captured ships, the pirates should take them to the Arabian port of Aden where, he was sure, company representatives would pay a considerable ransom for their ships and cargo. The pirates agreed, and the four ships sailed off to Aden. But port officials there refused to allow the company to deal with the pirates. They even refused the company permission to ransom any of its cargo.

Company officials had been particularly anxious to ransom a consignment of Arabian horses aboard the *Calicut Merchant*—an extremely valuable cargo that the pirates had no interest in stealing, but which would bring great profit in Europe. In spite of all pleas, the port officials remained adamant. The pirates, feeling themselves somehow cheated, then angrily burned both ships in full view of the shore, after removing their European masters and officers. The native crewmen were allowed to swim for their lives. The fate of the Arabian horses was not recorded.

The angry pirates then deposited their European captives ashore and resumed their cruise with impunity.

Rich company ships like the *Ruparel* and the *Calicut Merchant* fell to pirates throughout the 1690s, until it seemed that the pirates of Madagascar had declared implacable war on the East India Company. Further, it was a war that the company could not win, thanks to a series of factors beyond its control.

First, the pirate sanctuaries in and around Madagascar were too numerous, too far away, and too well defended for the company's inadequate naval forces to attack. It would require a squadron of Royal Navy warships to root the pirates out of their island bases, and the Royal Navy was not available.

Second, Admiralty law prohibited company ships from attacking a suspected pirate on the high seas until *after* it had committed a hostile act. Thus, a pirate could masquerade as a legitimate trader until it committed an overt offense. Further, even if the company did manage to capture pirates in the act, it had no power to try prisoners charged with the crime of piracy. Instead, prisoners had to be sent back to London for trial—a process that took time and effort and, more important, took up precious and expensive cargo space aboard company ships.

As a result of such restrictions, the company made little effort to take pirates as prisoners, and its ships engaged in combat with pirate vessels only when attacked, or when they had a distinct advantage in numbers and armament—*and were certain that the ship they were attacking was indeed a pirate*.

The third factor that contributed to the pirate ascendancy was the superior quality of the outlaws' ships and crews. In general, the merchant ships of the day were slow and vulnerable, built for carrying capacity rather than speed or striking power. One of the most common merchant carriers in the seventeenth century was the broad-beamed flute. The flute was of Dutch origin and was designed with capacious holds for cargo and with simple rigging for ease of handling. Generally, flutes were in the 300-ton class and measured about 80 feet from stem to stern. They could, at most, accommodate ten cannon, but they almost never carried that many. Because flutes required so little handling, they seldom needed a crew of more than ten or twelve. Before the pirate menace became a major economic factor, flutes were the favorite European merchant ship in the East since they were so cheap to build and operate and could carry so heavy a payload. But they stood virtually no chance whatever against a pirate attacker—and consequently began in the 1690s to disappear rapidly from the eastern trade.

Another popular cargo vessel of the time was the three-masted square-rigger merchant ship, which carried passengers as well as considerable cargo. At 280 tons and 80 feet in length, the square-rigger was faster than the flute, but not much more maneuverable. Ordinarily it carried only a dozen cannon and a crew of twenty to twenty-five men. Relatively slow and clumsy, the square-rigger, too, was easy prey for pirates. Like the flute, it began to disappear from eastern waters very rapidly after the outbreak of the pirate war.

By far the most popular, and potentially most powerful, of the merchant ships in service in the East was the East Indiaman. At 700 tons, it was 160 feet long, and 34 feet in the beam. It was built to carry fifty-four cannon and a crew of three hundred—and when properly armed and crewed, it could be a formidable opponent of any pirate who might attack it. Fortunately for the pirates, however, few East Indiamen ever carried full armament or a complete crew. Most merchants, including the wealthy East India Company, knew that if they made room in their ships for fifty-four guns and three hundred sailors, they would have to reduce the amount of profitable cargo they could carry. Furthermore, the expense of feeding and paying a large crew would eat up much of the proceeds of the voyage. For these reasons the company's East Indiamen usually carried only a very small part of their potential armament and crew. Thus the company preserved its profits but in the process rendered its East Indiamen almost as vulnerable to pirate attack as the smaller, slower square-riggers and flutes.[4]

(Company ships did, however, attempt to fool pirates into *thinking* they were carrying a full fifty-four guns by painting false gunports on their hulls. It was a tactic that sometimes worked.)

In contrast to the merchant vessels that plied the Indian Ocean, pirate ships were always swift, well armed, well maintained, and crewed by scores of first-class fighting men.

As a general rule, pirates preferred ships of shallow draft and narrow hull, capable of crowding on clouds of sail—ships built for speed. The favorite pirate vessels were schooners and sloops, usually of no more than 100 tons. Pirates also liked the three-masted square-rigger. But they would modify the square-rigger for speed by removing cabins and most other deckwork, creating the flush deck that added significantly to velocity and maneuverability under sail. Pirates often chose such modified square-riggers for their ability to cruise on long journeys and because they could carry a crew of 150 men, plus thirty or more cannon. Pirates would also modify East Indiamen for their own use. When altered for speed, both square-riggers and East Indiamen found favor with pirates, often as the flagships of pirate fleets.

With heavily armed, swift-sailing ships under them, pirates were able to strike quickly with overwhelming strength in their encounters with the ships of the East India Company, the Great Mogul, or other European merchant vessels. These tactics of speed and power almost always carried the day against the slow and clumsy ships pirates preyed upon. Only a Royal Navy man-of-war, usually a 110-foot, 360-ton frigate, carrying a crew of two hundred, plus twenty-five well-served cannon (and looking much like a square-rigger) could match the outlaw ships.

In addition to the fighting qualities of their ships, pirates enjoyed another advantage in their encounters with merchant vessels: The crew of cargo ships seldom had any stomach for a fight in defense of a rich man's merchandise. Sailors aboard merchant ships knew full well that if they resisted a pirate attack, the odds were that they would be killed, while surrender ensured their survival.

In contrast, pirates almost always fought furiously, aware that *their* survival, not to mention their enrichment, depended upon victory.

In addition to the superior fighting quality of their men and ships, the outlaws benefited from a number of very effective tactics that they had developed for use against merchant shipping.

Since the pirate aim was always to capture prey intact rather than to destroy it—and then to escape pursuit—pirates seldom tried to be heroes. They knew that battle was far from splendid and that a man struck by a musket ball in the kneecap would more than likely have to undergo the agony of having the surgeon saw his leg off at the knee. They had seen too many of their fellows blown to bits by cannonballs, or maimed by sword strokes, to regard combat as glorious. For pirates battle was always a last resort.

Pirates, therefore, had developed tactics aimed at capturing prey by means of speed, stealth, and threat.

Usually, as a pirate ship patrolled the sea-lanes, it would maintain a continuous sharp lookout for likely-looking prey. Virtually all pirate ships, when on the hunt, kept a sharp-eyed sailor perched high up on the mainmast; he thus had a view over the horizon for miles in every direction. Shorthanded merchant vessels often could not spare men to act as lookouts. For this reason, pirates almost always spotted potential victims before they were seen themselves. This gave the pirates in their swift ships the opportunity to close up rapidly and unobtrusively on their quarry.

Having closed the distance between themselves and their chosen victim, the pirates did not attack immediately. Instead they would now observe their victim carefully, trying to gauge her speed, possible armament, the kind of cargo she might be carrying, and—most important—whether she was likely to offer any serious opposition. This cat-and-mouse game might go on for days with the pirate ship usually continuing to better her position relative to the merchant. At some point, if the pirates decided to attack, the pirate vessel would suddenly pile on canvas and, with a surge of new speed, begin bearing down on her prey. Nine times out of ten, the swift pirate vessel would run down her victim in the open sea. At this point, having overtaken the quarry, the pirates would usually fire a warning shot and call upon the merchant to surrender. Almost always the victim, undermanned and underarmed and fully aware of the scores of cutlass-wielding bruisers crowding the pirate deck ready to board, struck her colors without resistance. Only if a prize refused to surrender would the pirates fire on it, and even then they fired first to disable masts and rigging. From a pirate's point of view, there was no point in sinking a cargo they hoped to capture.

It was, of course, always a favorite pirate tactic to fly false colors. Most pirate ships possessed a variety of appropriate flags taken from previous victims. Sometimes clever pirates, flying false colors, would even enter harbors or trading-station anchorages, drop their own hooks, and, at their leisure, choose a victim. Later, the disguised predator would exit the harbor as if to continue her voyage. Instead, she might lie in wait over the horizon for the unsuspecting victim to appear.

Tactics of speed and maneuver were also crucial in evading pursuit. Pirate captains not only made it a practice after taking a prize to flee swiftly from the scene, they also sought to maneuver their vessels into areas—island groups or low-lying coasts— where natural features such as shallow bays, rocky coves, and tidal swamplands offered shelter from possible pursuers.

As a basic complement to their tactics of deception, rapid attack, and swift retreat, the pirates also employed deliberate terror. The purpose was to gain so terrible a reputation that victims would surrender without resistance.

Toward this end, pirates almost invariably made it a point to inflict a terrible vengeance on ships that refused a demand to surrender. One example of this was the awful carnage that Henry Every allowed his men to inflict on the passengers and crew of the *Gang-I-Sawai*.

Sometimes the terror that pirate captains employed took bizarre forms. One pirate captain made the master of a captured cargo vessel drink bottle after bottle of rum until the poor man toppled unconscious into the sea where, presumably, he drowned. In another instance, a pirate captain, in order to punish recalcitrant captives, made them run around and around his ship's mainmast until they collapsed in exhaustion.

One of the most bizarre and cruel instances of pirate terror involved the punishment of a Captain Sawbridge, who was the master of an East Indiaman captured in 1696 by the pirate captain Dirk Chivers, for a time master of the famed Madagascar-based pirate vessel *Charming Mary*.

Chivers had burned Sawbridge's ship after a deal to ransom the vessel and its cargo had gone awry. The distraught Captain Sawbridge had then berated Chivers so bitterly that the pirate captain ordered the merchant master's lips sewn up with twine, using a sailing needle, to "stop his mouth from complaining." Chivers had then put the unfortunate Sawbridge ashore where he soon died of such barbaric treatment. Needless to say, the story of Sawbridge's horrible fate spread far and wide within a short time—and Chivers's next victim no doubt surrendered his ship and cargo without audible complaint.

Such tales of pirate brutality—almost all of them true[5]—made it easier for pirates to gain their aims without a fight. When the black flag—itself an instrument of terror[6]—rose on the masthead of a pursuing vessel, most merchant captains were quick to strike their own colors. (Sometimes, however, merchants *did* fight, and there are a number of instances in the record when pirates backed off rather than face determined resistance. But such opposition was relatively rare.)

It was through the use of such tactics as terror, speed, and maneuver that the Madagascar pirates were able to dominate the eastern seas in the 1690s, to the fury and chagrin of the officials of the East India Company.

The rage of the company was compounded by the knowledge that the pirates were bleeding the company to death not only because of superior fighting ability and tactics but also because they were, in effect, being financed by the merchants, and encouraged by the officials, of colonial America.

From the company's point of view, profiteering in piracy within the American colonies was not only a scandal, it was a crime. Yet month after month the criminal collusion between the Madagascar pirates and their colonial supporters grew more brazen and more frustrating for the company.

In one instance of colonial impudence, a cabal of enterprising Bostonians set up a mint to stamp gold and silver, plundered from the East India Company ships, into coins.

Officials in Rhode Island, to protect the Red Sea Men who supplied luxury goods to colonial ladies of fashion, not only refused to enforce the Navigation Acts, they even refused to allow an Admiralty court to sit anywhere within the colony's boundaries.

In Virginia, a judge, scandalized by the overt dealings of his fellow citizens with pirates, wrote: "If the pirates have not supplies and a market for the goods that they plunder and rob, they would never continue in these parts of the world."

In faraway Madagascar, Adam Baldridge, the ex-pirate turned merchant and king of St. Mary's Island, kept a diary that detailed the thriving commerce he carried on with colonial merchants.

In one entry Baldridge wrote: "Arrived the ship *Charles*, John Churcher, Master, Frederick Phillips, owner, sent to bring me certain sorts of goods, these being four pairs of pumps, six dozen worster stockings, three dozen speckled shirts, three dozen canvas trousers, twelve hats, some carpenters' tools, two stills, one grindstone, two crosscut saws, one whipsaw, three jars of oil, two iron pots, three barrels of cannon powder, some books being catechisms, horn books, primers, and bibles, some garden seeds, and some cocks and hens. For these goods I paid 1,100 pieces of eight, 34 slaves, 15 head of cattle and 57 bars of iron. . . ."

The Frederick Phillips mentioned in Baldridge's diary was by far the most active and most prominent of the colonial dealers in pirate goods.

A Dutch immigrant, Frederick Philipse (the correct spelling) was not only a merchant prince in New York City, he was also the owner of a huge and magnificent estate overlooking the Hudson River. He was a major benefactor of the Dutch Reformed Church, and had served for more than twenty years as a member of the City Council of New York.

Philipse and his son, Adolph, had no love for the English who had taken New Amsterdam from the Dutch in 1664. Nor had they any love for the East India Company, which, in their view, had unfairly excluded colonial merchants from the eastern trade. But the Philipses, father and son, had more than made up for any profit they might have lost because of the East India Company's exclusiveness by supplying the company's enemies, the Madagascar pirates, with everything from Bibles to hats—and all at a very healthy markup. (For example, Philipse regularly supplied the canny Adam Baldridge with copious amounts of rum bought in New York for two shillings a gallon and sold in St. Mary's for £3 a gallon—*a markup of 3,000 percent.*)

Philipse and the many merchants like him who profited from the pirate trade could not have operated without the active cooperation of colonial officials. Governor Benjamin Fletcher, Captain Tew's good friend, was of course the most notorious of the corrupt New World officials, but he was by no means the only one. In fact, the corruption epitomized by Fletcher had spread like a contagion.

In North Carolina it was generally known that Governor Seth Sothel, who had himself once been captured and held for ransom by Algerian pirates, would openly sell privateering commissions to pirates for as little as 20 guineas each. Moreover, Sothel let it be known he was always open for a deal in pirate booty.

William Markham, lieutenant governor of Pennsylvania from 1694 until William Penn himself arrived in 1699, and titular head of the Quakers of Philadelphia, was also such a good friend to pirates that a pamphleteer wrote of him: "These Quaker have a neat way of getting money by encouraging the pyrates, when they bring in a good store of gold, so that when Every's men were here in 1697, the Quaking Justices were for letting them live quietly, or else they were bailed easily."

Markham, in fact, liked pirates so well that he had allowed his daughter to marry one of Every's men, a James Brown by name. Brown, as Markham's son-in-law, later gained a seat in the Pennsylvania legislature.

One exemplary official who had not been corrupted was Edward Randolph, the royal surveyor of customs. Randolph, who struggled to enforce the Navigation Acts, complained in one of his reports that Governor Phips, of Massachusetts had threatened to drub him as a public nuisance because, by doing his duty, Randolph was interfering with the pirate trade. Furthermore, reported Randolph, the governor of Rhode Island, an illiterate named Caleb Carr, had "turned Rhode Island into a free port for pirates."

Officials of the East India Company knew that it was the skein of corruption in the colonies that made possible the profits that energized the pirate nation in Madagascar.

Once again the East India Company sent an appeal to London. This time they implored the British government to halt the colonial trade in pirate goods by enforcing the Navigation Acts.

The company also renewed its plea that a squadron of Royal Navy men-of-war be sent to clean out the pirate sanctuaries in Madagascar, and to drive the pirate fleets from the Indian Ocean. Company officials seemed to argue that detaching two or three warships from the European fleet was not likely to affect the war with France, while it was *very* likely that unless the Madagascar pirates were destroyed, England's influence in the East, so painfully built up over the course of almost a century, might be dissipated entirely.

In response, London, with the ponderous caution characteristic of all governments, took some tentative first steps toward suppressing the illegal trade in pirate booty in the colonies.

The Council for Trade and Plantations sent official communications to governors suspected of collusion in the pirate trade, warning them that "the King has given orders to the Governors of the Colonies to prevent the sheltering of pirates under the severest of penalties." The council's communication then went on to warn each of the concerned governors that their colony was "named as a place of protection to such villains."

At the same time, Edward Randolph had forwarded to the council a series of comprehensive and sensible recommendations for extirpation of the pirate trade in the colonies. The most important of these was his recommendation that the king replace corrupt governors with men committed to "regulating abuses in the plantation trade."

But if there were encouraging signs in London that the government was at last prepared to take steps against the colonial merchants, the Admiralty absolutely refused the company's request for a Royal Navy operation against the Madagascar pirates.[7]

King William's War against Louis XIV, begun in 1689, had cost the Royal Navy dearly.

In the first stages of the war, France's chief aim had been to topple England's new Protestant king, William III, and to restore the deposed Catholic king, James II, the ally of Louis, to the English throne.

Toward this end, Louis had sent his powerful fleet to seek battle against the English. On July 10, 1690, seventy French warships had met a combined English and Dutch fleet of fifty-six ships off the southeast coast of England near the Isle of Wight. In the battle that ensued—called the Battle of Beachy Head by the English—the French had badly mauled the combined allied fleet. But, inexplicably, the French fleet had failed to pursue and destroy the fleeing allied ships. The English-Dutch fleet had managed to escape, although heavily damaged.

In the meantime, on land, the deposed King James had stirred up rebellion in Ireland but had been defeated in the Battle of the Boyne by the Protestants of Northern Ireland. He had then fled to the court of Louis XIV.

Languishing in Versailles, James continually entreated Louis to invade England in order to restore James to his throne.

In 1692, the third year of what had begun to seem an endless war, Louis agreed to attempt an invasion of the south coast of England, to be led militarily by James, and to be made possible by the French fleet.

In May 1692, the French fleet, under the Comte de Tourville who had won the Battle of Beachy Head two years earlier, went out to seek battle with the English and Dutch fleet as the necessary first step to invasion.

De Tourville's fleet consisted of forty-four ships. Although James had boasted to Louis that the English ships would not fight against a French force that would be carrying James back to his throne in England, the Sun King was skeptical. He gave de Tourville direct orders to attack the combined English and Dutch fleet, even if some English ships defected in support of James. De Tourville was also reminded that his failure to follow up his victory at Beachy Head had allowed the defeated fleet to escape. De Tourville was determined that this time there would be no such failure.

On May 29, 1692, de Tourville sighted the enemy fleet, consisting of ninety-nine ships—a force that was, surprisingly, far greater than his own. Nevertheless, expecting English defections, mindful of Louis's direct order to attack the enemy, and recalling his failure at Beachy Head, de Tourville attacked the allied fleet with his forty-four vessels. The French fought bravely and inflicted much damage on their enemy, but it was clear that they could not overcome the English and Dutch superiority in numbers. During the night, therefore, having fought well, the French began to withdraw toward their own ports. But the allied fleet pursued. At La Hogue allied ships caught and destroyed a dozen French ships. Another three ships were caught and burned off Cherbourg.

France had lost a third of her fleet, and the English and Dutch had proved to themselves that they could, after all, defeat Louis XIV.

Although by the following year the French Channel fleet once again numbered more than seventy ships, it never again reached the fighting capabilities it had enjoyed at Beachy Head. Further, after the battle of La Hogue, the French fleet never seriously contemplated invasion of England.

For the English, however, this fact was far from apparent as they looked across the Channel at their enemy. To the English, the French fleet still seemed perfectly capable of invasion. For this reason the Royal Navy remained concentrated in home waters to block such an effort.

Moreover, in 1693 the French fleet had inflicted a terrible *commercial* defeat on the English. Surprising a huge guarded convoy of four hundred ships near the Straits of Gibralter, the French had destroyed or captured one hundred of them, and had scattered the rest.

In addition, as the war dragged on, French privateers operating out of Dunkirk and other Channel ports increasingly bedeviled English and Dutch commercial shipping. The most redoubtable of these Gallic privateers was the famed Jean Bart, who before the war ended, would lead his flotilla of daring privateers in six all-out battles against allied convoys and who would capture a total of eighty-one prizes. Called "the French devil" by the Dutch, Bart and his fellow privateers, in the years following the Battle of La Hogue, inflicted far more damage on English and Dutch shipping than did the regular naval forces of France. Bart and other French privateers even had the temerity to raid the English coast. In one famous episode, Bart was captured by the English and imprisoned at Plymouth. But somehow he escaped from his cell, stole an open boat, and rowed himself across the Channel to the French coast to resume his depredations against English shipping.

With such enterprising privateers to contend with and fearing the French capacity to invade England even with a badly wounded fleet, the Admiralty kept the Royal Navy concentrated in European waters. With English losses in the war having already amounted to an estimated four thousand commercial and naval ships, the Admiralty had no intention of detaching a squadron of warships to Madagascar for the benefit of the East India Company.

The East India Company, therefore, had no choice but to carry on, to fight the pirate war as best it could, and to hope that it could hold out until the Royal Navy was finally able to come to its rescue.

For the foreseeable future, however, the nabobs of the East India Company, whether in Surat or in London, could only regard the pirate nation—secure in its Madagascar bastions—with the rage of rich men balked by circumstances beyond their power to alter.

For the pirates of Madagascar on the other hand, the future seemed to promise only continued success. With each passing month their confederacy grew stronger as new recruits to the outlaw brotherhood sailed into the eastern seas and took up the pirate life.

What was that life like?

Above all, it was a *free* life.

7

On the Account:[1]
A Pirate's Life

In the late seventeenth and early eighteenth centuries, there was only one true democracy on earth: the pirate brotherhood forged in Madagascar.

Incongruous as it might appear, the cutthroats, who brutalized captives and who scoffed at the rules of society, were passionately democratic. They had a high regard for individual rights—and a burning hatred for the tyranny that had oppressed them in their days of "honest service."

Unlike privateer crews, who were still only hired hands despite the fact that they received fair shares of their ship's plunder, pirates regarded themselves as self-employed, collective owners of their own ships. They believed that since the crew of a pirate ship had acquired their vessel by their common effort, all should participate equally in making decisions aboard her. For this reason, pirates evolved a system that called for virtually all matters regarding life aboard their ship—whether to fight, where and when to anchor, division of spoils, even courses to be followed—to be subjected to a referendum, with each man, regardless of his rank, race, religion, or previous employment, entitled to an equal vote in the decision, as well as an equal right to voice his opinion. Only during battle did the pirates abandon this referendum system.

So pervasive was this insistence on individual rights—and so fearful were pirates of placing too much authority in the hands of any one man—that they even elected their captains and other high-ranking officers, retaining the right to depose them by vote whenever they wished. Occasionally, if the vote of a ship's crew was too close to allow a clear-cut choice for captain, the crew would split into two different crews, and each go its own way. On one pirate ship, according to Defoe, a total of thirteen captains were elected during a cruise of only a few months.

The pirate system of democracy, bordering on anarchy, also required the elimination of all marks of distinction aboard ship. Officers wore no special uniforms and had no special privileges. Pirates regarded such perquisites, common aboard "honest" ships, as hateful reminders of the upper-class despotism most of them had had to endure in their previous employment. They would permit none of it aboard their own ships.

For example, even though the captain was usually permitted a cabin of his own as a mark of his crew's esteem, he could not claim exclusive use of it. Crewmen could enter anytime they wished, and they could make use of any of the captain's furnishings as well, including dishes and cutlery.

As Defoe says of a pirate captain's "privileges": "They only permit him to be captain, on condition that they may be captain over him."

While the chance to win a treasure usually supplied the initial and immediate lure that attracted honest seamen to piracy, an objective examination of the lives actually led by pirates makes it clear that the *real* lure, implicit in the outlaw nation's values, rules, and style of life, was the chance that piracy offered to ordinary sailors to live as free men. In a world that permitted personal liberty only to the well-born and the wealthy—and tyrannized cruelly over the poor—the pirate brotherhood offered the common seaman a passage to liberty and self-respect, provided he possessed the courage to defy the law that would punish him severely if it caught him.[2] Most pirates, though simple men, realized full well that the key to the free life they wanted was their system of democratic decision making.

To ensure that democracy would prevail among them, almost all pirate crews subscribed to specific rules of behavior, which they embodied in "ship's articles," covenants that were, in effect, rough constitutions that spelled out the rights, duties, and powers of a ship's officers and crew. Every officer and crew member aboard a ship had to swear to abide by the articles.

Although the articles might differ in various particulars from ship to ship, their general aim was always to safeguard individual liberties, especially the right of each crew member to a trial by his peers and an equal voice in the ship's affairs.

The articles aboard Bartholomew Roberts's ship, as reported by Defoe, were typical:

I. Every man shall have an equal vote in affairs of moment. He shall have an equal title to the fresh provisions or strong liquors at any time seized, and shall use them at pleasure unless a scarcity may make it necessary for the common good that a retrenchment may be voted.

II. Every man shall be called fairly in turn by the list on board of prizes, because over and above their proper share, they are allowed a shift of clothes. But if they defraud the company to the value of even one dollar in plate, jewels or money, they shall be marooned. If any man rob another he shall have his nose and ears slit, and be put ashore where he shall be sure to encounter hardships.

III. None shall game for money either with dice or cards.

IV. The lights and candles should be put out at eight at night, and if any of the crew desire to drink after that hour they shall sit upon the open deck without lights.

V. Each man shall keep his piece, cutlass and pistols at all times clean and ready for action.

VI. No boy or woman to be allowed amongst them. If any man shall be found seducing any of the latter sex and carrying her to sea in disguise he shall suffer death.

VII. He that shall desert the ship or his quarters in time of battle shall be punished by death or marooning.

VIII. None shall strike another on board the ship, but every man's quarrel shall be ended on shore by sword or pistol in this manner. At the word of command from the quartermaster, each man being previously placed back to back, shall turn and fire immediately. If any man do not, the quartermaster shall knock the piece out of his hand. If both miss their aim they shall take to their cutlasses, and he that draweth first blood shall be declared the victor.

IX. No man shall talk of breaking up their way of living till each has a share of £1,000. Every man who shall become a cripple or lose a limb in the service shall have 800 pieces of eight from the common stock and for lesser hurts proportionately.

X. The captain and the quartermaster shall each receive two shares of a prize, the master gunner and boatswain, one and one-half shares, all other officers one and one quarter, and private gentlemen of fortune one share each.

XI. The musicians shall have rest on the Sabbath Day only by right. On all other days by favour only.

Whenever a man joined the pirate crew he had to take an oath on a Bible or an ax that he would obey the ship's articles.

Although the idea of pirate articles probably originated with privateering agreements covering division of spoils, the rules aboard pirate ships usually differed markedly from those aboard privateers, especially when it came to circumscribing the powers of various officers, and deciding policy by vote of the crew.

No privateer captain would ever have allowed the crew to restrict his power over his own ship. Nor would most privateer captains set up a system of dueling to settle quarrels.

One other important aspect of pirate life, covered only sketchily in most ship's articles but crucial to good order aboard ship, was the pirate judicial system. This rested on the concept of public trial—and upon the indelible pirate principle of majority decision.

As rough-edged as it was, the pirate judicial procedure was far more just than that of honest society where well-fed judges condemned defendants to hang for stealing a loaf of bread or a bit of cheese.

In general it was the quartermaster aboard pirate ships who had responsibility for enforcing the laws. Although serious offenses were always tried before a pirate jury, the quartermaster could order punishment without trial for minor offenses such as quarreling, mistreatment of equipment, or neglect of duties. The quartermaster even had the power to inflict a flogging on a miscreant, providing a majority of the crew approved. If there was a fight between two crewmen, the quartermaster had the duty of trying to reconcile the disputants. If he failed to attain reconciliation, it was the quartermaster's duty—as stipulated in most ship's articles—to take the quarreling men ashore and let them settle it among themselves with "sword and pistol", until one or the other drew blood.

Defoe reports one lively, flavorful example of how pirates conducted their trials. The incident also illustrates how free ordinary crewmen were to participate in the proceedings.

The trial took place aboard the ship of Captain Bartholomew Roberts, and involved one Henry Glasby, a skilled "sailing master" and navigator whom Roberts had impressed into service aboard his ship because he was in dire need of Glasby's skill. After a fair length of service with Roberts, Glasby had jumped ship in the West Indies—a capital offense. Caught later, he was tried for his life by his shipmates.

Glasby's trial was held belowdecks with all members of the crew crowded around, drinking rum and smoking. There was both a "prosecutor" and a "defense attorney."

In Glasby's case, the evidence was overwhelmingly against him. He *had* jumped ship, and there was no denying it. But before the pirate judges could pass sentence, one of them—a tough old salt who called himself Valentine Ashplant—declared that he wished to say something on behalf of Glasby. Allowed to speak, Ashplant declared: "By God, Glasby shall not die. Damn me, if he shall!"

This declaration, passionate as it was, did not sway the other judges, and so Ashplant spoke up again, this time at greater length: "God damn ye, gentlemen! I am as good a man as the best of you. Damn my soul, if ever I turned my back on any man in my life or ever will, by God! Glasby is an honest fellow, notwithstanding this misfortune, and I love him, Devil damn me if I don't! I hope he will live and repent of what he has done; but damn me, if he must die, I will die along with him!"

To drive home his point, Ashplant then took out a pair of loaded pistols and leveled them at his fellow jurists. Glasby was acquitted.

Other members of Roberts's crew, who had apparently accompanied Glasby in his attempt to escape the ship and who had also been recaptured, were less lucky than the sailing master. They had no Valentine Ashplant to argue for them behind a pair of cocked pistols. They were convicted. Their execution by firing squad followed within minutes.

Such punishments, while not rare aboard pirate vessels, were always reserved for the most serious offenses. For the most part, the punishments that pirates employed depended on the ship, and the nature of the crime.

For example, most ship's companies regarded it as a serious felony to smoke a pipe without a cap, or to carry a lighted candle without a lantern in the hold, especially because the feared calamity of fire at sea was one that could almost always be avoided with the prudent use of open flame. Yet as serious as it was to endanger the ship by careless use of fire, most ship's companies did not make it a capital offense but prescribed what was called the "punishment of Moses" for the crime—"40 stripes, less one, on the bare back."

Murder, however, was always a capital crime if it could be proved. Many ships prescribed, as the penalty for murder, that the murderer and his victim be roped together and thrown overboard. This was the punishment called for in the regulations of the Royal Navy as well.

Aboard the ships of Captain George Low the articles stipulated: "If any of the company shall adjure or speak anything tending to the separation, or breaking up of the company, or shall by any means offer or endeavor to desert or quit the company, that person shall be shot to death by the quartermaster's order, without the sentence of a court martial."

But the most common punishment by far was marooning.

The term itself comes from the Spanish word *cimarrones*, meaning "people who live in the mountains." Eventually it came to mean "fugitives." In time the name was corrupted to Maroons and applied to fugitive black slaves who had married Indian women—and had formed a Maroon community in the West Indies. (Only much later did the word *maroon* come to mean a specific color, presumably the fancied skin color of the black-Indian Maroons of the Caribbean.)

For pirates the punishment called marooning consisted of putting an offender ashore on some deserted island, in effect making him a Maroon or a fugitive—and leaving him to die. Usually the offender was provided with a pistol so that when hunger and thirst became unbearable, he could kill himself. It was a punishment that pirates usually applied only to traitors, and only after a majority vote.

Although there are a number of authenticated cases of men who survived marooning, or—more commonly—had the good luck to be rescued, most marooned men died alone and anonymously since the "islands" on which they were marooned were as a rule no more than tiny spits of sand, often under water at high tide.

Because of their predilection for this particular punishment, pirates themselves were sometimes called "marooners," especially in the West Indies.

There were, of course, times when democratic procedure aboard a pirate ship had to give way to practicality—in battle action, for example.

When the ship was engaged in a fight—and only then—the captain became the absolute master aboard her. According to Defoe, his power was "uncontrollable in chase or in battle, drubbing, cutting or even shooting anyone who does deny his command."

Once the fight was over, however, the captain had to revert once again to his usual position of "first among equals." Yet there were exceptions even to this fundamental and general rule. Captains like Henry Every, Bartholomew Roberts, Thomas Tew, and several others achieved such dominance over their crews by virtue of superior courage, cunning, or leadership, that they received from their men not only the captain's double share of booty but a measure of respect and privilege not granted to lesser pirate captains.

For the most part pirates chose their captains on the basis of merit. Because of the dangers inherent in their calling, they could not afford to apply any criterion other than ability to the selection of their leaders.

It is hardly surprising then, given the rough social Darwinism of a pirate ship, that outstanding leaders sometimes came to the fore—and claimed privileges not normally accorded to the common run of pirate captains.

Yet even these competent, charismatic few were ultimately under the rule of the majority. Every, for example, knew better than to interfere in his crew's rape of the *Gang-I-Sawai*. Tew understood how important it was to gain the consent of his crew before striking out for the Indian Ocean. Despite their respect for him, Roberts's men insisted on having free access to his cabin—and Roberts knew better than to forbid what he could not prevent.

As Roberts's own lieutenant, Walter Kennedy, once remarked about the relationship between captain and crew: "They chose a captain from amongst themselves who held little more than that title."

Pirates had still another custom designed to limit the power of captains. This was the elevation of the ship's quartermaster to a position of virtual equality with the captain.

The quartermaster, who was usually a veteran sailor and a skilled navigator, was also elected to his post and was expected to serve as a counterbalance to the captain. Toward that end, the crew assigned a number of critical duties to him—in addition to his role as chief judicial officer.

It was his duty to handle the helm when the ship was in action, and to lead the boarding party when a prize was taken. He had the responsibility for deciding what plunder—in addition to the obvious jewels, gold, and silver—was to be taken from the prize and transferred to the pirate vessel. (The quartermaster usually selected booty—silks, drugs, spices—that would fetch the best prices from pirate brokers in Madagascar or colonial ports.) It was also the quartermaster's job to keep a record of the plunder taken and to see that every man received his fair share. On some vessels the quartermaster was so well respected that he was in command whenever the ship was not in action.

Other posts on board a pirate vessel usually paralleled those of the Royal Navy. Only a few of these lower-echelon officers were elected, however. Most of them were appointed by the captain or the quartermaster on the basis of their special skills. One of the most important was the sailing master who was responsible for navigating the ship and keeping the sails properly trimmed. The boatswain was charged with the maintenance of the vessel, including provisioning. The gunner was responsible for keeping both the cannon and the crews that served them in fighting condition. Other important figures in the hierarchy of the ship were the carpenter, the sailmaker, and the surgeon.

Although surgeons were always in short supply, and always in great demand, they were—like most physicians of the day—all but helpless against the diseases from which pirates suffered most: syphilis, yellow fever, and malaria. As for surgery, it usually consisted of the amputation of a limb, and was performed as often by the carpenter as by the surgeon.

By far the most popular members of any pirate crew were the musicians, men who could coax a song out of a pipe or a horn, and who were often excused from the most onerous duties in recognition of their tuneful talent.

Musicians and such "sea artists" as navigators, sailing masters, carpenters, surgeons, and gunners were always the most valuable members of a pirate crew. No vessel ever seemed to have a sufficient number. For this reason captured sea artists were routinely forced into pirate service if they refused to volunteer.

For such forced men, accustomed to the strict discipline and straightforward command structure of honest vessels, life aboard a pirate ship often seemed at first like a cacophonous floating anarchy. At any hour of the day some men would be working, while others slept on deck or below and still others lolled around the deck, drinking, dancing, smoking and talking—in fact, doing pretty much whatever they fancied at the moment.

In reality, however, the "madhouse" atmosphere was not a symptom of breakdown. It was, instead, the certain sign of a well-functioning crew, for the purpose of the pirate enterprise was not to achieve a "shipshape" environment, but to ensure maximum personal liberty for each of its members.

While the commitment to personal liberty, always implicit in pirate laws and attitudes, seldom found expression in words, a few sea-outlaws *did* manage to verbalize their feelings on the subject. For example, according to Defoe, Bartholomew Roberts was accustomed to say: "Damnation to him who ever lived to wear a halter!"

A pirate captain named Charles Bellamy delivered himself of a magnificent skein of invective on the topic of freedom when the master of a captured cargo ship spurned Bellamy's invitation to come pirating with him. Cried Bellamy to the honest skipper: "You are a devilish conscious rascal, damn ye! *I am a free prince* and have as much authority to make war on the whole world as he who has a hundred sail of ships and an army of a hundred thousand men in the field. And this my conscience tells me; that there is no arguing with such sniveling puppies who allow *superiors* to kick them about the deck at pleasure, and pin their faith upon the pimp of a parson, a squab who neither practices or believes what he puts upon the chuckle-headed fools he preaches to."

In the apocryphal story of the idealistic Captain Misson and his Madagascar republic of Libertatia, there were numerous expressions of that yearning for freedom.

In one pretty passage Misson even condemns the slave trade, which was then regarded as a perfectly legitimate activity:

"The trading for those of our own species could never be agreeable to the eyes of Divine Justice. No man had power of the liberty of another, and while those who profess a more enlightened knowledge of the deity sold men like beasts, they proved that their religion was no more than grimace and that they differed from the barbarians in name only, since their practice was in nothing more humane."

Occasionally a physical act by an individual pirate illuminates more forcefully than words ever could the importance of personal liberty for pirates.

For example, one of Blackbeard's officers, a black named Caesar who was probably an escaped slave, attempted to blow up his ship when it appeared that Blackbeard would be beaten in an engagement, preferring to die rather than fall into the hands of the authorities and—very likely—be returned to slavery.

It is important to keep in mind, however, that while freedom was of paramount significance to the men of the outlaw brotherhood, their definition of it was based on the collective experience of untutored, angry men, concerned with earthy, sensual values. For the ordinary pirate, illiterate and inarticulate, the hunger for liberty found expression in doing what he wished, behaving in ways that would be unthinkable aboard honest ships. The average pirate was a simple man, lusty in his tastes and not very discriminating in his pleasures. For him freedom did not mean the chance to cultivate his mind, to enjoy music, or to contemplate beauty. It meant gratification of his appetites, license to do as he pleased, and a general recognition of his equality with others. This was the coarsest and most sensual kind of liberty, but it was liberty nonetheless—and in pursuit of it pirates usually made life aboard *their* ships the reverse image of daily living aboard merchant or naval vessels.

For example, pirates all ate together and partook of the same fare. There was no such thing as an officers' mess with special wines and foods aboard a pirate vessel.

The crew of a pirate ship worked only as much as was necessary to handle the ship. As a result they often omitted all but the most necessary maintenance. If, as sometimes happened, the ship became unseaworthy through neglect, pirates simply transferred to another ship. For them a ship was primarily a means to an end, not a property in itself.

On pirate ships men usually slept wherever they chose and whenever they chose. Aboard many brigand vessels regular watches were a matter of indifference except when the ship was on the prowl for prey, at which time their vigilance was famous.

Although forbidden on some ships by agreement, gambling with dice or cards was nevertheless a favorite pastime on many vessels, even though it quite often led to quarrels and bloodshed. Any pirate was free to call on the ship's musicians to "give us a jig" at a pirate revel.

But it was the freedom to drink as much and as often as he liked that the ordinary sea outlaw prized above all others.

Pirates considered it their right to drink constantly, whether under sail or at anchor. Drunkenness was not only the great solace for the boredom that was so much a part of life aboard ship— the antidote for days of endless blue skies and empty ocean—it was also, for the ordinary pirate, the undeniable proof that he was, indeed, truly free. It was the keystone of his personal liberty.

No pirate captain—not even the teetotaler Bartholomew Roberts or the clever, abstemious Henry Every—ever dared to deny drink to a pirate crew, or even to curtail the worst of the drunken excesses common aboard all pirate ships.

Consequently, alcoholism was rampant among pirates, and many in the fraternity—even some famous captains—died of it. Captain Edward England died an alcoholic. Drinking contributed to Blackbeard's grisly end. And drunkenness among Roberts's crew led to their entrapment by Royal Navy forces.

Pirates drank almost anything alcoholic. But rum was always a favorite. Its original name was "rumbullion," and it was described by the sailors who first drank it in Barbados as "a hott, hellish, and terrible liquor." The pirates often called it "kill devil."

Pirates were fond of mixing rum with wine, tea, lime juice, sugar, and spices to make a drink to which they gave the name "punch." They also enjoyed a blend of beer, gin, sherry, raw eggs, and spices, which for some reason they called "rumfustian." Drinking bouts of two or three days with such concoctions were a popular recreation when the ship lay at anchor.

Despite the ravages that alcohol inflicted on the health of individual outlaws and on the efficiency of a crew, drinking was the

most visible manifestation of the general pirate credo that a man should take whatever pleasure he could in the present moment— and let tomorrow take care of itself.

Even Bartholomew Roberts—who was far from a thoughtless or debauched man—subscribed to the eat, drink and be merry philosophy. Said Roberts, upon his election as captain of his ship: "A merry life, and a short one, shall be my motto."

While the right to drink himself into stupor when and as he pleased was the most important of the personal liberties the ordinary pirate demanded in his daily life, sexual freedom ran a close second.

Although the era of the late seventeenth and early eighteenth centuries was far from puritanical in matters of sex, most of the working poor of the time had little leisure—or inclination—for sexual experiences beyond those sanctioned by church, state, and custom. The licentious pursuits of the age were mainly the occupation of the rich—and of criminals like the rebellious brotherhood of sea outlaws.

In the enclaves on Madagascar, pirates made free with native women. Often—like Baldridge and other settlers in the place—they would "marry" several of them at the same time. At one time on Madagascar, the bastard offspring of pirate fathers seem to have grown so numerous that they almost comprised a separate social class among the natives.

Among many pirate crews it was the custom, when they careened their ships on remote beaches, to sweeten this necessary interval with orgies of drinking and sex with prostitutes and captive women.

One such famous orgy took place in October 1718, when Blackbeard and his crew met the pirate captain Charles Vane and his men on Ocracoke Island off the North Carolina coast—and enjoyed a weeklong carousal with local whores especially brought in for the occasion.

Wise captains made it their business to hold such parties for their men at regular intervals. Bartholomew Roberts, who was not himself a man to engage in lascivious play, nevertheless gave his crew a period of several weeks' rest and relaxation at Devil's Island—later to become the French penal colony. The party featured the varied ministrations of dozens of prostitutes as well as copious amounts of liquor.

Even Henry Every—who always appears too calculating and too cold-blooded to abandon himself even to the briefest of sexual urges—allowed his men to carry off the harem girls and the chaste Muslim wives discovered aboard the *Gang-I-Sawai*. While it is difficult to imagine Every approving the salacious turmoil that marked his ship's voyage of escape after the capture and sack of the *Gang-I-Sawai*, it is even more difficult to imagine him trying to halt the orgiastic revels of his crew.

The terrifying giant Blackbeard is supposed to have serially "married" fourteen wives—all of them teenage beauties. Reportedly, Blackbeard was also in the habit of sharing whatever wife happened to be nearby at the time with any members of his crew who had particularly pleased him.

Although the evidence from contemporary sources clearly indicates that the sexual liberty that pirates demanded and enjoyed was overwhelmingly heterosexual in nature, the circumstances of shipboard life in the age of sail would seem to imply the existence of at least some, possibly intermittent, homosexuality.

Not only were crewmen crowded together physically, and without women for long periods of time, the crews of the day also contained many boys. In honest service, these youngsters—usually only twelve or thirteen years of age—were apprenticed to the ship's officers and to craftsmen such as carpenters, to learn their trade. Many of these young apprentices found their way aboard pirate vessels when their older fellow crewmen mutinied and went on the account, or when sea outlaws captured them.

Thus boys were almost always present aboard pirate vessels, where they occupied the same apprentice niches they had formerly occupied aboard honest ships. In battle these apprentices played a most important role: They fed the powder and shot to gunners, a circumstance that earned them the nickname "powder monkeys."

The rosters of almost all pirate ships listed at least a few powder monkeys. Given human nature then, it is possible to infer that homosexuality was not entirely absent from pirate ships, despite the lack of any solid evidence for its presence.[3]

While the opportunity to enjoy the widest possible personal freedom was clearly the primary reason for turning pirate, a secondary reason was almost as important: the chance to take vengeance on the cruel and unjust society that most pirates had left behind. Almost all the seaborne outlaws of the era shared a profound hatred for *Authority*. From time to time this pervasive hatred emerged in words—usually directed toward the masters of captured ships. For pirates, these honest captains were usually the most visible representatives of that Authority they loathed.

One of these honest masters, George Roberts of the merchant sloop *Dolphin*, recounted the hate-filled invective that the pirate captain John Russel hurled at him while boarding his ship: "You dog! You son of a bitch! You speckle-shirted dog! I'll drub you, you dog, within an inch of your life and that inch, too!"

A similar raging abhorrence of Authority was more eloquently expressed in the speech of denunciation that pirate captain Charles Bellamy directed toward the merchant master who had scorned his invitation to join the outlaw brotherhood.

After extolling his own free life, Bellamy switched gears to excoriate a hypocritical society, crying out: "Damn you! You are a squeaking puppy, and so are all those who will submit to be governed by laws which rich men have made for their own security. For the cowardly whelps have not the courage otherwise to defend what they get by their knavery. But damn *ye*, altogether! Damn *them* for a pack of crafty rascals, and *you*, who serve them, for a parcel of hen-hearted numbskulls! They villify us, the scoundrels do, when there is only this difference: *they* rob the poor under the cover of law, forsooth, and *we* plunder the rich under the protection of our own courage; had ye not better make one of us, than sneak after the arses of those villains for employment?"

Some pirate captains conveyed this desire for vengeance even in the names of their ships: *Vengeance, Black Revenge, Revenge's Revenge, Holy Vengeance, New York's Revenge, Sudden Death, Defiance, Black Joke.* The black flag itself, with its skull and crossbones, spoke of hatred and retribution.

Lust for vengeance permeated pirate life. Most ordinary pirates, illiterate and far from poetic, satisfied *this* lust as they did all others: by straightforward physical action.

For example, whenever pirates took a prize, they immediately asked the crew of the captured ship if the captain of the vessel had treated them well. If the crew complained of the captain's cruelty, it was the usual practice to strip the clothing from the captured master's back, tie him up to the mainmast, and give him a dozen or more stripes with a tarred rope's end.

Such mistreatment of captive officers differed greatly from the deliberate tortures that pirates utilized almost as a matter of course to force captives to reveal the location of their valuables. It also differed markedly from the terror tactics employed to induce prey to surrender rather than fight. The mistreatment of captive masters and officers was a passionate discharge of the rancor that the sea outlaws felt toward a detested and feared civilization as personified by a cruel ship's captain.

An incident that took place in 1719, reported by Defoe, trenchantly illustrates the long-lived animosity that ordinary pirates harbored toward brutal masters. According to Defoe's account, it happened that off the west coast of Africa a pirate ship took the merchant vessel *Cadogan* whereupon the pirate captain ordered the captive ship's master to come aboard.

When the merchant master complied, Defoe says, "the Person that he first cast his Eye upon, proved to be his former Boatswain, who stared him in the Face like his evil Genius, and accosted him in the following manner: 'Ah, Captain Skinner! Is it you? The only Man I wish'd to see; I am deeply in your Debt and now I shall pay you all in your own Coin.' The poor Man trembled every Joint, when he found into what Company he had got, and dreaded the Event, which he had Reason enough to do; for the Boatswain immediately called to his Consorts, lay hold of the Captain, and made him fast to the Windlass, and there pelted him with empty Glass Bottles, which broke upon his Body and cut him in a sad Manner; afterwards they whipp'd him about the Deck, til they were weary then told him, because he was a good Master to his Men, he should have an easy Death, and so shot him thro' the Head, and tumbled him overboard into the Sea."

Even captains who had not inflicted cruel discipline on their men often became objects of pirate brutality because they were viewed as representatives of the society that pirates despised and feared.

An account by the English merchant captain William Snelgrave, who spent three weeks as a prisoner of pirates, tells how the outlaws tortured a French captain because, they said, the man did not strike his colors when ordered to do so. Reported Snelgrave: "They put a Rope about his Neck and hoisted him up and down several times to the Main yardarm, til he was almost dead."

Pirate cruelty to shipmasters sometimes took even more bizarre and horrible forms. One report tells of pirates who filled a captive's mouth with oakum, a flammable caulking material, and set it afire, inflicting a terrible agony on their victim.

If captains were the favorite, they were by no means the only targets of pirate vengeance. Any prisoner who seemed to represent Authority might find himself singled out for brutal treatment. Priests and monks were often victimized in this way not only because they represented Authority but also because pirates

associated them with Spain and Portugal, the most implacable enemies of piracy.

In some instances captives, especially clergy, were subjected to
a treatment called "sweating": made to run around the mizzenmast for a long period of time while being jabbed with cutlasses
and struck by tarred ropes.[4]

Pirates also expressed their hatred of Authority by jeering at
the civilization they despised, feared, and fought against. Examples of their rancorous mockery abound.

Though many pirate ships bore such names as *Revenge*, others
carried names intended to ridicule the values and the religion of
honest society: *Prophet Daniel, Happy Delivery, Most Holy Trinity, Blessings, Mayflower, Childhood, Amity, Merry Christmas,
Morning Star, Peace, Black Angel, Charming Mary*—and dozens
of others in a similar vein.

Another illustration of the ridicule that pirates directed toward
the society they hated can be found in the names they often gave
themselves. Senior members of Bartholomew Roberts's crew, for
example, referred to themselves as "The House of Lords," and
addressed each other as "Your Lordship."

Sometimes the derision was expressed by outright mockery.
When, after taking the *Cabo*, John Taylor turned the doughty
Portuguese ex-viceroy Dom Luis over to the French authorities,
he took the trouble to send the Portuguese grandee ashore with a
burlesque guard of honor, a sardonic salute, and longboat decorated like a viceregal barge.

Numerous pirates went to the gallows jeering at the court that had condemned them. "Give me Hell," said one unrepentant brigand. "It's a merrier place!"

The derision could take more subtle forms was well. It was, for example, a usual pirate practice to accept with solemn sincerity the royal amnesties that were periodically offered to ordinary pirates by colonial and naval authorities, to make great show of "repentance" for past crimes—and then, when convenient, revert once again to the old life on the account.

Some pirate captains and crews enjoyed tweaking the nose of Authority by issuing "receipts" to merchants when they ransomed their captured vessels. More often than not, these receipts were signed with fictitious and often ridiculous names such as "Aaron Whisslingham" and "Simon Tugmutton"—false signatures that members of Bartholomew Roberts's crew actually used.

One of the oddest—and most popular—forms of derision employed by pirates was the mock trial.

Held aboard ship—or ashore on deserted islets during careening—this game consisted of a macabre lampoon of an Admiralty court session, with ordinary seamen playing the roles of bewigged judges and prosecutors who would try their shipmates with rough humor on one fatuous charge or another.

Defoe tells the story of one such mock trial reported to him by an eyewitness.

Defoe says the sport began with appointment of the criminals in the case. Counsel were then also appointed, as were an attorney-general and a judge. Once these worthies were named, the judge climbed up a tree which he used as his bench. The judge then wrapped a tarpaulin around his shoulders for his judicial robe, and put a shaggy cap on his head instead of a wig. He also equipped himself with what Defoe calls a "large Pair of Spectacles upon his Nose."

Now, with the court ready and their grinning shipmates crowding around, the criminals were brought out "making a thousand sour faces." The attorney-general then revealed the charge against them.

Defoe reproduces the rest in a dialogue that he may very well have improved, but which nevertheless preserves the flavor and the atmosphere of the event:

ATTOR. GEN.: An't please your Lordship, and you Gentlemen of the

Jury, here is a Fellow before you that is a sad Dog, a sad, sad Dog; and I humbly hope your Lordship will order him to be hang'd out of the Way immediately—He has committed Pyracy upon the High Seas, and we shall prove, an't please your Lordship, that this Fellow, this sad Dog before you, has escaped a thousand Storms, nay, has got safe ashore when the Ship has been cast away, which was a certain Sign he was not born to be drown'd; yet not having the Fear of hanging before his Eyes, he went on robbing and ravishing Man, Woman and Child, plundering Ships cargoes fore and aft, burning and sinking Ship, Bark and Boat, as if the Devil had been in him. But this is not all, my Lord, he has committed worse Villainies than all these, for we shall prove, that he has been guilty of drinking Small-Beer; and your Lordship knows, there never was a sober Fellow but what was a Rogue. My Lord, I should have spoken much finer than I do now, but that as your Lordship knows our Rum is all out, and how should a Man speak good Law that has not drunk a Dram—However, I hope your Lordship will order the Fellow to be hang'd.

JUDGE: Heark'ee me, Sirrah—you lousy, pittiful, ill-look'd Dog; what have you to say why you should not be tuck'd up immediately and set a sun-drying like a Scare-crow?—Are you guilty or not guilty?

PRIS: Not guilty, an't please your Worship.

JUDGE: Not guilty! say so again, Sirrah, and I'll have you hang'd without any Trial.

PRIS: An't please your Worship's Honour, my Lord, I am as honest a poor Fellow as ever went between stem and stern of a Ship, and can hand, reef, steer and clap two ends of a Rope together, as well as e'er He that ever cross'd salt Water; but I was taken by one George Bradley (the name of him that sat as Judge) a notorious Pyrate, a sad Rogue as ever was unhang'd, and he forc'd me, an't please your Honour.

JUDGE: Answer me, Sirrah—How will you be try'd?

PRIS: By God and my Country.

JUDGE: The Devil you will—Why then, Gentlemen of the Jury, I think we have nothing to do but to proceed to Judgment.

ATTOR. GEN.: Right my Lord; for if the Fellow should be suffered to speak, he may clear himself and that's an Afront to the Court.

PRIS: Pray, my Lord, I hope your Lordship will consider . . .

JUDGE: Consider!—How dare you talk of considering?—Sirrah, Sirrah, I never considered in all my Life—I'll make it Treason to consider.

PRIS: But, I hope your Lordship will hear some reason!

JUDGE: D'ye hear how the Scoundrel prates?—What I'd have you to know, Raskal, we don't sit here to hear Reason—we go according to Law—Is our Dinner ready?

ATTOR. GEN.: Yes, my Lord.

JUDGE: Then heark'ee, you Raskal at the Bar; hear me, Sirrah, hear me—You must suffer, for three reasons; first, because it is not fit I should sit here as Judge and no Body be hanged. Secondly, you must be hanged, because you have a damn'd hanging Look—and thirdly, you must be hanged, because I am hungry for know, Sirrah, that 'tis a Custom, that whenever the Judge's Dinner is ready before the Tryal is over, the Prisoner is to be hanged of Course—There's Law for you, ye Dog,—So take him away, Gaoler."

By means of such mockery, the pirates reduced the institutions of the society they warred with to mere caricatures. By doing so they also diminished the lingering fears that they, as rebels against—but products of—that society, still bore in their hearts. Like all rebels, in order to free themselves of the past, they had to laugh at it.

It was an effective system for achieving psychological solidarity against the common foe. As such it was worthy of the professional revolutionaries of later, more ideological and sophisticated times. Yet the men who invented it, the outlaws who had evolved their own free brotherhood of the sea in defiance of the political powers of their time, were neither ideologues nor sophisticates—but only ordinary, uneducated seamen.

The mythology of piracy, composed by writers of romantic fiction long after the great outbreak, may depict pirates as wronged noblemen seeking justice, or as swashbuckling soldiers of fortune, or as gentry with a score to settle, but this is far from reality. In fact, virtually all pirates were simple seafaring men who had first gone to sea as boys. Even the most outstanding pirate captains all began their careers as ordinary sailors. Most of them discovered their ability to command only *after* turning pirate and entering an outlaw society in which merit, rather than birth, conferred leadership.

There were no wronged noblemen aboard pirate vessels, nor were there London pickpockets, Irish convicts, or displaced farmers in pirate crews, despite what fiction writers put in their stories. For no matter how lax the discipline aboard a pirate vessel, knowledgeable seafarers, men who understood the ways of a ship at sea and how to furl a sail and haul a line, were essential to its working. Landlubbers were not welcome. There were some exceptions to this rule: A doctor was always happily received, even if he didn't know a mizzen from a marlinspike, and musicians were also gleefully accepted. But most of those who served under the black flag were hard and seasoned men of the sea.

Generally speaking, there were three ways men became pirates: by voluntarily joining a pirate crew when captured, by mutiny, or by desertion from the Royal Navy.

Whenever pirates took a prize, they made it a practice to give the crew of the captured ship the opportunity of enlisting in the outlaw brotherhood. Usually the ordinary seamen volunteered with alacrity, glad to escape from bullying discipline. But these potential pirates were not automatically accepted. They first had to submit to an interview by the quartermaster, who explained the pirate ship's articles to them, and he could accept or reject candidates as he saw fit. For the most part, however, likely-looking able-bodied seamen were admitted to the brotherhood without much bother.

Mutineers were men who—like Henry Every's crew—had seized the ships of their masters for their own use. They were usually the toughest and most incorrigible of all pirates, since they were almost always wanted men, often not eligible for pardons, and usually subject to hanging if caught.

Recruits to the black flag from the Royal Navy were usually deserters from warships, who became pirates because it was the only alternative open to them. So acute was the problem of desertion among naval personnel in this era that some Royal Navy commanders did not permit their men to go ashore at all, but kept them virtual prisoners on board their ships for years at a time. (Even when they were not allowed to go ashore, however, the Royal Navy seamen *were* allowed a variety of creature comforts in port. These included the attentions of prostitutes who were rowed out to the anchored ships in boatloads.)

The chief causes of desertions from the Royal Navy were, first, the harsh discipline aboard men-of-war and, second, the resentment that many seamen felt at having been press-ganged into the service to begin with. In addition, some navy men felt strongly about the navy's unfair division of prize money, with officers getting most of it and the common sailors only a relative pittance.

The fact that throughout this era the pirate brotherhood never lacked for recruits testifies to the irresistible pull that the free pirate life exerted on untutored sailors. For, in most other respects, life aboard a pirate ship was as hard as that on any ship in the age of sail.

Physical conditions aboard a pirate vessel were certainly no better than those aboard other wooden ships. Pirates, like all sailors of the age, had to put up with wet bunks, overcrowding, filthy food, sickness, vermin, boredom, and—often—danger. Sailing ships were dark and damp. The smell of bilge water and rotten meat filled their holds. The sea constantly leaked in, even in good weather, and in heavy weather seas often washed down the hatchways. The fo'c'sle, where the ordinary sailors lived, was always wet. It was also gloomy with candlelight and smoke, and fetid with the overpowering odor of men crowded together in a small area. Because pirate crews were always large (to ensure that the ship would always dispose enough force to overcome even the most determined foe), there were often as many as two hundred men or more crammed into vessels that were ordinarily no larger than 130 feet long and 30 to 40 feet at the beam.

Disease was a constant companion. Despite almost medieval attempts to drive away the "humors" and "pestilential airs" that were believed to cause illness—usually by fumigation with pans of burning brimstone, or by sloshing the decks with vinegar and salt water—nothing could really defeat such afflictions as typhus, malaria, and the various forms of dysentery that were often epidemic. Rats, cockroaches, and other vermin that bred in the bilge—and in the wet refuse that piled up in out-of-the-way corners of the ship—also helped to spread sickness. Scurvy, caused by a lack of vitamin C, was also a plague, as were yellow fever and venereal disease.

Food aboard a sailing ship of that time was barely edible whether a sailor served aboard a pirate or aboard an honest ship. Biscuit was the staple food, along with salt beef. But the biscuits were usually rotten with mold while the beef was alive with worms and maggots.

Because there existed no way to store food and keep it both nutritious and palatable, seafarers in the days of sail sought supplies of fresh meat and vegetables at every port where they were available. Pirate vessels tried to provide fresh meat by hunting wild pig and sea turtles at any likely island or beach. Sometimes, to ensure freshness, they would take live animals aboard ship, keeping them tethered below until they were ready to use them. This was often impractical, however, given the limited space aboard a wooden ship. Madagascar pirates made it a practice to buy fresh fruit and cattle from natives or traders whenever possible.

Pirate cooks did develop one distinctive dish, which they called "salmagundi." Basically it was a salad concoction consisting of any marinated or cooked meats that happened to be available, tossed together with an array of pickled vegetables, eggs, anchovies— even grapes. The whole thing would then be seasoned with garlic, pepper, salt, vinegar, and oil. (There were apparently as many recipes for salmagundi as there were pirate cooks. The origin of the name is unclear. It has been suggested that it was a corruption of an old French word, *salmigondis*, a strongly seasoned stew. Some cookbooks say that whatever the origin of the name, the basic idea of salmagundi was invented in sixteenth century England where it was also known as Grand Salad.)

It was rare, however, that pirates got to enjoy fare as savory and nutritious as salmagundi when they were under sail. Usually they had to make do with biscuit and salt beef, just as they had in honest service.

Pirates—and all sailors—also had to endure long stretches of endless sea and sky, or weeks becalmed, cooped up with the same men, doing and saying the same things, day after day, week after week. (Pirates, at least, could fight off this boredom with liquor and music and, if the articles permitted, gambling.)

In addition to boredom, poor food, disease, and discomfort, there were a variety of hazards inherent in the seaman's trade: Storms could wash men overboard. Sailors often fell from the rigging. Shipwreck was not uncommon. Fire was always a terrifying possibility.

For pirates there was another danger: combat.

Although pirates made it their business to avoid a fight whenever possible, there were occasions when a clash of arms became unavoidable. Bartholomew Roberts and his crew fought a bloody battle with black tribesmen while ashore on the west coast of Africa. A pirate captain names Charles Vane, much feared in his time, blasted his way out of Nassau harbor in the Bahamas, in defiance of a Royal Navy squadron. Henry Every lost twenty men during his battle with the *Gang-I-Sawai*. Tew was killed in combat. Blackbeard fought and won a fierce duel with a Royal Navy man-of-war. The pirate captain Edward England engaged in a thunderous and bloody battle off Madagascar with the East Indiaman *Cassandra* in which forty of his men were killed or wounded.

These are only *some* of the combats recorded in pirate annals.

Most pirates recognized that the day might very well come when they would have to risk their lives in a hand-to-hand struggle with other men. For this reason, each pirate carried an assortment of heavy weapons, which he handled expertly and kept in excellent condition.

Most pirates favored as personal weapons the cutlass, pistols, the boarding ax, and often a couple of grenades. A few pirates also carried a musket, but the weapon was unwieldy and for that reason rarely used. The cutlass, which took its name from the "curtal ax" used by English warriors of medieval times, was about a yard long, slightly curved, and had both a sharp edge and a vicious point, allowing its user to deliver both a thrust and a cut. Pirates usually carried two flintlock pistols that could fire a solid one-ounce ball with deadly accuracy. At a range of twenty yards they were lethal. Even beyond that range they could still cripple a man.

With such weapons pirates were fearsome adversaries who usually gave more punishment than they took. Yet, given the nature of shipboard combat at close quarters, where oak splinters from explosions flew through the air like shards of shrapnel and men slashed at each other in a fog of smoke and confusion, pirates often suffered serious maiming wounds, frequently made even worse by the primitive surgical methods of the day.

So common was it for ordinary pirates to lose a limb or an eye in combat that most pirate ship articles routinely provided compensation to crewmen for such a loss.[5]

Added to the dangers and discomforts inherent in pirate life was the knowledge that only a few who followed the "sweet trade" would ever really succeed in obtaining riches. Of course all pirates had heard the tales of those who *had* made their fortune. Every sea outlaw from Madagascar to the Spanish Main knew the story of Tew's men and of the great score Henry Every's crew had made. In later years pirates told about Captain Condent's great strike in the Arabian Sea, and there was, naturally, the story of Captain Taylor, his crew, and the *Cabo*. But most pirates never found their Eldorado. If they were lucky enough to serve with a clever and lucky captain, they might enjoy, for a time, wealth beyond what honest seamen could earn in a lifetime, but few pirates ever amassed a fortune.

Furthermore, even when a pirate did make a big score, he was more apt than not to spend his loot wildly in debauch and in generosity, until he was once again penniless—and ready for another cruise. Pirate captains, too (with a few exceptions like Henry Every), usually failed to hang on to, or benefit from, their plunder. Most, like the ordinary seamen they sailed with, spent their money as fast as they could. (One of the most persistent myths about pirates is that they buried their treasure. This notion apparently got started because Captain Kidd did, in fact, temporarily bury some of his loot. Blackbeard, too, let it be known he had buried a treasure. But Blackbeard, among other things, was a very great liar, and there is no evidence he ever buried anything but corpses. Stories of buried treasure were really given credence and wide circulation by such fictions as Edgar Allan Poe's "The Gold Bug" and—of course—by R. L. Stevenson in *Treasure Island*. People still search for buried pirate treasure, but little is ever found, and for an excellent reason: The men of the outlaw brotherhood spent it all more than two hundred years ago.)

Not only did pirates, as a general rule, die broke, many—even the most canny and farseeing among them—also died miserably: of drink, an Admiralty rope, or wounds sustained in the pursuit of riches.

Captain England, for example, ended his days as a drunken beggar. Tew took a cannonball in his gut. Dozens of lesser captains danced at the end of a rope—as did literally hundreds of the common run of pirates.

Yet executions did not suppress piracy. Nor did the odds against success discourage it. Neither could the dangers nor the hardships of the life dissuade recruits from flocking to the outlaw nation, for the urge to live in freedom—no matter how crude its form or short its duration—burned so fiercely in the hearts of thousands of simple seamen of the day that no power of logic, no argument, no fear, could keep them from risking themselves in what was essentially a war against the world—a war that most of them knew they would lose in the end.

So compelling was the lure of the freedom available under the black flag that as the eighteenth century dawned, it seemed to many contemporaries that the outlaws of Madagascar had all but won the struggle in the eastern seas.

Yet even as the Madagascar pirates stood at the zenith of their power, events were under way that would at last present a serious challenge to the Libertatia emerging in the Indian Ocean. Slowly, ponderously, almost invisibly, the first movements in what would soon become a full-fledged counterattack against the outlaws were taking place in London, in New York, and in Ireland.

The counterstroke had actually been set in motion as early as 1695. In that year King William decided to replace the notorious Governor Benjamin Fletcher of New York.

The king was determined that Fletcher's replacement would be a trustworthy, proven servant of the Crown whom the king could count on to enforce his laws—especially the Navigation Acts. The king had also made up his mind that he would name his new appointee not only governor of New York, Massachusetts, and New Hampshire, but also captain-general of all the military and naval forces in Connecticut, Rhode Island, and New Jersey as well. The king's new man in America would be the most powerful royal governor ever to serve in the colonies.

William offered the post to a forty-nine-year-old Anglo-Irish peer, Richard Coote, the Earl of Bellomont—a man who enjoyed a reputation for flinty Protestant honesty and a sense of duty that made him "unbribable."

Bellomont, who had recently married a young wife, hesitated over the advisability of exchanging the comforts of his Irish estates and his London home for the dubious labors of an administrator in the far-off colonies. But he was a man with a highly developed sense of duty and he soon put aside his doubts and agreed to accept the appointment with the provision that he receive a salary sufficient to allow him to live without the necessity of taking bribes. The king's ministers grumbled over Bellomont's condition, but acceded to his demand.

In the summer of 1695, Bellomont went to London to receive his orders—and to begin the lengthy preparations for his move to the New World.

In his instructions to Bellomont, the king had enjoined his newly appointed governor to take whatever action he thought necessary to enforce the Navigation Acts and to suppress the brazen trade in pirate booty.

"I send you, my Lord, to New York," said the king, "because

an honest and intrepid man is wanted to put these abuses down, and because I believe you to be such a man."

Over at their headquarters in Leadenhall Street, the directors of the East India Company hailed the appointment. But they also knew that months—even years—would probably elapse before Bellomont accomplished his mission in America.

In the meantime, the Madagascar pirates were wreaking havoc out east—and the Royal Navy continued to refuse any help whatsoever.

It was at this point that Lord Bellomont heard a question that also contained an interesting suggestion: In view of the Royal Navy's reluctance to move against the Madagascar pirates, why not send a specially equipped, well-armed privateer against the outlaws?

Bellomont thought it a capital idea. It would show the nabobs of the East India Company that the government was indeed concerned about the pirate menace. Sending such a privateer east, Bellomont knew, would not constitute a major threat to piracy, but it was at least a step toward retaliation. And it might actually succeed in scaring off a few of the Madagascar outlaws. Best of all, it would pay for itself—perhaps even bring a tidy profit—out of captured pirate plunder. Yes, it was a capital idea.

But Bellomont, and those who became associated with him in the project, recognized that the success of the scheme would depend on finding an honest fighting sailor to captain their pirate-killer ship. In time, they managed to find the right man for the job: Captain William Kidd of New York.

8

The Trusty and
Well-beloved Captain

The idea of sending a specially equipped and crewed privateer against the Madagascar pirates had actually originated with King William himself.

William understood very well the cost in wealth and influence to England if the East India Company should fail. He was not as insensitive to the company's plight as he sometimes appeared to the directors. But he was a man with a mission. All his energies and all his powers of persuasion were directed toward one aim: the defeat of France and the curbing of the power of Louis XIV. With Dutch stubbornness and almost-fanatical commitment, he had pressed his war against Louis, excluding from his thoughts anything not relevant to that war. No amount of pleading from the wealthy men of the East India Company would cause him to alter his policy and dispatch elements of the Royal Navy to the East. The war against Louis came first. But there was a second factor that contributed to the king's stubborn attitude: He gen-

uinely doubted that warships were necessary to reduce the brigands of Madagascar. Pirates, the king was convinced, were mere
thieves—a rabble that would scatter at the approach of the law.
To deal with such scum, you did not need the navy, you needed
only a few seaborne policemen. If some private gentlemen of
means prepared such a police force—a well-armed privateer, for
example—and sent it against the pirates of Madagascar, the king
was certain it would quickly clean up that nest of thieves.

In making his suggestion, William had indicated that he himself
might be willing to buy a share in such a privateering venture.
But despite the fact that the privateer proposal had originated
with the sovereign himself, the idea had borne no fruit. It would
have required some enterprising individual with the ability to sell
the scheme to men of influence and wealth to organize the venture and get it off the ground—and no such person had come
forward. The king's suggestion had languished.

Then, in August 1695, Thomas Livingston arrived in London
from New York.

Livingston, forty, was a prominent landowner and merchant of
New York, connected by marriage to many of the colony's oldest
and richest families. A broad, powerful man, Livingston possessed a tenacious will and a clever, conspiratorial mind. From
humble beginnings he had risen high in the world, and like many
men who claw their way to fortune, he had developed a hard,
grasping, vindictive, and self-righteous character in the process.
Born in Scotland of a poverty-stricken family, Livingston had emi-
grated to New York where he had found employment as a bookkeeper. Energetic and self-disciplined, he had saved his money
until he had accumulated enough to invest in shipping ventures.
By the time he was thirty, Livingston had amassed a considerable
fortune. While attending to business, he had also devoted much
of his energy to creating a position for himself in New York society. By virtue of a marriage that was as shrewdly thought out as
any of his business deals, Livingston had formed marital ties with
both the Van Rensselaers and the Schuylers, families that had
long been prominent in New York. To go with his business success and social prominence, Livingston had acquired 160,000
acres of prime Hudson Valley real estate—and was the lord of a
magnificent home known as Livingston Manor.

In the course of his business career, Livingston had somehow made an enemy of New York's corrupt colonial governor Benjamin Fletcher. The pithy Fletcher liked to refer to Livingston as "the little bookkeeper," adding that Livingston had "screwed himself into one of the most considerable estates in the province."

Livingston despised Fletcher in turn. In fact, Livingston had even filed a lawsuit against Fletcher in London, claiming that the colonial governor owed him money for services rendered to the colony—and had refused to pay.

When Livingston learned that Lord Bellomont was to replace Fletcher, he was extremely gratified. He decided to sail to London in order to introduce himself to Bellomont—and to ingratiate himself with the new colonial governor. At the same time he would press his lawsuit against Fletcher.

For Lord Bellomont, dealing with the thousand-and-one details involved in arranging the affairs of his estates and business interests preparatory to taking up his new post across the Atlantic, it had been a very difficult summer. His gout had been acting up. His young wife seemed unhappy about the prospect of going to America. Almost every day reports of pirate depredations arrived from the East. Moreover, he was beginning to comprehend the full complexity of the task he faced in trying to suppress the trade in pirate contraband in America—a trade long established and generally approved by the colonials.

Further, the summer itself had been gloomy and full of portents. The weather had been wet and cold, more like November than August. Forged banknotes had been circulating throughout the town, making every shopkeeper suspicious of every customer. A wild-eyed soldier had appeared in the City, crying out that King William had died in Flanders, and snarling that he would shoot anyone who denied the news he had brought. The authorities had taken the poor man into custody, but not until he had spread panic in the streets. He was later found to be certifiably insane. The king, the City was assured, was alive and well, and as determined as ever to bring down Louis. But the crazy soldier, with his message of royal demise, had seemed to symbolize the gloomy strangeness of the summer.

In his fine London home, Lord Bellomont must have occasionally regretted his decision to forsake his comfortable Irish estates to accept the king's commission.

Then, on August 10, Thomas Livingston came to call on the new governor.

The tough, self-made American merchant and the haughty, often-irascible Establishment peer discovered that they had much in common. Both were shrewd men of business. Both enjoyed good wines and good horses. And both loved intrigue.

As the two men discussed colonial affairs, the king's idea of sending a privateer to the East came up. Livingston pounced on the proposal. There were great possibilities in such a project, he told Bellomont. In one stroke, he pointed out, and at little cost, Bellomont could please the king, give the East India Company the immediate action against the pirates that it was clamoring for, and show the American pirate brokers that he really meant to suppress the pirate trade. What better way for Bellomont to launch his career as governor? Furthermore, and not incidentally, said Livingston, the plan could bring considerable profit to investors.

Livingston suggested that Bellomont approach some of his powerful and wealthy friends in the British government to form a syndicate that would privately finance the "pirate killer" ship. Livingston suggested to Bellomont that he might point out to potential backers that the pirate killer would no doubt recover great piles of loot from captured vessels—and that most of this plunder would go to the backers of the enterprise. Bellomont, now fired with enthusiasm for the venture, felt confident that he would have no trouble finding investors in a plan that would accomplish the laudatory goal of reducing piracy while bringing profit and praise to its sponsors.

In the event, Bellomont brought four of England's most powerful political figures into the syndicate. They were Sir John Somers, lord keeper of the great seal; the Duke of Shrewsbury, secretary of state; Sir Edward Russell, first lord of the admiralty; and the Earl of Romney, master general of ordnance. A wealthy London merchant, Edmund Harrison, was also allowed into the consortium in exchange for lending Bellomont enough cash so that the new colonial governor could buy into his own proposal.

The powerful men whom Bellomont had recruited into his pirate-killer syndicate were not only highly placed figures in the English government, they were also close personal friends of the king himself. All of them had been in the forefront of the parliamentary "bloodless revolution" of 1688 that had deposed the Catholic King James II and had brought William to England. The participation of such high-ranking men would have cloaked the project with a respectability beyond dispute if the syndicate members had been willing to make their names public. However, Bellomont's partners insisted that they must remain anonymous—a proviso to which Bellomont and Livingston readily acceded.[1]

Although Bellomont and Livingston had quickly secured the necessary financial backing for their pirate killer, they still lacked the one component they deemed essential to the enterprise: a trustworthy and skilled commander. The captain of this very special vessel, Livingston felt, must not only be an outstanding seaman, he must also understand how pirates operated and— probably more important than any other requirement—he must be discreet enough to keep confidential the identities of his backers and sensible of the need for prudence and circumspection in carrying out his mission.

Livingston fretted that lacking a suitable captain, the venture that Bellomont and he had now set their hearts on might never come to pass.

Then, as if the fates were at work on his behalf, Livingston encountered an old acquaintance who had just arrived in London: a fellow New Yorker, a knowledgeable man of the sea, and a man of substance. Livingston was elated. This old colleague, he felt certain, would be the perfect man to captain the enterprise to the East. He was William Kidd, master of the merchant sloop *Antegoa*.

Kidd was then about fifty years old, not tall but solidly built, with wide shoulders and powerful, seaman's hands. Broad-faced, blue-eyed, brown from the sun, he had a beak of a nose that gave his bluff sea-captain's face an almost Roman look. Slow of speech and cautious in manner, he seldom smiled. He was never considered a clever man. But when he spoke, he spoke plainly and directly, holding to a seaman's rather simple view of the world: fair or foul, full or empty, friend or foe, honest or false. He was an honest man, too, a man of good repute—and a man of courage. (Some thought him too easily led by others, however, and for all his outward tranquillity, he was capable, when provoked, of outbursts of rage.)

In 1695 William Kidd was one of New York's most successful merchant captains, due in no small measure to his habit of plain speaking, his courage, and the simple integrity he brought to his dealings with others.

Born to poverty in Scotland, Kidd had gone to sea as a lad.[2] Nothing is known of his early career, but in 1688, when he was about forty-three, he had risen high enough in the world to be the owner of his own ship and to buy a fine house in New York City.

Around this same time he had also become involved in the political affairs of New York, and the colony's assembly had thought well enough of him to award him a purse of £150 in recognition of his services in helping to quell a short-lived political upheaval in the port.

The New York council also thought well of him. In a resolution the council had called him "gentlemanly," and had gone on to say: "Neither in his domestic relations nor in his personal history . . . could aught be said against him."

In 1691 William Kidd, ship captain, had taken a step that had transformed him from a respectable merchant mariner to one of New York's leading citizens: he had married a young, beautiful—and very wealthy—wife.

She was Sarah Oort, widow of shipping magnate John Oort, who had been her second husband. Sarah, born Sarah Bradley in less than affluent circumstances, was described by all who knew her as "lovely and accomplished." She had married her first husband, a city alderman named Cox, when she was only fifteen. Cox had died three years later, leaving Sarah well off. Subsequently

Sarah had married the rich Mr. Oort, who had died on May 5, 1691, leaving Sarah all he possessed, which was considerable. Only eleven days after Mr. Oort's demise, the grieving young widow had married Captain William Kidd.

Although the beautiful Sarah could neither read nor write, signing all her documents with her own peculiar "S.K." mark, she owned some of the finest properties in New York, including a beautiful house on Pearl Street and a farm called Saw Kill Farm, overlooking the East River.[3]

Thanks to Sarah's fortune, Kidd was able to live in exceedingly comfortable circumstances. His tall, gabled house looked out over New York's magnificent harbor. Sarah furnished the place luxuriously, with finely carved furniture and Turkish carpets for the floors, and saw to it that there was always plenty of good food and fine wine for the captain and his guests.

Kidd and his family became pillars of the church. It was William Kidd who donated the block and tackle with which Wall Street's historic Trinity Church was built—and Kidd and his family had their own pew in the finished edifice.

But even though he had won the love of a beautiful wife, had earned the esteem of his community, and possessed a comfortable home, William Kidd was not a happy man. He yearned to fulfill a dream—a dream that seemed to belie his blunt practical nature— that seemed so fanciful and so obviously unattainable that it rendered him absurd in the eyes of those to whom he had revealed it.

William Kidd, merchant master, who had had barely enough education to write a comprehensible letter, longed to captain one of His Majesty's men-of-war—hungered for the prestige and the dignity of a command in the Royal Navy.

Although he lacked virtually all the requirements necessary to attain such a post in that age of snobbery—social graces, political connections, and the proper background—Kidd would not allow such mundane considerations to dissuade him from his goal. He had convinced himself that he could become a captain in the Royal Navy—and he traveled to London in the summer of 1695 to persuade the Admiralty to grant him his heart's desire.

Toward that end Kidd carried a letter of recommendation from James Graham, attorney general of New York, addressed to William Blathwayt, a political figure who had a reputation as a man able to obtain "favors" for friends. Unfortunately for Kidd, Blathwayt was away from London—in Flanders with the king—when Kidd arrived in the city. Consequently, Kidd found himself at loose ends in London. Then Thomas Livingston happened upon him.

To Livingston, Kidd seemed the ideal man for the privateer voyage he had in mind. He was a respected man of property, and a more than competent seaman, who had considerable experience dealing with the moneyed classes and whose discretion could therefore be relied upon.

There was still another, most important reason why Livingston considered Kidd the right man for the job. The New York captain had successfully commanded privateers in the past. With the outbreak of King William's war with France in 1689, Kidd, in a sloop he had then owned—the *Blessed William*—had fought as a privateer auxiliary with the English fleet in the West Indies—and had participated gallantly in several actions. In fact, the fleet commander, Thomas Hewson, had later said of Kidd: "He was with me in two engagements against the French, and fought as well as any man I ever saw, according to the proportion of his men." (Perhaps it was this experience with the professional fleet in the West Indies, plus Hewson's praise, that had convinced Kidd that for all his lack of schooling and background, he *did* possess sufficient natural merit to realize his dream of a Royal Navy command.)

After action with the fleet, Kidd and *Blessed William* had put in at Antigua for provisions prior to returning to New York. While Kidd was conducting his business ashore, however, his crew, stirred up by the mate, Robert Culliford, had mutinied and sailed away with the ship. (Culliford eventually made his way to Madagascar and was elected captain of several pirate ships. The fate of the *Blessed William* is unknown.)

If this event embarrassed Kidd, at least it had cost him no financial loss. The British governor of the Leeward Islands, in recognition of his services to the fleet, had presented Kidd with a captured barkentine, the *Antegoa*, to replace the stolen *Blessed William*. Thereupon the grateful captain had sailed home to New York.

A few months later, the Massachusetts colony—mindful of Kidd's good work against the French in the West Indies—had hired him to chase a notorious French privateer away from the American coast—and Kidd had succeeded in that mission.

Although the intriguing Livingston probably saw Kidd as the commander of his pirate killer from the first moments of their meeting in London, he was careful not to broach the subject of his eastern enterprise too abruptly. Instead, he concentrated on ingratiating himself with the bluff seafarer, succeeding so well that Kidd even testified on Livingston's behalf in his suit against the retiring Governor Fletcher.

It is likely that Livingston encouraged Kidd's preposterous conviction that he could become the captain of a Royal Navy man-of-war. In doing so, however, Livingston further excited in Kidd a hitherto-inconsequential propensity for self-delusion, which was a basic, if not obvious, aspect of the captain's character. For there seems to have been in William Kidd a deep streak of stubborn fantasy, a penchant to believe a thing possible because he *desired* it, an inclination to regard something as true simply because he *wanted* it to be true. This tendency toward magical thinking, so clearly exposed in his dream of a Royal Navy command, seems to have operated by blinding Kidd to the reality of his situation when his deepest desires were engaged. It also seems to have led him often to misinterpret the intentions of others, as he had for example misinterpreted the character of the mate, Culliford, who had made off with his ship. It seems likely that this inclination toward wishful thinking also made it difficult for Kidd to see himself as others saw him. Thus, in his fantasy, he was able to envision himself with ease as the polished and dashing commander of one of His Majesty's men-of-war.

Probably, in his rough world of privateers and cutthroat merchants, this facet of Kidd's personality had not mattered very much. More than likely it was usually dismissed as a quirk, a rather laughable inclination of the captain's to put on airs. It did not, in any case, interfere very much with his professional performance as either a self-employed privateer or as a merchant captain.

But for a project like Livingston and Bellomont's, a commander was needed who was not only discreet and competent but also capable of acting on his own in remote waters, capable of weighing the reality of his situation, capable of making critical judgments under pressure. To put in command of such an enterprise a man whose view of reality might be determined by his desires was a prescription for disaster. Yet Livingston, although a shrewd man of experience, apparently failed to perceive this flaw in Kidd—or if he did recognize it, he did not believe it would adversely affect his enterprise, for he had now fixed on William Kidd as his captain.

Livingston waited for an appropriate moment—and then put forward his privateer proposition to his fellow New Yorker. Kidd professed himself uninterested. He had no wish to command a privateer, he explained to Livingston, even one with so lofty a mission as suppression of the Madagascar outlaws.

Livingston, however, refused to accept Kidd's negative response. Perhaps, as a crafty salesman, he sensed that the bluff sea captain could be pressured or cajoled into accepting the post offered.

Perhaps Kidd himself created this impression in Livingston's mind in order to retain Livingston's friendship. Like many unsophisticated people with ambitions beyond their talents, Kidd often thought himself more clever than he really was. He probably believed that if he did not *entirely* close the door to Livingston's project, he would be better able to cultivate Livingston and Bellomont, and perhaps even secure their help in obtaining his commission in the Royal Navy. In this sense Kidd himself opened the door to the pressure that, with single-minded tenacity, Livingston now exerted on him.

Livingston began his campaign by taking Kidd to see Lord Bellomont himself. The great man suggested to the duly impressed captain that perhaps the best way to achieve his life's dream of a Royal Navy career would be to accept the special privateering commission he and Livingston were now offering to him. It was a mission, after all, that had been proposed by the king himself, Bellomont no doubt pointed out, and it had the backing of some of the most influential men in the realm, not the least of whom was himself, soon to be governor of Kidd's own province and in a position to do him a great deal of good. On the other hand, Bellomont no doubt implied, to refuse such a service to the Crown might be construed by some as a disloyal act unworthy of a Royal Navy captain.

Even Kidd must have understood the message: Take the proposition offered to him by Bellomont and Livingston, and he would prosper; refuse, and his dream of a navy command might come to nothing.

The pressure on Kidd to accept immediately was enormous. But he did not buckle under. He pointed out that as an experienced privateer, he saw a number of major flaws in the proposed venture to the East.

Foremost among these flaws was the fact that even with a pirate-killer vessel, pirate ships would be most difficult to capture. Pirates were not only fast sailors, well armed, and crewed by tough fighting men, they were impossible to identify at sea unless they attacked or broke out a black flag. No pirate would be fool enough to willingly engage a fighting ship like Bellomont and Livingston's privateer. Nor would any pirate ever be stupid enough to show his true colors to such a fighting ship.

Moreover, even if the pirate killer did manage to overtake a pirate on the high seas, there would be little likelihood of finding booty aboard her since it was not the pirate custom to remain long under sail after making a big score but rather to get quickly to some safe haven and there share out the plunder. As for rooting the pirates out of their bases on Madagascar, no single ship, no matter how well armed, could possibly accomplish that objective.

Bellomont and Livingston brushed off these objections. They told Kidd that the commission they would arrange for him to receive from the king would also empower him to capture French ships, since England and France were at war. Thus, they assured their chosen captain, there would be plenty of opportunity for him to capture plunder even if pirate vessels eluded him.

It seems very clear that as his private conversations with Bellomont and Livingston proceeded, Kidd gained the distinct impression that he would be given great latitude in carrying out his mission. If he should find it necessary to commit any "irregularities" in the course of it, such as "requisitioning" supplies from the East India Company, the great men backing the project would protect him.

"Lord Bellomont assured me again and again," Kidd later wrote, "that the noble lords would stifle all complaints."

Whether Bellomont or Livingston deliberately fostered this impression in Kidd's mind, or whether it was due to Kidd's own propensity for fooling himself and for misconstruing the intentions of others, it is impossible to tell. It was probably a combination of Kidd's fantasy and Bellomont and Livingston's guile that created the perception that the mission would be carried out under special auspices and that the captain's role in that mission would be a lofty one: He would be, in effect, the king's own privateer.

With this fantasy before his eyes, Kidd consented to captain the enterprise.

On October 10, 1695, Lord Bellomont, Livingston, and Captain Kidd met to sign a final agreement covering their project. The contract called for Bellomont and his high-ranking partners to put up 80 percent of the cost of the venture. Livingston and Kidd would put up the rest, some £1,500. The document also spelled out how the booty was to be shared: 10 percent to the Crown; 55 percent for Bellomont and his backers; 22.5 percent to the crew; and 12.5 percent for Kidd and Livingston. If there should be no booty, Kidd and Livingston agreed to pay back all the money put up by their sponsors, retaining the ship as their own compensation.

There were other clauses as well: Kidd was to sign his crew on a "no prey, no pay" basis. He was to complete his cruise and report to Bellomont in Boston no later than March 20, 1697, with all his booty intact—at which time the spoils would be properly assessed and divided by an Admiralty court. Kidd was also required to put up a good conduct and performance bond of £20,000. A similar bond for £10,000 would be posted by Livingston.

As a veteran privateer captain Kidd must have realized that this agreement placed him in a dangerously vulnerable position: He *had* to find booty—or he would suffer grievous financial harm, since he and Livingston would have to make good any losses to their backers if the venture failed. Furthermore, if anything went wrong—if his crew mutinied, for example, or a friendly ship was attacked in error, he alone would be responsible.

Moreover, as a more than competent seaman, Kidd must also have recognized that it would be impossible for him to accomplish his mission by the deadline spelled out in the agreement. It was simply not feasible to prepare a ship, sail to the Indian Ocean, capture elusive pirates laden with spoil—almost all as well as or better armed than he would be—and then bring his prizes halfway around the world again to Boston—and do it all in fourteen months. Why, it would take at least two months just to reach the Cape.

What is more, it could not have escaped Kidd's notice that because of King William's War, much of France's merchant fleet was concentrated in European waters and operating as privateers against the English. Potential French prey in the eastern seas would not be plentiful.

Finally, topping all these negative factors was one further reality: To finance his share of the expedition Kidd would have to sell his sloop, *Antegoa*. From Kidd's point of view, the whole scheme seemed a poor risk indeed.

Nevertheless, he signed the agreement proffered by Bellomont.

Why did he accede to so dubious and unfair a contract? No doubt he felt trapped by Bellomont's veiled threats against him, as well as flattered by the thought that he would be serving the king and the great men of the realm. He may also have been confident that the strictures written into his agreement would not apply in reality, and hopeful that completion of his mission to the East would bring that which he hungered after: a command in the Royal Navy.

Captain Kidd, it would seem, was blinded by the peculiar defect in his makeup that caused him to believe a thing true because he *wished* it so. There is no other way to explain Kidd's acceptance of the deal offered to him by Bellomont and Livingston, except to say that he refused to acknowledge the reality of his situation.

Now, with Kidd signed up for the voyage, events moved rapidly. In December 1695 the Admiralty issued a commission to Kidd, empowering him to "apprehend, seize, and take the Ships, Vessels, and Goods belonging to the French King or his Subjects or Inhabitants within the dominions of the said French King; and such other Ships, Vessels, and Goods as are or shall be liable to confiscation."

In January 1696 Kidd received a special commission signed by the king himself.

"To our Trusty and well-beloved Captain Kidd," it began. It then instructed Kidd to seize pirates wherever he found them, but added: "We do hereby jointly charge and command you, as you will answer the same at your utmost Peril, That you do not, in any manner, offend or molest any of our Friends or Allies, their Ships or Subjects."

During this time Kidd also had had audiences with the Earl of Romney and with Admiral Sir Edward Russell, the first sea lord. These great dignitaries, both investors in the privateer scheme, applauded Kidd's mission. Their attentions no doubt further fed Kidd's fantasy of present protection and future preferment.

As Kidd himself wrote later about his state of mind during this period: "I, thinking myself safe with a King's commission and protection of so many great men, accepted, thinking it was in my Lord Bellomont's power as Governor of New York, to oppress me if I still continued obstinate. Before I went to sea I waited twice on my Lord Romney and Admiral Russell. Both hastened me to sea, and promised to stand by me."

For William Kidd the die was now cast.

He had already chosen his ship for the voyage. She was a 287-ton three-masted vessel named *Adventure Galley* that had been specially designed for speed, maneuverability, and armament. Ship's carpenters at Deptford on the Thames, where she was being fitted out, had equipped her with special adaptations for her mission: oars, for example, to allow her to maneuver during notorious Indian Ocean calms, and an enormous spread of sail to give her extra speed. Under full sail *Adventure Galley* could make fourteen knots. Even becalmed, her forty-six oars would give her three knots of speed. Only 124 feet from stem to stern, she had been built flush-decked, adding to her nimbleness when under way and permitting her to carry a greater spread of sail. She carried thirty-four guns, and Kidd was confident that she would prove the equal of any vessel she was likely to encounter in the Indian Ocean.

Kidd chose his crew with great care. He wanted no potential mutineers, no officer who would, like Robert Culliford, seize *Adventure Galley* and go off "on his own account."

Kidd carefully recruited 70 honest sailors, most of them married men with families in England. With this crew, less than half the ship's full complement of 150, he intended to sail across the Atlantic to New York where he would settle his personal business, visit briefly with his family, explain his mission to associates, and recruit an additional 80 men.

At the end of February 1696, *Adventure Galley* slid down the Thames to begin her fateful voyage.

Matters went wrong from the start.

As *Adventure Galley* proceeded downriver she encountered a Royal Navy yacht near Greenwich. Kidd failed to dip his colors to the naval vessel as custom dictated. The yacht then fired a shot across *Adventure Galley*'s bow as a reminder of the respect that a privateer owed to any ship of the Royal Navy. Kidd's crew then delivered an incredible insult to the naval vessel: They turned and slapped their backsides derisively in the direction of the yacht.

It was a stupid and gratuitous affront. It was probably traceable to Kidd's delusion that his commission made him the equal of an officer in the Royal Navy, and *Adventure Galley* the equal of a Royal Navy man-of-war. Thus he did not consider it necessary to salute the yacht—and his crew's insolent mockery had been no more than a sailor's rude statement in support of his captain. The incident, however, was to cost Kidd dear.

When he later anchored, still in the Thames, a Royal Navy press gang, probably under specific orders, came aboard *Adventure Galley* and carried off more than twenty of Kidd's handpicked crew. Furiously Kidd brandished his commission at the press-gang's officer. Angrily he protested that he was on the king's business and was not to be treated with such high-handed contempt. But the Royal Navy officer directing the press gang ignored all Kidd's protestations. He had his duty—and no doubt he took great pleasure in discomfiting the arrogant privateer who had insulted His Majesty's navy.

After the loss of his best men, Kidd, certain that his special commission exempted *Adventure Galley* from the ravages of a navy press gang, hurried off to complain to one of his powerful patrons, Admiral Russell. While he might not have agreed with Kidd that *Adventure Galley* was the equal of a navy frigate, Admiral Russell did order that Kidd's abducted crewmen be returned to him. In the event, the Royal Navy delivered twenty seamen back to *Adventure Galley*—but they were not the same men whom Kidd had earlier lost to the press gang. Instead they were a score of hardcases and troublemakers whom the Royal Navy was glad to get rid of.

Realizing that he was not likely to get any satisfaction from the

Royal Navy, Kidd set sail for New York. On the way he captured a French fishing boat, a lawful prize that he took to New York with him.

Arriving in New York in July, Kidd sold the French fishing boat and used the proceeds to purchase additional provisions for the long cruise to eastern waters.

Obtaining the additional eighty men he needed, however, turned out to be more difficult than Kidd had anticipated. New York was at that time a major port in the Pirate Round, a place where seamen were more interested in sailing as pirates than in sailing as pirate *catchers*. There was little interest in an expedition in which the crew's share would amount to less than one quarter of whatever booty they took.

In order to attract new hands, therefore, Kidd—in conscious violation of his agreement with his backers and acting on his own authority—drastically revised the ship's articles of *Adventure Galley*: The crew would now receive 60 percent of any profits rather than the 22.5 percent stipulated in Kidd's agreement with Bellomont and Livingston. Probably Kidd convinced himself that he could explain away this arbitrary decision when the time came. Perhaps he also felt that as the king's privateer, his mission was so important he was justified in changing the terms of his agreement with his backers in order to carry it out.

Eventually Kidd managed to sign on enough men to fill out his crew of 150. Many of them were the dregs of the New York waterfront: drifters, ex-privateers, deserters, and a variety of toughs. Benjamin Fletcher, who was still governor pending Lord Bellomont's appearance in the New World, observed the new crewmen of *Adventure Galley* with a cynical eye. "Many flocked to him from all parts, men of desperate fortunes, and necessities in expectation of getting treasure," Fletcher wrote of Kidd's New York recruits. "It is generally believed here, that if he misses the design named in his commission, he will not be able to govern such a villainous herd."

Although some observers, like Fletcher, suspected that there were outright pirates among Kidd's New York enlistees—and that many of these had signed aboard with the secret aim of seizing the ship for piracy—there is no clear evidence that this was the case. It is hard to believe that Kidd, an experienced privateer and a New Yorker himself, would be taken in by a conspiracy of ordinary pirates. He was too old a hand for that. It is equally hard to believe that any cabal of semiliterate pirates, no matter how desperate, would choose to sign on with the king's own privateer for purposes of fomenting a mutiny. There were far less risky ways to steal a ship.

Very probably Kidd knew full well that his New York crewmen were a bad lot. But he also must have known that there were no out-and-out brigands among them—and he must have felt confident of his ability to control them. In any case, he had no choice. He had to make do with the men available.

Throughout this period, while Kidd was provisioning *Adventure Galley* and signing up his new hands, he seemed to feel no urgency to get away from his home port and on to the task ahead. Instead he took advantage of this time to enjoy the company of his wife and children, spending many long summer days at the family's farm overlooking the East River. It was as if Kidd, dreading the voyage ahead, wished to put off his departure as long as possible.

But July turned into August and August into September—and finally the day arrived when Kidd could no longer delay. On September 6, fully provisioned and with a full crew of 150 aboard, *Adventure Galley* slipped her cable and drifted on the tide out of New York harbor, under way at last for the East.

It was a nine thousand mile run to the Indian Ocean. Kidd's course took *Adventure Galley* first due east across the Atlantic to Madeira off the northwestern coast of Africa. From there, by easy stages, Kidd sailed south along the west coast of the continent, slowly—almost reluctantly—making for the Cape of Good Hope. Now that the reality of the voyage was upon him, there must have been many times when Kidd confronted the chill secret knowledge that he carried deep within himself: His mission, so lightly agreed to in London, could not possibly succeed. But he must have just as often submerged that awful realization again, persuading himself that, somehow, he would find a way to bring it off. If his commission was a burden, it was also an opportunity. By accomplishing his task, even if only partially, would he not be proving to men of quality and power that he was indeed worthy of a Royal Navy command?

As the weeks passed, Kidd—with such thoughts no doubt boiling in his mind—brought *Adventure Galley* farther and farther south of the equator, closer and closer to the Cape. Then Kidd once again affronted the Royal Navy.

The incident began on December 12, 1696, when *Adventure Galley* encountered a squadron of four Royal Navy warships, under the command of Commodore Thomas Warren, off the western coast of Africa only one hundred miles north of Capetown. Kidd went on board Warren's flagship, where he showed the commodore his royal commission and demanded that Warren provide him with new sails to replace sails that *Adventure Galley* had lost in a storm. When Warren refused, Kidd again brandished his commission, claiming that he had a right to the navy's help. If Warren refused such help, Kidd would be forced to seize the sails he needed from the first merchant vessel he came across, but his actions would be Warren's responsibility. Kidd's high-handedness infuriated the commodore. Angrily, Warren informed Kidd that far from supplying him with sails, he intended to impress thirty of Kidd's men the following morning to fill out short-handed crews in his own squadron.

Chastened, Kidd pretended to agree to Warren's demand for his men—and he returned to *Adventure Galley*. During the night, however, with the seas calm, Kidd used *Adventure Galley*'s oars to sneak away from Warren's squadron. By morning he had an insurmountable lead over Warren's ships and easily got away. But he had deeply offended the Royal Navy again and his arrogance had earned him a negative reputation even before *Adventure Galley* rounded the Cape into the Indian Ocean.

In February 1697, *Adventure Galley*, after sailing past the Cape and beating her way north through the Mozambique Channel, arrived at the island of Johanna to take on fresh water.

While she was anchored in the harbor of Johanna, a well-armed East Indiaman also arrived to take on water. The East Indiaman was flying a naval pennant—a circumstance that seemed to vex Kidd greatly. He demanded that the East Indiaman's captain lower the pennant since he alone, as the king's privateer, was entitled to fly a navy ensign. The captain of the East Indiaman did not know what to make of Kidd, but he was deeply suspicious of this oddly arrogant pirate catcher with his crew of New York wharf rats—and he kept his guns trained on *Adventure Galley*, letting it be known that if Kidd was not soon gone from Johanna, he would be attacked.

Chastened again, Kidd filled his water casks and then made for the nearby island of Mohéli in the Comoros, northwest of Madagascar in the Mozambique Channel. But the captain of the East Indiaman soon carried the word far out into the Indian Ocean about the insolent privateer, William Kidd, and his evil-looking crew. Thus, before she had even well begun her mission, *Adventure Galley* was regarded with suspicion among East India Company merchant captains as well.

It was now March 1697, and Kidd careened *Adventure Galley* on the beach at Mohéli in preparation for the long voyage still ahead. Kidd was now in the general area where he intended to operate, but it was more than a year since *Adventure Galley* had departed Deptford, and although Kidd could claim his tardiness had been due to events outside his direct control—such as the difficulty in recruiting crewmen in New York—the fact was that his supplies were beginning to run low and his men (not to mention his backers) were growing impatient for the plunder they expected to earn.

At this point some of the hardcases Kidd had recruited in New York began to mutter against their captain, grumbling that *Adventure Galley* ought to forgo her original objective and turn to open piracy, earning equal shares for those who actually sailed in her. Why, they asked, should they further enrich wealthy men in London with their labor? Why not go on the account, and be done with it?

Kidd heard the grumbling. But it seemed, so far at least, only the grousing of a disgruntled few—and he dismissed it.

While they were careened at Mohéli, plague struck the crew. Within a week Kidd lost fifty of his men.

Apparently regarding this loss as just one of the unavoidable hazards of life at sea, Kidd and his surviving crew returned to Johanna where Kidd recruited thirty men "off the beach" to replace those who had died. These new crewmen were genuine pirates, a far tougher and more brazen lot than Kidd's New Yorkers.

Finally, with his crew replenished and his ship refitted, Kidd sailed northward in late April 1697 to seek the prey his commission entitled him to take: pirates or French shipping.

In July Kidd took up his station at the mouth of the Red Sea. Here, he knew, he would be well placed to intercept the pirates who preyed on the Moorish and East India Company ships that plied between the Arab port cities and India. Here he would also be in good position to attack any French merchants that might be in the area.

Day after day the *Adventure Galley* plowed back and forth at the narrow mouth of the Red Sea, fruitlessly seeking a prize. Every day now, with the new men aboard, the grumbling among the crew increased.

Kidd began to fret. Here, under the burning sun, looking out over an empty sea, the reality of his situation struck him with renewed force. How would he fulfill his financial obligations to his sponsors if—as seemed certain—he failed to find French or pirate shipping to attack? And how could he keep his increasingly mutinous crew in hand if he failed to find a ship? Was he justified, under the circumstances, in undertaking some illegal act, some act not permitted by his commission? But how could he reconcile such an act with his own vision of himself as Sailor of the King?

Then word reached *Adventure Galley* that a big convoy of some fourteen or fifteen ships, both Moorish and European, was forming up in the port of Mocha preparatory for the run to India.

Perhaps, the torn Kidd now thought, this convoy would provide the solution to his dilemma. Suppose he attacked one of the Moorish vessels of this convoy? Would such action, under the circumstances, *really* constitute a violation of his commission?

Now Kidd's propensity to fool himself must have come into play again. Surely his sponsors on the other side of the world would understand if—to satisfy his mutinous crew and preserve his command—he took a Moorish prize. After all, no one in England really gave a damn about Muslim losses, did they? Surely his powerful backers would protect him from censure if he overstepped his commission out of necessity. Surely his partners in the enterprise would look past his deeds toward his motives. They had promised him as much, had they not? And was the taking of a Moorish ship true piracy, in any case? Did the Great Mogul of India really qualify as a "friend or ally" of the king of

England—whom Kidd was forbidden by his commission to attack?

Such questions must have plagued Kidd continually as *Adventure Galley* patrolled the mouth of the Red Sea, waiting for the Mogul convoy to appear. Kidd must have prayed fervently that a suitable prize would materialize before the Mocha ships got under way so that he could avoid making the terrible decision their appearance would force on him.

But the convoy came into view first.

On August 14, 1697, lookouts spotted the fleet of fifteen ships moving slowly and ponderously down the narrows right toward *Adventure Galley*. The convoy appeared to consist mainly of merchant ships belonging to the Great Mogul. Three armed escorts were accompanying it. Two of the escorts, both flying Dutch colors, were sailing close to the merchant vessels, while the third, an East Indiaman, was running out ahead of the clustered cargo ships.

Now Kidd made the decision he must have dreaded.

He moved to intercept.

He ordered *Adventure Galley*'s topsails set and the crew to man the oars. Then, in an act that was certainly a gratuitous violation of his commission, he ran up a red ensign. Kidd certainly knew that among Eastern pirates, the red flag signified a demand for surrender—or no quarter given. Then Kidd flung himself in among the Mocha merchants like a wolf seeking a likely victim. Soon he picked out a slow Moorish merchantman as target and began maneuvering to come alongside her.

As other ships of the convoy became aware of Kidd's presence in their ranks, scattered shots began to ring out. Kidd, ignoring the desultory firing, loosed a broadside at the Moorish vessel he had targeted as his victim. His cannon damaged the rigging of the merchant but did not halt her.

Now the big East Indiaman that had been running ahead of the convoy came about and began making for *Adventure Galley*. This was the *Sceptre*, under the command of Captain Edward Barlo, a tough old sea dog. *Sceptre* now hoisted English colors. She fired at *Adventure Galley* with her bow guns.

Kidd, realizing that it was an English ship bearing down upon him, now decided to break off the action. It was one thing to attack and rob a Moorish vessel, but it would not only be an open breach of his commission to engage an English ship, it would be treason as well.

Adventure Galley thrashed away from the scene in full retreat.

But aboard *Sceptre*, Captain Barlo wrote a report of the incident in his log. There was no doubt in his mind that Kidd had intended piracy against the convoy—and from now on Indian Ocean mariners would consider him no better than any other pirate.

For Kidd the aborted attack on the Mocha convoy only worsened his situation. It made it impossible for him now, or in the future, to call upon the East India Company for aid or provisions as he had planned. Despite his commission, the company would now regard him as an enemy. The incident also demonstrated to Kidd that capturing sufficient prey to pay off his backers would be even *more* difficult than he had thought. Even Mogul shipping, it seemed, could only be taken at the risk of a fight with English or Dutch escorts. And Kidd was not yet desperate enough to risk such an open violation of his commission.

But he had to get results somehow. It was now eighteen months since he had left England, and he had absolutely nothing to show for it. He was already six months overdue on his contract with Bellomont. Furthermore, after the ignominious failure against the Mocha convoy, his prestige among his crew was lower than ever. Talk of mutiny was spreading. Added to all these troubles, the ship was beginning to leak.

Kidd now decided that, whether it constituted a technical transgression of the king's charge or not, he had no alternative but to widen his choice of prey to include Moorish and neutral ships as well as pirates and Frenchmen. He would just have to rely on his backers to put everything to rights later—after the successful completion of his mission.

Now Kidd headed *Adventure Galley* westward into the Indian Ocean.

Early in September he captured a small Moorish barkentine, captained by an Englishman. Kidd and his men got only a handful of coins, a bale of pepper, and a bale of coffee for their trouble.

Kidd now made for the Malabar Coast of India. But his luck continued bad.

He ran into two Portuguese warships near Goa. Although one of the Portuguese never got close enough to fire, the other fought

Adventure Galley for most of a whole day. When the Portuguese warship finally drew off, Kidd had sustained eleven casualties— and his ship was splintered, her sails cut to ribbons.

Adventure Galley limped on. Tensions between Kidd and his crew seethed. Kidd seemed to be acting now without any clear purpose in mind. Nor did he seem to understand that by now all the traders on the Malabar Coast saw him as a pirate. At one point Kidd put in at the trading station of Calicut and—despite all that had happened—demanded that the local East India manager provide him with food and water. When the company representative refused the demand, Kidd imperiously informed the man that "he was sent out by the King of England." The company man still refused to help.

Kidd also called at the East India Company post at Karwar. Here, too, he demanded—but did not receive—supplies. The company representative at Karwar later reported that at this time Kidd's men still went in awe of him because of his special commission from the king, but that the crew "are a very distracted company, continually quarrelling and fighting amongst themselves, so it is likely they will in a short time destroy one another, or starve, having only sufficient provisions to keep the sea for a month or more."

The situation aboard *Adventure Galley* had in fact become so tumultuous that Kidd was able to maintain such discipline as still existed aboard her only by going armed and threatening crew members into performing their duties. Screaming orders, using physical force, and—like a deranged man—forever flaunting his king's commission, Kidd seemed to be nearing a mental breakdown.

It was now November 1697—almost twenty-one months since *Adventure Galley* had set out on her voyage—and the rich prizes so desperately needed still eluded Kidd.

Then one sultry day, as *Adventure Galley* cruised off India, a rich prize at last hove into sight. She was a large merchant ship traveling alone and evidently fully loaded, judging by how low she rode in the water.

Adventure Galley pursued. But when she overhauled the merchant, the ship proved to be English: the *Loyal Captain*. Kidd, desperate as he was, still could not bring himself to attack an English ship.

But all at once the tensions aboard *Adventure Galley* boiled into the open.

Some of Kidd's men drew their pistols and leveled them at their captain. If Kidd would not take the English merchant, they would take her themselves.

Kidd, never lacking in courage, faced them down.

"I have no commission to take any but the King's enemies and pirates," he growled at the mutinous men who confronted him. "If you attempt to do any such thing, you will never come on board the *Galley* again. I will attack you and drive you into Bombay, and will carry you before the Council there."

Kidd then disarmed the would-be mutineers. The English merchant ship sailed on. The brief uprising was ended, but not the rancor that seethed aboard *Adventure Galley*.

Only two weeks later, the hostility between Kidd and his crew again flared into the open.

A gunner named William Moore, one of the most disaffected of Kidd's men and one of those who had wanted to take the *Loyal Captain* in spite of her English nationality, was sitting on deck grinding a chisel when the captain appeared.

Moore, who was surrounded by some of his sullen shipmates, suddenly called out to Kidd that they could have taken the *Loyal Captain* and "never been the worse for it."

Kidd glowered at the gunner and his mates, fury building within him.

But Moore went on berating Kidd for his failure to take the *Loyal Captain*.

"You have brought us to ruin, and we are desolate," cried Moore.

Now Kidd, furious, screamed back at Moore, calling him, according to one later account, "a lousy dog."

Now it was Moore who became infuriated.

"If I am a lousy dog," he shouted to the captain, "you have made me so. You have brought me to ruin, and many more!"

Now all the tension and anguish of the previous weeks and months seemed to erupt in Kidd. He trembled with rage at the insolent gunner who dared to upbraid him aboard his own ship. At that moment Moore must have appeared to Kidd the very embodiment of all his troubles.

"Have I ruined you, you dog?" Kidd howled at Moore.

Then he suddenly caught up an ironbound wooden bucket and smashed it against the side of Moore's head. The gunner pitched over into the scuppers. His mates carried him below to the surgeon.

"Damn him, he is a villain," Kidd cried after them.

When the gunner died the next day, Kidd was unrepentant. He told his surgeon that he did not fear legal reprisals for the death of a mutinous crewman, adding that he had "good friends in England that will bring me off that."

Now, in the wake of the killing of the gunner, an uneasy stillness descended on *Adventure Galley*.

But it was soon broken by an incident that marked Captain Kidd's first irrevocable descent into genuine piracy.

Adventure Galley was still sailing off the Malabar Coast at the end of November when her lookout sighted a sail.

Adventure Galley swept off after the potential prey. Kidd ran up the French flag as a subterfuge to encourage his quarry to show her own colors. As Kidd had hoped, the strange ship also ran up a French flag in answer to *Adventure Galley*'s pennant.

Adventure Galley now rapidly overtook the other ship. She was the *Rouparelle*, bound for Surat on the Malabar Coast. Her captain and officers identified themselves to Kidd as Dutch. Her crew were mostly Moors. The Dutch skipper came aboard *Adventure Galley* and explained to Kidd that the *Rouparelle* was owned by Moors and carried a cargo of baled cotton, quilts, and sugar. There were also two horses aboard her. The *Rouparelle*'s captain also produced a pass issued by the French East India Company—a fact that Kidd now seized on to claim that the vessel was French and therefore a legitimate prize according to his commission.

"By God, have I catched you?" he shouted, brandishing the pass. "You are a free prize to England!"

Despite his elated outburst, Kidd as an experienced ship's master knew very well that his claim that the *Rouparelle* was French would not hold water. While it was true that her Dutch captain carried a French pass, he also carried a number of additional passes—issued by other countries trading in the area. It was routine for merchant vessels to obtain such passes as a means of facilitating their movement from port to port and from trading station to trading station.

Nevertheless, Kidd claimed the *Rouparelle* as a prize. He turned her Moorish crew out of her, putting them into the ship's longboat. Then, with the connivance of her Dutch captain and officers, Kidd brought the *Rouparelle's* cargo ashore where he sold it to traders who asked no questions. He then shared the proceeds among his crewmen, something his commission did not empower him to do but the normal procedure among pirates.

Kidd renamed his "French" prize the *November*, marking the month he had captured her. He then put a prize crew aboard her—and she sailed away with *Adventure Galley*.

Now, having at last committed an authentic act of piracy, the tortured Kidd seemed to lose all his inhibitions. Starting at the end of December 1697, he seized a number of Moorish and Portuguese vessels off the Indian coast. But the plunder from these ships amounted to very little—barely enough to keep his crew appeased.

Kidd began to hunt for larger game. Apparently still viewing himself as "an honest man," still the "well-beloved captain" of his king, who had been forced against his will to engage in some minor piracy, Kidd clung to the belief that even at this late date he could satisfy his sponsors, win their promised protection, and even earn the gratitude of his monarch—if he could only find a rich, and legitimate, prize. (Clearly, despite all his setbacks, Kidd's tendency to believe a thing possible because he wished it so was still operative—and was soon to lead him even deeper into the morass.)

On January 30, 1698, *Adventure Galley* sighted a ship off the Malabar Coast that carried a load of destiny for Captain Kidd.

She was the 500-ton *Quedah Merchant*, bound from Bengal and flying an Armenian flag. *Adventure Galley* gave chase and fired a warning shot across her bow, at which point the *Quedah Merchant* hove to and waited for *Adventure Galley* to come abeam of her.

The *Quedah Merchant* carried a rich cargo that included chests of gold, silver, jewels, silks, sugar, iron, saltpeter, and guns. Owned by Armenians, she was captained by an Englishman named Wright. As Kidd approached her, he hoisted a French ensign, as he always did to conceal his true identity and to induce any potential French prize to identify herself in turn.

But when Captain Wright of the *Quedah Merchant* saw Kidd's

French colors, he attempted a clever trick that backfired on both him and Kidd: In an effort to pose as French, which he supposed Kidd to be, he ran up his own French flag and he persuaded an old French gunner in his crew to pose as the captain of the *Quedah Merchant*. The old gunner went aboard *Adventure Galley*, where he showed Kidd a pass issued by the French East India Company. At this point, convinced by the French accent of the gunner and by the French pass that he had finally come across a legitimate French prize, Kidd ran up his English flag and seized the *Quedah Merchant*.

Now the two Armenian owners of the *Quedah Merchant*, who happened to be aboard her, offered to ransom their ship for £3,000. Kidd, however, spurned their offer. By this time he knew that *Quedah Merchant* was worth much more than that. In fact she was, he felt sure, the great prize he had been seeking.

Kidd sold some of *Quedah*'s cargo ashore for £10,000 and divided the proceeds among the crew to assuage their mutinous greed. Overjoyed with his good fortune, Kidd felt sure that having at last made a rich and lawful score, he would be able to satisfy his backers—and salvage his career.

Then, to his horror, Kidd discovered that the Englishman, Captain Wright, was the actual master of the *Quedah Merchant*. His joy turned to a ghastly fear. He had captured a ship under English command. He wanted to hand the *Quedah Merchant* back to her captain, pointing out to his crew that the "taking of that ship will make a great noise in England." But the crew howled him down. After all their travail they were in no mood to surrender a ship full of treasure.

Kidd caved in.

With *Quedah Merchant* and *November* sailing in consort with *Adventure Galley*, Kidd made for the pirate's haven of St. Mary's Island. It was an odd destination for the king's own pirate catcher to choose. It may be, however, that Kidd had no other choice available to him. Perhaps his men demanded that he take them to St. Mary's. But it is possible that Kidd himself selected St. Mary's as the only refuge open to him in the Indian Ocean where he might rest and refit for the long voyage home without fear of interference by warships or armed merchants of the East India Company. Furthermore, St. Mary's lay along Kidd's homeward route.

Whatever the case, *Adventure Galley* arrived at St. Mary's on April 1, 1698. *Quedah Merchant* and *November* arrived a few days later.

While his little flotilla lay anchored in the harbor, a real pirate arrived at St. Mary's loaded with spoils for sale.

She was the *Mocha Frigate,* a former East India Company vessel now under the command of Robert Culliford—the same man who had stolen Kidd's own brigantine *Blessed William* eight years earlier in the West Indies.

Culliford, who had only forty men with him, took one look at the guns aboard the *Adventure Galley* and her two companions and decided that he was no match for Kidd. Like most of the Madagascar pirates, Culliford had heard of Kidd's pirate-hunting expedition, and he did not intend to fall into Kidd's hands. Furthermore, Culliford thought that Kidd would naturally want to take revenge for the *Blessed William* incident. Culliford, of course, could not know that Kidd—despite appearances—was in fact weaker than he. *Adventure Galley* was by now all but unseaworthy, and Kidd's crew, though still aboard, were openly mutinous.

Ignorant of the true situation, Culliford and his men, rather than face Kidd, went ashore and took shelter.

In the meantime Kidd imagined that Culliford's presence offered him a further opportunity to redeem his mission: If he could capture the *Mocha Frigate,* as his royal commission entitled him to do, he might still be able to claim that he had fully accomplished his task by taking both a French prize and a pirate loaded with plunder. Certainly the taking of the *Mocha Frigate* would help silence those who were calling him pirate.

But when he proposed seizing Culliford's ship, Kidd's crew laughed in his face, saying they would rather fire two shots at him than one at the pirate. The crew now also insisted on sharing out the spoils from the *Quedah Merchant.* Kidd could do nothing to stop them. Oddly enough, they stuck by the agreement they had made with Kidd in New York, taking 60 percent of the booty for distribution among themselves and leaving the other 40 percent for Kidd to dispose of as he wished. Supposedly, the share of the loot left to Kidd amounted to some 1,200 ounces of gold, 2,400 ounces of silver, several chests of precious stones, and bales of silks and other fabrics—a fortune.

After the share-out, ninety-seven of Kidd's men joined Culliford, who had by now come out of hiding after discovering Kidd's weakness. Kidd's former crew burned the *November* and stripped both the *Quedah Merchant* and *Adventure Galley* of all arms, guns, gear, supplies, sails, and anything else they could move, transferring all this material to the *Mocha Frigate*. Warning Kidd that if he tried to make trouble for them, they would put a bullet in his brain, Kidd's former crew now deserted entirely to the *Mocha Frigate*—leaving Kidd and thirteen honest crewmen holed up on the defenseless *Adventure Galley*.[4]

During the ensuing weeks, Kidd endured a bizarre purgatory. In constant fear of his life, he remained locked in his cabin aboard *Adventure Galley*, with bales of goods barricading his door and loaded muskets at his side, while all around him the pirates of Madagascar, together with Culliford and his men and Kidd's own former crewmen, indulged in an orgy of drinking and sex with native women.

Eventually Kidd must have recognized that he could not continue indefinitely under siege in his cabin. He must also have seen that Culliford was the dominant figure among the pirates—a circumstance that must have seemed to offer Kidd a chance to extricate himself from his little Hell.

In any event Kidd eventually emerged from his cabin and sought out Culliford, assuring his one-time mate that he had long ago forgiven him for the theft of the *Blessed William*. At one point Kidd gave Culliford a pair of pistols as a present—and went aboard *Mocha* with Culliford where the two enjoyed themselves, drinking and chatting like old friends.

Kidd even swore an oath of friendship with Culliford, "swearing that his soul might fry in hell-fire e'er he harmed his old comrade, and new found companion."

Did Kidd behave this way because he was tempted by the freedom and license he saw all about him to renounce his previous life and become, at last, the pirate that honest men said he was anyway? Or was he playing possum to save his life and the lives of his few loyal crewmen?

In the end it appears Kidd made some sort of deal with Culliford, perhaps buying him off with part of his share of the *Quedah Merchant*, for the pirate captain allowed Kidd to keep for his own use both the captured *Quedah Merchant* and the no-longer-seaworthy *Adventure Galley*—as well as his share of the *Quedah* booty.

In mid-June Culliford decided the time had come to put an end to the revelry of the previous weeks—and to get back to sea. Soon thereafter, *Mocha Frigate*—with most of Kidd's former crew aboard and bristling with guns taken from *Adventure Galley*—sailed away from St. Mary's, leaving Kidd behind with his two ships, his thirteen honest crewmen, and his fortune in loot.

With Culliford gone, Kidd resolved to return home as soon as possible. If he had ever been genuinely tempted during his revels with Culliford to go on the account, it was now forgotten. He stripped *Adventure Galley*, already half full of water, of everything useful, even burning her hull in order to get at her iron stays and spikes. He then recruited what additional seamen were available among the Madagascar gentry and did what he could to ready the *Quedah Merchant* for a transatlantic voyage.

In November 1698, having waited for the favorable monsoon winds, Kidd, in *Quedah Merchant*, set sail from St. Mary's harbor, homeward bound.

No doubt he longed to be reunited with the beautiful Sarah and his children. And he yearned for his comfortable home in New York.

Clearly Kidd felt confident that in spite of everything, he would be able to explain away his questionable behavior, perhaps blame his crew for his troubles, call upon his sponsors to protect him for the sake of their own good names—and above all, be able to distribute sufficient spoils to quell any criticism.

What Kidd, in his wishful ignorance, did *not* know was that he was no longer in a position to excuse, or explain, or even buy his way out of trouble. For Kidd and his cruise had become the subject of a vicious political scandal in England.

As reports of Kidd's depredations in the East had reached England over the past three years, it had become clear that Bellomont's pirate-killer scheme had failed. Not only had piracy in the East *not* diminished, it was obvious from reports submitted by the East India Company and the Royal Navy that William Kidd had betrayed the king's trust by turning pirate himself. Kidd was being portrayed in England as an archcriminal.

At this point, the names of Kidd's aristocratic backers had become public. Suddenly these great men, among the highest dignitaries of the realm, became fat targets of their enemies in Parliament. If Kidd was the worst pirate in history, these parliamentary critics cried, his haughty sponsors were at least as bad.

The embarrassment of Kidd's backers was profound. Washing their hands of William Kidd, they declared they were as determined as their enemies were to condemn the terrible pirate.

Kidd was declared an outlaw. The Royal Navy was ordered to capture him. The governors of the American colonies were also alerted to arrest Kidd and his crew in order that they might "be prosecuted with the utmost Rigour of the Law."

Thus, even as Kidd was sailing confidently home, he had been proclaimed a criminal, a traitor, a wanted man.

In April 1699 *Quedah Merchant* made landfall in Anguilla in the Caribbean. Kidd and his crew discovered—to their horror— that they were wanted in every port in the New World.

Some of Kidd's men panicked. They wanted to drive the *Quedah Merchant* against a reef and then flee as best they could. But Kidd refused. He still clung to his belief that ultimately he would be vindicated or, barring that, at least protected by his powerful friends. Furthermore, he did not really *feel* like a pirate. He had been forced to contend with extraordinary circumstances. He had had to quell a mutinous crew. And yet, had he not taken two French prizes? Did he not have in his possession their French passes to prove it?

He decided his best course would be to make for New York where he knew Lord Bellomont—his good friend—was now colonial governor. But first he had to rid himself of *Quedah Merchant*, now too clumsy and worn for his purposes.

Luckily he found a sleek fast ship—the *Antonio*—becalmed out at sea, and he bought her on the spot from her owner-captain. He then transferred mysterious chests—rumored full of gold, coins, and jewels—from the leaky old *Quedah Merchant* to the *Antonio*. After this he gave the former owner of the *Antonio* some money to sail the *Quedah Merchant* to a secluded spot in Hispaniola and to keep her there under guard for three months, or until Kidd should contact him.

Then, with only twelve men still willing to sail with him, Captain Kidd set out northward for New York.

9

A Voyage to Wapping

On June 10, 1699, Captain William Kidd, now master of the sloop *Antonio*, anchored in Oyster Bay on the New York side of Long Island Sound.

He was home at last after a voyage that had covered 42,000 miles and had taken more than three years. In the course of this voyage he had engaged in highly questionable behavior, had killed a member of his crew, had sworn friendship with a pirate captain, and had made himself rich with stolen goods.

He was also an outlaw.

But he did not regard himself as an outlaw, and he was convinced that once he told his side of the story, others would not long continue in that opinion of him. They would see that he had done only what had seemed best.

And so, full of confidence in his own rectitude and certain that the French passes he had taken from his two main prizes would eventually exonerate him of piracy, Kidd set out to vindicate himself.

He began by sending word of his arrival in the New York area to an old friend, James Emmott, a lawyer. Emmott joined Kidd aboard the *Antonio* and informed Kidd that Lord Bellomont was in Boston rather than New York. Kidd then asked Emmott to go to see Bellomont as Kidd's agent—and explain Kidd's innocence to the colonial governor. Emmott agreed. Two days later he met privately with Bellomont. He put Kidd's case to the colonial governor, even turning over the two French passes that Kidd believed were proof of his innocence.

Bellomont, who had sent Kidd on his mission in the first place, listened noncommittally. He was under orders to arrest Kidd. He knew that his own career and reputation might be smashed if he mishandled this affair. Bellomont, fearing that Kidd might flee if he appeared less than friendly, then assured Kidd's emissary that the captain had nothing to fear if, as he claimed, he had not dishonored his commission from the king.

Bellomont, who was a much craftier man than either Kidd or Emmott, then wrote to Kidd, saying as much and suggesting that a pardon could no doubt be obtained. First, of course, Kidd would have to present himself to Bellomont in Boston. (In a report to London, Bellomont made it clear that his letter was merely a device to lure Kidd into his hands. "Menacing him had not been the way to invite him hither," Bellomont wrote, "but rather wheedling.")

Bellomont's letter to Kidd was delivered by Duncan Campbell, Boston's postmaster and another close friend of Kidd's.

Kidd agreed to come to Boston. He wrote back to Bellomont: "I doubt not that I shall be able to make my Innocency appear, or else I had no need to come to these parts of the world."

Now Kidd, a simple sailor still, and never clumsier than when he tried to be clever, undertook a series of actions that could only arouse deep suspicions about his motives. Ignoring the Admiralty law that required him to turn over all booty for evaluation by Admiralty court, Kidd instead dispersed his swag like a man who did not trust the future. He hid a bag of gold bars in the home of a Rhode Island friend. He buried chests of gold and jewels on Gardiners Island in Long Island Sound, with the consent of the island's proprietor. He also sent bales of cloth and other materials to friends and associates around the New York area. It was as if he intended to use his spoils as bargaining chips, if his confrontation with Bellomont did not work out as he hoped. But it was a stupid maneuver because it made him appear guilty despite his protestations of innocence.

He also did something else he thought clever. He sent a number of jewels in an enameled box to young Lady Bellomont. It seemed an obvious bribe, and it embarrassed the colonial governor at a time when he was already feeling exceedingly discomfited by his relationship with Kidd.

On his way to Boston aboard the *Antonio*, Kidd put in at Block Island where he was reunited with Sarah and their two daughters, who had been only three and four years old when he had set out on his fateful journey more than three years earlier. It was a touching reunion, with many tears. Together the family sailed to Boston, where they landed on July 2, 1699.

In Boston Kidd once again made a bumbling attempt to ingratiate himself with Bellomont through the Governor's wife. He sent Lady Bellomont a green silk bag containing gold bars worth £1,000. Lady Bellomont returned the unsubtle gift.

On the day after Kidd's arrival in Boston, Bellomont summoned him to an interview.

Kidd met with Bellomont and members of his colonial council in Bellomont's house. The colonial governor treated Kidd with cool formality. He requested that Kidd provide a full account of his activities since embarking down the Thames aboard *Adventure Galley*.

Kidd apparently had not expected Bellomont to receive him so coldly. He told Bellomont and his council, truthfully but with some belligerence, that his crew had destroyed the log of *Adventure Galley* and he was therefore unable to provide a detailed account of his adventures. The governor and the council then directed Kidd to put together a written report from memory, and dismissed him temporarily.

For two days Kidd stalled over the requested written report. Perhaps he feared self-incrimination. Perhaps he felt that without precise times and places as set forth in his log, his story would sound vague and unconvincing. More than likely, however, he merely hoped that if he could avoid the task long enough, Bellomont and his council might take some other tack with him—and he could avoid the pitfalls of writing out what might be construed as a confession.

After two days of Kidd's stonewalling on their request for a written statement, and fearing that Kidd might try to flee their jurisdiction, the council ordered Kidd's arrest.

He was arrested on July 6 outside Bellomont's house. Apparently he had had it in mind to see Lord Bellomont alone and was on his way to do so when he was stopped by the police officers, for he drew his sword when seized and broke away from the arresting officers, running into Bellomont's house crying out that he wanted to speak to his one-time patron.

Whatever Kidd may have wanted to convey privately to Bellomont, he never got the chance. He was taken away and clapped in irons in the Stone Prison in Boston. Probably it would have done Kidd little good even if he had succeeded in meeting Bellomont alone. The colonial governor had washed his hands of the king's privateer, for in his report to London on the affair, Bellomont referred to Kidd as "a monster."

Throughout July 1699, while Kidd languished in prison, Bellomont's agents tracked down and confiscated all Kidd's loot—from the chests buried on Gardiners Island to the gifts to various friends to the cargo stowed aboard the *Antonio* and hidden elsewhere. Even Kidd's clothes, and his gifts to Sarah, were hauled off.

One inventory of the recovered loot showed 1,111 ounces of gold, 2,353 ounces of silver, more than a pound of precious stones, 57 bags of sugar, and 41 bales of expensive brocade and other fabrics.

Bellomont also sought to discover the fate of the *Quedah Merchant*—which Kidd had left, supposedly under guard, at Hispaniola.

Bellomont, believing that the *Quedah* cargo would actually be worth far more than the goods he had already recovered from Kidd, eventually sent a ship to find her and to salvage whatever cargo might be left. But the mission was unsuccessful. *Quedah Merchant* had "disappeared." (Later evidence indicated that her "guards" had sold her cargo to passing ships at a good profit and had then fled. One witness reported that after her cargo had been sold, *Quedah Merchant* had been burned to the keel and destroyed off the coast of Hispaniola. But there was never any proof of her actual fate, or of the fate of her cargo, and the mystery was never cleared up.)

While in Stone Prison, Kidd himself had offered to go and find the *Quedah* for Bellomont. He had claimed that her recoverable cargo would be worth £50,000 or more. But Kidd's offer was probably no more than a desperate effort to tempt Bellomont into freeing him from the solitary confinement and chains of his prison. (Perhaps Kidd also hoped that once free of jail, he would find a way to escape altogether. Certainly Kidd would not have left goods worth £50,000 on a ship he had entrusted to strangers. In any case Bellomont ignored Kidd's offer—and the captain remained in prison.)

When Bellomont was at last satisfied that he had found all there was to find of Kidd's booty, and that all the necessary legal paperwork had been completed, he shipped the recovered plunder back to England under heavy guard—to be added to the Royal Treasury if and when the law permitted.

As for Kidd himself, on February 16, 1700, after seven months in prison, he was taken aboard H.M.S. *Advice* for transport to England and trial. During the voyage, he occupied a steerage cabin. The *Advice* was also carrying thirty-one other prisoners back to England for trial on various charges. Among them were members of Kidd's crew who would stand trial with him. These thirty-one prisoners, all ordinary seamen, did not rate cabins. They were chained together in the ship's gun room.

While Kidd was en route to his destiny, Parliament was boiling over with the scandal of the Kidd affair. Basically it was a case of the newly elected Tory majority in Parliament taking advantage of an opportunity to blacken the now-minority Whigs—whose leaders had been the secret backers of the Kidd adventure.[1]

The Tory members of Parliament were determined to root out and expose the story of the Whig leadership's role in the Kidd affair. Toward this end Parliament had ordered the Admiralty to deliver to it for investigation all papers and information pertaining to the voyage of Captain Kidd.

Inevitably, the real names of Kidd's sponsors had been revealed in Parliament. Thereupon the Tory members had not only expressed shock and shame, they had also proposed a motion censuring the pirate-catching scheme as "dishonorable to the King, against the law of nations, contrary to the laws and statutes of this realm, invasive of property, and destructive of trade and commerce." Despite the Tory majority, this motion was defeated by a vote of 189 to 133. But the parliamentary political pudding did not stop boiling. Parliament was scheduled to adjourn in April and not sit again for months. The Tories feared that the Whigs would somehow manage to hush up the Kidd affair while Parliament was in recess. They therefore petitioned the king not to allow Kidd to be "tried, discharged, or pardoned, until the next session of Parliament." The request was granted.

On Thursday, April 11, 1700, Parliament recessed.

On that same day William Kidd had been transferred from his locked cabin aboard H.M.S. *Advice* to the Royal yacht *Catherine* in the Thames estuary—to be taken, under heavy guard, to the Admiralty office in Greenwich.

The *Catherine* arrived in Greenwich with her infamous prisoner early on the morning of April 14. But when officials opened his cabin door to examine him, Kidd was found to be nearly insane. He cried out for a knife with which to end his life. With a trembling hand he proffered a gold piece, begging his hearers to send it to Sarah. He implored all who heard him to spare him the ignominy of the hangman's noose. He wished to be executed by shooting.

Later in the day Kidd recovered sufficiently to make a deposition at the Admiralty. After signing it, he was transported to Newgate Prison in London to await trial.

Newgate, already an ancient pile of damp stone when Kidd was brought there, was a foul overcrowded warren of dank corridors and dark cells. It stank of the fetid odors of unwashed prisoners' bodies and of piles of excrement. So bad was the stench that it was the custom for visitors to bring a bunch of flowers with them to inhale while inside the noisome place. Prisoners had to be doused in vinegar to kill the odor before court appearances.

Here Captain William Kidd, crawling with lice and, according to his jailers, "troubled with a great Paine in his Head, and shaken in his Limbs," lay month after month in what was called "safe" and "close" confinement. He was not permitted to write any letters—not even to his wife. His only visitors were an aunt and an uncle who were allowed to see him only when a guard was present. He was not even allowed to communicate with anyone about his trial—except to write directly to the Admiralty board. Such deprivation of rights was unusual. In fact, safe and close confinement was ordinarily reserved for men accused of treason.

Nevertheless, it was under such conditions that Kidd was expected to prepare for his coming trial. It is little wonder, then, that he wrote plaintively to the Admiralty, saying about the trial that sooner or later he would have to undergo: "I am wholly un-

prepared, having never been permitted the least use of pen, Ink, and paper to help my Memory, nor the advice of friends to assist me, in what so nearly concerns my life."

On March 27, 1701, after he had spent almost a year under horrendous conditions in Newgate Prison (and months before that in Stone Prison in Boston), Kidd was taken from his cell—but not for trial.

Instead he was taken before the House of Commons to testify not in his own case but in an inquiry that Parliament, pressed by the Tories, was conducting into the conduct of Kidd's Whig backers. The Tories made no secret of their expectation that Kidd's testimony would help impeach his sponsors, the Whig ministers. As Bishop Gilbert Burnet later recalled Kidd's parliamentary testimony: "All endeavors were used to persuade him to accuse the Lords. He was assured that, if he did it, he should be preserved; and if he did not, he should certainly die for his piracy; yet this could not prevail on him to charge them."

Kidd, shuffling and confused after his long incarceration, appeared to understand little of what was happening. Instead of taking the deal offered him and giving the Tories the testimony they wanted, he insisted that he had not committed piracy. Like a man obsessed, he defended his actions. In the process he appeared stubbornly self-righteous. He even seemed to resent the questions directed to him by House members—an attitude that offended many Tories who had been prepared to offer him a pardon had he given the testimony hoped for, and had he thrown himself upon the mercy of the House.

As one member put it: "I had thought him only a knave. Now I know him to be a fool as well."

Instead of a *victim* of dishonest, but powerful, Whig ministers, the truculent fumbling Kidd made himself appear their accomplice. If *he*—as he insisted—had committed no piracy on the high seas, how could the House accuse his sponsors of financing his crimes? Unless Kidd testified to his own crimes, there was no case against the Whigs—and Kidd held tenaciously to his claim of innocence.

Disappointed and irritated with Kidd, the House dismissed him, returning him to Newgate. By his stubborn mishandling of his parliamentary testimony, Kidd had destroyed his value as a witness. Parliament washed its hands of him, declaring that he should be "proceeded against according to law."

Now Kidd finally seemed to understand what it was the Tory members wanted of him. He wrote to the Speaker of the House, Robert Harley, claiming that his Whig sponsors had made him "the Tool of their Ambition and Avarice." But even in this letter he refused to admit guilt—a fact that rendered all else in his letter useless to the Tories.

Ironically, the House eventually passed motions impeaching Kidd's Whig backers, but Kidd himself no longer had any role to play in the proceedings. The Tories had lost interest in him. He was now a discredited witness. Even if he were to confess to everything, it would be regarded as nothing more than a desperate man's lying effort to extricate himself from peril.[2]

On May 8, 1701, Captain William Kidd went on trial for his life at the Old Bailey. He was grossly unprepared.

Kidd had been informed of his trial date only two weeks earlier. The court had appropriated £50 for him to retain defense attorneys, but the £50 had not been delivered until the night before the trial was scheduled—and Kidd's two attorneys had refused to handle his case until their fee was in their hands. Thus Kidd had been able to hold only one brief meeting with his defense lawyers—an hour before the start of his trial.

Kidd still believed that the two French passes, which had been turned over to Bellomont two years earlier, were the key to his defense because, in his view at least, they proved he had acted within the bounds of his commission. But unfortunately for Kidd, the passes could not be found among the voluminous documents that Lord Bellomont had forwarded to the Admiralty on Kidd's case. As Kidd went to trial on the morning of May 8, 1701, the passes still had not been located.

Even though Kidd felt he had no real defense without the missing French passes, his trial went on as scheduled.

Under the rules of court that applied in that era, Kidd would not be allowed to testify in his own defense. Nor would his lawyers be allowed to cross-examine witnesses against him. Only Kidd, in his clumsy, angry, self-righteous and blundering way, would be permitted to cross-examine.

The first charge against Kidd was for the murder of the gunner, William Moore, on board the *Adventure Galley*. The Crown's two chief witnesses were Joseph Palmer, one of the most mutinous of Kidd's men aboard *Adventure Galley*, and Robert Brandinham, *Adventure Galley's* surgeon.

These two, among those who had deserted Kidd at Madagascar to join Culliford's pirates, were themselves charged as pirates—and had turned King's evidence against Kidd in order to save their own necks.

Palmer painted Moore as a peaceful fellow whom Kidd had killed without provocation.

Kidd cross-examined—and made a mess of it. He tried to get Palmer to admit that Moore was fomenting a mutiny.

"There was no mutiny," Palmer insisted. "All was quiet."

The clumsy Kidd could not shake Palmer's story.

Bradinham testified that he knew of no quarrel between Kidd and the dead gunner.

Kidd's own witnesses, also crewmen, proved ineffective.

Kidd pleaded that the gunner had provoked his fury.

"I had all the provocation in the world given me, and I had no design to kill him," Kidd declared. "It was not designedly done, but in my passion, for which I am heartily sorry."

In his charge to the jury, the judge declared: "I cannot see what distinction can be made, but that the prisoner is guilty of murder."

Not surprisingly, the jury, after only an hour's deliberation, returned a guilty verdict.

On the next morning Kidd and nine of his men shuffled again into the courtroom, this time for trial on the piracy indictments.

The prosecutor for the Crown referred to Kidd as "an arch-pirate, equally cruel, dreaded, and hated both on the land and at sea. . . . No one in this age has done more mischief, in this worst kind of mischief, or has occasioned greater confusion and disorder, attended with all the circumstances of cruelty and falsehood. . . ."

The prosecutor condemned Kidd for piracy in taking the *Quedah Merchant*, and *November*, and three other, unnamed, ships. He also argued that Kidd had been derelict in his duty by not seizing Culliford and *Mocha Frigate* while at Madagascar.

Again the two men who had testified against Kidd in the murder trial—Bradinham and Palmer—were the Crown's chief witnesses. They told their thoroughly rehearsed stories in convincing detail, careful to paint Kidd as a man who had intended piracy all along.

Kidd, inevitably inept in his cross-examination, kept returning to the question of the French passes, pleading that if only they were found they would prove his innocence. As for the ships he took that had *not* been sailing under French passes, Kidd tried to convince the court that he had seized them only when compelled to do so by his rebellious crew. Even Kidd's own witnesses could not definitely testify to the existence of the crucial French passes.

In the end, Kidd seemed to despair.

"This man contradicts himself in a hundred places," Kidd said of Bradinham. "He tells a thousand lies."

In his charge to the jury, the judge noted that even if the

French passes had been placed in evidence, Kidd had clearly committed a series of felonies upon the high seas: by attacking the Moorish convoy at the mouth of the Red Sea; by taking other Moorish ships and Portuguese ships off the coast of India; by consorting with Culliford; and by sharing out plunder before condemnation by an Admiralty court as required of legal privateers. There was also reference to Kidd's "mistreatment" of natives when *Adventure Galley* had briefly put into the Maldive Islands during the early days of her cruise off India.[3]

The judge then returned to the subject of the French passes.

"As to the French passes," he declared, "there is nothing of that appears by any proof; and for aught I can see, none saw them but himself, if there were ever any."

Not surprisingly the jury found Kidd guilty, taking only half an hour to deliberate. Of the nine men tried with Kidd, six were found guilty along with their captain. Three others, who had been employed primarily as servants aboard *Adventure Galley*, were acquitted.

Asked if he had anything to say before sentence was passed, Kidd declared: "I have been sworn against by perjured and wicked people."

He was then sentenced to be hanged. "My Lord," said Kidd, "it is a very hard sentence. For my part, I am the innocentest person of them all, only I have been sworn against by perjured persons."

Kidd's execution was set for May 23 at Wapping—a marshy tenement area on the Thames mud flats where the Admiralty customarily hanged its criminals on gibbets visible to all the traffic on the great river.

In the days preceding his execution, Kidd was visited by the Reverend Paul Lorrain, chaplain of Newgate Prison, who offered him the comfort of religion.

But Kidd, far from asking forgiveness for his crimes or throwing himself upon the mercy of his Creator, continued to insist that he was innocent of all crimes. Lorrain, however, did not despair of Kidd's soul. On the day that Kidd was scheduled to die, as Lorrain himself later reported it, the chaplain applied himself with "particular exhortations" until, at last, according to the clergyman, Kidd "readily assented and said he truly forgave all the world."

The chaplain, thereupon, left Kidd alone to meditate on the death that awaited him in only a few hours.

At 3:00 P.M. on May 23, 1701, however, when Kidd emerged from Newgate for his ride to Wapping, he was not intoxicated with the hope of everlasting life. Instead he was falling-down drunk on alcohol that some kindly benefactor—apparently lacking the chaplain's clear-sighted sense of what was fitting for a condemned man—had smuggled in to him.

Kidd was transported to the place of execution in a black-draped cart. The king's deputy marshal preceded him in an open carriage, resting a silver oar (the symbol of the Admiralty) on his shoulder. A crowd, hooting and shouting with glee, followed Kidd's cart as the little parade moved through the district of shabby hovels and cheap taverns toward the execution ground.

Finally, after two hours, the cavalcade arrived at Execution Dock at Wapping on the tidal flats of the dismal riverside.

Even now, in the shadow of the gallows, Kidd, still unsteady from drink, continued to insist that he had committed no piracies.

Chaplain Lorrain, grieved by his charge's drunken condition, renewed his campaign to achieve Kidd's repentance. Even at this late hour, the chaplain exhorted Kidd, there was time for redemption, if he would say he repented of his crimes. But the stubborn Kidd, true to his own vision of himself, would only say he was sorry for his sins in general.

"He expressed abundance of sorrow for leaving his wife and children, without having the opportunity to take leave of them," the chaplain reported later, "so that the thoughts of his wife's sorrow at the sad tidings of his shameful death was more occasion of grief to him than that of his own sad misfortunes."

Now Kidd was made to stand on the rickety platform of the gallows. The noose was tightened around his neck. He was then pushed off. But the rope snapped. He fell to the ground.

White-faced and shaken, he had to be hanged a second time. This time he was made to climb a ladder. Again Chaplain Lorrain called upon Kidd to confess his evil deeds. In response Kidd spewed forth some words of sorrow which the Chaplain was pleased to regard as the long-sought repentance.

Now, with a swift motion, the constables pulled away the ladder. Kidd fell. The rope held.

Kidd's body, tarred to preserve it, was displayed on the bank of the Thames for years—caged and hung from a gibbet—as a "deterrent" to other malefactors.[4]

So perished Captain William Kidd. Within months he had become a legend. Songs were written about him. One of them, "The Ballad of William Kidd," gives the flavor of the legend that grew up around him and his fate:

> My name was William Kidd, when I sailed, when I sailed.
>   My name was William Kidd, when I sailed.
> My name was William Kidd,
>   God's laws I did forbid.
> And so wickedly I did, when I sailed.

That William Kidd did wickedly is beyond dispute. He was guilty of most of the charges against him. He *did* kill the gunner, Moore. He *did* disobey the orders contained in his commission. He *did* engage in piracy—despite his claim regarding the missing French passes.[5]

Yet, despite his guilt, Kidd was far less a conscious criminal than a victim—of circumstances, of bad luck, of social pressures exerted by powerful men, of a mutinous crew, and above all, of his own propensity for wishful thinking.

Throughout his long descent into the inferno, he continually committed acts that were not only wrong but against his own best interests. All these self-destructive acts—from his insolence to the navy to his attempts to cozy up to Lady Bellomont—flowed from this fundamental defect in his character: his disposition to see things as he *wished* them to be. It was this flaw that first set Kidd on his journey to the gallows at Wapping—by permitting him to dream of becoming a Royal Navy commander. If he had not saddled himself with *that* unreal ambition, he probably would not have traveled to London in the summer of 1695, would not have met with Livingston and Bellomont, would not have acceded to the impossible mission they pressed on him—and would not have blundered into the crimes that eventually brought him to Execution Dock.

Or perhaps, being what he was, William Kidd might have found some other road to some other Wapping.

In any event, Kidd *did* commit murder and piracy. He *was* a criminal.

But he was *not* a pirate. The pirates of the outlaw nation were conscious, deliberate outlaws—rebels against society. Among them there could be no such thing as a "trusty and well-beloved" Sailor of the King—which was what Kidd tried to be, and thought he was, right up to his last moments.

It is possible that while reveling with Culliford at Madagascar, Kidd was tempted by the free and lusty life of piracy, but he was also clearly disgusted by it. His innate respect for order, his sense of duty and mission, his past life as an honest, successful seaman, as faithful husband and loving father, and above all, his ambition for the future—all these factors precluded Kidd from ever becoming a true pirate. If he committed piracies, they were acts of expediency, even acts of survival. But they were not acts of rebellion, not acts of war. Kidd simply did not have it in him to rebel against society. He was too much a part of it.

Yet Kidd, and the cruise of *Adventure Galley*, occupy an important place in the annals of the outlaw brotherhood.

Kidd's story illuminates the pervasiveness of piracy among the common sailors of his time—and makes plain the power of its allure for simple seafarers.

Although his crewmen were not outlaws when Kidd signed them aboard *Adventure Galley*, they were soon infected by the genuine pirates that Kidd later brought into the crew. In time almost all of Kidd's men—except for a handful of loyalists—became open rebels who defied their captain and their king by forcing Kidd to piracy, thereby in effect making him a prisoner aboard his own ship while on the king's own business. The vast majority of Kidd's men, when offered the chance, joined Culliford in Madagascar to go pirating, once again demonstrating that for many sailors it was better to be a free pirate than the honest servant of any Authority, even the king's.[6]

Kidd's voyage was also important because it showed contemporaries just how futile would be any further private efforts to stem piracy in the East. The failure of Kidd's cruise helped to convince many of those in power that only a determined effort by the Royal Navy and an honest effort by colonial officials to enforce the king's writ at sea and ashore would eradicate piracy in the eastern seas.

As for Kidd himself, in death he became known as one of the most fearsome pirates of history. Even in this he was a victim. Encapsulated in his false legend, he remains as much a captive of the outlaw nation today as he was during the long, luckless, and fatal cruise of *Adventure Galley*.

10

Counterstroke and Intermission: The War Moves West

Even before Captain William Kidd had returned from his ill-starred voyage, the forces of law and property had begun an effective counterattack against the outlaw nation based on Madagascar.

The initial blows had been economic, designed to deprive the Madagascar outlaws of the two essential pillars of their existence: their sources of supply and markets for their stolen goods.

Lord Bellomont, the new colonial governor, fresh in his post and full of highly visible zeal against the trade in pirate contraband, had embarked on a campaign to remove corrupt officials from the colonies. He had begun by sending the notorious Benjamin Fletcher back to England under arrest. He had also had numerous other officials whom he suspected of trading with pirates ("pirate brokers" he called them) dismissed from their positions.

Bellomont had let it be known far and wide that unlike previous colonial governors, he could not be bribed. Nor would he countenance evasion of the Navigation Acts, no matter how onerous they were to the general population.

To enforce his policies Bellomont had deployed the small naval forces available to him to guard the coastal waters, to board suspected vessels, and to seize illegal cargoes.

Although pirates had continued to operate by sneaking past Bellomont's coast guards, the sweet trade had soon begun to sour both for the pirates themselves and for the businessmen who purchased their booty. So effectively had Bellomont cut into the piratical trade that in 1698 New York merchants had petitioned London to recall him—and to send back Fletcher!

The New York pirate brokers had had more cause than any others to complain of the new colonial governor, for Bellomont had directed most of his energies at them. In fact, Bellomont had managed to force out of business New York's premier pirate trader, Frederick Philipse, who had been for many years the chief supplier and dealer for the Madagascar-based pirate broker Adam Baldridge.[1]

To halt Philipse's illegal trading in pirate goods, Bellomont had ordered his coast guards to seize several of Philipse's ships, each of them laden with plunder purchased from the pirates. Bellomont had also dismissed Philipse from his post on the governor's council on the very good grounds that Philipse, by dealing with pirates, had been for many years violating the very laws he was sworn to uphold.

Nor had Bellomont been the only colonial governor to act against piracy in America.

Governor Francis Nicholson of Virginia, had also taken effective measures against the trade.

In November 1697, for example, Nicholson had sent an armed party over the Virginia border into Pennsylvania to capture a gang of pirates who had taken shelter there under the protection of Pennsylvania's corrupt Governor William Markham. (Markham was one of the officials later dismissed through the efforts of Lord Bellomont.)

In June 1700—a year after Kidd's return from his infamous cruise, and only four months after Bellomont had sent the notorious captain back to England for trial—Governor Nicholson had personally directed a coast-guard ship in a successful battle with a pirate vessel that had been cruising off the coast of Virginia.

Throughout the bloody combat, one witness reported, Governor Nicholson "never stirred off the quarterdeck, but by his example, conduct, and plenty of gold which he gave amongst the men, made them fight bravely, til they had taken the pirates' ship, with a hundred and odd prisoners, the rest being killed."

Because of the zeal of Governor Nicholson and other honest colonial officials—and especially because of Lord Bellomont's policies—the pirate trade had by 1701 all but withered away, and pirate vessels had become rare off colonial shores where once they had proliferated.[2]

In addition to economic measures against the pirate trade, the British government had attacked piracy by changing the laws to make it easier to prosecute seaborne outlaws.

Under the new laws, men charged with piracy no longer had to be returned to England for trial—as Kidd had been, for example. The new acts had authorized Admiralty courts to try pirates in the colonies themselves. This change had been a great improvement over the old system, which had been both time-consuming and costly, and which in practice had often meant that the accused went free because prosecution required more time, expense, and effort than it was worth.

However, stern new antipiracy laws had not been the only measures adopted by the London government. It had also tried to induce at least some of the Madagascar-based outlaws to cease their activities voluntarily. Toward this end King William had proclaimed a general amnesty for all pirates who sought pardon before June 1699. (William Kidd and Henry Every had been specifically excluded from the amnesty offer, however.)

The combination of proffered amnesty, new legal sanctions against piracy, and suppression of colonial markets had soon inflicted serious damage on the outlaw brotherhood. What good, after all, was loot that you couldn't sell, or trade for rum or women?

Many Madagascar pirates, especially those who had depended most heavily on traders such as Baldridge in Madagascar and the colonial pirate brokers of New York, Newport, and Boston, had abandoned the sweet trade altogether. Others had begun to look elsewhere for markets for their plunder. A number had been taken by the East India Company—and tried and convicted under the new Admiralty acts. Many others, reading the handwriting on the wall, had accepted pardons and had returned to honest service or settled on Madagascar.

But despite the effectiveness of government programs against piracy, a number of pirates had remained in the East and had continued to prey on merchant shipping in the Indian Ocean, accepting for their plundered goods reduced prices from smugglers and from petty traders.

The enemies of piracy had had to recognize that this hardcore remainder—still a formidable force and still able to strike with impunity from its Madagascar sanctuaries—could be exterminated only by Royal Navy action.

And beginning in the latter half of 1698, such action had become, for the first time in nearly a decade, a distinct possibility, for in that year the political landscape had begun to alter, and with it the role of the Royal Navy.

In the summer of 1698 King William's war against France, which had kept the English fleet engaged for nine years, had come to an indecisive end with the signing of the Treaty of Ryswick.

While the treaty had halted hostilities, it had not resolved any of the political, religious, and economic problems between the warring parties. It had merely acknowledged that both sides had reached near exhaustion and required a respite. All parties to the treaty, especially King William himself, had recognized that war might break out again at almost any time.

For this reason William had continued to resist the incessant pleas of the East India Company and other merchants to dispatch Royal Navy men-of-war to Madagascar. In addition to renewed war with France, William feared that war might break out in the Baltic between Sweden on one hand and a combination of Russia, Poland, and Denmark on the other. He wanted to be able to intervene with the Royal Navy if such an outbreak did occur— while still maintaining sufficient fleet strength to fend off any challenge from France across the Channel.

William had still another reason to retain the fleet in home waters: The Tories had won a majority in the House of Commons in the parliamentary elections of 1697 on a pledge to reduce taxes for the maintenance of the army and navy, and on a promise to pursue a policy of peace in opposition to William's own determination to oppose Louis XIV of France. The Tories had wasted no time in reducing the size of the Royal Navy—and William had argued that in view of the cuts in the naval budget and the dangers of the international situation, it was more imperative than ever to husband the reduced fleet at home. But the Tories had disagreed with William. In spite of the king's concern about the possibility of war's breaking out again, and despite their own pledge to cut back on naval expenditures, the Tory government had decided it was in England's interest to use the Royal Navy to suppress the Madagascar pirates. The nabobs of the East India Company had at last won their fight for Royal Navy help in the Indian Ocean.

Accordingly, in January 1699, the Admiralty had dispatched eastward four naval vessels—*Anglesea, Hastings, Harwich,* and *Lizard*—under Commodore Thomas Warren, the same officer whom Captain Kidd had tried to bully in their encounter off Africa two years earlier.

The Admiralty, which agreed with William that a new war was imminent, had been loath to spare even these four armed vessels from the main fleet. But it had done so out of political necessity.

Regarding the expedition as no more than a modest counterstroke designed to check the most serious of the pirate depredations—and to scare the less bold among the pirate captains out of the Indian Ocean altogether—the Admiralty ordered Warren to use whatever force was necessary to break up the pirate concentrations but, at the same time, to extend the king's pardon to any pirates willing to give up their outlaw life peacefully.

Warren and his flotilla of four ships had arrived at the island of St. Mary's in May 1699.

According to Warren, the virtually landlocked harbor was filled with pirate ships when his squadron approached. Apparently the outlaws had been taken by surprise, but they had made haste to defend their base. They had manned the forty guns of Adam Baldridge's old fort overlooking the harbor, and they had blocked the bottleneck of the harbor entrance by sinking old ships in the shallow water.

They also sank and burned all the other ships in the harbor, destroying whatever plunder they had aboard and many stores as well.

Commodore Warren, standing offshore with his guns trained on St. Mary's harbor, reckoned that there were some fifteen hundred outlaws on the island and that a battle would be costly to both sides. Prior to initiating hostilities, therefore, he had sent an emissary ashore to offer the king's pardon to all who would surrender. Most of the pirates, recognizing the impracticality of taking on the Royal Navy (and always willing to accept amnesty temporarily to escape a dangerous situation) gave themselves up. Many others, however, refused the offer of pardon. These crossed by various means to the main island of Madagascar and took refuge among the natives and ex-pirate settlers, apparently willing to wait until better days returned.

In the event, the Royal Navy squadron had not had to fire a shot. Warren's men had dismantled the harbor defenses of St. Mary's. The commodore had then resumed his search-and-destroy cruise in eastern waters.

For the better part of a year, the Royal Navy squadron had patrolled the eastern seas, seeking pirate vessels. But the squadron had not found a single pirate ship, nor had it fired a shot at any of the shore installations the pirates had built and now had abandoned. Finally, two of Warren's four vessels had gone home, leaving two ships to continue on patrol in the East.

By the middle of 1701 the pirate nation had all but disappeared. Pirate captains, deprived of both their base and their markets and unwilling to face the guns of the Royal Navy, abandoned the Indian Ocean. Some shifted their activities farther east to the Dutch East Indies, and even to the China Sea. A few gave up the sea altogether, settling down on Madagascar or in the islands of the Indian Ocean. Some wandered where the winds took them.

It was certain, however, that the great days of Madagascar were over.

The outlaw nation was near extinction.

Then Louis XIV saved it.

In far-off Europe, Charles II of Spain had died without an heir in direct line to the throne. In his will, however, he had designated a grandson of Louis XIV as inheritor of the vast Spanish Empire that stretched from the Americas to the Pacific and included possessions in Italy and the Netherlands. For the enemies of the Sun King—England, Holland, Austria, Prussia, Sweden, and Denmark—a union of the Spanish Crown with the military might of France constituted an intolerable threat. England and Holland backed a rival claimant to the Spanish throne, Archduke Charles of Austria.

Despite the opposition of much of Europe, Louis's grandson— prodded and protected by the Sun King's power—ascended the throne of Spain as King Philip V, infuriating and terrifying the enemies of royal France. Louis outraged England even further by recognizing the Catholic heir of the dethroned Stuarts as the rightful king of England. In addition, Louis laid heavy duties on English trade with France and Spain.

The result was the bloody War of the Spanish Succession, which broke out in 1701 between England, Holland, and their allies on one side, and royal France and Spain on the other.

In England the Tories and the Whigs, parliamentary opponents, finally found a cause they could agree upon. They rallied to King William's call for a national effort against Louis. Even after William died early in 1702, England's resolve to fight the war as part of a Grand Alliance against Louis did not flag.

In May 1702, England's new queen, Anne, who had been designated by Parliament as William's successor, issued a proclamation designed to boost Britain's naval strength—depleted by Parliament's budgetary constraints in the last years of William's reign. The proclamation authorized the use of privateers against the shipping of Spain and France.

Suddenly the Madagascar pirates, almost extinguished a year earlier, were back in business, this time as lawful brigands of the queen of England.

For the ordinary pirates of Madagascar, the privateering life might not have been as enjoyable as the pirate life, but it paid well. And even more important, enlistment aboard a privateer exempted a man from impressment into the Royal Navy where discipline was cruel and plunder almost nonexistent.

In the course of the long war, which lasted a total of eleven years, British and American privateers were immensely successful, capturing more than two thousand prizes. One fleet of thirteen privateers operating out of New York took thirty-six enemy prizes in three years, sharing a total of £60,000 in booty.

In 1708, when the war was at midpoint, Parliament passed a new law that permitted the owners and crews of privateering vessels to share *all* the plunder, without having to forward 10 percent of the take to the Crown. As a result, privateering became even more popular, primarily because it became more profitable.

Although England and her allies held the upper hand in the sea war from the beginning, the War of the Spanish Succession was essentially a land struggle, decided by a series of mighty, and bloody, battles. In the Battle of Blenheim, John Churchill, the Duke of Marlborough, inflicted on France her first military defeat in more than four decades. Upwards of forty thousand French soldiers were killed or captured at the battle, which taught the English that they possessed the power to defeat Louis on land as well as at sea.

By the time the war came to an end in 1713, England had become the dominant power in Europe. France was broken militarily and economically. At the peace of New Utrecht, which ended the struggle, Louis's grandson, Philip V, was allowed to remain on the throne of Spain, but he was stripped of all his territories in the Netherlands. England was triumphant on land and sea.

At the end of the war, the pirate brotherhood, left for dead on Madagascar, had also achieved a vigorous new life. Youthful seamen who had served for years on privateers and who had no experience other than sea raiding, now struck out "on their account." The War of the Spanish Succession had trained thousands of new recruits in piracy.

As they had in earlier times in the East, the new pirates of 1714 sought a base from which to operate. With most colonial ports still firmly closed to pirates, and with Madagascar still under watch by the Royal Navy, the new pirates—who had spent most of the war preying on Spanish shipping—searched for their base in an area they had come to know well during the war: the Caribbean.

And there they found their new sanctuary: the Bahama Islands.

The Bahamas consist of some seven hundred islands and islets, stretching from a point approximately fifty miles off Florida's southeastern coast almost to Haiti, six hundred miles farther to the southeast.

The main island of the group, New Providence, is about twenty-one miles long and only seven miles wide.

The doleful history of the Bahamas—at least as far as Europeans are concerned—goes back to 1492 when, it is generally believed, Christopher Columbus stepped ashore on San Salvador, before going on to explore Cuba and Hispaniola. Within twenty-five years of Columbus's landing, the native Indians of the Bahamas—the Arawaks—had disappeared from the islands, enslaved by the Spaniards and transported to work on larger islands in the Caribbean.

For more than a century thereafter the islands had remained virtually uninhabited.

Then, in 1648, a band of English Puritans attempted to establish a colony on the Island of Eleuthera. Other settlers from Bermuda, and elsewhere, settled on New Providence. The colonists on both islands struggled against poor soil, Spanish hostility, hurricanes, and the indifference of the English government. In 1670, the government assigned the Bahamas, with their struggling little settlements, to the lords proprietors of the Carolina colony on the mainland of North America. The proprietors, however, took little interest in the Bahamas, generally leaving its inhabitants to eke out a living as best they could.

During the War of the Spanish Succession there was fierce fighting in and around the sparsely inhabited islands, most of it centered on the island with the most commercial importance, New Providence.

In 1703 the French and Spanish virtually destroyed Nassau, the seat of government and main harbor of New Providence Island. Although they burned and looted the town, they made no effort to take possession of New Providence or of any other islands in the Bahamas group.

In the year after the sack of Nassau, the governor of the colony abdicated. In the years that followed, many of the town's inhabitants also gave up the struggle to make the colony pay and fled to the mainland. As the population continued to decline, the lords proprietors of Carolina seemed to come to the conclusion that the islands were useless and they made no effort to reestablish government in Nassau.

In 1713, when the war ended, the pirate brotherhood moved in.

The first pirate captain to recognize the usefulness of New Providence as a base had been one Henry Jennings, of Jamaica, who first dropped his hook in the harbor of Nassau while the War of the Spanish Succession was still on, and while he was serving as a privateer in the queen's service.

When the war ended, Jennings, who had turned pirate, decided to make Nassau his headquarters. Other ex-privateers who had turned to the sweet trade soon followed. Like Jennings, they were drawn to New Providence and Nassau harbor because of a number of obvious attributes. The island was located in the center of heavily traveled sea-lanes between the Spanish possessions to the west, the North American coast only a short sail to the north, and the European trade routes between France and England and their rich sugar colonies in the West Indies.

The numerous islands of the Bahamas offered wood, water, and safe areas for careening, as well as numerous creeks and inlets where swift pirate sloops could dodge away from men-of-war.

Furthermore, there were only a few people living on the islands to dispute possession with the pirate brotherhood. According to the governor of Bermuda, the islands at this time were inhabited by approximately two hundred families, who, he reported, were "scattered up and down" and who lived "without any face or form of government, every man doing only what's right in his own eyes."

Finally, the island of New Providence offered one amenity that outweighed all others: The harbor at Nassau was perfect for pirate use. According to Defoe it was "big enough to hold 500 sail of ships; before which lies a small island, making two inlets to the harbor. At either way there is a sandbar over which no ship of 500 ton can pass."

Moreover, hills overlooked this ideal harbor, allowing a clear view of any enemy (or possible prey) while it was still far out at sea.

The area around Nassau was also furnished with ample supplies of fresh water and fruit, as well as fish and wild pigs.

By 1715, two years after the end of the War of the Spanish Succession, more than two thousand ex-privateers, new enlistees under the black flag, had invaded New Providence in the wake of Captain Jennings.

The handful of local inhabitants who had remained on the island after its abandonment by government welcomed the pirates as sources of income.

According to contemporary sources, only one man tried to resist the pirate invasion. He was a certain Captain Thomas Walker who had at one time served as a vice-admiralty judge on the island. Although his commission had long since expired, Walker boldly arrested some of the first pirates who landed at Nassau and sent them under guard to Jamaica. Needless to say, they escaped en route and made their way back to Nassau. Walker must have realized soon enough that there was no future in Nassau for honest men like himself. He fled the Bahamas for South Carolina. There he reported that the pirates had taken over the town of Nassau, even mounting guns in the fort "for the defense of their republic." But there was little disposition in the Carolina colony to expend money and effort to expel the pirates. "Let the outlaws have it; it's useless anyway" seemed to be the attitude in Carolina.

Another inhabitant of New Providence, John Vickers, who had also fled the pirate invasion, stated in a deposition to the colonial governor of Virginia that the leader of the pirates of Nassau was a captain named Thomas Barrow.

"He is the 'Governor' of Providence and will make it a second Madagascar," Vickers reported.

Vickers's prediction proved to be deadly accurate. By 1716 the pirates based on New Providence Island had become a menace to shipping from the coast of Maine to the Spanish Main. But even this was only the beginning of the revived pirate war on the world.

The outlaw nation—born on Madagascar and nearly dead in 1701 until resurrected by war in Europe—was about to reach its zenith under the relentless sun that shone upon the island of New Providence.

11

Republic of Rogues

The town of Nassau, once a torpid waterside hamlet, had by 1716 become the capital city of the reborn pirate confederacy.

Nassau reflected both the values and the style of the brigands who made it their headquarters: impermanent, licentious, and chaotic. A shantytown—a zany collection of stores, shacks, whorehouses, and saloons, cobbled together from driftwood and canvas with palm thatch for roofs—stretched in a half circle along the sandy shore of the harbor.

The wreckage of captured prizes lay rotting on the beach, their ribs exposed like long-dead carcasses. Dozens of vessels—pirate sloops and captured merchants—crowded the harbor, their masts looking like a leafless forest from the shore.

In this place, their own crazy metropolis, the pirates of the western world drank, argued among themselves, gambled away fortunes, paid in stolen coin for the bodies of the prostitutes who flocked to the town, and lived in an uproarious present until their coin was gone and they had to go to sea once more.

It was said that the stench from Nassau—a combination of roasting meat, smoke, human offal, rum, unwashed bodies, and rotting garbage, all stewing together under the tropical sun—could be detected far out to sea, long before the island itself was visible.

New Providence and its wild harbor town were in many ways a pirate heaven as well as a pirate haven. Free from all laws other than the laws of piracy, it made available all the rough joys that the outlaw brotherhood held dear. Although, as with most pirate organizations, there was no strict or formal structure of command, the New Providence pirates *did* make provision for defense of their realm, raising a battery and appointing a guard of fifty to man it should any enemy appear. In addition, any pirate captains who happened to be in the port were expected to look to its defense should Nassau come under attack.

As more and more freebooters came to regard Nassau as their home port, the pirate capital flourished so greatly that Governor Alexander Spotswood of Virginia began to refer to New Providence as a "New Madagascar."

It was an apt description, for many of the forms and customs that the outlaw fraternity had first developed there almost twenty years earlier now bloomed again on New Providence.

Defoe makes it clear that as with the Madagascar pirates of earlier days, the brigands of New Providence were also passionately democratic, insisting on majority rule. Says Defoe: "Each Captain and Company were regulated by their own Laws, independently of the rest; nor were the Captains themselves always obey'd, every thing of Moment being carried by the Vote of the Company."

Nevertheless, despite the fundamental independence of each pirate ship (and of each individual pirate), a rough-and-ready republic was formed under the direction of a council of captains and quartermasters. According to Governor Spotswood, who had informers on the island, the pirates also chose a "governor" for themselves, although it appears the title was more honorary than real.

Although actual government on New Providence was exceedingly lax, since individual crews settled their own disputes and for the most part made their own decisions, many of the pirate usages and attitudes first in evidence on Madagascar were easily

transplanted—and sometimes took on new life—in the rogues' republic of New Providence. For example, the black flag, the Jolly Roger, had by now become the universal and standard ensign of the outlaw brotherhood.

Like their predecessors, the pirates of New Providence put loyalty to the brotherhood above any loyalty to nation, religion, or race. Ethnic and racial freedom was the rule, and the ship's articles of many New Providence crews contained forthright declarations of war "against the whole world."

Pirate tactics of speed, stealth, and terror—first developed in the East—had become standard operating procedure. Furthermore, their effectiveness was greatly enhanced by the fact that the New Providence pirates occupied a highly favorable strategic position from which to carry on their sea war.

From their capital of Nassau the pirates of New Providence could sail north to patrol the busy harbors of South Carolina and Virginia, or to intercept ships bound for ports on the Gulf of Mexico. They could sail westward to Central America in search of Spanish plunder, or south into the Caribbean to take the shipping

of European merchants supplying the plantation colonies of that region. And always after any raid, they could speed away to lose themselves among the isles and inlets of their Bahamas home, or betake themselves to their impregnable sanctuary at Nassau.

Although they attacked the shipping of all nations, the pirates of New Providence made Spanish shipping, and Spanish treasure, a special target.

An incident that took place in 1716, involving an immense amount of Spanish silver, illustrates why the freebooters of the Caribbean were particularly attracted to Spanish prey. (The Story of the Spanish Silver also illustrates, in an almost incidental way, how natural and even inevitable it was for the ex-privateers of the War of the Spanish Succession to become pirates in time of peace.)

Defoe says that the Story of the Spanish Silver actually began in 1714, when a fleet of Spanish galleons carrying a great load of silver sank in a storm in the Gulf of Florida. Two years later, Defoe continues, several Spanish vessels from Havana located the sunken fleet and began working with diving equipment "to fish up the silver that was on board the galleons."

The Spaniards had managed to recover millions of pieces of eight, most of which they had transported to their fortress at

Havana. But there were some 350,000 pieces of eight still awaiting transport. This silver was being held in a guardhouse on shore
under the watchful eyes of sixty armed men.

Unknown to the Spanish, word of their salvage operation had
reached the ears of several enterprising ex-privateers based on
the English-held islands of Jamaica and Barbados. Despite the
fact that the war had been over for three years, these freebooters
still thought of the Spanish as "the enemy." It seemed natural to
them that they should try to take some of the Spanish Silver for
themselves. They therefore set sail in five ships for the Gulf of
Florida.

Defoe tells, in his own inimitable style, what happened next:
"The Rovers came directly upon the Place, bring their little Fleet
to an Anchor, and in a Word, landing 300 Men, they attack'd the
Guard, who immediately run away; and thus they seized the
Treasure, which they carried off, making the best of their Way to
Jamaica."

Defoe adds in a casual aside that on their way to Jamaica with
their booty, the freebooters took another Spanish ship carrying
some additional 60,000 pieces of eight.

In Jamaica, however, the enterprising ex-privateers were
shocked to discover that they were *not* welcomed with open
arms. The Spanish had complained to the governor of Jamaica,
pointing out that there was a peace treaty in force. They demanded the return of their silver.

Since the war *was* long over, the English governor of Jamaica,
according to Defoe, let the freebooters know that he would not
let them go unpunished.

Says Defoe: "Therefore they saw a Necessity of shifting for
themselves; so to make bad worse, they went to Sea again, tho
without disposing of their Cargo to good Advantage, and furnishing themselves with Ammunition, Provisions, etc., and being
thus made desperate, they turned Pyrates."

Eventually each of the captains involved in the raid on the
Spanish Silver made his way to Nassau. Some of them became
major figures in the roguish republic.

Although Spanish treasure was the favorite prey of the New
Providence raiders, galleons overflowing with gold and silver
were relatively rare. As a result, the largest number of Nassau

brigands concentrated on the trade between England and her American colonies.

So heavy were the concentrations of pirates who preyed on this commerce that James Logan, colonial secretary of Pennsylvania, wrote in 1717 that he estimated that there were at least fifteen hundred pirates cruising at any one time off the coast of North America and that no one could travel safely by ship.

The governor of Antigua wrote in 1718: "I do not think it advisable to go from hence except upon an extraordinary occasion, not knowing but that I may be intercepted by the pirates."

Commented Defoe: "The Pyrates in the West-Indies have been so formidable and numerous, that they have interrupted the Trade of Europe into those Parts; and our English Merchants in particular, have suffered more by their Depredations, than by the united Force of France and Spain in the late War."

One peculiar effect of the pirate presence in the Caribbean—often complained of by planters and merchants—was the unrest it spread among the black slaves who worked in the cane fields of the sugar islands. These slaves, hearing that they would be welcomed in the pirate republic, began to run away in ever-increasing numbers, bent on becoming pirates.

One of the former colonists on New Providence, who had fled from the pirate invasion of his island, reported that slaves in the islands had become "very impudent and insulting," and that many planters feared an insurrection.

The largest recorded mass escape of black slaves at this time took place in Martinique, where fifty blacks, supposedly stirred up by a white man, had risen against their French master and had fled the island "to seek a career in piracy."

Many runaway slaves did eventually find their way to Nassau. And blacks formed a substantial minority in a number of pirate crews based on New Providence. In fact, blacks, who usually feared a return to slavery even more than they feared death, were often far more willing than white pirates to fight and die in defense of their ships and their freedom.

Inevitably, as the pirate republic flourished, powerful personalities and dominant figures emerged from the ranks of the brigands who flocked to the free life in Nassau.

Among those who, around 1715, began to use Nassau as their home port was the fierce giant, Edward Thatch, or Teach, who was soon to become better known as "Blackbeard," and who would be wanted by the authorities from Honduras to Nova Scotia. Bloody and cruel, Blackbeard was a terror not only to his victims but even to fellow pirates who consorted with him in taverns and brothels.

Another pirate captain who made his headquarters in Nassau and who later became infamous was Edward England. An effective privateer in the War of the Spanish Succession, England was unusual among the pirates of Nassau in that he did not believe in mistreating captives. Described as a somber and gentlemanly man, England had been one of those involved in raiding the Spanish Silver in the Gulf of Florida. A man of unquestioned bravery, England would eventually forsake New Providence, lead his crew in an epic battle with two merchant vessels in the Indian Ocean, and end his days in poverty.

Another captain who came to Nassau around this time was Christopher Condent, who was destined to make one of the greatest scores in the history of piracy. A clever manipulator of men, Condent had been only an ordinary seamen aboard a privateer during the war, but he soon rose to a position of leadership among the men of New Providence.

Other captains who rose to prominence in the Republic of Rogues were Ben Hornigold, captain of the sloop *Mary*, who was to end his career on the side of the law—and Charles Vane, who became one of the most successful and active of the Nassau pirates.

A veteran of the war like most of the other Nassau pirates, Vane too had participated in the raid on the Spanish Silver. A stubborn and daring—but prudent—man, Vane specialized in preying on shipping bound for North American ports and was among the first of the New Providence captains to cruise off the coast of the Carolinas. Vane often sailed with other captains in a flotilla, regarding this as the most effective way to ensure numerical superiority in battle. Although he was a close friend of the explosive Blackbeard, he knew better than to sail in company with the black-visaged giant whose enormous appetites and erratic behavior made him a less-than-reliable ally.

A man who never allowed rage, drink, or lust for women to cloud his judgement, Vane enjoyed years of success as a Nassau captain because he knew when to fight and when to run—a trait that eventually caused some of his crew to question his leadership qualities. But in the early days of the pirate republic Vane was one of the best known—and most successful—of the New Providence captains.

Still another ex-privateer who came to Nassau during this era and later became notorious was "Calico Jack" Rackam. A brash figure fond of splashy waistcoats, bright ribbons, and colorful breeches, the handsome Rackam was nicknamed by his fellow pirates Calico Jack because of his taste for loud garments made of that material.

Rackam's rise in the piratical ranks began some time around 1717 when he was elected quartermaster aboard Vane's ship. But his real fame and reputation was to come later when he met and wooed a flamboyantly beautiful Irish lass named Anne Bonny—and took her pirating with him.

Anne, described as a girl of "fierce and courageous temper," also came to New Providence around 1715 or 1716, as the wife of a poor young sailor. Although she was only sixteen at the time, this future mistress of Calico Jack yearned for the free life of adventure at sea, and despite her married state, she often sought out the company of pirate captains like Vane, Blackbeard, and Hornigold, among others, drinking with them and soaking up their way of life.

When Anne Bonny eventually met and fell in love with the swaggering Calico Jack, she fought at his side as fiercely as any male pirate.

Not all the pirates who operated in the waters around New Providence were as romantic as Anne Bonny or as colorful as Calico Jack Rackam or as prudent as Charles Vane—or as fierce as the terrible Blackbeard.

A few were not even competent. There was, for example, the case of the bumptious Stede Bonnet, who turned pirate to escape an unhappy marriage.

When Bonnet, a paunchy retired army major, decided to go pirating, he began by *purchasing* a ship instead of stealing one—a most *un*piratical thing to do.

Bonnet was of good English family and owned a successful sugar plantation on the island of Barbados, where, according to Defoe, he was regarded as "a gentleman that has had the Advantage of a liberal Education, and being generally esteemed a Man of Letters."

Middle-aged, married, and deemed one of the leading men of Bridgetown, the capital of Barbados, Bonnet had suddenly announced his intention of becoming a pirate. He had then gone into the taverns of Bridgetown and had signed up some seventy hands to serve aboard a little sloop he had just bought for his pirating venture.

Defoe says, with his usual insight, that the major's decision to go a-pirating was due to a "Disorder of the mind."

In any case, after signing up his seventy crewmen, Bonnet had christened his ship the *Revenge*, apparently believing this to be a fashionable pirate name. He had then ordered his men to lash ten cannon to the ship's single gun deck. He was ready to sail—as soon as his crew signed the articles he had drawn up. These articles were as unorthodox and unpiratical as the major himself. They called for Bonnet to pay his crew wages rather than shares of plunder. It may be that Bonnet thought that in this way he could—despite his lack of experience at sea—maintain some kind of ascendancy over the roughnecks who crewed his little sloop. Whatever he thought, his crew signed on cheerfully enough— and Major Bonnet, to the horror of his wife and neighbors, set off in his little *Revenge* from Bridgetown harbor, bent on joining the pirates of Nassau in the sweet trade.

Despite his less-than-perfect knowledge of the sea, Bonnet had some immediate success preying on small ships off the North American coast.

In time Bonnet would fall in with the formidable Blackbeard himself, who, contemptuous of the chubby ex-major, would take over command of Bonnet's ship and forcibly join Bonnet's forces to his own in a fateful cruise off the Carolinas.

But in 1716 that event was still far off and Bonnet was free to try to emulate the many competent captains of Nassau who were already ravaging shipping from Honduras to Nova Scotia.

Although, except for the occasional Spanish treasure ship, the Caribbean and the American coast offered no rich quarry comparable to the ships of the Great Mogul or the East India Company, the New Providence pirates made up for this lack of quality by taking enormous quantities of booty.

By the end of 1717 the Nassau pirates had so savaged Caribbean shipping that the governor of Jamaica bitterly bemoaned the economic toll that the pirates were taking on his island's trade:

"There is hardly one ship or vessel coming in or going out of this island, that is not plundered."

Nor did the Royal Navy seem interested in driving the pirates out of their Nassau stronghold. But this time the London government was not at fault for the Royal Navy's inaction.

Unlike the situation that had obtained two decades earlier when King William had refused to send warships against Madagascar because they were needed for the war in Europe, the Admiralty in the second decade of the eighteenth century was extraordinarily responsive to the cries of colonial governors for help against pirates. Since there was no war or even threat of war to keep warships in home waters, the Admiralty regularly dispatched Royal Navy men-of-war to Caribbean and North American coastal waters when requested. These vessels were often given specific orders to patrol the sea-lanes and intercept pirates. But in spite of the good intentions of the Admiralty, the Royal Navy proved peculiarly ineffectual against the pirate enemy. The reasons for this were twofold. First, the proud Royal Navy commanders as a general rule refused to accept orders from colonials who were invariably far more knowledgeable about pirates and their operations than the navy was. As a consequence of this stiff-necked attitude, the navy missed many opportunities to strike blows at the Nassau freebooters. Second, and far more important, many Royal Navy commanders had learned to profit from the existence of the pirates—and from the merchants' fear of piracy.

Some naval commanders hired out their warships for convoy duty, charging as much as 12.5 percent of the value of a merchant's cargo as a fee for a naval escort. Although this was legal under the accepted usage of the times, the profit to be made from such convoy duty made many Royal Navy captains less than zealous to destroy the pirates who were the indirect source of their profits.

Other naval commanders engaged in profitable activities that were flagrantly illegal. For example, when, because of the threat of piracy, the cost of sending cargo in an ordinary merchant ship became exorbitant, some unscrupulous navy captains offered to transport cargoes in their warships for a flat fee that, while still hefty, was far less than that charged by cargo vessels. Traders leaped at the chance to transport their goods in navy ships. Not only were the rates, however illegal, actually cheaper than the rates charged by cargo vessels, the chances of a naval ship's being attacked by pirates were practically nil. Some merchants and naval captains became virtual partners in the business—and hoped the pirates would fatten on their competitors.

Some Royal Navy captains even went into the freight business for themselves. They would charter sloops, fill them with purchased cargo, and then, after manning them with naval personnel and arming them with naval cannon, operate them as civilian cargo carriers.

Because of such scams, naval commanders had little real interest in suppressing the piracy from which they profited, and Admiralty attempts to relieve the pressure on Caribbean and North American trade had so far failed.

Even when, in response to complaints from local governors, the Admiralty replaced profit-taking captains with new commanders, the situation did not improve. The new men soon learned the ropes, and cut themselves in for a piece of the action.

As the situation in the Caribbean continued to worsen—and as it became apparent that the Royal Navy would not, or could not, suppress the Nassau pirates, a syndicate of English merchants joined together for the purpose of dealing with the problem—and turning a profit while doing so.

As a first step in their project, the merchants leased the Bahamas from the Crown, explaining that they intended to colonize the islands with honest settlers, farmers, and artisans who would be grateful for the chance at a new life in the New World.

They explained that it was also part of their plan to drive the pirates of Nassau out of their newly leased colony—or to tame them—even if, to accomplish this aim, it became necessary to wage a military-naval war against them. For this reason the merchant syndicate petitioned the Crown to appoint as governor of the new colony one of the finest sea captains of the time. He was Woodes Rogers: a man whose personal bravery, steadfast leadership, and dogged determination would make him one of the great unsung heroes of British history.

12

Nemesis of Pirates: Woodes Rogers

No one looked less like what he was—a genuine hero—than Woodes Rogers.

Tall, more than a little paunchy, with soft auburn hair, Rogers had about him an almost preternatural tranquillity.

His portrait shows a man with a near-cherubic face, a cordial but unsmiling mouth, and gentle dark eyes peering out from under elevated eyebrows. It is a picture of a man who has seen much of the world's wickedness, who is still slightly surprised by it, but who will, of course, deal with it as required.

Rogers, according to contemporaries, dressed well but soberly. He rarely raised his voice and was slow to anger. Though never familiar in his business with others, he was always fair and polite. He guarded his emotions, never showing fear when in danger or satisfaction when he had attained a goal. A man who respected the laws of man and God, Rogers kept his word and expected others to keep theirs. He took care of his own honor, and es-

NATIONAL MARITIME MUSEUM, GREENWICH, ENGLAND

teemed virtue in himself and others. He was also a devoted husband and father.

Yet this paragon was capable of the most draconian measures when necessary. He once hanged eight men who had betrayed their word to him, and he pistol-whipped a naval officer who had challenged his right to command.

In fact, this pudgy man calmly observing the world under his perpetually arched eyebrows was, beneath his unprepossessing exterior, a man of steel, unflappable and indomitable.

He was also a most effective leader of men. This was so not only because of his innate qualities but also because he had learned the secret of command: to give only the most necessary orders, to give them as if it were the most natural thing in the world to carry them out, and never to demand that men act against their own convictions, no matter how shallow or false those convictions might be.

By 1718, when Woodes Rogers was appointed governor of the Bahamas, his character had already been formed by many years at sea—and by an early life spent among the bluff, honest, and self-sufficient people of the west of England.

Rogers's family came from Poole, in Dorset, where an ancestor, John Rogers, had served as sheriff in Queen Elizabeth's time—and had been knighted by her. Rogers's sea captain father, however, had moved his family to the port town of Bristol. And it was there that Woodes Rogers was born in 1679.

Rogers followed his father's calling. He went to sea as a boy and learned his trade well. At twenty-six, an impressive and prosperous young man with an excellent future, he married Sarah Whetstone, daughter of Admiral Sir William Whetstone, Commander-in-Chief of England's West Indian fleet.

It was a happy marriage, and the couple were soon parents of three children: Sarah, born in 1706; William, born in 1707; and Mary, born in 1708. (Mary, however, died in childhood.)

When Rogers's father died, Rogers inherited sufficient property and funds to keep him and his little family in comfort.

Although contented with family life, Rogers was also a man of the sea. He could not stay long ashore without experiencing a yearning to be under sail. For this reason Rogers expressed great interest when, in 1708, a syndicate of Bristol merchants asked him to lead a privateering expedition.

It was approximately the midpoint in the War of the Spanish Succession—and England and her allies were sending privateers to all corners of the globe to attack the shipping of the French and Spanish enemy. The Bristol merchants who had approached Rogers had it in mind to send two ships on an expedition that would take them around the Horn of South America and into the Pacific where—they were sure—they would find rich pickings among the Spanish treasure ships. Rogers, already a veteran sea captain at twenty-nine, readily agreed to lead the enterprise.

The expedition's ships, referred to as "private men-of-war" and fitted out for a total of £15,000, were the *Duke* (320 tons, 80 feet long and 25 feet in the beam, mounting 30 guns and carrying a crew of 117), and the *Duchess* (260 tons, slightly less than her consort in length and beam, mounting 26 guns, and carrying a crew of 108). The Admiralty issued commissions that empowered the *Duke* and *Duchess* to take the shipping of both France and Spain wherever their vessels might be found.

As overall commander of the expedition, Rogers was named captain of the *Duke*. The *Duchess* was captained by Stephen Courtney, who had invested heavily in the enterprise. In addition to Rogers and Courtney, the two ships were officered by a motley collection of gentlemen-investors, veteran seafarers, medical men, and youthful adventurers. Many of these men had had only minimal experience of the sea, but all were enthusiastic about the coming adventure. Some of them would even become good officers.

The most important figure in the expedition, besides Rogers himself, was William Dampier, who was to act as chief pilot. Lean, long-jawed, and moody, Dampier had already circled the globe twice and knew the currents and winds of the Pacific.[1]

There was one peculiar aspect of the venture that Rogers had accepted only with great reluctance. This was the insistence on the part of the investors in the enterprise, some of whom were actually sailing with it, that major decisions during the cruise—including those affecting combat and sailing routes—be made by a council of the officers of both ships. Rogers, foreseeing that this would inevitably lead to wrangling among the officers, tried to talk the backers out of the council arrangement. But the investors, who viewed the council system as a way to ensure that their interests would be protected, refused to budge on the issue.

The *Duke* and *Duchess* set sail from Bristol in August 1708. The first crisis took place only six weeks later. The expedition had reached the Canary Islands off the northwest coast of Africa and was preparing for the long southwesterly passage across the Atlantic and around the Horn of South America, when the crew of the *Duchess* mutinied. Rogers, after rowing over from the *Duke*, quickly subdued the mutineers by seizing their leader and forcing one of his companions to whip him.

Rogers recorded the incident laconically in his journal, saying he thought that forcing one mutineer to whip another would be "best for breaking any unlawful friendship amongst them."

In January 1709 the *Duke* and *Duchess* rounded the Horn and sailed north along the coast of South America for some two thousand miles until, at the beginning of February 1709, they made landfall at the uninhabited islands of Juan Fernandez, approximately six hundred miles west of what is now Santiago, Chile. Here Rogers rescued a white man with long wild hair and a beard, who spoke English but was clothed in skins like a savage.

The wild man turned out to be Alexander Selkirk, a Scottish sailor who had been marooned on these desolate sea isles four years earlier. The expedition's pilot, Dampier, recognized Selkirk as an old shipmate, and Rogers made the former castaway an officer of the *Duke*. Selkirk's adventures while stranded on Juan Fernandez later served as the inspiration for Defoe's *Robinson Crusoe*.[2]

After refitting at Juan Fernandez, the *Duke* and the *Duchess* resumed their cruise northward until they reached waters off the coast of Peru. Here they operated for several weeks, taking a number of small Spanish vessels.

It was during this period that Rogers, with cool resolve, led a raid on the rich Spanish town of Guayaquil in what is now Ecuador. After looting the town of supplies and possessing themselves of some £16,000 worth of gold chains and jewelry from the Spanish ladies of the town, Rogers demanded that the Spanish authorities come up with a ransom of 30,000 Spanish dollars—or he would burn the town to the ground. The Spaniards paid. Rogers then departed.

Now the expedition, refreshed and resupplied, resumed its northward cruise along the coast of Central America. At the end of May they captured a small Spanish ship, which they renamed the *Marquis* and kept with them.

By December the expedition was operating off the coast of Baja California. Here, a few days before Christmas, they sighted a Spanish galleon bound for Acapulco. Guessing that the galleon—which was armed with twenty cannon and twenty smaller swivel guns—was en route from the Philippines and might therefore be carrying at least a portion of the treasure that those islands annually sent to Spain, Rogers ordered a chase.

After a day and a night of pursuit, the *Duke* caught up with the galleon. It was early morning. The *Duke* was alone. The *Duchess* had fallen behind in the chase. Without hesitation, Rogers ordered the *Duke* to engage.

In his journal, Rogers describes the brisk battle that ensued: "At first the enemy fired at us with their stern-chase guns, which we returned with those in our bow, till at length we got close on board each other, whereupon we gave her several broadsides, plying our small arms very briskly, which last the enemy returned as thick for a time, but did not fire their great guns half so fast as we did."

When the Spaniard lowered her colors, Rogers and his men boarded her. They found that she was indeed carrying a rich cargo: treasure valued at more than two million Spanish dollars. Rogers also learned from the crew of the captured galleon that a second, even richer, treasure ship was on its way to Acapulco. Moreover, it was sailing directly toward the English ships.

Rogers had been badly wounded in the battle with the galleon. A pistol ball had lodged in his upper jaw, shattering the bone and most of his teeth. Although in agony, he maintained an amazing calm. He called together his council of officers to discuss whether to attack the oncoming Spanish galleon.

Rogers advised against attacking the second ship. He pointed out that the Spanish officers they had captured described the oncoming galleon as a monster of 900 tons, mounting forty cannon and forty swivel guns, and carrying a crew of 450 men. Rogers expressed his opinion that she was too large and powerful for the English ships to overcome. But he was overruled by the council of officers. Reluctantly Rogers ordered his ships to begin searching for the other Spaniard.

They soon found her—and she proved more formidable than even Rogers had expected. She was the *Begonia*, newly built of Manila teakwood and served by gunners who knew their business.

For more than seven hours the English ships engaged the Spanish galleon. During the battle *Duchess* was badly mauled, her rigging and masts severely damaged, and twenty of her men were killed. *Duke* suffered fourteen men wounded, among them Captain Rogers, who was again hit, this time by shrapnel that tore away part of his left heel. Unable to shout commands because of the wound to his jaw, and unable to stand because of his torn-up heel, Rogers nevertheless continued to conduct the battle. Seated, with his foot propped up on a cushion, Rogers used hand signals to give his orders.

In the end, the *Begonia* beat off her attackers and escaped. In his journal Rogers estimated that during the battle *Duke* and *Duchess* had struck the Spanish ship with approximately five hundred rounds of solid shot without doing more than superficial damage.

Typically, Rogers did not blame his subordinate officers for the debacle even though their misjudgment in insisting on battle had badly damaged their venture.

Instead, despite his own pain, Rogers ordered the expedition to make ready for the long voyage across the Pacific. After effecting what repairs they could, and gathering provisions ashore, the expedition set out on January 11, 1710, for the island of Guam, six-thousand miles to the west.

Rogers's flotilla now consisted of the *Duke*, the *Duchess*, the *Marquis*, and the captured Spanish galleon, which Rogers had renamed the *Batchelor* in honor of a friend from Bristol.

During the voyage Rogers suffered a high fever and his jaw and throat were so swollen from his wound that he could barely whisper. He was so weak that he was unable to stand up. Yet he endured his agony with amazing humor and courage. He wrote in his journal every day. One remarkable entry, for February 14, 1710, illustrates the extraordinary strength of Rogers's character:

"That same day, in Commemoration of the Antient custom in England of chusing Valentines, I drew up a list of the fair ladies in Bristol, that were any ways related to or concerned in the Ships, and sent for my officers into the Cabbin, where everyone drew, and drank the Lady's Health in a Cup of Punch, and to a happy Sight of 'em all; this I did to put 'em in mind of Home."

Three days later Rogers managed to cough up slivers of his jawbone that had been lodged in his throat since he had received his wound. From that point on his condition improved rapidly.

The expedition arrived at Guam on March 11. Here they rested, took on water, and put their prisoners ashore before continuing to the Dutch-held island of Java.

In Java, Rogers sold the *Marquis*. After refitting, he sailed with his remaining three ships across the Indian Ocean to South Africa. Here they joined a Dutch convoy with whom they completed the voyage home. The expedition finally reached England on October 1, 1711.

Rogers and his men had circumnavigated the world in a voyage that had taken more than three years. They had also brought back a huge treasure, amounting to more than £170,000 in the final reckoning.

But after the expedition's investors were paid off, and the crew compensated, Rogers's share of the proceeds amounted to only some £1,600—hardly adequate recompense for his pain and suffering, let alone for his outstanding leadership.

Rogers, however, made no complaint. He published his journal of the voyage. The book was a literary success. Rogers became the friend of London coffeehouse lions like Addison and Steele.

In addition to gaining him fame and a modest financial reward, Rogers's round-the-world voyage had given him insight into the political, military, and commercial value of empire. Rogers was convinced that countries that possessed colonies in all regions of the world, as Spain and Holland did, were destined to dominate the future.

With this in mind Rogers tried to interest the Admiralty and the Board of Trade in a scheme to establish British settlements on remote islands in all the oceans. Despite his popularity and the respect in which he was held, Rogers could make no headway with his proposal.

In 1713 he even made a voyage to Madagascar in order to scout the great island as a possible site for the first of his proposed colonial settlements. But Madagascar, still regarded in England as the home of pirates, savages, and half-breeds, seemed to hold no attraction for anyone but Rogers himself—and nothing came of his idea.

In 1717, at the age of thirty-eight, Rogers turned his eyes toward the pirate-infested Bahamas. It seemed to him that these islands, all but abandoned by their proprietors, might be the ideal place to test his ideas about empire. He became an enthusiastic member of the syndicate that leased the islands from the Crown for the purpose of reclaiming them from their pirate overlords.

Rogers was confident that with a new infusion of honest artisans and farmers, this neglected corner of the Crown's colonial empire could be made to bloom. He was equally confident that the pirates who had made New Providence their base could be suppressed with a modicum of determination and force.

The Board of Trade gave its support to the Bahamas proposal—probably because it did not involve any great expenditure of government funds. As requested by the syndicate that had leased the islands, Rogers was appointed by the Crown as the unsalaried "Captain-General and Governor-in-Chief" of the Bahamas colony. The Admiralty promised to furnish Rogers with an escort of warships to New Providence. The War Department put 100 soldiers under his command to garrison the island. Rogers would also have with him 250 European farmers, most of them Protestant refugees from the Continent, who would be the key to establishing the plantations that would give the Bahamas a viable economy.

As Rogers worked through the early months of 1718, preparing his expedition for departure, dispatches continued to arrive in England reporting a worsening crisis on the sea-lanes of the New World as the pirates continued to increase in both numbers and boldness.

Many, even those who were his closest supporters, wondered how Rogers planned to deal with the pirates of New Providence. Although his commission as governor gave Rogers authority to suppress them in any way he chose, it was clear that he lacked sufficient forces to defeat them militarily. (In addition to his commission Rogers also carried a royal proclamation that promised pardon to the New Providence outlaws for any piracies committed prior to January 5, 1718, provided they came in and surrendered themselves to Governor Rogers. But, given the power of the pirates in the Bahamas, it was thought that only a few would accept these pardons.)

Rogers himself betrayed no concern about the brigands awaiting him across the Atlantic. He might not have had a specific tactical plan in mind for defeating the pirates, but he most definitely had a *strategy*. He knew seafaring men. He understood pirates, and he was confident that when he arrived at Nassau harbor, he would manage the situation as it presented itself to him.

On April 11, 1718, Rogers set sail for New Providence Island in his 460-ton East Indiaman *Delicia*. He was escorted by four small Royal Navy warships—the frigates *Milford* and *Rose* and the sloops *Buck* and *Shark*. (He had left his wife and children at home in Bristol, intending to send for them when he had pacified his colony.)

On the other side of the ocean, the pirates of Nassau had gotten wind of Rogers's expedition. The reactions to the news varied.

About half the two thousand pirates who made their headquarters in Nassau decided to depart for other waters, conceding Nassau—at least temporarily—to Rogers and his Royal Navy support. This faction, aware of Rogers's reputation for honesty and fearlessness and, like most pirates, always anxious to avoid unnecessary and unremunerative combat, would go elsewhere and await developments. They would—or would not—return, depending upon the military strength Rogers brought with him and upon his determination to use it.

Another large segment of the Nassau pirates, however, seemed to view Rogers as just another corruptible colonial governor. With their usual disdain for authority, these pirates were ready to receive Rogers peaceably and to accept the royal pardon he offered. It would appear that this group expected Rogers's rule to last only as long as the Royal Navy stayed around to prop him up. The navy, they anticipated, would not reain long in Nassau. There were more important things for men-of-war to do than guard a colonial governor. When the Royal Navy had gone, this faction thought, Governor Rogers would soon be doing business with the pirates, for the Bahamas had no *real* value as a colony. They felt sure that in order to support himself, Rogers would soon be issuing bogus privateer commissions and serving as a broker for pirate loot. In the long run, they seemed to feel, Rogers's arrival in Nassau could prove a boon to the sweet trade. In the meantime, it made prudent sense to cooperate with the new governor—until a better course showed itself.

But at least one pirate captain, the redoubtable Charles Vane, decided he would neither flee, nor welcome, the new governor. Instead he vowed to resist when Rogers appeared.

On July 24, after an uneventful fifteen-week journey, Rogers's flotilla dropped anchor just outside the narrow entrances of Nassau harbor.

Rogers soon learned from local residents, who rowed out to him with the news, that many of the worst pirates had already left New Providence and that most of those remaining would receive their new governor peaceably. But he also learned that Charles Vane, who had sworn to resist Rogers, was still in the harbor. Before Rogers could decide on any course of action however, an emissary from Vane arrived, carrying a letter addressed to Rogers. In his letter Vane haughtily said he would accept the king's amnesty from Rogers only if Rogers allowed him and his men to keep the plunder from a prize ship they had just taken and brought into Nassau harbor. If Rogers refused, Vane threatened, there would be a fight.

Rogers disdained even to reply.

Instead, he blockaded the main entrance to the harbor with his ships. When night fell he sent two of his warships, the frigate *Rose* and the sloop *Shark*, into the harbor. Under cover of darkness they were to approach and take Vane. But the pirate captain had prepared for such a maneuver. He had filled his captured prize with explosives and combustibles. When he spotted the two men-of-war approaching down the channel, he slipped the cable on his prize and set fire to her. Within minutes she was a roaring inferno. Booming with explosions that sent huge gouts of flaming debris into the night sky, she drifted down upon the nearest of the two warships, the *Rose*. To avoid Vane's fire ship, both men-of-war retreated from the harbor out to the open sea.

With the daylight, Vane ran up his black flag and daringly ran out of the harbor through its lesser-used channel not guarded by the warships. Firing a derisive salute to Rogers, Vane, with all

sails flying, soon reached the open sea. Two of the navy ships were not well placed to chase him down. The other, *Buck*, pursued but soon fell far behind.

Vane later sent word he intended to return and burn Rogers's ship the *Delicia* in revenge.

Rogers knew that Vane would prove troublesome in the future, but there was a more immediate task to deal with: He had to take official possession of his colony.

Knowing now that most of the pirates awaiting his arrival in Nassau intended to receive him amicably, Rogers was even more confident of success than he had been at the start of his venture. He understood the simple appetites and needs of seafaring men. And pirates were, after all, simple seafarers at heart, wilder than most and more dangerous—but still seamen. Rogers had once written: "Good liquor to sailors is preferable to clothing." He was sure he would know how to talk to the pirates who awaited him on shore. He would know how much line to give them, when to leave it slack, and when to draw it taut.

Nevertheless, he intended to tread carefully in the first weeks of his administration. Sailors, pirates especially, could easily turn from a good-natured pack of scoundrels into a bloodthirsty mob.

He recognized better than anyone that he lacked the resources to conquer his new colony by force. And he was aware—as were the pirates—that his four Royal Navy men-of-war would not remain perpetually on duty in Nassau harbor. If he was to win control of his colony, it could not be at the point of a pistol, or a Royal Navy culverin.

With these considerations in mind, Rogers seems to have worked out a threefold strategy for the conquest of his islands. First, he planned to claim from the outset all the prerogatives of a governor. He would issue proclamations, grant pardons, enact laws—and in general use his powerful position, and what forces he possessed, to establish the legitimacy of his authority. If he *behaved* as if he were strong, Rogers seemed to believe, the pirates would assume he *was* strong.

Second, Rogers planned to avoid open confrontation by leaving the pirates of New Providence free to live pretty much as they pleased, and pretty much as they had been doing—as long as they acknowledged his authority and abstained from overt piracy or other acts against the law. Clearly he hoped, with this policy, to achieve an interval of peace necessary for his colonist-farmers to get themselves organized on the island.

Third, Rogers would try to induce at least some of the pirates to give up the sweet trade. He would attempt to persuade as many of them as he could that they could live just as freely as honest Bahamian citizens as they ever had on the account. He would also seek active allies among the pirates, even inviting a few key figures among them into his government.

With these general principles to guide him, Rogers went ashore on July 27, only two days after Vane's explosive departure, resolved to conduct himself with the dignity and firmness befitting the king's representative.

Instead of a crowd of grumbling brutes sullenly tolerant of their new situation, Rogers found a celebration.

The pirates of Nassau greeted their new governor with a drunken reception, which included cheers for the king, volleys of musketry, and pledges of goodwill. There was even an honor guard and a welcoming committee headed by the roguish republic's own "governor"—a mad old ex-pirate named Sawney, who lived in the town's dilapidated fort and who was accorded sarcastic deference by the pirates.

If the welcome tendered the new governor contained in it elements of the customary piratical derision of Authority, Rogers was too astute to take notice of it.

With his usual aplomb, he read out the king's proclamation of pardon and his own commission of appointment. He then swore an oath to obey his commission as governor, shouting the words with a flourish so that all who heard him—the half-drunk pirates, their whores, the tavern keepers, traders, settlers, and soldiers—would know beyond doubt that he was, from that moment on, the legitimate representative of the king of England in those benighted islands. He thus took possession of the colony.

During the first few weeks of his tenure as governor, Rogers worked furiously in the brutal summer heat to establish himself in his capital. Nassau's harbor was a wreck, unkempt and neglected, in keeping with the shantytown nature of the town itself. There were no roads, no agriculture, no wells or sanitation. Nevertheless, Rogers set to work to bring some order out of the chaos that was Nassau.

He brought his company of soldiers ashore, quartering them in makeshift huts inside the town's fort, which he made his headquarters. He housed his 250 settlers in tents that ringed the fort.

He created a civil government from an amalgam of his settlers and the few New Providence natives who had been living in the colony before the pirates had arrived and who could prove they had not trafficked with the outlaws. To help him run his government, he appointed a chief justice, an admiralty judge, justices of the peace, constables, and overseers of the roads.

Rogers also let it be known that he would be liberal in granting the king's pardon to any and all pirates who applied. (Eventually he would issue amnesties to more than six hundred of his freebooters.) The new governor, however, was under no illusion about the significance of these pardons. He knew that for the most part those who accepted them tended to be the older men, the hopeless alcoholics, the sick, and—by far the majority—those who regarded a pardon as a convenience, a ticket to remain at large and comfortable in Nassau until a better berth came along.

But despite the fact that there were relatively few genuine penitents among those to whom he extended the king's grace, Rogers continued to offer pardons as a matter of policy. He even decided to allow pardoned brigands to keep the spoils they had accumulated by their wrongdoing. Apparently, in the wake of his clash with Vane over this issue, Rogers had concluded that peace had to take precedence over principle, given the circumstances of his situation.

His tolerant attitude soon won Rogers a number of important allies among the pirate population. These were, generally speaking, older captains like Ben Hornigold—men who had already made their fortunes in the sweet trade and who were therefore now amenable to a more lawful life (provided they were permitted to hold onto their past plunder, and were not required to give up their free and easy ways.)

As part of his policy to wean pardoned pirates and their friends away from the reckless lives they lived in the dives of Nassau, Rogers offered free plots of land in and around the town to anyone—ex-pirate, whore, or poor trader—who would build a permanent house on it. But few took him up on his offer. Rogers thought he knew why. He wrote in his journal: "For work they mortally hate it, for when they have cleared a patch it will supply them with potatoes and yams and very little else, fish being so plentiful . . . they thus live, poorly and indolently, seeming content. . . ."

He also attempted to enlist some of his ex-pirates in a militia he was trying to form. Rogers hoped that an armed troop of ex-pirates would not only add to his own slender force of regular soldiers but also help channel the energies of his unruly ex-brigands into positive activities. But the pirates made poor soldiers. As Rogers put it in his journal: "These wretches can't be kept to watch at night, and when they do, they come very seldom sober, and rarely awake all night."

Nevertheless, he persisted in his efforts to make soldiers out of his "reformed" pirates.

Rogers did not always fail in his attempts to turn his outlaws to constructive pursuits. In one brilliant stroke of persuasion and perseverance, he induced two of Nassau's best-known pirate captains, Ben Hornigold and Thomas Burgess, to accept pardons and to serve as privateer commanders, with the mission of guarding New Providence against attack by pirates or by the forces of other countries. The appointment of these well-known pirates convinced many of the denizens of Nassau, who had previously regarded Rogers as only a temporary irritation, that the new governor would be a permanent presence to be taken seriously.

Rogers also set to work building a small, eight-cannon battery to cover the eastern entrance of Nassau harbor, which was currently unguarded and out of which Vane had escaped. Repair of the long-neglected main fort that served as his headquarters, which overlooked the western, and most heavily trafficked, entrance to Nassau, would be a major long-term task.

During these early days of frenzied activity there was no overt opposition. Most of the pirates openly acknowledged Rogers's authority, even if grudgingly, and watched his performance with often-bemused interest. Many still clung to their belief that when the Royal Navy departed—as it must eventually—Rogers would prove as corruptible as any other colonial governor, and that the sweet trade would make a comeback.

Meanwhile, word came in that Captain Charles Vane, after his escape from Rogers and Nassau, had sailed north along the American coast, even as far as Long Island, taking and plundering numerous cargo ships and gaining a great reputation in those parts. Rumors were soon rife that Vane had turned south again and that he was still planning to raid Nassau, throw Rogers out, and burn the Delicia in the harbor. It was also said that another brigand, the gentleman pirate from Barbados, ex-army major Stede Bonnet, would join with Vane in his planned raid.

Apparently subscribing to the adage "set a thief to catch a thief," Rogers sent one of his new privateering captains, Ben Hornigold, out to search for Vane. Hornigold's mission was to find

Vane if he could, induce him to surrender if possible—and capture him if necessary.

Hornigold went out on his search. Nothing was heard of him for several weeks. Rogers began to fear that Hornigold and his crew might have reverted to piracy. However, Hornigold did at last return to Nassau to report that although he had not been able to find Vane, he *had* spread the word that Vane was now a wanted man, and that Governor Rogers was determined to take him should he return to Bahamian waters. Hornigold's faithful completion of his task was a great satisfaction to Rogers. It confirmed him in his policy of integrating ex-pirates into his little government.

If Rogers achieved some unexpected successes during these first frantic weeks of his regime, he also suffered a near catastrophe. An epidemic of fever swept through the island, killing many of the farmer-settlers and skilled artisans that he had brought with him, as well as a score or more of his soldiers and dozens of the sailors who manned his warship escort.

The death toll from the epidemic was so high among his immigrant settlers that Rogers knew he would have to forgo—at least for many months to come—his cherished plan to create a self-sufficient colony on New Providence. And, what might prove even worse, the strange illness had so crippled the crews of Rogers's Royal Navy ships that their commanders decided to sail away from Nassau before all their men died. (One of the navy ships, the frigate *Milford*, had been scheduled to depart for other duty in any case.)

With the departure of the Royal Navy, Rogers was left to deal as best he could with the epidemic and with Nassau's rowdy populace.

As autumn approached, the fever that had oppressed the colony waned. At the same time Rogers's pardoned pirates began to grow troublesome. With the Royal Navy gone, more and more of them began to resume their former style of life. Some sailed away to join pirate crews elsewhere. Many of those who remained began to fall back into the old ways of drunken, brawling lawlessness.

Soon Rogers, with his little band of surviving soldiers and settlers, found himself isolated in his ramshackle capital, surrounded by hundreds of grumbling pirates who were now quickly reverting to type, even if they were not yet prepared for open confrontation. Any small incident, a misunderstood word, an insult, even a moment of drunken bravado, Rogers realized, might set off an explosion of violence.

Rumors persisted that several pirate captains who had left Nassau, both before Rogers's arrival and after, were now cruising in Bahamas waters with the aim of attacking the island. To make matters worse, there were also rumors of another war between England and Spain. If war did break out, Rogers reckoned, Nassau would certainly be a target of the Spanish.

Rogers, who was himself recovering from a bout of the mysterious fever, knew that he could not put up much of a fight, whether it was the Spanish or vengeful pirates who attacked.

For defense at sea he had only his own ship, the *Delicia*, and the privateer sloops skippered by the ex-pirate captains Burgess and Hornigold, who might in the crunch prove less than reliable. On land Rogers could count on his newly built little redoubt of eight guns overlooking the eastern channel of the harbor. But the fort, which would have to serve as the island's main defense in time of attack, was still a dilapidated jumble of tumbled walls, hodgepodge tents, and temporary shacks, manned by a few sick soldiers, untrained volunteers, and several boozy ex-pirates who had, so far at least, remained loyal.

Despite the setbacks he had suffered and the pressures under which he had to labor, Rogers now proceeded, with outward calm, to do what he could to repair the fort. Yet for all his exterior tranquillity, Rogers must often have wondered as that summer of 1718 turned to fall, what would happen if Spanish men-of-war, loaded with real soldiers, suddenly appeared off Nassau and trained their heavy cannon on his little settlement. He must also have worried that Charles Vane, alone or with others, would make good his threat to return to Nassau and blast Rogers and his colonists off the map to reclaim the pirate lair for himself.

But if Rogers worried about Vane, he must have worried even more about a second pirate captain, a man who had departed from New Providence Island before Rogers had arrived but who, according to reports from the mainland, had been terrorizing the coast of America for months. For all his demonstrated pluck, Governor Rogers must have realized in his heart that should *this* captain attack Nassau, he would prove far more formidable than Vane. He was the savage giant, the terrible Captain Teach, better known as Blackbeard.

13

Blackbeard Himself

He was a monster.

Tall, burly, enormously strong, he spoke in a booming voice, and his appetites were as ferocious as his temper. He derived his name from the matted sable-colored beard that grew from just below his dark eyes to the middle of his belly.

Defoe says Blackbeard would twist his enormous growth of beard into "small tails" and decorate them with tiny ribbons. In time of action, Defoe adds, he would stick "lighted matches" under his tricornered hat. These were long, slow-burning hempen cords used in those days for firing cannon and grenades. When lit and thrust under the brim of his hat, these slow matches would create a swirl of smoke around his fierce head, giving him the appearance, according to Defoe, "of a Fury from Hell." To complete the picture of the fiendish firebrand, Blackbeard usually carried a naked cutlass in his wide leather belt—and three pairs of cocked and loaded pistols tucked in a bandolier across his chest.

Many who knew him thought him insane. He had an explosive nature that could lurch from evil irritation to murderous rage in a moment. He enjoyed humiliating other men, and he never hesitated to use his fists to impose discipline on his crew. He resorted to the most outlandish terror tactics to cow his victims. It was said that he once forced a captive to eat his own ears.

According to popular belief, Blackbeard "married" no fewer than fourteen wives, most of them teenage girls. Defoe recounts that at least one of Blackbeard's "wives"—a sixteen-year-old North Carolina girl whom Blackbeard had wed in a ceremony performed by his good friend the corrupt governor of North Carolina—was regularly made to have sex with members of Blackbeard's crew who had pleased him in some way.

As Defoe put it: "He would force her to prostitute her self to them all, one after another, before his Face."

In his brief two-year career as a pirate captain, Blackbeard terrorized the American coast, took dozens of prizes, formed a powerful pirate fleet under his sole command, betrayed his companions, and created a legend that etched for all time the popular image of the pirate: roaring, bloodthirsty, recklessly brave, cruel, crazed in battle, hard-drinking, outlandish, and larger-than-life.

His personality and his crimes were equally prodigious—and if only half the stories told of him are true, he was, beyond doubt, the madman that many thought him to be.

The origins of this astounding malefactor are unknown.

Defoe states as a fact that he was born in Bristol. Other accounts, however, give his birthplace as Jamaica, or Virginia. His real name is also unknown, although Defoe states he was baptized Edward Drummond. By the time he came to public attention, however, he was calling himself Edward Teach, or Thatch.

It is know that he served aboard a privateer in the War of the Spanish Succession. According to Defoe, during the hostilities Blackbeard "distinguished himself for uncommon boldness and personal courage," although he never achieved any command. Calling Blackbeard a "courageous brute," Defoe adds that, in a good cause, he might have been a hero.

But Blackbeard was not a man to respond to a good cause. When the war ended in 1713, Blackbeard showed no interest in finding a berth aboard an honest vessel. No doubt, like many others who had served as privateers, he had spent too many years as a freebooter to follow any other calling. Like many others he drifted to Nassau sometime around 1715. Here he enlisted in the crew of the pirate captain Benjamin Hornigold, who was later to become Woodes Rogers's own privateer.

In 1716 Hornigold, impressed with Blackbeard's toughness and ship-handling abilities, gave him command of a sloop in a small pirate fleet that Hornigold was then leading in a foray along the American coast.

At some point in this cruise Hornigold's fleet engaged and captured a big French prize. Hornigold, as leader of the pirate fleet, gave this ship to his favorite subordinate, Blackbeard.

Blackbeard christened his new command *Queen Anne's Revenge*. Returning in her to Nassau, he mounted some forty guns in her, transforming her into one of the most formidable pirate vessels then operating out of the Bahamas. Then, in the early spring of 1717, Blackbeard set off on his own to plunder shipping in the nearby Caribbean—and he began almost immediately to build his legend.

Within weeks after leaving Nassau, Blackbeard took his first prize in *Queen Anne's Revenge*. She was the English merchant vessel the *Great Allan*, which he captured off the island of St. Vincent. Blackbeard plundered her, transferring most of her cargo to his own hold. Then he marooned her crew and set the *Great Allan* afire.

When intelligence of the *Great Allan's* loss reached the Royal Navy, the thirty-gun frigate *Scarborough*, stationed in Barbados, was sent out in search of *Queen Anne's Revenge*.

Sighting Blackbeard's ship after several days, the naval vessel bore down on the pirate, expecting *Queen Anne's Revenge* either to flee or to strike her colors—as pirates usually did when encountering a ship of the Royal Navy. Blackbeard, however, far from fleeing, swung into battle. For hours *Queen Anne's Revenge* exchanged heavy broadsides with *Scarborough*. Finally *Scarborough*, wounded and outgunned, withdrew from the engagement and limped back to Barbados.

Blackbeard's victory over a ship of the Royal Navy, following upon his savage capture of the *Great Allan*, made his name known in short order throughout the Caribbean.

In May 1717, not long after his victorious encounter with *Scarborough*, Blackbeard set sail for the Bay of Honduras, where he cruised successfully for several months. Then one day he encountered the gentleman pirate and ex-army major, Stede Bonnet, who was working the same territory with his little ten-gun sloop *Revenge*.

According to one story Blackbeard took one look at the chubby, bewigged Bonnet and burst into contemptuous laughter. Whether

the tale is true or not, there is no doubt that Blackbeard regarded Bonnet as an incompetent. Without much ceremony, he relieved Bonnet of his command and took him aboard *Queen Anne's Revenge.* He then put one of his own lieutenants in charge of Bonnet's sloop. After that the two ships operated in tandem, taking numerous prizes together in the Bay of Honduras and West Indian waters.

Although he was for all intents and purposes a prisoner aboard

Blackbeard's ship, Bonnet apparently accepted his secondary role. Perhaps his acceptance was made more palatable by the fact that Blackbeard awarded him a full share of the plunder and treated him with rare tact, telling the deposed amateur captain, according to Defoe, that "as he had not been used to the Fatigues and Care of such a Post [as captain], it would be better for him to decline it and live easy at his Pleasure."

In January 1718, Blackbeard, with Bonnet still in company, was back in Nassau. Here he heard that the famed circumnavigator Woodes Rogers was planning to come to New Providence with an armed militia and the Royal Navy to make himself governor.

Blackbeard, having no desire to confront Rogers, or to beg the king's pardon either, departed Nassau. He set sail northward toward the American coast on the first leg of a cruise that would earn him a permanent place in the annals of the outlaw nation.

At the end of January 1718, Blackbeard, with Bonnet and the *Revenge* still accompanying him, reached the town of Bath, North Carolina, where he had a good friend and ally: the governor himself, Charles Eden. Although most of the other English colonies in North America had long ago closed their ports to pirates, North Carolina—poor and lacking in trade—still welcomed freebooters and allowed them to market their plunder openly.

When Blackbeard and his men arrived in North Carolina, they applied to Governor Eden for a "pardon." This was, in fact, no more than a legal fiction that allowed Blackbeard and his men to use the colony as a base of operations. In return for a share of the profits, Governor Eden and Tobias Knight, secretary of the colony and collector of customs, looked the other way while Blackbeard disposed of his booty to the public and merchants of Bath. As men who had been pardoned by the governor for their crimes, Blackbeard and his crew were free to dispose of their goods as they wished—as any other honest citizens of North Carolina were. The pardoned Blackbeard and his band of pirates were also free to careen their ships and to refit and resupply for any further voyage they might contemplate.

After a few weeks' respite in North Carolina, Blackbeard and Bonnet set sail again. This time they headed southward for the Bay of Honduras, which had become a favorite hunting ground for Blackbeard. Here Blackbeard captured another vessel, the sloop *Adventure* out of Jamaica, and added it to his growing flotilla. As captain of the *Adventure* he appointed one of his own favorite officers, Israel Hands. (The name was later appropriated by Robert Louis Stevenson.)

Over the next two months, Blackbeard made a series of captures, adding another sloop and several smaller vessels to his growing fleet. Then, after a patternless crisscrossing of the West Indian sea-lanes, which included a pause in Havana to dispose of plunder and at least one stop at Nassau, Blackbeard headed north once again to the American coast.

In May 1718, he and his now-formidable fleet stood off the harbor of Charleston, South Carolina. Blackbeard was about to carry out one of the most audacious acts of piracy ever committed.

Aware that there were a dozen or more ships in Charleston preparing to get under way, Blackbeard and his consorts set up a blockade beyond the mouth of the harbor and waited for prey to come to them.

Within a day or two, three unsuspecting merchants, all bearing rich cargoes, fell into the net. Before a week was out half a dozen smaller vessels had also been captured.

Aboard one of the larger vessels that had run afoul of his blockade, Blackbeard had discovered four passengers, including one important individual: Samuel Wragg, a member of the governor's council of South Carolina, who was traveling to England with his four-year-old son. Blackbeard took Wragg, his son, and two other passengers as hostages. The town of Charleston, he decided, could ransom Mr. Wragg and the others only by supplying the pirates with medicine to treat the syphilis that was tormenting them. Blackbeard sent a delegation of his men into Charleston to deliver this ransom demand to the governor. He allowed one of the prisoners, a man called Marx, to accompany the pirate delegation in order to bear witness to the facts of the story—and to urge his fellow citizens to comply with Blackbeard's demand.

Along with the demand for medicine, Blackbeard's emissaries delivered a gruesome threat: If the governor did *not* pay the ransom within two days, Blackbeard would murder his captives, including the four-year-old boy, and deliver their heads to the town. He and his men would also destroy the port and burn the ships that lay in the harbor.

The governor and his council had no alternative but to comply with Blackbeard's ultimatum. There were no warships anywhere in the neighborhood, and Blackbeard's blockading fleet could easily have sailed into the port and leveled the city with their cannon.

The governor and his council turned over some £300 worth of medical supplies, but bad weather kept Blackbeard's delegation from returning to their fleet until after the deadline for the transaction had expired. But when his men brought the medicine to him, Blackbeard had not carried out his threat to behead the prisoners. They were released as promised, but not until Blackbeard had stripped them of all their belongings, including their clothing—and £6,000 that Samuel Wragg had been carrying. Shivering in their underclothing, the four hostages were set ashore.

Blackbeard and his fleet lifted their blockade of Charleston. They set sail for the hospitable environs of North Carolina, leaving in their wake hundreds of wrathful citizens who swore to avenge themselves on the terrible Teach.

In June 1718, Blackbeard and his fleet reached one of his favorite havens: Topsail Inlet, North Carolina. He had given it out that he meant to rest and refit here before resuming operations. But in fact, he had quite a different plan in mind.

Blackbeard now stood at the zenith of his power. He controlled a formidable fleet. He had more than three hundred men under his command. He had seized dozens of prizes in the West Indies and off the southern coast of the American mainland. He had made his name a terror from Honduras to Virginia. Now, despite all this success, Blackbeard had decided, in his terrifyingly erratic way, that the time had come to divest himself of his fleet. Operating with so many ships had become unwieldy. The flotilla was too easily seen at sea and impossible to disguise. There were also too many crewmen. By the time the booty was divided among all hands, each man's share was hardly worth the counting.

For these reasons he was determined to rid himself of all but his best vessel and a small select crew. He had also resolved to dispose of his hostage colleague, the gentlemanly Stede Bonnet.[1]

Accordingly, Blackbeard now devised a scheme—typically full of both guile and menace—to accomplish his aims.

First, with a great show of goodwill, he allowed Bonnet to resume command of his ship *Revenge*. Then, mixing cajolery with the threat of reprisal, Blackbeard suggested that Bonnet travel overland to Bath to obtain a pardon from the obliging Governor Eden. Blackbeard suggested to the gullible Bonnet that this legal fiction was essential before their fleet could set out again after prey. Bonnet departed. Now Blackbeard implemented the rest of his plan. He dismissed most of the 320 men under his command, selecting only 40 to serve with him in the future. He then loaded the plunder and supplies belonging to the whole fleet aboard the sloop *Adventure*, which he considered the most seaworthy of his vessels, as well as the craft most suitable for the smaller crew he intended to work with.

When some of Blackbeard's dismissed crewman had the temerity to object to his seizure of their common goods, the black giant exploded with rage. He marooned the objectors on a barren sandbar (from which they were later rescued by Bonnet). The rest of Blackbeard's former crewmen acceded without argument to his confiscation of their property. Fearful of their ex-captain's fury, most of them simply fled inland.

Now Blackbeard, with his pared-down crew, his plunder, and his swift sloop *Adventure*, left Topsail Inlet and made his way once again to Bath where he again "surrendered" to his friend Governor Eden and obtained another "pardon" for all his previous illegal activities, including the blockade of Charleston.

After concluding this business—and no doubt making a substantial payment to the governor—Blackbeard departed Bath once more to cruise in *Adventure* off the American coast.

By now the legend of Blackbeard was spreading rapidly. Stories about his enormous appetites and his unpredictable cruelty were circulated in waterfront cities from Cartagena to New York. Most of the stories were not much exaggerated.

Fragments of a journal—supposed to be Blackbeard's—tell of a life aboard Blackbeard's ship centering around violence and alcohol:

"Such a Day—Rum all out:—Our Company somewhat sober: Rogues a plotting;—great Talk of Separation:—So I look'd Sharp for a Prize."

Another fragment tells how the capture of a merchant ship, with a supply of liquor on board, mollified his men:

"Such a Day took one, with a great deal of Liquor on board, so kept the Company hot, damn'd hot, then all Things went well again."

To keep his turbulent crew in line Blackbeard resorted to often-grotesque outbursts of violence. According to one story, he was drinking in his cabin one night with his navigator, Israel Hands, and another crew member, when, for no discernible reason, he furtively drew out a pair of small pistols under the table and cocked them. The other crewman saw what was going on and went up on deck, leaving the unsuspecting Hands and Blackbeard alone in the cabin. Suddenly Blackbeard blew out the candle and fired his pistols. One of the pistol balls struck Hands in the knee, crippling him for life.

When asked why he had shot Hands, Blackbeard answered that if he did not now and then kill one of his men, they would forget who he was.[2]

Some tales about Blackbeard had a supernatural aura. Defoe, for example, tells one such story that he says he got from surviving members of Blackbeard's crew.

During one of Blackbeard's cruises, Defoe relates, the crew became aware that there was a strange extra man on board. For several days the men glimpsed this shadowy figure "sometimes below, and sometimes upon Deck, yet no Man in the Ship could give an Account who he was, or from whence he came." The stranger never spoke, never showed his face. One day the mysterious extra crewman simply disappeared and was seen no more. Blackbeard's men were convinced that the Devil had boarded their ship—to examine and wonder at their own diabolical captain.

In September 1718—three months after ridding himself of Bonnet and setting off with his forty picked men in the sloop *Adventure*—Blackbeard again returned to North Carolina for rest and refitting. This time he chose as his hideout Ocracoke Island, off the tip of Cape Hatteras—a low-lying sandy strip, but with numerous inlets, shallows, and sandbars. There were also stands of tall trees growing on the high ground. It was an ideal place to hide out. It was virtually inaccessible to warships because of the shallow waters and because it was crisscrossed with channels navigable only by those who knew the way through the tricky currents and shifting sandbars. In addition, the trees helped camouflage the masts of anchored ships.

Blackbeard, who knew Ocracoke well, dropped *Adventure*'s hook in a shallow, hidden inlet. With him also was a prize ship he

had recently taken. Snug in their concealed haven, Blackbeard and his men prepared to enjoy a period of drinking and ease before resuming their brigandage off the American coast.

During this interlude at Ocracoke, Blackbeard and his crew were joined by the redoubtable Charles Vane and his men, for a week-long orgy of drinking, sex, and feasting. Vane had also been operating off the coast of America in recent months after escaping from Nassau harbor and from Woodes Rogers and was glad to spend some time with Blackbeard, whom he had known since the early days of the pirate republic on New Providence. But he had no intention of joining forces with the mad giant.

According to witnesses, the Ocracoke orgy—one of the largest gatherings of pirates ever held—was a nonstop revel of riotous drinking, roaring bonfires on the beach, sex with whores from the mainland and with captive women, and wild dancing to music provided by fiddlers from Vane's crew and musicians invited over to Ocracoke by Blackbeard.

Eventually the tumultuous celebration came to an end. Vane sailed away on his own business. Blackbeard, however, continued to lie at Ocracoke, taking his ease and conducting desultory business with officials and merchants from the mainland. Regarding himself as safe from attack while sheltered in Ocracoke's maze of shallows, Blackbeard made no secret of his presence in the island hideout.

Unknown to Blackbeard, however, many of the honest planters of North Carolina had agreed among themselves that despite their governor's illicit relationship with the terrible giant, Blackbeard represented a danger to the future of the colony. They had come to this conclusion after hearing a rumor that Blackbeard intended to build a fortress at Ocracoke Island and to turn the area for many miles around into a kind of "pirate kingdom," with himself as lord of it. The planters knew better than to ask their own corrupt governor to act against Blackbeard. Instead they appealed to Governor Alexander Spotswood of Virginia to chase him from their midst.

Spotswood, whose own colony had lost scores of ships to Blackbeard and to other pirates, was a vigorous ex-army officer of forty-two who hated all pirates, and Blackbeard more than any. Born in Tangiers, Morocco, in 1676, Spotswood was a strong-minded, unsmiling man with direct dark eyes. Tall and broad, he bore himself with a military correctness. Spotswood had served with Marlborough in the War of the Spanish Succession. Appointed governor of Virginia in 1710, he had discharged his duties with integrity and with an unusual concern for the future development of the colony. During his tenure as governor, Spotswood had established a Virginia merchant company to carry on trade with the Indians, had encouraged the construction of forts along the colony's western frontier, and had personally conducted an expedition of exploration into the Shenandoah Valley in 1716.

Governor Spotswood leaped at the chance to capture the diabolical Blackbeard, even though it meant circumventing the jurisdiction of North Carolina's own governor.[3]

Spotswood had two Royal Navy men-of-war available to him. They were the H.M.S. *Pearl* and H.M.S. *Lyme*, stationed in Virginia's James River. But when the governor conferred with the captains of these two ships to draw plans for capturing Blackbeard, they pointed out that their heavy men-of-war could not possibly navigate the shallows or manage the winding channels of Ocracoke Island. But Spotswood was not daunted. He would, at his own expense, provide shallow-draft sloops for the enterprise if the Royal Navy captains would furnish the seamen from their own crews. It was agreed.

Acting on his own authority, Spotswood had already sent an agent into North Carolina to gain information on Blackbeard's location and armament. The agent was also to bring back to Virginia two pilots who knew the tricky waters of the area where Blackbeard had holed up. Their help would be crucial in getting to the pirate.

Spotswood also persuaded the Virginia legislature to appropriate funds so that he could offer rewards for the capture of Blackbeard and his men. The reward for Blackbeard was set at £100.

In utmost secrecy Spotswood met with the Royal Navy officers to draw up the final plans for the expedition. Fearing that intelligence of the coming operation would somehow reach Blackbeard and that he would escape, Spotswood did not discuss his plan even with his own colonial council.

On November 17, the expedition set off in the two sloops Spotswood had provided. Lieutenant Robert Maynard of H.M.S. *Pearl*, in charge of the expedition, commanded one sloop with thirty-five men. A midshipman named Baker, from H.M.S. *Lyme*, commanded the second sloop with an additional twenty-five men.

On the late afternoon of November 21, the expedition arrived off Ocracoke.

Because the distance on Ocracoke were not great, the navy men could easily see Blackbeard's sloop *Adventure* and his captured prize at anchor only a few hundred yards away in one of the island's larger inlets.

Yet, as close as Blackbeard lay to them in terms of space, Lieutenant Maynard and his men knew that their quarry, protected by the maze of waterways that lay between him and his pursuers, was still far away in terms of time.

Despite the fact that the day was already nearly spent, the naval sloops began their stalk of Blackbeard. Slowly, yard by yard, they began to feel their way through the channels and shoals.

When darkness fell, however, they anchored where they lay, fearing to go permanently aground in the treacherous shallows. At first light, Maynard told his men, they would resume the hunt.

Across the few hundred yards of sandbars and shallows that separated him from the naval sloops Blackbeard must have observed the struggling approach of his would-be captors. It is certain that he knew who Maynard and his men were and why they had come to Ocracoke, for his friend Tobias Knight, North Carolina's corrupt customs collector, had heard of Spotswood's expedition, despite the governor's secrecy, and had sent a warning to Blackbeard. But the black giant had not acted on the warning. And even when Maynard anchored for the night less than a cannon-shot away, Blackbeard seemed unconcerned.

Although it was clear that the naval force hoped to attack him on the following morning, and although he had only eighteen men with him aboard *Adventure*, Blackbeard made no effort to escape, or even to prepare for a possible battle. He did not send for the rest of his crew who were scattered on various errands ashore. Instead, he sat up all night drinking with a few cronies and with the master of a merchant ship whom he had invited aboard. His roaring voice must have been easily audible to the naval forces lying in wait across the shallow water.

According to Defoe, it was during this nightlong drinking bout, that one of Blackbeard's men asked him whether—in case anything should happen to him in battle the following morning—his wife knew where he had buried his money. Says Defoe: "He answered, that no Body but himself, and the Devil, knew where it was, and the longest Liver should take all."

Blackbeard's extraordinary lack of concern, despite his obvious peril, may have been due to confidence that the navy men would not be able to negotiate the tricky waters of Ocracoke and would therefore never get near enough to engage him at close quarters. Or was he, in his mad brain, actually looking foward to a combat and a chance at Hell?

In the gray light of dawn, Lieutenant Maynard ordered his two sloops to hoist anchor and resume the effort to close with Blackbeard. There now ensued for the navy men a grueling struggle in the maze. Time after time their sloops went aground and had to be backed off sandbars. Tossing water casks overboard in order to lighten their vessels, the navy men used oars to work their way over the shallows. Inexorably, Maynard and his men drew nearer and nearer to Blackbeard.

According to Defoe, Blackbeard now came to life. He cut his own cable and he began to carry on a running fight with the approaching naval force—"keeping a continual Fire at his Enemies, with his Guns," as Defoe put it. Maynard and his men, despite their labors in the maze, managed to answer Blackbeard, keeping up a steady barrage of small-arms fire.

At one point Blackbeard hailed the oncoming navy force.

"Damn you for Villains. Who are you?" he roared, although he knew very well who his tenacious enemies were.

Maynard pointed to the British ensign hanging limply from his mast in the light wind and shouted: "You may see by our Colors, we are no Pyrates."

Blackbeard then roared out an invitation for Maynard to come on board *Adventure* so that he could see who his enemy was. Maynard shouted in reply: "I cannot spare my boat, but I will come aboard of you, as soon as I can, with my sloop!"

At this, Blackbeard lifted a glass of rum to Maynard in a sardonic gesture and, after drinking it, roared out: "Damnation seize my soul, if I give you quarters, or take any from you!"

Maynard hollered back that he expected no quarter from Blackbeard, nor would he give any to the pirate.

Now Blackbeard, with his black ensign flying, headed away from Maynard's rowing sloops, as if, at last, he had decided to escape. It is likely that he knew of some nearby channel that would lead him to open water and escape, and he was heading for it. But the wind was very light and the current of the inlet very slow, and *Adventure* moved sluggishly in these conditions.

In any event, the second naval sloop, under the command of Midshipman Baker, managed to close up on Blackbeard and threatened to intercept him. Blackbeard, seeing this threat, suddenly hauled around toward Baker and unleashed a tremendous broadside "charged with all manner of small shot." The sudden blast killed Baker and a number of his men. It also disabled Baker's sloop. She fell quickly astern and took little part in the action that followed.

Now what little wind there had been failed completely. Maynard's men continued to labor at their oars to catch up to *Adventure*, now moving even more sluggishly, apparently carried only by the current of the inlet.

Soon Maynard had dramatically closed the distance between his sloop and Blackbeard. All at once Blackbeard fired another broadside of small shot. The lethal hail swept viciously across Maynard's deck, putting twenty-one of his crew of thirty-five out of action.

Maynard, fearing that a second broadside from Blackbeard would put an end to the enterprise, ordered his remaining crewmen to take shelter by hunkering down belowdecks. Only he, the helmsman, and the pilot, remained on deck. Crouched low, Maynard kept his sloop headed toward Blackbeard. Now, as they closed up on *Adventure*, Maynard ordered his men in the hold to get their pistols and their swords ready for close fighting—and to be ready to rush up on deck at his command.

But when the two ships were alongside, it was Blackbeard who attacked first. His crew hurled hand grenades—bottles full of gunpowder, shot, and chunks of iron—onto the navy sloop. Exploding with great gouts of thick smoke, the hand grenades spewed deadly shrapnel in all directions. But because Maynard's men were still below, the grenades had little effect.

Blackbeard, however, peering through the smoke from his own deck and seeing the almost-empty deck of the navy sloop, thought his grenades had destroyed his pursuers. He roared out to his own crew that their enemies were "all knock'd on the head, except three or four, and therefore, let's jump on board and cut them to pieces."

No sooner had Blackbeard shouted this information than he himself swung across to Maynard's sloop. His men, screaming and cursing, followed their giant leader.

Now Maynard gave the signal to his waiting men to attack the boarding pirates. With a shout, Maynard's crew poured out on deck through the swirling smoke and flung themselves upon the astonished outlaws.

At this moment Blackbeard and Lieutenant Maynard confronted each other. In the midst of the swirling combat between the two crews, with the clanging of cutlasses and the crack of pistol shots punctuating the shouted oaths of men fighting for their lives, Maynard and Blackbeard drew pistols and simultaneously fired at each other from point-blank range.

Somehow Blackbeard's shot missed. But the naval lieutenant's bullet found its mark, striking Blackbeard in the body.

Incredibly, however, the giant seemed not to notice. Roaring curses, spewing blood, Blackbeard came at Maynard with his cutlass. In the duel Maynard's sword broke. Leaping back from Blackbeard's swinging cutlass, Maynard cocked another pistol. Hoping to put a final ball between the giant's eyes, Maynard aimed his heavy pistol while Blackbeard drew back his cutlass to strike off Maynard's head. But Blackbeard never struck the fatal blow. Instead, before Blackbeard could strike or Maynard fire,

one of Maynard's crewmen slashed Blackbeard across the throat. The pirate staggered back, streaming blood and screaming curses. At this moment Maynard fired his pistol. The heavy ball struck Blackbeard in the chest. Still the roaring giant would not fall. Instead, like a wounded elephant, he charged his enemies. Again and again the navy men fired at him and slashed at him with their swords. Struck at least five times by pistol balls, and cut at least twenty times by the swords of his antagonists, Blackbeard continued to roar defiance. Then, as he was drawing another pistol from his belt, he began to stagger. His weapons fell from his hands. Slowly, like some great beast, he toppled to the deck. He was dead.

Immediately his crew threw down their arms and surrendered.

But the drama was not yet over.

Down in the hold of the *Adventure*, one of Blackbeard's most trusted lieutenants, the former black slave Caesar, now attempted to carry out instructions Blackbeard had given him to blow up the *Adventure* if Maynard should win the battle. In accordance with his captain's orders, Caesar had laid a gunpowder trail to the ship's magazine. He had only to touch a match to the gunpowder in order to blow them all, Maynard and all the survivors, pirates and navy men alike, to eternity. But as Caesar moved to carry out his final task, a prisoner being held belowdecks leaped on Blackbeard's faithful officer and, in a desperate wrestling match, managed to keep him from igniting the gunpowder until Maynard's men came aboard and took the ex-slave into custody.

In the exhausted aftermath of the battle, Maynard counted up the cost of taking Blackbeard. Ten men of the naval expedition, including Midshipman Baker, had been killed and another twenty-five wounded. (One of these later died of his wounds.) Ten of the pirates had also been killed, including Blackbeard himself. Of the nine surviving outlaws—three white men and six blacks—all had been wounded, most of them more than once.

Maynard ordered Blackbeard's head cut from his gigantic body—and the headless corpse flung overboard. The head, its great beard matted with blood, was then hung from the bowsprit of Maynard's sloop. Maynard and his men set sail homeward for Virginia with this grim trophy as testimony to their epic victory over the most terrifying pirate of them all.[4]

Even in death, however, Blackbeard was the stuff of legends. The story soon got around that after Maynard threw Blackbeard's headless corpse into the water of the Ocracoke inlet, it swam several times around the sloop, as if searching for its missing head.

But it finally sank out of sight—and Blackbeard was no more.

14

Rogers at Bay

In his headquarters in Nassau, Governor Woodes Rogers—clinging to his precarious hold on his Bahamas colony—must have heard the news of Blackbeard's death with gratification.

While Blackbeard's demise did *not*, by any stretch of the imagination, mean that Rogers could now rest secure on New Providence, it *did* mean that one more threat to his colony had been removed. Further, the news of Blackbeard's grisly end no doubt helped sober many of those pirates who, although they had elected to stay in Nassau under Rogers's nominal rule, had never in their hearts renounced their allegiance to the outlaw nation. These pirates—among them longtime acquaintances of Blackbeard—had followed the giant's rampage along the American coast and in the Bay of Honduras with growing interest. It is possible that if Blackbeard had continued to enjoy success, his example might have encouraged many more Nassau pirates to resume careers on the account. But the news of Blackbeard's death had dampened any revival of enthusiasm for the sweet trade in Nassau—at least for a while.

Around this time, news reached Rogers that the gentleman pirate Stede Bonnet had also met his end. This intelligence, too, must have been most welcome to Rogers, holed up in his unfinished fort. For although Bonnet—unlike Blackbeard—had never posed a serious threat to Nassau, the circumstances of his death had a further chilling effect on the pardoned brigands of New Providence.

According to the story that reached Nassau, the bumbling Bonnet had again gone pirating on his own after Blackbeard had so abruptly dissolved their incongruous partnership.

During the summer of 1718, Bonnet, once more the captain of his little ten-gun sloop *Revenge,* had managed to take several prizes off the American coast. Although these prizes were of no outstanding value, the governor of South Carolina, apparently still smarting from Blackbeard's outrageous blockade of Charleston, had commissioned two sloops to hunt down Bonnet and his thirty crewmen.

Bonnet, still an amateur at pirating, had been trapped by his pursuers when he had foolishly entered the Cape Fear River. Although the gentlemen pirate had fought back briefly, he and his crew were captured and taken to Charleston for trial. Somehow Bonnet had then contrived to escape. But he was soon recaptured. He had then been swiftly tried and convicted in November 1718. In a despairing letter, he had pleaded with the governor for a pardon, promising to render himself unable to pursue piracy again by "separating all my Limbs from my Body, only reserving the Use of my Tongue, to call continually on, and pray to the Lord." But his plea had fallen on deaf ears. The people of Charleston regarded Bonnet not as a gentlemen planter who had inexplicably gone mad, but as a partner of the terrible Blackbeard in the blockade of Charleston.

Bonnet, clutching a nosegay, had been hanged during the same week that saw Maynard's victory over Blackbeard.

With Blackbeard's destruction and Bonnet's execution, Rogers probably felt that there was only one more pirate captain he needed to worry about. This was Charles Vane, who was still at large and whose oath to avenge himself on Rogers was not forgotten in Nassau.

The last reports on Vane indicated that he was operating off the American coast, and had eluded several attempts to capture him. Rogers believed it was entirely possible that Vane would still try to carry out his threat to invade New Providence. If he did so, Rogers was convinced that most of the Nassau pirates would side with Vane.

"Should their old friends have strength enough to design to attack me," Rogers wrote at this time, "I must doubt whether I should find one-half of the Nassau pirates to join me."

In addition to the threat from Vane, Rogers fretted about re-newed hostilities with Spain. For months rumors had persisted that war with Spain was imminent. In such an eventuality, Rogers was certain the Spanish would attempt to invade New Provi-dence. In that event, however, he was sure that his pirates would join with him and his few armed men to defend the island against the Spanish.

"I don't fear but they'll all stand by me in case of any attempt except pirates," he wrote. The question in his mind was whether a ragtag force of boozy pirates, untrained farmers, and a handful of soldiers could resist an invasion by professional troops.

With his usual indomitable coolness, however, Rogers contin-ued the slow and laborious task of rebuilding the fort of Nassau, necessarily the main defense against any attack, whether by Cap-tain Vane or by Spanish ships and soldiers.

Then, in December 1718, only a month after Blackbeard's death, Rogers faced a new crisis, one whose outcome, he knew, would probably determine his own fate as well as the future of his struggling little colony.

The roots of the crisis stretched back several weeks to when Rogers, faced with a shortage of food supplies and with his naval escorts departed, had sent off three ships—manned and com-manded by pirates he had previously pardoned—to trade for fresh supplies in Hispaniola and other nearby islands.

When they were only two days out from Nassau, Rogers's pi-rates had reverted to their old habits. They had gone off on their own account.

When Rogers had gotten wind of this betrayal, he had dis-patched the dauntless—and now loyal—Ben Hornigold to pursue the backsliders.

Hornigold had eventually caught up with his quarry. But when he did, he found that they had been badly mauled by Spanish warships and only thirteen of the turncoats were still alive —and three of those were badly wounded.

Hornigold had put his prisoners aboard his own sloop and had loyally transported them back to Nassau. Rogers, pleased that Hornigold had so demonstrably justified his faith in him, wrote: "I am glad of this new proof Captain Hornigold has given the world to wipe off the infamous name he has hitherto been known by, though in the very acts of piracy he committed, most people spoke well of his generosity."

After placing the thirteen backsliders under guard aboard the *Delicia,* Rogers had decided to take a daring action —one that if successful would enhance his authority, but if unsuccessful, could spell the end of his efforts on New Providence. He decided that instead of sending the pirates to Jamaica for trial (as a strict interpretation of the law demanded) he would stretch his prerogative as governor and try them himself.

Three of those caught by Hornigold died of their wounds before they could be tried. The other ten had to face Roger's justice.

On December 9 and December 10, 1718, Rogers convened his court in the guardroom of his still unfinished fort. The court consisted of eight judges, among them the governor himself and two of Rogers's pardoned pirate captains, Thomas Burgess and Peter Courant.

To conduct such a trial, under the circumstances, was an incredibly bold stroke. Here was the beleaguered governor, lacking naval support, with only an inadequate militia to rely on, surrounded by hundreds of armed pirates in his colony, and with many more loose among the islands—and lacking authority to hold such proceedings to boot—convening an open Admiralty court to try pirates, with ex-pirates as judges.

If any action of Rogers's ever demonstrated his unflappable audacity and self-assurance, this trial of the turncoat pirates of Nassau was it.

For the rest of the pirates of Nassau, who were free to observe the trial of their former colleagues, Governor Rogers's cool aplomb at this time must have seemed still another sign of England's determination to suppress piracy. If Governor Rogers did not fear the pirates of Nassau, it must be because England did not fear them and because the governor knew that—now or later—he had the might of the Royal Navy behind him.

During the two-day trial, incontrovertible evidence was presented against the defendants. In the end nine of the ten were found guilty. The court exonerated one defendant, concluding that he had been forced by the others to participate in their criminal behavior.

The nine convicted men were sentenced to be hanged two days later—on the morning of Friday, December 12, 1718.

On the appointed day, the convicted pirates, guarded by one hundred picked men from Rogers's soldiery, were taken to the gallows, which had been specially built for the occasion on a strip of beach under the ramparts of the fort.

According to Defoe, several hundred of the Nassau pirates gathered to watch their comrades hang. Rogers, no doubt, sweated out this crucial hour of the executions. Would the sullen pirate audience watch their fellows swing without an eruption of violence?

At the last moment Rogers granted a reprieve to one of the nine condemned, George Rounsivil, eighteen, who was from Rogers's own home county of Dorset and who had "loyal and good" parents still living there.

For the other eight, however, there was no reprieve. In the shadow of the gibbet the eight condemned were given time for their final words and last prayers. Although Rogers knew that he was risking a possible riot among the onlookers by permitting this customary final ritual, he probably reasoned that to deny the condemned the chance to utter their last words in public would be riskier than to allow them.

According to Defoe, at least some of the convicted men tried to stir up their fellows to rescue them, crying that "they never thought to have seen the Time, when such Men as they, should be ty'd up, and hanged like Dogs and four hundred of their sworn Friends and Companions, quietly standing by to behold the Spectacle."

Defoe goes on to say that another of the condemned taxed his audience with "Pusilanimity and Cowardice, as if it were a Breach of Duty in them not to Rise, and save them from the ignominious Death they were going to suffer."

But it was all in vain. There was no riot. The pirates of Nassau only grumbled and shuffled their feet while the ropes went around the necks of the convicted men.

Now, as the fatal moment neared, each man confronted his fate in his own fashion.

John Augur, forty, haggard, unwashed, and dressed in rags, expressed sorrow for his misdeeds. His last request was for a glass of wine, which he drank, toasting "the good success of the Bahama Islands and the Governor."

Will Cunningham, forty-five, who had once served as a gunner in Blackbeard's crew, also expressed remorse for his life of crime.

Dennis Macarthy, twenty-eight, who had once served as an ensign in Rogers's militia, was jaunty. Wearing a new suit of clothes "adorned at neck, wrist, knees, and calf, with long blue ribbons," he kicked his shoes over the parapet of Rogers's fortress, saying he had "promised not to die with his shoes on."

Another, Thomas Morris, twenty-two, wearing bright red ribbons, when asked whether he repented of his wickedness, replied: "Yes, I do heartily repent. I repent I have not done more mischief, and that we did not cut the throats of them that took us, and I am extremely sorry that you aren't all hanged, as well as we."

William Dowling, twenty-four, an Irishman whose past crimes included the murder of his own mother, also refused to repent, as did George Bendall, eighteen, who insisted that he was not a pirate.

One of the condemned, William Lewis, thirty-four, an ex-boxer, said he had always wished to die drunk and he bellowed for a drink to ease him into Hell.

At this, another of the condemned, William Ling, thirty, who was one of those who had expressed remorse for his crimes, said he thought "water was more suitable to them at that time."

When all the speeches of defiance and contrition and bravado were finished, the gallows stage fell—and each of the eight men danced at the end of his rope, until he died. They had paid the full penalty for breaking the law and their word to Woodes Rogers.

Instead of rising in revolt, the pirates who had watched the hangings slunk away to get drunk in the dives of Nassau. Rogers had once again demonstrated his ascendancy over his colony.

But his authority, as he soon discovered, was still to be challenged. Only two weeks after the execution of the eight backsliders, a small group of Nassau pirates, together with some of the soldiers whom Rogers had brought with him from England, hatched a plot to assassinate the governor. Their object was to restore pirate rule to New Providence. But an informer warned Rogers of the plot, and he seized the three ringleaders. After having the trio flogged for conspiring against the king's government, he released them, as if to underscore the contempt with which he regarded such amateur assassins, and as if to illustrate the ease with which he could always foil such simpleminded conspiracies.[1]

As the New Year of 1719 began, Rogers, despite the considerable success he had achieved in establishing his authority in Nassau, regarded his labors as a failure. The plague had put an end to his hopes for planting a self-sufficient colony on New Providence. His naval escorts had deserted him. The fort, key to the island's defense and perhaps to his continued ascendancy over the Nassau pirates, was still far from finished. The soldiers he had brought with him from England were beginning to prove as unreliable as his ex-pirate militia. In addition to the hundreds of pirates who grumbled against him in Nassau, there were hundreds more still at large, preying on the commerce of the Caribbean and the American coast—and one of the worst of them, Charles Vane, had not been heard from for months and might, at any time, appear off the bar at Nassau to lead a rebellion against Rogers's hard-won authority.

It was an uneasy New Year for Governor Rogers.

In point of fact, however, Rogers need not have worried about Vane. That canny old brigand had fallen on evil times.

After his celebrated orgy with Blackbeard and his crew at Ocracoke Island back in October, Vane and his men had resumed operations off the American coast. At first they had enjoyed considerable success. Vane had even dared to cruise off the coast of Virginia, despite Governor Spotswood's widespread reputation as an implacable hunter of pirates. Then matters had quickly soured for Charles Vane.

His troubles had begun one day when Vane, still cruising off the American coast, had sighted what looked like a fat, slow merchant flying the French flag—a perfect target. He gave chase. But as his ship neared the supposed merchant, she suddenly let go a powerful broadside, revealing herself to be a heavily armed man-of-war.

Vane, always careful to avoid unequal encounters, immediately came about to flee from the French warship. Now it was the Frenchman who gave chase. At this point Vane's quartermaster, Calico Jack Rackam, with the support of the majority of the crew, vociferously urged the captain to engage the Frenchman. According to Defoe, Rackam acknowledged that the French man-of-war "had more Guns and a greater weight of Mettal," but even so, he was certain that "if they could board the Frenchman, the best Boys would carry the day."

But Vane refused. He pointed out to Calico Jack that the man-of-war, twice their size, could sink them long before they could ever get close enough to board her.

As captain, Vane had the right to make decisions during combat, and thus he won the argument. But after Vane and his men had eluded pursuit, the disgruntled faction of the crew, led by Calico Jack, called a council of war and accused their captain of cowardice. In a vote of the crew, Vane was deposed as captain. He was then set adrift in a small boat with fifteen members of the crew who had voted with him in the matter of boarding the French man-of-war. Rackam was elected captain in Vane's place.

Because their old captain had led them so successfully in the past, Rackam furnished Vane and his loyal followers with supplies of food, water, and ammunition, so that they might have the means to begin a new piratical career. Rackam then sailed off in his new command.

Vane in his open boat had made his way south toward the Caribbean. Off the northwest coast of Jamaica he succeeded in capturing three boats—probably fishing boats only a little larger than the boat he had received from Rackam. Nevertheless, after looting these three small craft of their supplies and anything else that might be useful, he recruited several members of their crews into his ranks. Then, keeping one of the boats with him, Vane made his way westward to the Bay of Honduras. Here, during the first two months of 1719, while Woodes Rogers worried about him in Nassau, Vane operated in obscurity. Sailing with only two small boats under his command, he was able to take only a few prizes, none of them of any great worth. Vane was barely able to keep his crews together. (It is likely that given his reduced circumstances, Vane had not even heard of the demise of his old friend Blackbeard or of Rogers's execution of the eight turncoat pirates in Nassau.)

But as if matters were not bad enough, Vane's luck took another bad turn in March 1719. The two small boats with which he was operating ran into a fierce tropical storm. Both were wrecked and most of Vane's crew were drowned. He himself was cast away on an uninhabited island. Here he lived for some weeks, in rags, begging for food from Indians who came to the island to fish and catch turtles.

Then, after he had with difficulty kept himself alive for several weeks, a ship from Jamaica captained by an ex-pirate and a onetime friend of Vane's, a Captain Holford, arrived to take on water. Vane pleaded with Holford to rescue him.

But the wary ex-pirate, recalling Vane's reputation as a crafty schemer, feared that his old friend would organize a mutiny against him and seize his vessel. He refused Vane's plea, saying, "Charles, I shan't trust you aboard my ship, unless I carry you a prisoner; for I shall have you caballing with my men, knock me on the head, and run away with my ship a-pirating."

Vane protested vigorously that he had no such intention. Holford then assured Vane that if, when he returned to the island the following month, Vane was still there, he would take him off—and carry him to Jamaica to be hanged. Holford sailed off.

A few days later, however, a second vessel put into the island, bound for Jamaica. Again Vane pleaded for rescue. But he now gave a false name, and claimed he was only a poor shipwrecked sailor who would prove his honesty and worth in return for a passage off the island. The captain of this vessel, who had never met Vane, took the pirate captain aboard and continued on his way. Vane was saved.

But in fact, fate had now set its face permanently against Charles Vane.

The ship that had rescued him was hailed one hot day by a passing vessel. After exchanging news and pleasantries, as was the custom, the captain who had rescued Vane invited the master of the other ship to come aboard.

The visiting master turned out to be none other than Captain Holford, who had earlier refused Vane passage on his ship. Holford spotted Vane among the hands and revealed his identity.

Vane, despite his protestations, was placed in irons. Holford then volunteered to take Vane to Jamaica in his own ship, apparently reasoning that since he had more experience with pirates,

Vane would be less likely to cause problems aboard Holford's ship.

Brought safely to Jamaica, Vane was tried at Port Royal and found guilty. He was hanged in the late spring of 1719.

In Nassau, Woodes Rogers must have given a private sigh of relief at the news of Vane's execution. With Vane's removal from the scene, the last of the old New Providence pirates capable of leading a seaborne attack on Nassau was gone. The threat of a pirate invasion of the Bahamas colony was over.

But the feisty governor had little time to enjoy this fact before a new menace loomed, one that was far more formidable than any that Charles Vane had posed: a Spanish invasion.

At long last the oft-rumored war with Spain had become a reality. A formidable Spanish fleet had been gathered in the Caribbean, together with thousands of well-armed soldiers. Their purpose was to overrun England's island colonies, many of which had once belonged to Spain and which Spain was now determined to repossess.

Governor Rogers, excruciatingly aware of the poor state of his colony's defenses, begged London for more soldiers and warships. But none were forthcoming.

If the Spanish struck, the Bahamas colony and its dauntless governor would—as usual—be on their own.

15

The End on
New Providence

Expecting a Spanish invasion at any time, Rogers threw himself
into preparing a resistance.

As it had been for months, his prime concern was still the main
fort overlooking the harbor. Even after eight months of desultory
work on its walls, gun emplacements, magazines, storage areas,
and interior buildings, the fort was not yet ready to withstand a
serious attack by well-trained soldiers and sailors.

Although he had employed both cajolery and threat, Rogers
had not been able to persuade the indolent residents of Nassau
that finishing the fort was critical to their own well-being. As a
result the project had languished for lack of labor.

Now, playing on fears of a Spanish invasion—and liberally dol-
ing out liquor and food—Rogers managed to obtain more work
than ever before from the boozy inhabitants of his capital. But
progress was still painfully slow, and it looked as though it would
be months before the fort would become the impregnable strong

point that Rogers envisioned. In the meantime, he could only try his best to keep his men at their tasks—and hope that the Spanish would be slow to press the war north of Cuba. For Rogers knew that if the Spanish arrived at Nassau harbor before the fort was ready, the Bahamas colony would be theirs for the taking.

If progress on the fort was painfully slow, Rogers had much better results putting together a fleet for the seaborne defense of his colony.

In addition to the loyal Ben Hornigold, he commissioned two more ex-pirates as privateers in his service. These captains were men who, like Hornigold and Burgess, had proved their loyalty by carrying out assignments Rogers had given them.

During this period of frenzied activity in anticipation of a Spanish invasion, Rogers received notice that the British government had issued a new royal proclamation extending the king's pardon to all Carribbean pirates who would come in and surrender to colonial governors. The purpose of this act was to induce freebooters to enlist as privateers in the war against Spain, something that most of them were only too happy to do.

Before long, pirates were turning themselves in to the governors of English colonies from Bermuda to Jamaica to New Providence—and receiving in exchange pardons for past crimes and immediate commissions to go right out again and attack the ships of Spain.

One of those who came into Nassau harbor to surrender to Governor Woodes Rogers was Calico Jack Rackam, the man who had deposed Charles Vane from his command.

Following Vane's forced departure, Calico Jack and his crew had taken some good, if not spectacular, prizes. They had captured and ransomed a vessel loaded with convicts destined for labor in the West Indies. Operating off Bermuda, they had seized two ships homeward bound from Carolina and New England. They had also plundered some vessels off Cuba. But when they had heard of the war with Spain, and of the new pardons being offered, they had made for the Bahamas.

Arriving in Nassau harbor in May or June of 1719, Rackam and his men were granted the king's pardon as promised. But if Calico Jack had expected that it would be easy for him to obtain a privateering commission from Woodes Rogers, he was soon disappointed. Rogers seemed in no hurry to hand out a privateering

license to a man like Calico Jack, who had been a trusted officer of the notorious Vane and a friend of the terrifying Blackbeard. To Rogers there were certainly more trustworthy candidates for privateering commissions than Calico Jack Rackam.

Rackam, however, remained in Nassau, probably convinced that sooner or later, Rogers would be forced to commission as many ex-pirates as he had available in order to meet the Spanish threat. For word had recently come to Nassau that the king of

Spain had already named a new Spanish governor for the Bahamas, and that this grandee was even now preparing an invasion force in the harbor of Havana that consisted of two men-of-war, three galleys, and sixteen hundred soldiers—all destined for an early onslaught against Nassau and the Bahamas colony.

To defend his colony, Woodes Rogers had only his half-finished fort, his half-trained militia, two score soldiers, his own *Delicia*, and a handful of ex-pirate privateers.

It was a pitifully inadequate force. Rackam must have felt confident that Rogers would eventually come forward with the privateering commission he sought.

Calico Jack, therefore, enjoyed a period of leisure in Nassau, drinking in the waterfront taverns, visiting old friends, spending the hot humid nights in the shantytown's brothels. It was the classic way for men in the sweet trade to spend their intervals ashore. But for Calico Jack Rackam this shore leave brought an event that changed his life. He fell in love.

The object of his passion was the beautiful, fiery Anne Bonny, the nineteen-year-old wife of a young sailor, James Bonny.

Anne, who was far from a blushing bride, had already had a number of lovers among the pirate captains of Nassau, and was a familiar figure in the town's harbor-side dives. When Calico Jack fell wildly in love with her, she soon let him know that the feeling was mutual. Anne was a woman who knew what she wanted.

Born in Ireland, she was the illegitimate daughter of a prominent Cork attorney, William Cormac, and a maid in the family household, Peg Brennan. Cormac, whose wife had left him because of his "dissolute way of life," lost so much of his practice because of the scandal of his affair with his housemaid—and the birth of his illegitimate daughter—that he decided to leave Ireland forever. Taking his mistress and their daughter, he set sail for a new life in Charleston, South Carolina.

While continuing to practice law, Cormac also set himself up as a merchant. He soon became so successful that he was able to buy a large plantation in the countryside. When Anne's mother died, the young girl, now a beautiful redheaded lass of thirteen or fourteen, became the the mistress of her father's household.

Within another year or two there were numerous suitors for Anne's hand—despite her growing reputation as a spitfire. It was said that in one of her monumental fits of rage, she had stabbed a serving girl with a knife. Another story told how one young man, burning with passion for the tempestuous Anne, tried to rape her. Infuriated, Anne turned the tables on her would-be rapist and assaulted him with such ferocity that he remained bedridden for weeks afterward.

In time Anne met and married—against her father's wishes—a penniless young sailor named James Bonny. With her passionate nature, Anne yearned to escape the staid life of Charleston—and to throw herself into a life of adventure. Anne must have seen young Bonny as the means to attain the free life she longed for. When Bonny took her off to the pirates' nest of Nassau, on the island of New Providence, Anne became fascinated by the sweet trade—and especially by the men who practiced it. At the same time, she began to lose interest in her youthful husband. The young man seemed out of his element among the wild and wicked pirate captains. When Bonny, broke, desperate, and unable to find employment, became an informer for Woodes Rogers, Anne recoiled from him in revulsion.

At this point the dashing, handsome Calico Jack Rackam came into Nassau to claim the king's pardon in anticipation of a privateering commission. Perhaps she saw him first swaggering in the street, a brace of pistols in his belt and a cocky plume in his hat. Perhaps they met again later amid the raucous diversions of a tavern, the redheaded spitfire and the laughing, lusty pirate captain who must have seemed to Anne the very embodiment of the free and heroic life she hungered for.

If Calico Jack fascinated Anne, the pirate captain was even more enthralled by the wild young vixen. She might have been the darling of many before, but he was determined that she would henceforth belong to him alone. He wooed her passionately, presenting her with extravagant gifts of jewelry from his booty. He even offered to buy her from her husband. This was a form of divorce that was fairly common in that age. It was accomplished, usually, by paying an agreed-upon sum of money to the offended party. But the young man refused Calico Jack's generous offer for Anne. Instead, he complained to Governor Rogers that Rackam had seduced his wife from his bed. Rogers, always determined to uphold the law and family values, ordered Anne to return to her husband, warning that if she did not do so, he would

have her whipped as an adulteress—according to the law of the day. (Rogers apparently made no such threat to Rackam, however.)

But Anne was never one to surrender to Authority—not even to the formidable Woodes Rogers. She absolutely refused to return to Bonny. Instead, she called on Calico Jack to carry her away with him. Together they would go pirating and defy the world. The lustful Rackam agreed.

Now Anne and Calico Jack, in their first piracy as a team, executed a clever scheme to seize, for their own use, a swift merchant sloop that happened to be anchored in the harbor of Nassau. First, Anne used her charms to get aboard the sloop. She was able to estimate the number of crewmen guarding the ship, and to discover the hour at which the watch changed. She then managed to slip away again, probably leaving several disappointed sailors behind her.

In the middle of the night, Anne, Calico Jack, and some of his old crewmen crept aboard their intended victim. Anne, wearing an ordinary seaman's garb and carrying a sword in one hand and a pistol in the other, sneaked up behind the two men on watch aboard the sloop. Showing them her weapons, she whispered that she would blow their brains out if they uttered a sound or tried to stop the takeover of their ship.

The astonished sailors on watch did as they were told. (They were later put ashore.) Because most of the officers and crew of the sloop were enjoying themselves in town, the rest was easy. Rackam's old crewmen quickly cast off from the ship's moorings. The sloop slid silently out of the harbor, past the quiet shapes of other ships rocking at their cables, toward the open sea. Once beyond the bar, Rackam set her sails, and the speedy sloop took the wind.

By sunrise they stood far out to sea. Anne Bonny and Calico Jack Rackam were now well embarked on a voyage that would be fraught with destiny for both of them.

For the next six months Anne and Calico Jack cruised the Caribbean, taking and plundering a number of small prizes, and even raiding some shore installations. During all this time Anne dressed in men's clothing and fought in the ship's combats like other members of the crew. Apparently she and Calico Jack had decided to keep Anne's sex a secret, probably because Calico Jack feared the presence of a woman aboard would upset his crew. Keeping Anne's secret was probably not as difficult as it might seem. There were always a number of powder monkeys in pirate crews. Anne might have passed for one of these boys. Given the confusion and the chaotic lack of discipline that prevailed, it might have been relatively easy for Anne to maintain this disguise indefinitely. (On the other hand, it is equally possible that the crewmen knew that Anne was a woman, but knew also that she was their captain's woman, and not to be touched.)

Living a life of adventure aboard the pirate ship of her lover, it must have seemed to Anne Bonny that she had finally found the wild sweet life she had longed for.

Then the idyll of Anne Bonny and Calico Jack Rackam took another bizarre twist. Rackam's ship had captured a Dutch merchantman. Needing hands for his own vessel, Calico Jack had recruited several strong young sailors from among the crew of the Dutch ship. One of these Dutch volunteers was a handsome young man, blue-eyed and flaxen-haired.

Anne, never able to resist her passions, immediately fell in love with the youthful Dutch sailor.

At the first opportunity, Anne, despite her professed love for Calico Jack, contrived to be alone with the youth. Perhaps this encounter took place one quiet night when the two were assigned to stand watch together. In any case, Anne revealed herself to the boy, possibly by baring her breasts. In her own way she also made it clear that she felt a strong attraction to the young man.

She was amazed, however, when the object of her desire revealed *his* secret: "He" was neither Dutch, nor a man, but a twenty-seven-year-old Englishwoman named Mary Read.

It must have been an appalling moment—and a comic one, too—as the two women discovered each other aboard a pirate ship crewed by some of the toughest and the roughest sea brigands of the day.

Like Anne Bonny herself, Mary Read had been passing as an ordinary sailor. No one aboard the Dutch ship, she told Anne, had penetrated her disguise—and she begged Anne to keep her secret now. Anne quickly agreed, and the two women pledged undying friendship to each other.

In the weeks that followed, Anne Bonny and Mary Read, maintaining their disguises as powder monkeys, became inseparable friends. They fought side by side in all the ship's actions, as fiercely as any of the men. They could curse with the best of them, and neither of them ever hesitated to use their weapons to defend themselves. As Defoe put it, none among Calico Jack's crew "were more resolute or ready to Board or undertake any Thing that was hazardous as Mary Read and Anne Bonny."

Eventually, Mary Read must have begun to tell her life's story

to her friend. It was a story that sounded like the most romantic of novels, and perhaps Mary herself had made up some of it. In any case the tale she told to Anne, and to others in later days, began with her illegitimate birth in England sometime around 1693.

According to Mary's story, her mother conceived her after her lawful husband had gone to sea. For this reason she felt it necessary to conceal the fact of Mary's birth from both her own relatives and from her in-laws. To accomplish this, she dressed Mary in the clothes of a recently deceased legitimate baby—a son—whose death she had not revealed to anyone. The trick worked. Mary Read was thereafter raised as a boy. After a time, the deception became second nature to her.

When she was about eleven or twelve, she served as a "footboy" aboard a Royal Navy man-of-war. Later, still in her teens, she became a cadet in an infantry regiment. During the War of the Spanish Succession she served as a cavalry soldier in Flanders. Although a brave soldier, Mary's enthusiasm for military life began to fade when she fell in love with a handsome young soldier with whom she shared her tent. According to Mary's account, the young man was overjoyed when she revealed her sex to him, apparently under the impression that Mary intended to become his mistress on campaign. But Mary resisted all his advances until he married her.

Now Mary at last put on woman's clothing in order to take her marriage vows. The marriage itself created a sensation. Officers and men alike took great delight in this case of "two troopers marrying each other." Good-naturedly the men of Mary's former regiment contributed money for Mary and her new husband to set up a tavern near Breda, in Holland. The tavern, known as The Three Horseshoes, prospered, and Mary and her husband were as happy as any newlyweds could be. But then tragedy struck. A mysterious fever killed her husband. The Three Horseshoes failed. Mary was devastated. But despite her grief, Mary could not endure playing the role of a young widow. She decided that she preferred to seek her fortune as a man rather than as a wife. Once again she put on male clothing and went boldly into the world.

After another interval of service as a foot soldier, Mary disguised herself as a sailor and shipped out aboard a Dutch merchantman bound for the West Indies. When that vessel ran afoul of Calico Jack Rackam, she decided to take a flyer on the pirate life—and her friendship with Anne Bonny had flowered from that decision.

The shipboard friendship of Anne and Mary inevitably came to Calico Jack's notice. Jealously he observed that his love, Anne, was spending far more time than was necessary in the company of the handsome young Dutch sailor he had taken aboard some weeks earlier.

Convinced that his passionate spitfire was cheating on him, Rackam confronted her and her supposed lover one night as the two women were relaxing together on deck. In a jealous rage, Calico Jack threatened to kill his "rival." To protect her friend, Anne revealed Mary's true identity.

Calico Jack went along with Mary's secret—until love once again played its tricks. Mary Read fell in love.

The object of her desire was a young English sailor whom Calico Jack had forced into his crew from a prize taken off Jamaica. This reluctant pirate, Tom Deane by name, is described as a good-looking, honest fellow with an engaging manner. Mary, always direct, let the young man see that she was a woman "by carelessly showing her breasts, which were very white." Mary and Tom Deane became lovers.

Sometime later Deane, who was not a good hand with weapons, became embroiled in an argument with another member of the crew, one of Calico Jack's veteran cutthroats. According to pirate law, Deane and his adversary were slated to settle their differences by a duel onshore at the first opportunity. Mary, realizing that her lover would most likely be killed in the duel, provoked her own quarrel with the pirate who had challenged her man. She then insisted that her duel with their common antagonist take place in advance of her lover's. It was agreed.

Following the usual procedure, Mary and her enemy were taken ashore to settle their quarrel as soon as a suitable uninhabited island could be found. The duelists, observing strict pirate ritual, first fired pistols at each other—and missed. Then they fell to with cutlasses. Mary, knowing that it was her lover's life as well as her own that hung in the balance, slashed savagely at her opponent, forcing him to retreat under her onslaught. Now her years of service as a soldier proved their value. When her foe gave her an opening, Mary thrust home—and killed him.

After her victory Mary abandoned the disguise she had worn for so long and consorted openly with young Deane as a woman. Anne Bonny also acknowledged her true sex. Although the two women now donned female clothing, they continued to function as members of the crew. They also continued to take part in all the ship's combats. But during such actions, according to one account, they still "dressed in men's jackets, and long trousers, and handkerchiefs tied about their heads."

This romantic spell of passion, friendship, and battle was interrupted sometime around the New Year of 1720, when Calico Jack took Anne, who was in the last few weeks of pregnancy, to Cuba to bear their child. There is no record of this child's fate. Perhaps, like many infants born in that era, it died soon after birth. Perhaps Anne gave it to another woman to raise. Whatever happened to Anne's child, the record shows that by the early months of 1720, Anne was back with Calico Jack Rackam and her friend Mary Read, cruising the Caribbean for prey.

Meanwhile, back at Nassau, the indomitable Woodes Rogers had finally completed work on the harbor's fortress. In January 1720, the last of the bastion's fifty guns was put into place. To serve these guns and man the parapets of his stronghold, however, Rogers still had only a handful of soldiers and his unreliable pirate militia. Neverthless, despite the small number of quality troops available to him, he was sure that his fifty cannon, firing from behind now-impregnable walls, would be more than a match for any attacking force. Rogers now waited confidently for the long-anticipated Spanish invasion to materialize.

He did not have to wait long.

On February 24,1720, a Spanish assault force that included four men-of-war, a number of auxiliary vessels and transports—and thirteen hundred soldiers—appeared off Nassau harbor. But the Spaniards did not attack. Clearly surprised and dismayed to find the former pirate base now strongly defended by powerful new fortifications, the Spanish stood off the harbor, out of range of the guns of Nassau, to consider how to proceed.

Apparently deciding that direct assault on the island—which would have to be carried out under bombardment by fifty cannon—would be suicide, the Spanish decided to attempt a surprise landing under cover of darkness. On the night of February 25, a force of Spanish soldiers, transported in small boats, attempted to come ashore in the dead of night. But they were spotted by sentries—who blazed away at them in the blackness. The Spaniards fled back to their ships in ignominious disarray.

After this failed nighttime thrust at Nassau, the would-be invaders cruised aimlessly in Bahamian waters for some time, as if unwilling to acknowledge the miscarriage of their plan. Finally the frustrated Spanish sailed away.

Woodes Rogers had won. But it was not only the Spanish he had defeated. He had also defeated piracy.

Nassau, once the most notorious of pirate havens, was now defended on land by fortifications over which flew the British flag, and protected at sea by loyal ex-pirates such as Ben Hornigold and Thomas Burgess, who now flew not the Jolly Roger but the flag of St. George. Nassau—and all the Bahamas—was finished forever as a base for the outlaw nation.

By the midsummer of 1720 most of the pirates of the West Indies had abandoned their old haunts—and were searching for a new theater of operations. Only a handful of diehard brigands continued to follow the sweet trade in the Caribbean, and they were for the most part confined to the waters around Jamaica and Hispaniola.

One of that dwindling number was Calico Jack Rackam. For Calico Jack and his crew—which still included Anne Bonny and Mary Read—the hunting had been poor all that summer. They had taken a few fishing boats off Hispaniola. They had raided a few plantations for supplies. And they had captured a couple of trading sloops of no great value.

By October Rackam was operating off the north coast of Jamaica where his luck improved somewhat: He took a schooner and one or two small trading vessels.

But Calico Jack's luck was about to turn bad forever.

The governor of Jamaica, determined to put an end to piracy off his coasts, sent a fast sloop, under the command of a Captain Barnet, to hunt down Calico Jack.

Barnet caught Rackam at a place called Dry Harbor Bay. Calico Jack had anchored in this sheltered cove to allow his men to recover from their labors by drinking themselves into oblivion. Thus the pirates were far gone in drink when they finally spotted Barnet standing toward them. With his men sodden with rum and clearly in no condition for a battle, Calico Jack tried to escape. His besotted crew managed somehow to weigh anchor and raise sail. But it was no use. Barnet was soon alongside the pirate sloop. A moment later his men swung aboard. Calico Jack's drunken pirates fought poorly. Most of them stumbled away from the fight and tried to hide in the ship's hold. But Anne Bonny and Mary Read, attired in male clothing, fought like hellions. Firing pistols with furious rapidity and slashing wildly with their cutlasses, the two women held off Barnet's boarding party while the male crewmen cowered below.

But the odds against them were too great. The women had to give ground. When Mary Read saw that she and Anne could no longer contain their attackers, she ran to the hatch and screamed at her drunken mates to "come up and fight like men." But the craven crewmen ignored her call. Enraged, she then fired her pistols down into the cringing throng, killing one man and wounding several others. The battle, however, ended a moment later when Anne and Mary were overwhelmed.

Captain Barnet put the surviving pirates in chains and took them to St. Iago de la Vega (now Spanish Town), Jamaica, to stand trial.

It was another month before Calico Jack and his crew came before a judge. During this time, Anne and Mary continued to wear male clothing, apparently convincing their jailers and other officials that they were ordinary sailors like their fellows. At the trial, however, the truth came out, for they were identified in court records as "Mary Read, and Anne Bonny, late of the Island of Providence, Spinsters," and charged with "Piracies, Roberries, and Felonies."

At the trial Mary Read's young lover won acquittal when he was able to prove that Calico Jack had forced him to join the pirate crew. Although there is no record of it, Mary must have rejoiced to see her lover escape the noose. As for herself, she had often disclaimed any fear of the hangman. According to Defoe, she had on one occasion opined to Calico Jack "that as to hanging, she thought it no great Hardship, for, were it not for that, every cowardly Fellow would turn Pirate, and so infest the Seas, that Men of Courage must starve, and no Merchant would venture out; so that the Trade, in a little Time, would not be worth following."

In the end Mary *was* sentenced to be hanged—along with Anne, Calico Jack himself, and eight other crewmen. But when the judge inquired of the condemned if they had anything to say that might cause him to mitigate their sentences, Anne Bonny and Mary Read replied: "Milord, we plead our bellies."

Both women, it now turned out, were pregnant. The judge in the case then granted stays of execution to the mothers-to-be, since English law prohibited the killing of an unborn child, whatever the guilt of the mother. For Mary Read, however, the reprieve from the gallows was reduced to a grim irony when she caught a fever in prison and, after a few days of suffering, died— and her unborn child with her.

Anne Bonny was luckier. A number of Jamaican planters who had done business in the Carolina colony and knew and esteemed Anne's father interceded with local authorities on Anne's behalf. Thanks to their efforts she escaped execution.

No one interceded for Calico Jack Rackam, however. He went to the gallows early in December 1720. On the day that he was to hang, Calico Jack asked for, and received, special permission to pay a final visit to Anne. It was apparently Rackam's purpose to express his eternal devotion to his fiery mistress. But Anne, as tempestuous as ever, gave only cold comfort to her pirate lover, saying, according to Defoe, that she was "sorry to see him there, but if he had fought like a Man, he need not have been hang'd like a Dog."

With these unkind words ringing in his ears, Calico Jack Rackam climbed the scaffold to keep his date with the hangman.

Anne Bonny, it is said, returned to her father's house in South Carolina. Whatever her eventual fate there, it is certain that she never again went pirating. It is difficult, however, to imagine that her turbulent spirit ever found fulfillment in domestic life.

With the hanging of Calico Jack Rackam in Jamaica, piracy in the Caribbean virtually ceased.

Against all odds Woodes Rogers had succeeded in suppressing piracy—not only in his own Bahamas colony but throughout the Caribbean. By closing Nassau to the brigands, he had deprived the outlaw nation of its capital city, its center, its main base in the New World—and had thereby assured its eventual defeat in the West Indies.

There were several important reasons why Rogers succeeded in defeating the pirates of New Providence.

First, he always kept the pirates of Nassau off balance and in disarray by offering pardons to most of them but punishing a few others, by enlisting some in his own service, by alternately threatening and cajoling. As a consequence, the unruly citizens of Nassau were never able to agree among themselves whether to regard Rogers as an enemy or a friend. This made it impossible for Rogers's pirate enemies to muster a united opposition to the feisty governor.

Rogers also succeeded because of the strength of his character. Immensely brave, resolute, brimming over with self-assurance, Rogers always seemed to sense precisely when to take bold action—such as the hanging of the eight recalcitrants—and when to hold his peace. He knew when to bend the law to his purposes and when to ignore it. But for all that, he never allowed the outlaws, the whores, and all the other flyblown citizens of Nassau to forget that he represented the dignity, power, and majesty of England.

But the chief ingredient in Rogers's success was one he never acknowledged but always practiced: his willingness to tolerate, within bounds, the brawling, careless, unrestrained life-style of his pirates. For the most part—as long as they did not openly impede his designs or practice piracy—Rogers let the seadogs of Nassau live their lives as they chose. In this way the pirates remained almost as free under Rogers as they had been before his arrival. The brigands of Nassau, left relatively free, could never really work themselves up to rebel against Woodes Rogers. And so Rogers conducted his governmental business, established his authority, built his fort, planted his surviving settlers, even made some converts among the pirates—and one day the old seadogs of Nassau discovered that the Bahamas had become a real colony that no longer had a place for their lawless breed. They could either leave for other climes, or stay and—truly—reform.

Yet, having tamed his pirates, and having sent the Spanish invaders packing, Rogers now came face to face with an obstacle he could not overcome: the ingratitude of His Britannic Majesty's government.

Since his arrival in Nassau, Rogers had been paying the expenses of the Bahamas colony from his own funds. It had cost him approximately £11,000 to pay his soldiers, purchase food for the settlement, and provide for the defense of Nassau. Although he had kept careful accounts and had written often to the Board of Trade in London requesting reimbursment and support—in the form of money or supplies—he had been ignored.

In November 1720, alarmed by the lack of response from London, Rogers's colonial council wrote to the secretary of state in Westminster: "Governor Rogers having received no letter from you dated since July 1719, and none from the Board of Trade since his arrival [has] given him and us great uneasiness lest this poor colony should be no more accounted as part of his Britannic Majesty's dominions."

Still Rogers received no response.

In February 1721 he wrote to London: "It is impossible that I can submit here any longer on the foot I have been left ever since my arrival."

In March 1721 he finally reached the end of his patience. He left Nassau, sailing first to Carolina where he ordered provisions for his colony sufficient to last until the end of the year. Then he sailed for London, worn out and disillusioned, but determined to put his affairs in order.

Back in England, he found to his dismay that neither the government nor his backers in the Bahamas colony syndicate would make good the financial losses he had suffered during the previous three years. Humiliated, heartsick, and worn out physically, Woodes Rogers was declared bankrupt and dismissed as governor of the Bahamas colony. A new governor, George Phenney, was appointed in his place and sent to Nassau.

Rogers went to debtor's prison.

His work in the West Indies, however, endured. The outlaw nation was scattered and no longer a serious threat to Caribbean or American trade.

But if the outlaw brotherhood was defeated, it was far from annihilated. It still possessed numerous enterprising commanders. These spirited captains—many of them veterans of Nassau— had turned eastward once more.

16

King of Madagascar

Captain Christopher Condent had—over a long piratical career—
gained a well-deserved reputation for both cool courage and
shrewd judgment. A native of Plymouth who had gone to sea as a
boy, Condent—like most of the pirate commanders of Nassau—
had fought as a privateer in the War of the Spanish Succession,
and had drifted to the Bahamas after the war.

Condent—who must have been a bantam cock of a man—was
the sort of captain of whom it could be said: "He never fought
when he could talk, but never ran when he had to fight."

Veteran hands who had served with him were fond of recalling
one particular incident in which Condent most clearly displayed
the combination of bravery and sharpness that marked his character.

The story goes that during one of Condent's predatory cruises
through the Caribbean, an Indian crewman got into a dispute
with some other members of the crew and was badly beaten in a

fight. For days afterward the Indian brooded and muttered about "revenge." One day, while the rest of the crew were busy on deck, the Indian surreptitiously stacked barrels of gunpowder, arms, and flammable materials in the hold. He then began to shout and gesticulate, making it clear that he intended to set fire to this pile—and blow up the ship. The rest of the crew, peering down into the hold, could see that the Indian was mad with rage and meant to carry out his threat. Some of them proposed abandoning ship immediately, which also meant abandoning all their hard-won loot. Others suggested tossing smoke bombs down at the Indian. But it was pointed out that this would no doubt precipitate the very action they were trying to prevent.

At this juncture, according to the story, Captain Condent arrived on the scene and took in the situation in a flash. Cautioning the rest of his crew to make no sudden moves, and to do nothing to "help" him, Condent began to speak soft and soothing words to the distraught Indian, all the while edging closer to the brink of the hold, until he stood almost directly above the wild-eyed would-be incendiary. When he judged that the Indian had been sufficiently distracted by the mellow tones of his voice, Condent suddenly launched himself down into the hold, at the same time drawing both his pistol and his cutlass. The startled Indian managed to get off a shot just as Condent fired his own pistol. The Indian's shot struck Condent in the arm, breaking it. Condent's shot killed the Indian.

This was the man who early in 1719—when Woodes Rogers had been governor of his Bahamas colony for barely six months— foresaw that the doughty governor would inevitably triumph over the pirate republic in Nassau, and that the Caribbean would soon become both unsafe and unprofitable for sea raiders.

Certain that he had read the future accurately, Condent convened his crew and suggested that they abandon the West Indies and instead set sail in his ship, *Flying Dragon,* eastward across the Atlantic to see what luck they might have in those waters. As usual his crew supported Condent's judgment, despite the fact that for all *they* could tell, there were still plenty of good pickings in the Caribbean.

After crossing the Atlantic, Condent cruised southward along the west coast of Africa, taking a number of prizes as he went. By easy stages, he rounded the Cape and made for Madagascar. He arrived off the great island some time in June or July of 1719.

Although the outlaw nation had not been a force in the Indian Ocean since the great days of Madagascar nearly twenty years earlier, Condent thought there might be good hunting along the old sea-lanes between the Red Sea and India. He headed *Flying Dragon* north toward the mouth of the Red Sea, where Tew and Every and dozens of others had made their fortunes a generation earlier.

Although he patrolled vigilantly across the Gulf of Aden, no fat Mogul vessels or rich East Indiamen showed themselves. Condent then set his course for the west coast of India. For months *Flying Dragon* plowed between the Gulf of Cambay, on the Indian coast north of Bombay, and the Maldive Islands, twelve hundred miles to the south. But she took only a few small prizes. Condent and his men began to wonder if the stories of the fabulously rich cargoes of the East were perhaps no more than the tall tales of old men.

Then, in October 1720, more than a year after he had arrived in eastern waters, Condent's luck changed dramatically. While cruising off the Indian coast in the vicinity of Bombay, he sighted a large Arab ship headed eastward toward the East India Company trading center at Surat. Condent pursued her. He overtook her long before she reached the safety of the shore. The Arab ship surrendered without a fight.

As Condent's men ransacked her holds, they discovered that she was carrying an immensely valuable cargo: drugs, spices, silks—and £150,000 in gold and silver. Condent was determined to moderate—as far as possible—the wrath that the Great Mogul and the East India Company would no doubt feel when they heard of the loss of this great ship and her rich cargo. He was careful, therefore, to ensure that his men treated the Arab ship's passengers and crew with a certain amount of consideration. No violence was committed against any of those aboard the captured vessel—and passengers and crew alike were deposited safely ashore. Condent then beat a hasty retreat across the broad ocean with his prize, making for the old pirate sanctuary of St. Mary's.

There Condent and his men shared out the gold and silver. Each man's share came to approximately £2,000. Leaving much of the ship's luxurious cargo scattered on the beach of St. Mary's,

Condent and about forty of his crew then set sail for the French island of Bourbon, 450 miles east of Madagascar. At Bourbon they applied for, and received, pardons from the French governor, who was always pleased to give aid and comfort to any gentlemen of fortune who had harmed—or even embarrassed—Britain's East India Company. This was especially so when there was some little profit in it for the governor himself.

Defoe says that the shrewd Condent, having made a once-in-a-lifetime score, now retired from the sweet trade. He married the sister-in-law of the governor of Bourbon and returned with her to France where, according to Defoe, he parlayed his pirate loot into a fortune. He died a wealthy shipping magnate, respected by all who knew him.

Most of Condent's men followed their shrewd captain's example and never again went to sea. Many of them settled down in Bourbon, where they were regarded as valuable citizens of the island and lived contented, peaceful lives. The last of Condent's men, it was said, died in Bourbon in 1770, a half century after taking the prize that had made them all rich.

Christopher Condent was not the first of the Nassau pirates to head eastward in order to escape Woodes Rogers. He had been anticipated by the Irishman Edward England. One of the most successful of the New Providence pirates, England had been one of those who had chosen to depart Nassau in advance of Woodes Rogers's arrival. But unlike Blackbeard and Charles Vane, who chose to operate off the American coast, England had set sail eastward. It was a decision with momentous consequences, not least for England himself.

Like most of his colleagues, Edward England had served as a privateer in the War of the Spanish Succession and had headed to the Caribbean afterward. But unlike many others, it appears that he did not turn immediately to piracy. Headquartered at first in Jamaica, he seems to have avoided any overt acts of piracy until 1716 when he joined with other Jamaica captains to raid the Spanish Silver in the Gulf of Florida. It was after that score that England became a declared outlaw and made Nassau his headquarters.

A big man, slow moving and slow to anger, England seemed to lack that hatred of civilized society that was so characteristic of pirate leaders. Defoe describes him as "one of those men who seemed to have a better share of reason which should have taught him better things." Saying that England was not "avaricious" and was always "averse to the ill-usage" of prisoners, Defoe claims that England would have been contented with "moderate plunder and less mischievous pranks, could his companions been brought to the same temper." But England, he adds, was usually over-ruled by his crew and "obliged to be a partner in all their vile actions."

This was the man who—early in 1718—decided that with Woodes Rogers on his way to Nassau supported by Royal Navy warships, the time had come to leave the Bahamas—and to search elsewhere for prey. As Condent would a year later, England thought the Indian Ocean might offer good hunting. Accordingly, England set out eastward across the Atlantic, arriving off the coast of Africa in his ship, *Fancy*, in late March or early April of 1718.

Here England and his men took a number of vessels, including one called the *Cadogan*, whose brutal skipper was recognized by some of England's crew who had served under him in their days of honest service. Whooping with delight at having captured the master who had mistreated them in the past, these members of England's crew murdered the *Cadogan*'s captain "to avenge themselves and other poor sailors he had ill treated."

England worked along the coast of Africa for many months before finally heading into the Indian Ocean. By the time *Fancy* arrived at the mouth of the Red Sea in December 1719, Christopher Condent had already departed for the Indian coast where he would make his great catch. England, however, remained in the Gulf of Aden and took several rich Indian prizes.

Soon other pirate captains, most of them refugees from Nassau who had followed Condent and England's wake eastward, also began to take up stations in the Gulf of Aden. Among these were the French pirate Oliver La Bouche and the Englishman John Taylor, who was later to capture *Nossa Senhora Do Cabo* and score the greatest coup in the annals of piracy. At this time, however, Taylor was still an obscure figure in command of a small vessel, probably a brig, called *Victory*.

Taylor was well acquainted with England. (It is probable that Taylor had served in England's crew before becoming skipper of the *Victory*, and that *Victory* was a ship originally captured by

England and subsequently given to Taylor.) In any event, by the early part of 1720, England, in *Fancy*, and Taylor, in *Victory*, were hunting as partners.

In August 1720, England and Taylor, having pulled back to Madagascar waters to share out loot and to take a break from their labors, encountered two large East Indiamen lying in the bay of the island of Johanna.

The East Indiamen were the *Cassandra,* under the command of a Captain Macrae, and the *Greenwich,* under the command of one Captain Kirby. Both ships, well armed and provisioned, had been sent to Madagascar by the East India Company to search for pirates. The company—acutely aware that piracy was once again on the rise in the Indian Ocean—was determined not to allow the outlaw nation to reestablish itself in Madagascar. The *Cassandra* and the *Greenwich,* therefore, had been dispatched specifically to drive pirates away from Madagascar and its environs. The two pirate-hunter ships had come into the harbor of Johanna Island searching for the Frenchman La Bouche, who was rumored to have made his headquarters there.

When Captain Macrae of the *Cassandra* spotted *Fancy* and *Victory* approaching the harbor, however, he decided that these were even better prizes than the Frenchman. He signaled Captain Kirby of his consort *Greenwich* that he was preparing to engage the oncoming pirates. Kirby replied that he understood and would also engage. Now a third ship that happened to be in the bay, a Dutch merchant, beat a hasty retreat away from the harbor that obviously would soon become a scene of battle.

Meanwhile, the approaching pirates were under the impression that they had caught two fat and vulnerable East India Company merchant ships watering in the bay—perfect victims.

Aboard the well-armed and swift *Fancy,* Captain England now ran up his Jolly Roger, as well as a red flag. Ignoring the fleeing Dutch merchantman, England bore down on the two East Indiamen. His consort *Victory* trailed after him.

As soon as *Fancy* was close enough, *Cassandra* loosed a broadside that brought the pirate vessel up short. Soon *Fancy* and *Cassandra* were heavily engaged in a gun duel. *Victory* was soon closing also to join in the fight against the *Cassandra.*

Frantically Captain Macrae signaled to Captain Kirby, on the *Greenwich,* to join in the fight. But incredibly, Kirby, rather than joining in, sheered away from the combat—and headed for the safety of the open sea. After she had gotten half a league offshore and was safe from the battle, *Greenwich* suddenly came about again, as if intending to return to the harbor where *Cassandra* was now under attack by both pirate vessels. But *Greenwich* did not rejoin the fight. Instead she hovered offshore, apparently content merely to observe the battle.

Aboard *Cassandra,* Captain Macrae was enraged at the defection of *Greenwich.*

"He basely deserted us," Macrae later charged in his report on the battle. "He left us engaged with barbarous and inhuman enemies with their Black and Bloody flags hanging over us and no appearance of escaping being cut to pieces. But God in his good Providence provided otherwise."

The battle, which had begun sometime around midday, swayed back and forth for hours. Clouds of gunpowder smoke drifted across the harbor. The booming of cannon reverberated through the jungles of Johanna.

By late afternoon Captain Macrae knew that he was losing the battle. Most of his officers had been hit. There were thirty or more casualties among the crew. In addition, the pirate *Fancy,* though clearly damaged and with many wounded men aboard her, was continuing to maneuver closer and closer to *Cassandra.* Soon the pirate would be close enough to board her. The other pirate, *Victory,* had not been much of a factor in the battle so far, partly because she was guarding against the return of the *Greenwich*—which was still standing offshore aloof from the struggle—and partly because it was difficult to maneuver in the harbor.

Now Captain Macrae, convinced the battle was lost, decided on a desperate action to save his men if not his ship. He would run *Cassandra* onto the beach and attempt to escape into the jungle. Without hesitation he gave the necessary orders. Suddenly *Cassandra* sheared off from the fight and headed toward the shallows. *Fancy* followed.

Although *Cassandra* drew more water than the pirate ship, *Fancy* ran aground first, apparently on a sandbar. *Cassandra* ran onto the beach as her captain had intended.

Now, with *Fancy* aground, the pirates were unable to come alongside *Cassandra* to board her. In fury they kept up a steady fire at *Cassandra.* Macrae returned the fire fiercely.

(Still standing offshore, Captain Kirby in the *Greenwich* must have seen that the grounded pirate would now have been an easy mark if he had come in to add his fire to that of *Cassandra.* But still he refused to join the battle.)

Now, while the grounded *Fancy* and *Cassandra* continued to blast away at each other, Taylor in *Victory* saw his chance. He sent three small boats into the shallows, full of fresh men, with the idea of boarding the grounded *Cassandra*.

(Inexplicably, the *Greenwich* chose this moment—about five o'clock in the afternoon—to sail away from the scene of battle, leaving *Cassandra* and her crew "struggling in the very jaws of death," as Captain Macrae put it.)

Captain Taylor aboard *Victory* no longer had to worry that the other East Indiaman would enter the battle. He joined fully in the attack on *Cassandra*. He maneuvered to come under the larger ship's stern in order to board her.

Captain Macrae realized that the game was up. He implemented his plan to escape into the jungle.

"I ordered all that could to get into the longboat under cover of the smoke from the guns," Macrae reported later. "So that, what with some did in the boats, and others by swimming, most that were able got ashore by seven o'clock. When the Pirates came aboard they cut three of our wounded men to pieces. I with a few of my people, made what haste I could to the African King's house some 20 miles from us and there arrived next day almost dead with fatigue and loss of blood, having a musket ball wound in the head."

Macrae had lost thirteen men killed and twenty-four wounded in the battle. The pirates had sustained more than ninety casualties, including at least two dozen killed.

When England and Taylor's men finally boarded the abandoned *Cassandra*, they discovered that she carried a cargo worth some £75,000. But according to one account "no part of the cargo was so much valued by the robbers as the doctor's chest, for they were all poxed to a great degree."

The loot from the *Cassandra* did not, however, allay the pirates' rage against Captain Macrae for having killed and wounded so many of their fellows. So wrought up were England's and Taylor's crewmen against Macrae that they offered a reward of £2,000 to anyone who would bring the *Cassandra*'s captain to them for punishment.

For ten days Macrae and his surviving men lay hidden in the jungle. During this time the pirates refloated and repaired the *Cassandra* and the *Fancy*. They also used the respite to treat their wounded and to sift through their booty. Then, with astonishing boldness, Captain Macrae emerged from hiding and presented himself to the pirate captains England and Taylor. His purpose, he told the pirates, was to negotiate a ransom for his ship and her cargo. Macrae, who certainly knew that the outlaws had offered a princely reward for his capture, must have had remarkable confidence in his powers of persuasion to risk his life in this way—or else he was supremely sure that the ransom he planned to offer them would quickly dampen the pirates' rage against him.

In the event, the pirates were deeply divided over how to treat Macrae and his offer. One faction, led by Captain England, was much impressed by Macrae's audacity and favored negotiating with him. A second faction, led by Captain Taylor, wanted to cut Macrae down on the spot.

As the outlaws argued over the captain's fate, several of the pirates revealed that they had served with Macrae in the past— and still had great respect for him. This lucky coincidence proved a weighty factor in Macrae's favor, for these former crewmen of his took full advantage of their democratic rights under pirate law to speak up lustily in Macrae's behalf. One ferocious-looking old seafarer, according to a contemporary account, took Macrae by the hand and bawled at his colleagues: "Show me the man that offers to hurt Captain Macrae, and I'll stand to him [fight him], for an honester fellow, I never sailed with."

In the end, England's faction carried the day over the hardliners led by Taylor. They not only spared Macrae's life, they allowed him and his men to sail away in the damaged *Fancy*, and to take with them half the *Cassandra's* cargo. However, they kept the powerful *Cassandra*, as well as the other half of her cargo, for themselves.

Macrae and his men eventually managed to sail the crippled *Fancy* back to India. It was a horrendous journey that took forty-eight days under the broiling sun. Macrae and his men suffered terribly from thirst and starvation. When he reached India, however, Macrae was hailed as a hero. For his valor he received several important promotions in the service of the East India Company. (Eventually he rose to become governor of Madras and retired from that post after eight years of service with a fortune of £800,000—although the stated salary for the appointment was only £500 per year.)

For Edward England, whose faction had prevailed in the voting to spare the indomitable East India captain, the Macrae affair proved an albatross that finally led to his undoing. His partner, Taylor, and others in the pirate company continued to complain about what they considered England's unwarranted clemency toward Macrae. So effectively and so often did Taylor and his cohorts take England to task for his "softness" that they finally convinced the majority of the company that England was unfit to command. In a vote taken upon Taylor's insistence, England was deposed as captain—and Taylor elected in his place. With a few men who chose to remain with him, England was put aboard a small boat to fend for himself.

Taylor now sailed off as captain of the *Cassandra*, with *Victory* as his consort. (Over the next few months Taylor would range widely over the Indian Ocean, taking a number of prizes, until he made his great coup with the capture of the *Cabo*.)

England and his few companions managed to sail their small boat to St. Augustine's Bay in Madagascar where England knew a number of ex-pirates were living in retirement.

But deprived of his command and virtually penniless, Edward England would soon go into decline. For the rest of his life, England would live on handouts from ships that called at St. Augustine's Bay, and on charity from old companions. Drifting from place to place, cadging drinks, and telling stories of his days as the daring captain of the *Fancy*, England would degenerate into a half-comic waterfront "character" in the pirate hangouts of the great island.

But one of England's crewmen, who had chosen to accompany his old captain after his deposition, would flourish even as England fell further and further into decay.

This was a young sailor named John Plantain. And he would one day become the virtual king of Madagascar.

Plantain was born of English parents, in Jamaica, some time about 1700. At thirteen he went to sea as a cabin boy and served aboard a privateer. Later he fell into small-time piracy, serving aboard a number of pirate vessels that preyed on loggers off the Campeche coast of Mexico.

Jumping from ship to ship, Plantain found himself ashore in Rhode Island, and dead broke, sometime around 1718. Here he fell in with a certain Captain John Williams, master of the sloop

Terrible, and sailed with Williams for West Africa, possibly on a slave-trading mission.

Off the coast of West Africa the *Terrible* was taken by Captain England, who had just entered those waters after departing the Caribbean. Plantain volunteered for England's crew and sailed with him during all his subsequent adventures—until England was replaced by Taylor.

When Plantain chose to accompany England into exile on Madagascar, he took with him the considerable booty that he had gained during his years of pirating. He also persuaded two comrades to accompany him. These were a Scot named James Adair, and a Dane named Hans Burgen.

Adair, the son of a good Presbyterian family, was unusual for a common sailor in that he could read and write. He had run away to sea as a boy. Captured by pirates, he had joined voluntarily with them, eventually finding himself in England's crew. He was generally considered good-natured, but "a young man of very hard countenance" when crossed.

The Dane, Hans Burgen, was a native of Copenhagen, and a skilled cooper. He had become a member of England's crew when his ship, the *Coward,* was taken by England off the coast of Africa.

Both Adair and Burgen deferred to John Plantain. For despite Plantain's youth, there was about him a sort of jaunty self-assurance, as well as a hardness of will that made him a leader. More easygoing men sensed that John Plantain was a young man who knew exactly what he wanted—and how to get it. They followed him, as Adair and Burgen did, because he was able to give shape to their lives.

After his arrival on Madagascar, Plantain immediately set in motion a plan he had long had in mind. He made his way to Ranter Bay on the northeast coast. Here, using his store of pirate loot to purchase native labor, he had a stockade fortress built— and went into business as a trader. Plantain's enterprise was soon thriving. He became friendly with a local native chief known as Mulatto Tom, who claimed to be the son of the Arch-Pirate, Henry Every. Plantain's fort, much frequented by Mulatto Tom and his people, became the center of political and social life for the surrounding area.

It was not long before Plantain and his companions—Adair and

Burgen—were able to expand their initial establishment to include well-appointed living quarters for themselves—and for the numerous wives and servant-girls they soon added to the household. Plantain was the lord of this household. His harem included the most beautiful of the local women—to whom he gave such homely English names as Moll, Kate, Sue, and Peg. He decked his harem favorites in the silks and jewels that he had won in his piratical career. He took to calling himself the King of Ranter Bay.

Despite his success, however, John Plantain was not content. There was a woman he wanted—and could not get.

She was Holy Eleanora, the lovely half-caste granddaughter of a nearby native chieftain named King Dick. Called "Holy" Eleanora because she had been taught to recite the Lord's Prayer and the Ten Commandments, the girl was the daughter of a long-dead English pirate and King Dick's own beloved daughter. The object of many men's desire, Holy Eleanora must have been a magnificent beauty, perhaps a dusky rose with large dark eyes, a fall of black hair over her shoulders, and a natural sensuality in her movements.

John Plantain yearned to possess her. But her grandfather adamantly refused to allow Holy Eleanora to join John Plantain's harem.

Plantain was not a man to endure frustration for long. The love-sick king of Ranter Bay decided that if King Dick would not give him Holy Eleanora, he would take her by force. With the help of Mulatto Tom and other chieftains in the area, Plantain recruited three large companies of tribesmen. He armed many of them with muskets and pistols, purchased with his pirate plunder.

With Adair and Burgen each leading a company, and himself leading the third, Plantain marched on King Dick. But the native chieftain was not cowed. He had his own well-armed militia, which included in its ranks a number of retired European pirates. King Dick's forces went out to meet the invader.

In a bloody battle, Plantain defeated—but did not destroy— King Dick's army. The wily native monarch, realizing that the battle was going against him, fled from the field with as many men as he could take with him. Unfortunately for King Dick, many of the ex-pirates who were the "officer corps" of his army had been killed in the battle—and were sorely missed in subsequent actions.

Plantain, furious at King Dick's escape, pursued his defeated antagonist. There was a second battle. Again Plantain won. King Dick did not escape this time. Taken prisoner by Plantain, he had to watch as Plantain burned down his village—and at last took Holy Eleanora as his own.

But even now Plantain had to endure frustration. He discovered that his coveted bride was already pregnant by an English pirate killed in one of the battles. Furious, Plantain blamed King Dick for Holy Eleanora's condition. He had King Dick put to death in revenge. His love for Holy Eleanora, however, remained unabated. He took her back to Ranter Bay with him. She became his favorite wife and the mother of several of his numerous progeny.

Plantain was now, in fact as well as in name, the king of Ranter Bay. But still he was not content. Although his success against King Dick had made him the most powerful figure in the northern half of Madagascar, it had also ignited within him even larger ambitions. He now yearned to make himself king of all Madagascar. To accomplish this, however, Plantain knew he would have to conquer Port Dauphin—a dominant enclave on the southwest coast ruled by a native prince whose name has not been recorded but whose power eclipsed that of King Dick.

With singleminded purpose Plantain began to prepare his forces for war against Port Dauphin. Victory in this struggle, he was sure, would make him truly king of Madagascar.[1]

Meanwhile, the East India Company, smarting from the depredations of such pirate captains as Condent, England, Taylor, and La Bouche—and fearing a revival of the near-ruinous commerce raiding of the 1690s—had appealed to London for help against the new pirates of the Indian Ocean.

London, by now convinced of the importance of the eastern trade to Britain's economy and political status, responded with alacrity. The Admiralty, late in 1721, dispatched a squadron of four men-of-war, under the command of Commodore Thomas Mathews, to eastern waters.

Mathews had actually been given a dual mission: to make sure that the eastern pirates did not reestablish themselves on Madagascar, and to aid the East India Company in one of its interminable local struggles with the Portuguese for control of trading posts on the Indian mainland.

Commodore Mathews, in his fast flagship, reached Madagascar before the other ships of his squadron. But he found no pirates. Unwilling to waste time in a search for pirates, Mathews decided to get on with the other part of his mission: He would proceed to Bombay and do what was necessary against the irritating Portuguese—and return later to take care of the pirates. With this in mind, Mathews left a letter at St. Augustine's Bay for his other captains, explaining his decision and instructing them to follow him to India. He then sailed off.

Although Commodore Mathews had failed to detect them, there *were* pirates operating in the area around St. Augustine's Bay—and the commodore's letter to his captains fell into their hands. Thanks to Mathews's letter, the pirates learned the Royal Navy's mission—and that the men-of-war would be returning to waters around Madagascar, probably within a few weeks. Many of the eastern pirates—including Taylor and La Bouche, who had already made their big score against the *Cabo*—now decided to leave the Indian Ocean to the Royal Navy and to seek prey elsewhere.

In the spring of 1722 the East India Company's hostilities with the Portuguese in India were suspended by an armistice. Commodore Mathews and his squadron made for Madagascar, as planned, to hunt for pirates.

On April 22, 1722, Mathews anchored off the once-notorious pirate haven of St. Mary's. Prudently he sent a boat ahead to scout the island. The scouting party found the place deserted and the beach strewn with discarded booty: drugs, spices, porcelains, silks, and other goods that the pirates of St. Mary's had rejected as unsalable. The scouting party also found that sunken wrecks littered the harbor, blocking the entrance. One of the wrecks was Taylor's old ship, the *Victory*.

The pirates of St. Mary's had gone.

But John Plantain had not. He was still flourishing in nearby Ranter Bay.

Although he was, at this time, in the midst of his struggle with King Dick for possession of Holy Eleanora, Plantain heard that Commodore Mathews and his squadron had arrived at St. Mary's. He therefore took time out from his busy affairs to go and greet the Royal Navy.

According to one eye witness, Plantain and his two confederates, Adair and Burgen, simply emerged from the jungle one day—and introduced themselves to Commodore Mathews and his officers while they were ashore at St. Mary's. It was clear, according to the witness, that Plantain, who cockily carried two pistols in his sash, was the dominant figure of the trio. Plantain jauntily admitted that he had been a pirate. He had served with England's crew, he told the commodore and his officers, and he had even helped take the *Cassandra*.

At this point one of Commodore Mathews's officers apparently gave orders to arrest Plantain. But before the navy men could lay hands on the self-assured ex-pirate, an armed guard of approximately twenty natives materialized out of the jungle and threw a protective cordon around Plantain. Plantain then explained, apparently with some good-humored satisfaction, that he was not merely a retired pirate, he was a self-made sovereign. In fact he was the king of Ranter Bay.

During his visit with Commodore Mathews, Plantain cheerfully discussed his own history, from his lowly birth in Jamaica to his elevation to royal status in Madagascar. In the course of this conversation, he also informed Mathews that most of the pirates he was seeking had already left the East with the idea of sailing back to the Spanish-controlled areas of the Caribbean, where they hoped to purchase Spanish pardons. Plantain also invited Commodore Mathews and his officers to visit him at Ranter Bay after they had satisfied themselves that Captains Taylor, La Bouche, and others they might be seeking had indeed departed Madagascar.

In the event, Commodore Mathews and his officers *did* pay a visit to Plantain's establishment at Ranter Bay.

Plantain, in honor of his guests, ran up the flag of St. George over his fort and laid on a sumptuous entertainment that included great quantities of food and drink, as well as—very probably—the attentions of the sovereign's women.

(One of the guests at Plantain's party, it was said afterward, was the deposed Captain Edward England. Reduced to penury and in declining health, England was now in the last months of his life. According to contemporary witnesses, he spent these last days drifting from place to place, begging the white men of Madagascar for subsistence. It was also reported that England "seemed very penitent . . . and hoped that God would forgive him his sins and [he] desired his companions to leave off that [piratical] course of life.")

During his stay with Plantain at Ranter Bay, Commodore Mathews apparently took the opportunity to purchase from the pirate king—at cut rates—a quantity of luxury items that Plantain had plundered during his career.

Eventually Commodore Mathews, convinced that the Madagascar outlaws were in fact gone, as Plantain had told him, sailed for home. Plantain resumed his war against King Dick.

When Commodore Mathews reached England again he came under severe fire from critics who felt his behavior in Madagascar had been less than exemplary. Pointing out that he had failed to capture even one pirate, his critics charged that Mathews had not exercised sufficient enterprise in hunting down the Madagascar outlaws. Many felt that he could—and should—have kept pirate captains such as Taylor, La Bouche, and others from escaping the net.

Mathews also came in for much censure when it was revealed that he had traded privately with Plantain and other pirates. Eventually Mathews was relieved of his command for "neglect of duty."

But in spite of Commodore Mathews's alleged shortcomings as a commander, he did accomplish his mission: the suppression of piracy in the Indian Ocean. The mere presence of Mathews and his Royal Navy squadron in the waters around Madagascar had been sufficient to disperse the pirates there and to ensure that there would be no resurgence of the old-time outlaw nation.

In reality, of course, there had never been any serious chance that the pirates could reestablish themselves on Madagascar in the 1720s. Despite the huge depredations of Condent, England, Taylor, and others who had returned to the Indian Ocean from the West, the pirates of the 1720s were much diminished in both number and in effect upon trade when compared to their predecessors. In the 1720s the brotherhood of the black flag lacked the economic base it had enjoyed in the 1690s.

In 1720 there were no big traders like Adam Baldridge on Madagascar to buy pirate booty, no big brokers like Frederick Philipse of New York to deal in plunder and to finance pirate expeditions—and there were no colonial governors like Benjamin Fletcher to sell privateering commissions for a fee and to look the other way while pirate contraband was unloaded in their ports.

The merchants who dealt in pirate plunder in the 1720s were—generally speaking—free-lance operators, small businessmen who had to do their trading clandestinely, keeping themselves one jump ahead of the navy and the police forces of the large trading companies.

Without the substantial economic support provided by large brokers and by hungry markets, the outlaws of 1720 could not defy the authority of London or of the East India Company, as had the pirates of the 1690s.

There were other factors that also militated against reestablishment of any extensive pirate presence in the Indian Ocean. In 1721 Parliament had declared that anyone who trafficked with pirates, or furnished them with supplies, was himself guilty of piracy. This law greatly reduced outlets where pirate captains could obtain necessary provisions. At the same time, Parliament enacted regulations that called for rewarding merchant sailors who resisted attacks by pirates and for punishing any who *failed* to do so. The effect of these laws was to give ordinary sailors, for the first time, substantial incentives for remaining in honest service.

These changes in the law—together with the eradication of colonial economic support of piracy—seemed to many observers of the day to herald the end of the sweet trade. Commodore Mathews's squadron had driven the pirates from the East, and the indomitable Woodes Rogers had made them unwelcome in the West Indies. The outlaw brotherhood—what was left of it—seemed finished.

But those who thought so soon found that they had been premature in their assessment. For there was one last stretch of coast and ocean where freebooters might survive—and even thrive: the west coast of Africa, the Guinea Coast as it was called.

Here—along this feverish shore—slave dealers conducted their cruel but lucrative traffic with the powerful black tribes of the mysterious continent.

Here European trading companies milked the wealth of Africa.

Here outlaw traders still bought stolen goods—and sold contraband supplies to brigand sailors.

And it was here that a dwindling number of pirate captains—as fierce and as resourceful as any who preceded them—fought the final battles of the pirate war on the world.

17

Where White Men Die

The Guinea Coast—as it was called by white men—is the curving western seaboard of tropical Africa, stretching some 2,800 miles from Senegal in the north to Cape Lopez just south of the Equator in present-day Gabon.

For eighteenth-century Europeans, the Guinea Coast was not only a place of oppressive heat, it was also the home of fearsome mysteries, brutal customs, and deadly diseases. It was a place where white men came to win wealth—and where they often died broken in body and spirit.

All along this vast stretch of low-lying shoreline, the pale green waters of the Gulf of Guinea and the darker swells of the deep Atlantic rolled and crashed against narrow beaches of brownish sand. Beyond the foaming surf and the thin strip of sand stood the endless jungles—dark, damp, silent, and forbidding.

In some places the tapestry of surf, sand, and jungle parted to disgorge great rivers—among them the Niger, the Volta, and the

Gambia. In other places the rivers formed deltas of swamp, with the huge mossy trees rising out of briny shallows.

All along the coast a fiery tropical sun sucked vapor from the sea and the rivers into the air, making the atmosphere so humid that even the slightest movement drenched a man in his own sweat—and the skin was never free of its film of moisture.

Everywhere the heavy air stank with the mixed smells of the forest, the sea, and human occupation. The vapors from rotting vegetation and fish, the odor of salt spray, the smell of cook fires and of human offal—all were broiled into a ripe miasma beneath the equatorial sun.

The coast stank of fever too. Mosquitoes and flies swarmed out of the swamps and jungles, spreading virulent disease. Men trembled with dengue fever, sweated and shivered with malaria, and died of "fevers that had no name" and seemed to exist nowhere else on earth.

"This land is a hell," one Dutch trader to the Guinea Coast wrote home in the 1660s. Yet for all its hellishness, this coast and its hinterland supported a thriving population of indigenous black tribes.

In the jungle that stretched away for hundreds of miles into the unknown heart of the continent, powerful black kingdoms flourished. Among the most famous were the realms of Benin, Dahomey, and Ashanti.

In addition, populous tribal groups—all with complex and distinctive cultures—prospered here. The three dominant tribal peoples were the Ibo, the Fanti, and the Mandingo. These tribes generally supported themselves by fishing, by farming, and by carrying out some limited trading into the interior.

All the peoples of the Guinea Coast and its hinterland were fierce warriors. Many of the tribes and kingdoms of the region were also wealthy. All had highly developed political systems.

For many centuries Europeans had shied away from this coast of darkness, leaving it not only unexplored but virtually untouched.

Because the coast lacked suitable anchorages for ships, few Europeans visited it—unless driven ashore by necessity. Further, the rivers of the region appeared to be unnavigable—either pouring precipitously out of the jungle into the ocean, or oozing through a maze of swampy channels to the open water.

Clearly such rivers could not be usable pathways for the exploration of the unknown interior of the vast continent, and European adventurers passed them by.

Moreover, the handful of Europeans who had, by some mischance, been washed ashore on this dank coast and who had later returned to civilization had brought back tales of fierce, xenophobic African tribes, and of diseases that weakened and killed.

Yet, though unexplored, the Guinea Coast began to take shape on European maps sometime in the fourteenth century when western geographers adapted information from Arab sources for their own use. It was also about this time that the name Guinea Coast came into use. Applied first by the Portuguese, the name was derived from the Berber word *aguinaw*—meaning "black man"—which the Portuguese rendered as *guiné*.

In the fifteenth century, the Portuguese, who had earlier founded a colony in Angola, south of the mighty Congo, began to hear reports that this dark land they called the Guinea Coast produced goods that the white man coveted: pepper, ivory, and gold that was purer than any other in the entire world.[1]

Late in the fifteenth century the Portuguese became the first Europeans to attempt to establish themselves there. Portuguese traders constructed an outpost approximately fifteen hundred miles north of their Angola colony, in what is now Ghana.

Called Elmina, the post was actually a fortress since, in addition to being a trading center, it also had to serve as a bastion of defense in case of attack by local black tribes—and as a deterrent to European interlopers.

The Portuguese soon followed the establishment of Elmina with other fortress trading posts. Throughout the late fifteenth and early sixteenth centuries, Portuguese trade with the local tribes flourished, as European manufactured goods, such as guns, cloth, and metals, were exchanged for African gold and ivory.

Although the Portuguese prospered on the Guinea Coast and although they managed to make fruitful contacts with many of the black tribes in the region, their attempts to expand their trading footholds into the interior ended in dismal failure. This was due primarily to the inhospitable terrain and to the prevalence of disease. Portuguese expeditions sent into the jungles to "pacify" and to "bring civilization" to the indigenous peoples disappeared,

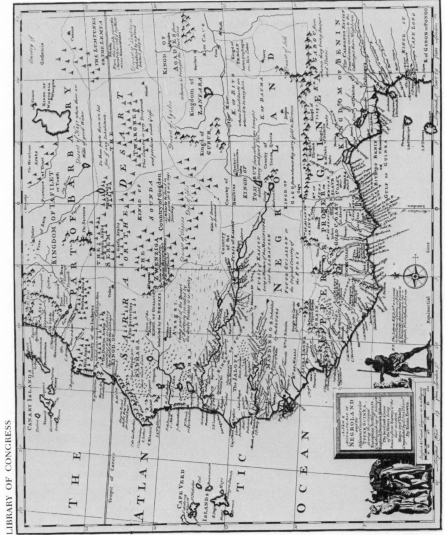

wiped out by "fever." Even expeditions aimed primarily at exploration of the interior were defeated by swamp, jungle, hostile tribes, and malaria.

The Portuguese experience on the Guinea Coast taught later European traders the futility of attempting to conquer and control the country—which was their usual method when dealing with "lesser" peoples. Instead, European traders followed the Portuguese example, contenting themselves with building fortified enclaves on the coast in which they could live and work safely and from which they could trade on a more or less equal basis with the powerful local black kings and chieftains.

In the first quarter of the seventeenth century, the Portuguese monopoly of Guinea Coast trade was decisively broken when the Dutch, English, French, Spanish, and Swedish all began constructing their own trading forts in competition with the Portuguese and with each other. By the mid-1650s there were dozens of European trading enclaves, from Senegal in the north to Cape Lopez in the south.

Throughout the seventeenth century, as European maritime nations fought each other for ascendancy in Europe and on the sea-lanes of the world, the Guinea Coast was a theater of war. Reflecting the ebb and flow of the worldwide struggle, trading forts were besieged, captured, lost, recaptured, and lost again. It was an age of ferment and turmoil in that area.

It was also an era that saw a drastic change in the nature of the trade between Europe and Africa. For it was in the late 1600s that slaves became the prime commodity bought and sold on the coast.

Although the Portuguese had in the past carried on a limited trade in Guinea Coast slaves for the New World, the trade had never become a major component of Portugal's commerce.

In the seventeenth century, however, with the establishment of plantation colonies—especially by the English—in the Caribbean and in North America, cheap labor to cut the sugar cane and to pick the cotton became a sought-after commodity.

Soon black human beings, captured and enslaved by black kings and black chieftains and then sold to white traders for transport to America, became the most profitable "product" on the Guinea Coast, replacing gold, ivory and spices.

It is estimated that by 1700, approximately 25,000 slaves were being shipped annually from the Guinea Coast to New World markets.

The trade in human beings, with all its moral and social consequences for the white men who took part in it and for the future of the Americas, also gravely marked and distorted the development and history of the black African nations that so willingly participated.

So frenzied was the demand for slave labor, and so lucrative did the trade become, that by the early years of the eighteenth century, many African kings along the coast had banned traditional pursuits in commerce, agriculture, and culture in order to devote themselves and their people completely to the task of supplying captives for purchase by European traders.

This policy led to brutalization of the people of the region, depopulation of the hinterland, loss of cultural values and skills—and severe economic dislocation when the trade came to an end. In essence, the Africans involved in the slave trade sold not only their people but their future to the white slavers.

But in spite of their involvement with, and dependence upon, the European traders, the black rulers of such powerful local kingdoms as Dahomey and Ashanti still maintained political and military control over the coast and over the trading forts in their territory. Both the Europeans and the Africans realized that while these well-armed forts could protect European interests for a time, they could not be held indefinitely if local chiefs turned hostile.

Most of the Europeans established on the shores of Black Africa still remembered that in 1637 the Dutch—after taking Elmina from the Portuguese—had tried to subjugate the tribes around this formidable fort. But they had been soundly defeated, with much loss of life, by the local kings. Similar efforts by whites to dominate various areas along the coast had also failed.

In the eighteenth century, with the slave trade thriving as never before, white traders acknowledged their vulnerability to the local black kings and did all that was demanded of them to secure the goodwill of the surrounding tribes and kingdoms. For example, white traders almost invariably paid a tribute, or a rent, for the right to maintain their forts on the coast. In addition, the traders usually had to recognize local chiefs and kings as the sole agents supplying slaves to the white men. White traders were forbidden to purchase their "merchandise" from any other source, although the chieftains themselves were free to get the best price they could from other European bidders for their slaves. The white traders were also required to pay homage to local kings and to acknowledge their sovereignty in many public ways. For example, ships arriving to trade at coastal forts had to fire salutes in honor of the local monarch. Any captain who failed to do so was subject to arrest and fine.

In Whydah, a major English slave-trading station on the coast, the local king insisted upon acting as arbiter if any dispute arose among the European traders who visited his little realm. His decisions were final and there was no appeal. Any European—English or otherwise—who made any objection whatsoever to the king's decision on disputes within his dominion, was summarily expelled from the coast.

In the court of the king of the Fanti, all European traders were required to remove their hats in the royal presence and to execute an obeisance to the king—exactly as if he had been a European autocrat. The king of Dahomey would shake hands with a European only as a "very uncommon mark of royal condescension."

Europeans may have smarted at the necessity for bowing before rulers whom they regarded as little more than barbarians, but they did whatever was required of them, for the commerce that was enriching them depended entirely upon the goodwill of such "savages."

In the first quarter of the eighteenth century the booming slave trade along the Guinea Coast was largely in the hands of the British—thanks primarily to British maritime supremacy. But British ascendancy had not been achieved overnight.

During the 1600s the English, like other European trading nations, had built a number of powerful forts on the coast. They had also seized others from rival nations. But the English government, unlike its rivals, found a way to maintain these important installations without draining its manpower reserves or its national treasury: It turned them over to the Royal African Company, a trading enterprise founded in 1672 along the lines of the powerful and successful East India Company.

In exchange for manning and maintaining English forts along the seaboard, the company received a monopoly over all trade, including the slave trade, on the Guinea Coast. In this way the Royal African Company became not only the largest single commercial enterprise on the coast but also the military and political surrogate of the British government. When the slave trade boomed, the Royal African Company was well placed to dominate it.

By 1713, when the War of the Spanish Succession ended and England stood supreme over her rivals, the Royal African Company controlled the trade in slaves, gold, ivory, and any other commodity from Senegal to Angola.

The company held forts at the mouth of the Gambia River; at Cape Coast Castle in what is now Ghana; at Whydah and Anamabu in present-day Benin; and at half a dozen other locations. Through these heavily fortified trading centers flowed the wealth, and the blood, of Africa.

To places like these also came white men, usually young and poor, intent on making their fortunes. They lived lonely lives in an oppressive climate, and in an alien culture. Surrounded by damp black forests, always fearful of treachery, they had to endure long empty days under the blinding sun and sticky nights of boredom. Engaged in the inhuman slave trade, subservient to brutal African tribal leaders, they soon became hardened to anguish—their own and that of the victims of their enterprise. Almost always these white fortune seekers sickened—spiritually as well as physically. Many died of the fevers that seemed to live in the very air. Many turned to alcohol and to native women for solace. More than a few went mad.

One way or another Africa marked those engaged in raping her.

Yet so great were the potential profits from trade along the Guinea Coast that hundreds of white men braved its hazards and miseries to man the trading posts of the Royal African Company and to funnel into the ships of Europe and the Americas the sons and daughters of the continent whose dark interior still defied all efforts by *civilized* man to penetrate it.

In addition to danger, disease, loneliness, and oppressive climate, the white traders who clung to their encampments on the fringe of Africa were also burdened by an inexpressible—but profound—sense of menace. Not only was Africa cruel, she was mysterious, and therefore dangerous and threatening. Only a few miles beyond the strip of sand, surf, and jungle where the white

traders lived and labored, began the *real* Africa, the "heart of darkness" that might contain any nightmare, that might erupt at any moment into any madness.

Tales about the deep invisible Africa that lay within the jungles circulated among all who lived on the coast. It was said, for example, that Prester John, the great Christian king of a nation of warriors, lived in splendor in the center of the continent—and that herds of unicorns ran wild on the vast open plains of his kingdom. Farther to the south, they said, was the land of Monomotapa where gold lay on the earth like shells on a beach. At the headwaters of the Niger lived elephants who knew how to use fire and who carried torches in their trunks. There were giant birds in the interior too, so big they could carry off elephants. There was a nation of Pygmies only six inches high. There were giant warriors who rode into battle on the backs of wild beasts. There were the Mountains of the Moon, and the Fountains of the Nile.

A land that contained such marvels, the white traders sensed,

must contain horrors as well. The blacks knew it, too. That was why they propitiated their gods with blood and fearful rites. *They* knew the horror was there. And who was to say that the horror would not, one day, come roaring from the black heart of Africa to take vengeance upon the strangers who were robbing the continent of her children? It was a weighty, unarticulated burden, this sense of Africa's strangeness and concealed menace—and it added greatly to the already difficult job of everyday life on the Guinea Coast.

For in this place even the mundane tasks connected with the business of trading—such as loading and unloading goods from ships and looking after cargo—presented the white traders with peculiar hardships.

For example, since there were no harbors to speak of, ships had to anchor well offshore, beyond the surge of surf and the danger of submerged rocks. Cargo, including human cargo, had to be ferried by canoe to and from the beach. In rough water goods were often lost in the sea. Helpless, but valuable, slaves—chained together to prevent their escape—were often drowned in the surf, or taken by sharks before they could be pulled from the sea.

Slave ships often had to lie at anchor offshore for weeks while their holds were slowly filled with slaves purchased ashore in small consignments. Meanwhile, their groaning human cargoes, chained belowdecks under the broiling sun, lay in their own excrement. The smell of the slave ships filled the air—and could be detected many miles out at sea, long before the coast itself was visible.

There was the humiliation of haggling and trading with black slavers who were, more often than not, thieves and cheats who would not keep their word.

Another trial for the white traders along the coast—those of the Royal African Company at any rate—were the English and American interlopers, independent merchants who refused to acknowledge the Royal African Company's monopoly. Trading when and where they could, in defiance of the "official" traders, the interlopers were a constant thorn in the side of the company. They were often able to offer better deals for slaves or other merchandise, and the black chiefs were not the least bit hesitant about breaking their agreements with the company when an interloper's proposition seemed more attractive.

Starting around the year 1719, the white traders on the Guinea Coast began to encounter still another serious problem: pirates.

Although freebooters had occasionally been reported off the Guinea Coast since the early days of the trade there, it was only after Woodes Rogers shut down the pirates' nest of Nassau that sea raiders in any significant numbers began to operate off the coast. But when the outlaws discovered how vulnerable the trading posts of the region actually were, their ranks swelled dramatically until they became, for the first time, a genuine menace to commerce.

Although pirates preyed on all types of merchant vessels, they particularly sought to seize slavers. As a general rule, pirates who captured a slave ship permitted her owner or her captain to ransom the vessel and cargo for a reasonable sum, usually £1,000. So valuable were the human cargoes of slave ships that most owners paid the ransom without much protest, regarding such payments as just another hazard of the trade.

It is a peculiar fact that although personal freedom was a fundamental value in pirate life, and pirates usually welcomed escaped
slaves into their crews, they exhibited little sympathy for the
wretched human cargo carried in the holds of the slave ships they
captured. It is possible that to the pirates, the terrified captive
blacks, jammed belowdecks, naked and primitive-appearing, and
jabbering in an "uncivilized" tongue, seemed not quite human. In
any case, they differed greatly from the English-speaking blacks
in pirate crews—almost always savvy and violent men who had
escaped from their masters to be free, who would fight madly to
maintain their liberty.

Even though, as products of their time, pirates had little sympathy for the human cargoes of the slave-ships they captured,
very few actually engaged in the slave trade themselves, preferring to sell captured ships back to their masters rather than attempting to dispose of their contents. But when pirates took a
merchant vessel other than a slaver, they *would* plunder her
cargo—and then seek out a free-lance merchant or an interloper
along the seaboard to sell their stolen goods for the best price
they could get.

Defoe—in one of his colorful passages—depicts how the outlaw
merchants who traded with pirates lived and operated on the
coast. He describes a secret trading settlement hidden deep in
the delta of the Sierra Leone River where approximately thirty
"English-speaking men," most of them ex-privateers and ex-pirates, conducted their illegal business in defiance of the Royal
African Company. Characterizing these dealers in contraband as
men who "still retain and love the Riots, and Humours" common
to the pirate's life, Defoe goes on to say that these English free-
lance traders had become very friendly with the natives, many of
whom had become their servants.

"The [native] Men are faithful, and the Women so obedient,"
Defoe reports, "that they are very ready to prostitute themselves
to whomsoever their Masters shall command them." Noting that
the Royal African Company fort in the region is too far away to
threaten the free-lance trading settlement, Defoe continues:
"Here lives at this Place an old Fellow, who goes by the Name of
Crackers (his true Name he thinks fit to conceal,) who was formerly a noted Buccanneer, and [who] had robb'd and murdered
many a Man; he keeps the best House in the Place, has two or

three Guns before his Door, with which he Salutes his Friends, the Pyrates, when they put in, and lives a jovial Life with them, all the while they are there.

"Here follows a List, of the rest of those lawless Merchants, and their Servants, who carry on a private Trade with the Interlopers, to the great Prejudice of the Royal African Company. . . ."

Defoe then gives the names of all thirty of the traders who made their headquarters in the swampy delta. He concludes his description of the settlement by pointing out that in addition to the pirates, "honest" merchant vessels also called at the settlement to exchange cargoes of beer, cider, and strong liquor for slaves and ivory—commodities the honest merchants would have had to purchase at much higher prices from the Royal African Company.

By selling their plunder to traders like old Crackers, and by utilizing such concealed bases to refit, rest, and hide out from the authorities, a considerable number of pirates began to find prosperity on the Guinea Coast starting around 1719. One of these was a devil-may-care Welshman named Howell Davis, whose daring exploits made him famous from Senegal to Angola.

Davis, a handsome, cocky man with dark hair, blue eyes, a ready smile, and a charming manner, seems to have become a pirate more by force of circumstance than by design—and to have pursued piracy more as a glorious game than as a grim vocation.

Davis's story begins in 1718 when he was serving as the mate of the ill-starred Bristol merchantman—the *Cadagon*—captured by Captain Edward England in the Gulf of Guinea.

During the looting of the *Cadagon*, Davis apparently charmed his pirate captors with his light-hearted manner, for England offered to take the smiling Welshman as mate aboard his own ship *Fancy*. Davis demurred. Whereupon England promptly made him a present of the captured *Cadagon* and sailed away.

The crew of the *Cadagon*, however, refused to recognize the validity of England's gift to the mate. Instead, they clapped Davis into irons and continued on course to their original destination, Barbados. Here the authorities wondered whether the affable Davis had been in league with the notorious Captain England to take the *Cadagon*. To check out this possibility, they put Davis in prison, releasing him after three months when it was decided no overt act of piracy could be proved against him.

But despite the fact that Davis had not been convicted—or even charged with—any act of piracy, the incident of the *Cadagon* hung around his neck like an albatross. Honest masters were loath to sign on a man who was so friendly with his pirate captors that they ended up *giving* him their prize. They were also deeply, if unfairly, suspicious of Davis's possible role in the vengeance slaying of the *Cadagon*'s captain.

Unable to obtain a berth in honest service, Davis now drifted from Barbados to the Bahamas, fetching up at Nassau, apparently in the desperate belief that he might find a pirate berth there.

However, the feisty Woodes Rogers had already arrived and was in the process of cleaning up the port. Pirate vessels still engaged in the sweet trade had already departed for waters where the hunting was better.

But in Nassau, Davis found his past record was near immaculate when compared with those of other seafarers in the port. Consequently, the master of the sloop *Buck*, which sailed in company with another sloop called *Mumvil Trader*, was glad to sign Davis aboard his vessel as an ordinary seaman.

For several weeks Davis worked diligently as a member of the crew of the *Buck*. He was a model sailor on the outside. But in his heart Davis had become a pirate. He had decided that since he would always be suspected of piracy because of the *Cadagon* incident, he might as well become a pirate in fact.

Accordingly, while the *Buck* and the *Mumvil Trader* were anchored at Martinique one night, Davis and a handful of accomplices whom he had talked into joining him seized the *Buck* before her surprised master knew what was afoot. Then, moving swiftly in the darkness, Davis and his men surprised the *Mumvil Trader*, transferring most of her cargo to the *Buck*. Davis put aboard the *Mumvil Trader* any men from the two crews who did not wish to go pirating with him. He then sailed away northward with the *Buck* and made a clean getaway. It was Davis's first act of piracy and it had gone off without a hitch, greatly enhancing his confidence in his piratical abilities.

On the day after his capture of the *Buck*, Davis called a council of war at which he was unanimously elected captain. "As soon as he was possessed of his Command," Defoe says, "he drew up Articles, which were signed and sworn to by himself and the rest, then he made a short speech, the substance of which was a Declaration of War against the Whole World."

Now, with his little vessel hardly larger than a fishing boat, and his crew of thirty, Davis set sail for the waters around Hispaniola and Cuba. Here he took a couple of French prizes, transferring their stores and equipment to the *Buck*.

It was now late in 1718. Blackbeard had been killed. Woodes Rogers was clearly in command in Nassau. The Caribbean was becoming a bad place for pirates. Davis had no trouble persuading his men that their future lay to the east, on the Guinea Coast.

The *Buck* arrived at the Portuguese-held island of São Nicolau, in the Cape Verdes off the coast of Africa, early in 1719. Flying the English flag, the smiling, clever Davis now posed as a merchant who had come to the island to trade. The Portuguese of São Nicolau were happy to exchange their wine and other local products for the goods Davis had aboard the *Buck*—which was, in fact, loot from his French prizes. Davis's easygoing manner earned him an invitation to the home of the island's Portuguese governor, where Davis was treated with almost royal hospitality.

After conducting business at São Nicolau for five weeks, Davis and his men sailed away to the island of Maio, also in the Cape Verde group.

Here Davis made no attempt to disguise his piratical intentions. Finding a number of vessels anchored in the harbor, he boarded and plundered each of them without encountering serious opposition. He then seized one of these ships for his own use. Renaming the chosen vessel *King James*, he mounted twenty cannon in her and transferred his crew and his plunder to her, abandoning his little sloop *Buck*.

Then, after recruiting additional men from the ships he had just plundered, Davis and his crew—now expanded to seventy men—set sail in their formidable new vessel for the nearby island of São Tiago where Davis intended to obtain a supply of fresh water.

As he entered the harbor and anchored, he was again posing as an inoffensive merchant. But when Davis went ashore to introduce himself to the island's governor, that gentleman made no secret of his suspicion that the smiling Welshman was something other than he seemed. Davis, pretending to be affronted by the governor's doubts about his honesty, went back to his ship with a great show of indignation.

Late that night, when the island was dark and silent, Davis and his men stealthily rowed ashore. They crept to within a few yards of the well-armed fort. Then, upon Davis's signal, they stormed the walls. But the fort was empty. Davis realized at once that the distrustful governor, anticipating Davis's nocturnal attack, had probably withdrawn the fort's garrison to his own stout house situated on a nearby hill. From this vantage point the soldiers of the garrison, no doubt well barricaded, would be able to lay down a murderous fire on any attackers.

Nevertheless, Davis led his seventy men in an attempt to storm the governor's house—and as he had expected, he and his men were met with a wicked barrage of muskets and pistols that killed three of Davis's men.

The clever pirate knew when he was beaten. He called off the attack but only after he had managed to toss several grenades into the governor's house, causing a number of casualties and a considerable amount of damage to the governor's furnishings. Davis and his men then looted the fort of whatever they could find. When dawn came, Davis spiked the island's guns and sailed off to visit the Guinea Coast.

Davis, whose knowledge of the region was considerable as a result of his years of honest service in the merchant trade, set the *King James* on a course for Gambia, where the Royal African Company maintained one of its strongest and richest trading posts.

All things considered, Davis had concluded that stratagem would be more effective than force in obtaining what he wanted from the Royal African Company fort. By now he and his men had their merchant-vessel act down pat. Accordingly, when *King James* approached the roadstead under the guns of the Gambia fort, the proper English ensigns were fluttering from her masts and only a few crewmen—the number that would be employed aboard an honest vessel—were visible on deck. The rest were hidden below. Captain Davis, his mate, and the ship's doctor, however, were all out on deck in full view of those who might be watching from the shore. Moreover, they wore the clothing of gentlemen—as the master and officers of any honest merchant vessel would, preparatory to going ashore at a Royal African Company installation.

After anchoring, Davis and his two officers were immediately rowed to the beach by a crew of hearty, honest-looking seafarers.

Ashore, Davis, smiling and confident, requested an audience with the governor. Taken before that gentleman, Davis told a plausible story. He was, he said, a merchant and he had been bound from Liverpool to the Senegal River to trade iron and other metal plate for ivory and gum. But a pair of French warships had chased him illegally, apparently to seize his cargo. He had barely outrun the Frenchmen. He had put in to Gambia, Davis said, his handsome face clouded with honest indignation, because it was the nearest English refuge. He went on to tell the sympathetic governor that now that he and his associates had learned they were not welcome in Senegal, he would be happy to trade his metals here in Gambia for a cargo of slaves—if the governor could provide them. The governor readily agreed and inquired if Davis might have any European liquor available. Smiling, Davis assured the governor that although his supply was short, he would certainly spare him a few bottles. At this the governor invited Davis and his two colleagues to stay ashore and have dinner with him and his staff. Davis agreed. First, however, he had to return to *King James* to make sure that she was properly anchored. But he would return shortly—and he would be certain to bring with him the governor's liquor. During his long pleasant talk with the governor, the clever Davis had been carefully noting the positions of the sentries, the number of guards, the locations of guns and arms in the fort, and had concluded that with daring and the right plan, the fort could be taken.

Returning to *King James*, Davis explained the plan he had devised while conversing with the governor. First, he and his officers would return to the fort with a dozen picked men who would each have concealed under his clothing two pairs of pistols. While Davis and his two officers were dining with the governor, these twelve men would casually fall into conversation with the soldiers on duty in the fort's guardroom. When they heard Davis's signal—a pistol fired from the governor's window—they were to draw their pistols, capture the soldiers in the guardroom, and open the gates of the fort. Meanwhile, the rest of the crew, fully armed and waiting aboard *King James*, were upon Davis's signal to come rapidly ashore in the ship's boats and storm into the fort. If all went well, it would all be over in a half hour.

As an extra precaution, Davis now seized the only other ship lying near *King James* in the anchorage: a small sloop. Acting in

near silence, he and his men not only captured the sloop but also took her officers and crew on board the *King James*, securing them below in order to keep them from sounding any warning to the fort.

Now, with all his plans laid, Davis returned to the fort bearing his gifts of liquor. While waiting for dinner to be served, Davis and the governor shared a bowl of punch and some light conversation.

Suddenly Davis, still pleasant and civil in his demeanor, drew a cocked pistol from under his waistcoat and leveled it at his astonished host. Without raising his voice, Davis politely informed the governor that he was the prisoner of the pirate Captain Howell Davis. It is easy to imagine the incredulous governor with a glass of punch at his lips, staring over the glass at the pistol in Davis's hand. Perhaps the governor is dumb with surprise. Perhaps he is not quite certain what he has just heard from the lips of this charming Welsh merchant. Is it a joke, perhaps? But when both the doctor and Davis's first officer also drew pistols and aimed them, any doubts about the situation must have swiftly evaporated.

With the governor now his captive, Davis—according to plan—ran to the window and fired his pistol. At this, his men lounging in the guardroom sprang into action. They surrounded the on-duty soldiers with their pistols cocked and ready. Disarming the soldiers and locking them in the guardroom, Davis's men seized the cannons of the fort and opened the gates to the reinforcements from the *King James.*

In a few minutes Howell Davis and his men had taken possession of one of the major forts belonging to the Royal African Company—and they had accomplished this feat without firing a shot, except for Davis's signal.

On the following day, while the men of the *King James* transferred plunder from the fort to their ship, they amused themselves by firing salutes to each other from the fort and their vessel. Although the loot from the fort was not as great as expected because most of the year's receipts for the Gambia operation had recently been shipped home, the booty was nevertheless ample. It included some £2,000 in gold as well as large quantities of trade goods.

Departing from Gambia, Davis sailed southward. He had not gone far when he encountered two other pirate ships. The masters of these ships, admiring Davis's methods, joined with him under his command. The three pirates then attacked the company fort at Sierra Leone, and were completely successful.

After the Sierra Leone victory, Davis and his consorts rested and repaired their ships for almost two months. Eventually, with Davis as commodore, the pirate squadron got under way again, continuing south along the coast, plundering whatever vessels came their way.

Now Davis, sensing that the rough tactics of his companions were unsuitable to his own style, parted company with the other two ships. He sailed on alone into the Gulf of Guinea. Here he encountered a large merchant flying the Dutch flag. Although the merchant carried thirty guns—ten more than *King James*—Davis attacked, believing that her Dutch crew would surrender rather than fight. He soon discovered his mistake.

The Dutch ship, a swift sailer, fought fiercely. She fired one broadside that killed nine of Davis's men. It was an epic fight that went on for thirty-two hours—from 1:00 P.M. on the first day to 9:00 A.M. on the second. In the end it was the Dutch vessel that surrendered. Davis, whose own ship had been damaged in the fighting—and had started to leak in any case—decided to take possession of the Dutch vessel. He transferred his flag, much of his crew, and all the company's loot to her. He then mounted guns from the *King James* in her—in addition to her own cannon. When he was done, Davis had transformed the Dutch merchant into a formidable brigand bearing thirty-two cannon and twenty-seven swivel guns. He renamed her the *Royal Rover*. Then, with the now-diminished *King James* as consort, he continued his voyage along the coast.

At the trading station of Anamobu he captured three English slave ships, one of which he presented to the Dutch captain from whom he had just taken his new *Royal Rover*. The other two slavers he kept with him, probably intending to ransom them back to their masters at the first opportunity.

On the very next day Davis captured another Dutch vessel. This one surrendered after a chase—and after he had emptied one broadside into her. Aboard this Dutch merchant, besides valuable cargo, Davis found £15,000 in sterling—making her the richest prize he had taken to date.

Full of high spirits, Davis now released the two slave ships to their masters, but only after he had recruited another thirty-five hands from their crews. He also released his latest Dutch prize after stowing all her valuable cargo aboard *Royal Rover*.

Finally, he decided that the *King James* was now too unseaworthy to continue. Accordingly he brought her crew aboard the *Rover* and abandoned *King James*.

Now Davis, with a powerful, swift-sailing ship served by a crew that was as tough, numerous, and bold as any on the Guinea Coast, continued his southward voyage, fetching up at the Portuguese island of Principe, located approximately 150 miles off the coast of what is now Gabon.

This time Davis employed a variation of his merchant act.

Flying Royal Navy ensigns and donning an appropriate uniform, Davis told the Portuguese officials who came out to the roadstead to greet him that his ship was an English man-of-war in pursuit of pirates who had lately been active in the area. As usual, his open demeanor and his sheer brazenness convinced the Portuguese that he was what he claimed to be. The island's fort fired a salute in honor of its English visitor. Davis had the *Rover* return the salute.

Davis and his officers were invited ashore where they were received by a military escort and taken to the house of the governor, who treated them with all the courtesy and hospitality due the Royal Navy. During his visit to the governor's home, Davis— as usual—spent much of his time surreptitiously reconnoitering the defenses of the fort.

Back aboard the *Royal Rover*, Davis was busy planning his coup against the fort when a fat French merchant ship came into the harbor. True to his piratical calling, Davis could not resist this opportunity. He and his men—notwithstanding their pose as English sailors—immediately boarded the Frenchman and plundered her cargo. This unexpected and brutal action planted some considerable doubt in the Portuguese governor's mind about the true identity of Captain Howell Davis. But Davis, with sublime self-confidence, buttressed by the invincible charm of a natural mountebank, airily explained that he had boarded the Frenchman because she had been trading with pirates—and it was his duty to punish her officers and crew for this illegality. He had, therefore, confiscated her illegal cargo. It was this act of confiscation, Davis said, that the governor must have misinterpreted as looting. The governor commended Davis for his zeal.

But his doubts must have remained unassuaged, for the governor did not invite Davis and his officers to dine—as Davis had expected. Such an invitation was essential if Davis was to seize the governor and sack the island.

Davis was undaunted, however. If the governor would not invite *him* to dinner, he would arrange a banquet on board the *Royal Rover* for the governor and his chief officials. During the festivities they would be seized and held hostage—and forced to have the fort opened to Davis and his men. Accordingly, Davis dispatched his invitation—and was gratified when the governor and his staff accepted.

Unknown to Davis, however, the governor was now on to him. An officer aboard the plundered French ship had somehow discovered both Davis's true identity and his plan. Contriving to get ashore, the Frenchman had told his tale to the governor.

That worthy man was not entirely devoid of Davis's kind of brass. Thus, when Davis suggested that as a mark of honor he would personally escort the governor to the shipboard banquet, the governor expressed his delight and agreed.

On the night of the festivities, therefore, the unsuspecting Davis went happily to pick up his guests in the ship's boat. Perhaps Davis intended to spring his trap even before he got the governor well aboard the *Royal Rover*. Instead it was Davis who was trapped. The governor greeted him affably and invited Davis and his men to come ashore for a drink before they all returned to the *Rover*. Davis agreed. But no sooner had his party landed than soldiers hidden in the underbrush near the shore opened up with a deadly fusillade of musket fire.

Although mortally wounded in the stomach by the first blast, Davis nevertheless drew his pistols and fought back furiously. He managed to kill at least two of his assailants before he himself fell dead on the beach, his smoking pistols still in his hands.

Only one member of Davis's landing party escaped the ambush. Leaping into the water of the harbor, he swam back to the *Royal Rover*, where he blurted out the news that their daring commander had been treacherously shot down.

Immediately, *Royal Rover* weighed anchor and made for the safety of the open sea.

Having outrun any pursuit, Davis's men held a council to decide how they should proceed now that the cunning Davis was dead.

It happened that there was aboard the *Royal Rover* another Welshman, a tall, dark-eyed, unsmiling man who had been serving as third mate aboard one of the slave ships Howell Davis had captured at the trading station of Anamabu.

Some of Davis's crew now remembered that there had been something about this man that their fallen leader had liked. Perhaps it was merely the fact that the mate was a Welshman like

Davis himself. Or perhaps Davis had sensed in this dour thirty-seven-year-old officer some quality that might prove useful to the company. In any event, Davis—who had never before forced a man to join him—had taken his fellow Welshman aboard the *Royal Rover* at the point of a pistol.

The grim mate from the slaver had, however, kept himself aloof from the crew, letting it be known that he had no intention of turning pirate. Yet somehow his personality had registered profoundly on the men of the *Royal Rover*. Despite the dark-eyed mate's cool demeanor toward them, they respected him—and they recognized his quality.

Now, at the crew's council following the death of Davis, one grizzled old member of the *Rover's* complement suggested that the Welshman from the slaver, despite his glowering and his teetotaling, might make a fitting successor to the dashing, exuberant Howell Davis.

The perceptive crewman made his nomination in these words: "Should a captain be so saucy as to exceed prescription at any time, why down with him! It will be a Caution after he is dead to his successors of what fatal Consequences any sort of assuming may be. However, it is my Advice, that, while we are sober, we pitch upon a Man of Courage and skilled in Navigation, one who by his Counsel and Bravery seems best able to defend the Commonwealth and ward us from the Dangers and Tempests of an instable Element, and the fatal Consequence of Anarchy; and such a one I take Roberts to be. A Fellow, I think, in all Respects worthy of your Esteem and Favor."

The rest of the crew, with only one dissenting vote, hailed the somber mate as their new captain.

And he, suddenly moved by some ferocious want that caused him to turn his back on all he believed in, accepted.

So began the piratical career of Bartholomew Roberts, the most formidable—and strangest—of all the captains who ever flew the black flag.

18

The Black Captain

He had about him a brooding, Celtic look: black hair, eyes like night, a swarthy face, bleak and clean-shaven.

Defoe calls his aspect "black"—and says he derived his pirate name from this somber quality. "Black Bart," his crew—and soon the world—called him.

As his meteoric and doom-driven career exploded across the vast oceans he traveled, it became clear, both to those who loved him and to those who hated him, that the blackness about him was more than physical. There was darkness in his soul as well, a black roaring emptiness in his center where Hope had once lived. He believed in God and the Devil—and therefore in Sin and in Hell. He seemed to know that he had committed sins beyond forgiveness—and that therefore the Fire must be his destiny. It seemed that it was this knowledge—that he had forfeited Heaven—that had created the void in his soul, the Despair that seemed to be an emptiness seeking to fill itself with pain and punishment. As much as the world condemned him, he condemned himself more.

It was as if Roberts knew that only in Hell could he finally fill the void that howled within him—and that to find Hell, he must rush madly through his days, seeking over every horizon for the doom he awaited.

Yet it appeared that if he could not forgive himself, he could not forgive the unjust world either—and so he punished it with all the wild energy he could muster.

To many who sailed with him during the incandescent months of his career, Roberts seemed touched with some strange and splendid madness that transformed him into a Demonic Prince who rode the wind seeking vengeance and his own destruction.

Described as tall and slim, he is depicted in one contemporary illustration as a dandy. In the drawing he is dressed in a crimson damask waistcoat, breeches, and a broad hat festooned with a red ostrich feather. He wears a diamond-studded cross on a thick gold chain around his neck. Two pairs of pistols are jammed into a silk sash draped over his shoulder. He stands with one sturdy leg forward, a naked sword in his right hand, as if challenging the world to combat.

Even this peacock dandyism—which he adopted only after his pirate career began—seems to have been basically an expression of the demonic self he had loosed when he became Black Bart, captain of the *Royal Rover*.

It was as though, by wearing their finery, Roberts was proclaiming his scorn for the powerful of the world who had made the rules of the game—rules that, as Black Bart, he defied with unquenchable fury and undeniable success. Dressed in his gaudy apparel, he declared his equality with, and freedom from, the "gentlefolk" who wanted Black Bart dead—and in so doing he also soothed the wounds Bartholomew Roberts had carried with him all his life because he had been born poor and thus, for all his intelligence, rendered forever inferior. Decked out in his stolen raiment, Black Bart was the avenger of Bartholomew Roberts.

This strangest and deadliest of all pirate captains was born in Pembroke, Wales, in 1682, the son of indigent but "respectable" parents who gave him a strict religious upbringing.

No drinking or dancing or swearing was allowed in his parents' home. The Sabbath was always stringently observed with prayer and church services in which hellfire, iniquity, and salvation were prominent themes.

From boyhood, Bartholomew Roberts absorbed the austere piety of his parents into his very bones. Their conception of righteousness stayed with him all his days. Even when he began to follow the sea, he remained faithful to his upbringing. From time immemorial it had been the practice of seamen to get drunk, to curse each other and God, and to laugh at preachers. But Roberts was a teetotaler who read the Bible, did not swear, and kept holy the Sabbath day by prayer and by refraining from labor.

Like many of the sons of the genteel poor of Wales, he had gone to sea as a lad, serving first as a cabin boy on a merchant vessel. "Smart and lively," he learned navigation and shiphandling and rose quickly from the ranks of ordinary seamen to become a mate. After service in the War of the Spanish Succession, he signed on as a mate aboard a sloop trading out of Barbados.

By the time he was in his mid-thirties, Roberts had earned a well-deserved reputation as a master mariner. Yet despite his proven ability, he was still only a ship's officer, with little prospect of achieving a command of his own—a goal that virtually all ship's officers of the day yearned after.

In that era, to become a ship's master was also to become firmly established as a member of the middle class. A ship's captain, unlike other officers aboard a merchant vessel, was not a mere servant of the owner but his trusted agent. The captain was responsible not only for navigating the ship but also for maintaining the business interests of the ship's owner while the vessel was far removed from the owner's control. The captain was a trusted man, a man of honor whose word was considered as good as a gentleman's. A ship's captain could bind the ship's owners for debt, make decisions in their stead regarding cargoes and prices, and had the power to represent the owners before any tribunal— in any port in the world.

Usually a ship's master was also a part owner of his vessel and its cargo. Most owners gave—or sold—their captains a substantial share of a ship in order to ensure the captain's concern for preserving both the ship and its profitability. Many ship's masters earned fortunes by their voyages. Many also became valued business and social associates of the wealthy and powerful.

Bartholomew Roberts, with his outstanding professional capacity, nurtured a fierce ambition to become captain of his own ship.

After more than twenty years' service as a second-in-command, he longed not only for the money and status that a captaincy would confer upon him but also for the freedom it would bring him. As captain of his own ship, he would no longer have to endure incompetence, no longer have to defer to lesser men. He would no longer have to bow and bob before men who possessed far less wit and quality than he. He would gain the recognition he deserved. He would at last be free to become what he knew he was meant to be: one of the elite.

Yet in that age, ability and desire were never sufficient by themselves to secure command of a ship. A mate might win the respect of the captains he served under and earn a great reputation among his peers. But it was not the respect and goodwill of peers that counted, but rather the good opinion of the merchant princes who owned ships—and who backed, with their fortunes, what were often perilous wagers against the sea.

For such men, gambling fortunes on each voyage, a man like Bartholomew Roberts, for all his skill and seamanship, seemed somehow *risky*. Roberts made such men uneasy with his restless energy and his moodiness, and especially with his scarcely disguised contempt for more cautious, steadier men. He seemed to most shipowners who came in contact with him not merely imprudent—which was bad enough—but unstable, even a little *dangerous*, a man who might do almost anything if the moon or tides were wrong. Most shipowners thought that such a man might serve very well as a chief mate, but only a fool would ever entrust a ship and its cargo to such a restive spirit. The shipping business was gamble enough, most merchants felt, without lengthening the odds by employing a Bartholomew Roberts as captain.

Roberts himself, it appears, began to realize as the years passed that he was unlikely ever to attain his dream of command. Judging by words later attributed to him, he seems to have ascribed the failure of his hopes to an inability to flatter and utter soft words to influential men—an inability to act the gentleman.

Yet in spite of his frustration, Roberts continued to follow the sea, the only mistress he ever seems to have had, taking whatever berth offered, holding on to his faith, and awaiting fortune's turn. So it was that on a hot day in June 1719, Roberts was serving as mate aboard the slave ship *Princess*, anchored at the Guinea Coast trading station of Anamabu, when fate, in the person of the daring Captain Howell Davis of the pirate vessel *Royal Rover*, plucked him from one world and dropped him into another.

Although taken aboard the *Royal Rover* at the point of a pistol, Roberts was not treated as a captive by Davis and his crew. Instead, Captain Davis, much impressed with Roberts's navigational skills and experience, tried hard to induce his fellow Welshman to join in his enterprise. But Roberts refused. He took no part in the life of the ship—and he made no effort to hide his contempt for the drunkenness and the lack of discipline aboard her. For Roberts, the free and democratic life as a member of a pirate crew exerted little attraction.

Then the charismatic Howell Davis was killed. The crew of the *Royal Rover*, guided by some extraordinary instinct, offered Roberts the command of their ship.

Suddenly the dream he had pursued all his life was within his grasp. Never mind that the ship was a floating anarchy of outlaws; it was a command. He could have his heart's desire. But he knew it would cost him his soul, his salvation. It was the temptation of Lucifer that confronted him: Was it better to rule in Hell than to serve in Heaven? Like Lucifer, Roberts chose to rule. And like Lucifer, he knew himself damned.

He himself later explained his decision in laconic words: "It is better to be a commander, than a common man, since I have dipped my hands in muddy water and must be a pirate."

He was—at last—a captain, and he knew his job. With characteristic energy, he moved immediately to impose some sense of discipline on the unruly crew of the *Royal Rover*—and to create an aura of authority about himself, which he deemed necessary for the good of his ship.

He drew up new articles for the crew. Generally his aim was to regularize duties and eliminate the worst of the disorder. He made every man swear to obey his rules. (He knew better than to forbid drink to his crew, but he did manage to impose new rules that did much to curb the most atrocious of the alcoholic excesses.)

It was also in these early days of his captaincy that Roberts began the practice of decking himself in the gentlemanly finery that soon became his trademark.

To validate his authority, Roberts challenged any man of his crew who resented his regulations and his insistence on discipline to fight him with sword or pistol, making it clear, according to Defoe, that "he neither valued or feared any of them."

He soon made his men understand that as captain he expected to be obeyed and that he would not suffer fools gladly. If a man was inept, or merely slow to carry out orders, Roberts would fly into a fit of fury that usually cowed anyone within reach. Although these rages eventually became part of his legend among his crewmen, they were, in the beginning of his captaincy, the occasion for several deadly confrontations that almost cost Roberts both his command and his life.

In one such incident, a crewman who had been drinking heavily offended Roberts with some abusive epithet. Roberts exploded at the insult. He pulled a pistol and shot the sailor to death where he stood. The dead man's friends were infuriated. But they also feared their captain—and did nothing. But another friend of the dead man, who had been ashore at the time of the killing, was less reticent when he learned of the captain's action. This sailor, Thomas Jones by name, cursed Roberts roundly and loudly and shouted out that Roberts himself ought to be put to death. Again Roberts flew into a rage. Drawing his captain's sword, he plunged it into Jones's body, wounding him severely but not mortally. Although bleeding profusely, Jones grabbed Roberts, threw him over a cannon, and beat him up "handsomely," as Defoe puts it.

When Roberts and his assailant were pried apart, a tumultuous argument ensued, with some of the crew believing Jones was justified in attacking the captain, and others backing Roberts.

In the end, according to pirate custom, the matter was put to a vote. Roberts won. Jones, it was decided, had had no right to curse the captain in spite of the provocation of his friend's death—and no right whatsoever to do violence to the captain of their ship. Jones was sentenced to receive two lashes from every member of the crew, as soon as he recovered from the wound that Roberts had given him. (Jones survived his punishment, and jumped ship with a handful of cronies soon thereafter.)

If Roberts's monumental rages, his fearlessness, and his seafaring skills soon won him the edgy respect of his men, his boldness in battle elicited their awe.

Within a week after taking command of the *Royal Rover*, Roberts—already Black Bart to his crew—undertook a madly valiant act of vengeance. He sailed back to the island of Principe, where

Howell Davis had been killed. He sailed the *Rover* right into the harbor, under the guns of the fort. Then, taking a force of armed men with him, Roberts went ashore and marched directly up a steep hill toward the fort. At this the flustered Portuguese, who had so far held their fire, unleashed a volley from their muskets at Roberts and his men. But the contemptuous Roberts and his determined pack of cutthroats kept on coming. The terrified Portuguese soldiers then fled their posts, abandoning guns and supplies in their haste to get away.

Roberts coolly entered the fort. He ordered his men to spike the cannon and to throw them over the parapet into the sea, rendering the fort useless. Roberts then led his men back to their ship, taking with them anything that seemed of value. Shortly thereafter the *Rover* departed as swiftly as she had arrived. Roberts had his crew fire a few cannon shots into the town for good measure.

Having avenged Davis, Roberts set sail southward along the Guinea Coast. Here he took a Dutch merchant ship and a slaver belonging to the Royal African Company.

After these initial successes, and after a number of authority-establishing confrontations with his crew, Roberts felt sufficiently at ease in his new role as Black Bart to launch what many would regard as his personal war against the world.

He began this whirlwind campaign with a stunning exploit of seamanship. He sailed the *Royal Rover* from the Guinea Coast of Africa westward across the Atlantic to the vast and wealthy Portuguese-held territory of Brazil—a voyage of 2,300 miles, accomplished in the incredible time of twenty-eight days. Moreover, he brought *Royal Rover* precisely to the destination he had chosen: the uninhabited island of Fernando de Noronha. Here he took on water, cleaned and repaired the *Rover*'s hull, and prepared to seek out Portuguese prizes in Brazilian waters.

In September 1719, after cruising for a number of weeks off the coast of Brazil without locating a prize, Roberts encountered a fleet of forty-two Portuguese merchant vessels off the port of Bahia. The merchants, most of them carrying cargoes of gold, sugar, tobacco, wood, guns, and hides, were in the midst of forming a convoy for the long voyage across the Atlantic to Lisbon. Anchored nearby were two Portuguese warships slated to act as escorts to the convoy.

Roberts never hesitated. With flags flying and all sail unfurled, the *Royal Rover* waded right into the merchant convoy and bore down on the largest of the cargo vessels. While the other Portuguese merchants fired their cannon and tried to signal to the two warships, Roberts brought the *Royal Rover* alongside her prey. Coolly ignoring the booming cannon of the other ships, Roberts's men swung aboard their victim. They quickly overcame the token resistance put up by the captured vessel's officers and crew. The men of the *Royal Rover* plundered the merchant with professional thoroughness and speed, transferring most of her cargo to their own ship. The loot included gold coins worth approximately £50,000.

Casting off from the plundered Portuguese vessel, Roberts made swiftly for the open sea. It was all over before the Portuguese warships could even weigh anchor to come to the aid of the convoy.

Now, still skirting the coast of Brazil, Roberts headed northward, putting in at Devil's Island off the coast of Guiana. Then a backwater Spanish possession—it did not become a French penal colony until 1852—Devil's Island was a place where gentlemen of fortune could buy anything from rum to women, and where they could solace their cares undisturbed by Authority so long as their money lasted. Here Roberts and his crew spent several weeks in a prolonged bout of gambling, drinking, and fornication with captive and paid women.

Following this interval at Devil's Island, Roberts sailed boldly into the Caribbean, although he knew that the Royal Navy, to say nothing of French and Spanish warships, had recently been active in the area. He also knew—as all pirates did—that thanks to Woodes Rogers, pirates no longer had available to them their old sanctuaries in the Bahamas. But Roberts seemed indifferent to the dangers in these sunny waters. Making no effort to disguise the *Royal Rover*, he sailed insolently across the well-traveled sea-lanes of the Caribbean, hewing to a northward-tending course, as if challenging any warships on patrol to catch him if they could.

To his crew—amazed at his defiant brass and dash—Roberts seemed touched with some special magic. He could take them anywhere. They began to think of Black Bart as "pistol proof." Even Roberts's rancor toward the civilized world began to rub off on his men. They took to calling themselves "The House of Lords," addressing each other as "Your Lordship."[1]

But for all its boldness, Roberts's foray into the Caribbean proved uneventful. The *Royal Rover* took only a few prizes in the course of her transit of the island-marked sea. The pirates had to fight no battles and they encountered no warships.

Continuing their northward course from the Caribbean, Roberts and the House of Lords worked their way in slow progression along the Atlantic Coast. Here, too, only a few small prizes came their way.

In June 1720, Roberts and the *Royal Rover* hove to outside the port of Trepassey in Newfoundland. It was almost exactly a year since Roberts had been taken, unwillingly, aboard the *Royal Rover*. Now, as a pirate captain whose brazen courage had made him known from Brazil to Africa to the American coast, he and the House of Lords were about to carry off one of the most audacious raids in pirate annals.

In the harbor of Trepassey lay 22 merchant ships that were preparing to cross the Atlantic. Many of them were armed with cannon. Their crews numbered well over twelve hundred men. Also in the harbor were some 125 to 150 fishing boats, part of the great fleet that fished the prolific Atlantic waters off Newfoundland and the banks to the south.

Roberts, outgunned and far outnumbered, plunged into the harbor with an almost manic recklessness. As a Boston newspaper later put it, the *Royal Rover* came charging into the harbor with "drums beating, trumpets sounding, English colors flying, and the pirate flag at the topmast with death's head and cutlass."

This sudden appearance of the *Rover* with her grim flags flying and her deadly cannon visible in gunports—in contrast to the gay music being played by her band—must have seemed to many who saw it a work of the Devil. Panic spread aboard the anchored ships. Instead of defending themselves, their crews fled to the safety of the shore.

Roberts and the House of Lords now began systematically to loot the anchored vessels as well as another four ships that blundered unknowingly into the harbor during the operation. Working methodically and at their ease, Roberts's men stripped whatever was valuable, and salable, from the captive ships. Just to show that he meant business, Roberts sank a number of the fishing boats that were in the harbor.

It was at Trepassey that Roberts also decided the time had come to change flagships. The *Royal Rover* was beginning to show her age, becoming leaky and encrusted with marine growth. Roberts chose one of the prizes he had taken in the harbor, a Bristol galley, as his new flagship—and rechristened her *Royal Fortune*.

After completing the plundering of the Trepassey fleet, Roberts, in his new *Royal Fortune*, sailed out of the harbor as brazenly as he had entered it. The governor of New England, reporting later to London on the Trepassey raid, said of Roberts: "One cannot withhold admiration for his bravery and daring."

Now Roberts cruised off the Newfoundland banks, taking six more ships, all of them flying the French flag. One of these vessels attracted his eye. He thought she would make an even better flagship than the one he had already captured. Again he transferred his flag. He called his new flagship, too, *Royal Fortune*. She was a sleek, swift sailer—and with twenty-eight guns mounted in her, she was as formidable as she was swift.

Now, in this newest *Royal Fortune*, Roberts set off southward again.

Operating off New England, he captured a series of English ships, among them the sloop *Samuel* en route from London to Boston. In addition to its cargo, the *Samuel* carried a number of passengers whom the House of Lords robbed of all their money and valuables, threatening to kill any who held anything back. These passengers later gave eye-witness accounts to a newspaper called *The Boston News Letter*, which printed them in detail. According to the *News Letter*'s story, the pirates behaved "like a parcel of furies, breaking open every bale, and packing-case aboard the *Samuel* in their search for plunder."

In addition to stealing approximately £10,000 worth of cargo, the pirates stripped the *Samuel* of sails, guns, powder, and rope. Uttering fearful curses, they tore open every locker and searched every possible hiding place on the ship, looking for hidden gold or jewelry. They then—wantonly, according to the *News Letter*—threw everything they did not want into the sea.

Although they did not find any hidden treasure in their search of the *Samuel*, the pirates *did* find *Samuel*'s chief mate, Harry Glasby, hiding below—and they dragged him up on deck. Glasby, who was a skilled and experienced sailing master, was then taken by force aboard the *Royal Fortune*. This was a notable action because Roberts rarely impressed any captives into his crew. Roberts must have been in dire need of another sailing master to have done something so much against his usual practice.

The *News Letter* account of the assault on the *Samuel* also made it clear that the pirates—no doubt reflecting the attitude of their Black Captain—had only contempt for the forces of law and order. They swore to the captain of the *Samuel* that they would never accept pardons, "may the King and Parliament be damned with their Act of Grace." They might look for a pardon, they mocked, only when they had each gained a fortune of "seven or eight hundred pounds."

They also scoffed at the notion that they might be captured and hanged. As one member of the House of Lords put it to the captain of the *Samuel:* "If we are captured, we will set fire to the powder with a pistol, and all go merrily to Hell together."

Clearly Roberts's own demonic spirit had by now taken full control of the *Royal Fortune* and those who sailed in her.

Continuing on his southward rampage, Roberts—in September 1720—was back in the Caribbean, despite the fact that by now he was the most sought-after pirate in the world—and despite the squadrons of English, French, and Spanish warships that had made these waters extremely dangerous for sea outlaws.

Roberts, however, had no intention of remaining there long. It was actually his plan, after taking on fresh water and supplies at the little island of Désirade (Deseada) in the Lesser Antilles, to sail due east across the Atlantic to Africa where he intended to resume operations off the Guinea Coast.

Accordingly, as soon as the *Royal Fortune* was fully provisioned at Désirade, Roberts set sail for the Cape Verde Islands. But far out on the Atlantic, the *Royal Fortune* was beset by contrary winds that drove her far north of her course. Roberts tried to beat southward in the face of prevailing southerly winds, but he was unable to make any headway toward his destination. Roberts finally had to admit failure.

He now decided that since they were far out on the Atlantic and unable to make any nearby landfall that would be safe for them, there was no other choice but to return to the Caribbean and await more favorable winds to take them to Africa. It was a dangerous choice to make. It was entirely possible that Roberts and his men would exhaust their supplies of water and food before they sighted land again. But Roberts, always prepared to rush toward whatever destiny lay ahead of him, made the decision to return without a second thought. Bringing *Royal Fortune* about on a reversal of course, he began the long journey back to the Caribbean.

Riding the prevailing trade winds toward the southwest, Roberts and his men could only hope they would make landfall before the ship's meager supply of water—a mere sixty-three gallons for 124 men—ran out.

Over the following weeks, as the *Royal Fortune* crept to the southwest on an empty endless ocean, the water dwindled. Eventually each man was allowed only one mouthful every twenty-four hours. Now, under the broiling sun, men began to go mad. "Many of them drank their urine," says Defoe, "or sea water, which instead of allaying, gave them an inextinguishable thirst, that killed them." They began to die of dysentery and fever, "fluxes" and "apyrexies," according to Defoe. Finally the water was completely gone. Roberts, it seemed, had found the doom he had been seeking.

But then, as the crew sounded the seabed beneath them, the ocean became shallower each day, indicating that land could not be far off. With hope reborn, *Royal Fortune* plowed on. Then one day, as if announcing a miracle, the lookout sang out: "Land!" They had arrived at Surinam on the northern coast of South America. Roberts sent a boat ashore. Before sunset it returned with fresh water. Roberts and the House of Lords were saved.

Now, as if in vengeance for the suffering that he and his crew had just endured and escaped, Roberts—instead of trying for Africa again—went on a rampage from Barbados to Martinique— "and damn the Royal Navy." With an almost contemptuous boldness, he swept across the Caribbean, capturing prize after prize—and eluding all efforts to catch him.

Roberts was also becoming—for the first time—cruel in his treatment of his prisoners. It was said that he had hanged a captured master from a yardarm, and that he had allowed his men to use prisoners for target practice. He was, they said, like a demon—or like a man who, believing deeply in sin and punishment, nevertheless sins, and then sins ever more heinously, begging the punishment he knows must fall upon him.

During this campaign, Roberts also took chances as never before.

In one incident reminiscent of his assault on Trepassey, Roberts sailed the *Royal Fortune* defiantly into the harbor of St. Kitt's in the British Leeward Islands, ignoring the fire of the cannon from the island's fortress. Insolently flying his own specially designed Jolly Roger, Roberts returned the fort's fire while his men went about plundering the ships anchored in the harbor. He even sent a boat ashore to take some sheep from a meadow for fresh meat while the fortress guns fired impotently.[2]

During this period of almost uninterrupted onslaught in the Caribbean, Roberts attacked English and French shipping—and shore installations—with equal aggressiveness.

Not long after his impudent attack on St. Kitt's, the governor of the French Leewards reported that Roberts had "seized, burned, or sunk, 15 French and English vessels and one Dutch interloper of 42 guns." So great was the damage Roberts inflicted on French shipping around Martinique that the governor of that island appealed to the British governor of Barbados for help. (However, when the British governor of the Leeward Islands tried to order the Royal Navy man-of-war *Rose*, one of the ships that had arrived at Nassau harbor with Woodes Rogers, to chase down Roberts, the navy captain refused to obey.)

Despite the fact that he had no permanent base in the Caribbean and that he faced forces many times more powerful than his own, Roberts continued to range freely throughout the West Indies for many more months.

In the spring of 1721, however, having almost halted shipping in the Caribbean, and with the holds of his own and two captured ships bulging with loot, Roberts called together the House of Lords to decide their next move.

He pointed out that they had practically exhausted the Caribbean. He noted also that sooner or later their enemies would mount a concerted effort to hunt them down. At the same time, the American mainland to the north was more heavily defended than it ever had been before. Governor Spotswood of Virginia, for example, had recently planted batteries totaling fifty-four pieces of cannon to guard strategic places along his coast. Furthermore, although they had taken a great deal of loot over the past few months, their plunder was of no real use unless it could be turned into ready money. Since the ports of America and the Caribbean were now closed to pirate contraband, there was no point in seeking to sell their goods in those areas. But on the Guinea Coast of Africa, he pointed out, independent merchants still operated in defiance of the Royal African Company—and would pay hard cash for their plunder.

The House of Lords voted to return to Africa.

In April 1721 Roberts set sail for the Guinea Coast where his career had begun, and where—as he well knew—it might be destined to end.

19

Demon's Destiny

This time Roberts made an easy passage eastward across the Atlantic, making landfall at Senegal. Then he took *Royal Fortune* and her two consorts south to the Royal African Company trading post at Sierra Leone. Here he anchored and ordered the fort to surrender. But the Royal African Company commander, described as a peppery old veteran trader named Plunket, refused—even though his supplies of gunpowder were too depleted for him to defend himself. Roberts began to bombard the fort with broadsides from *Royal Fortune*.

Plunket may have been "peppery," but he was also, apparently, realistic. He struck his colors and the pirates came ashore. Angrily Roberts confronted Plunket and berated him for having so foolishly resisted. Plunket, an old Africa hand, responded with such a thunderstorm of oaths and curses that members of the House of Lords—all of them connoisseurs of profane language—burst into appreciative laughter and Roberts spared the old man's life. But he looted the fort, nevertheless—and burned several empty slave ships that had been waiting for consignments.

Going on farther south, Roberts put in to one of those Guinea Coast enclaves frequented by free-lance traders. Here he stayed for approximately six weeks, conducting business and careening and refitting his ships.

While Roberts and the House of Lords were taking their ease among the interloper traders, word reached them that two formidable English warships, the *Swallow* and the *Weymouth*, both bearing sixty guns, were patrolling the coast, searching for Roberts.

Roberts declared that he was not at all worried about the presence of the two heavy men-of-war. After all, he had easily eluded warships in the past.

In late August 1721, having concluded his business among the traders and having refitted his vessels, Roberts set off once more, sailing along the eastward-curving coastline, plundering trading stations as he went, even capturing the Royal African Company's frigate *Onslow*. Liking the captured frigate, he again transferred his flag to his latest prize, renaming her *Royal Fortune*.

Roberts, like a man who feared nothing, least of all the Royal Navy, plundered his way eastward until he reached the mouth of the Calabar River in what is now Nigeria. In this swampy low-lying delta region, he again careened and cleaned the ships of his little fleet.

While careened here, Roberts's men attempted to trade with the local blacks. But the people of the region had been so brutalized by slave traders that they repelled attempts to contact them. The situation quickly escalated into a series of physical confrontations between the pirates and the natives who were trying to drive them back into the sea. Eventually the skirmishing became a battle. Roberts and his men, angered by what they considered ill-treatment from the blacks, fought fiercely, inflicting numerous casualties. As a result of this savage combat the name Black Bart became part of the tribal legends of that region.

Roberts continued his voyage for another four hundred miles along the now-southward-curving coast. Then, around Christmas, he decided to go north again.

He had learned from informants that the Royal Navy warships hunting him had had orders to return to their base at Sierra

Leone by Christmastime. Clearly, if they had obeyed their orders, the two warships were no longer searching the coast. Roberts felt confident that he could head back north without encountering the men-of-war.

Nevertheless, he thought it prudent not to return along the coast he had just devastated. He chose a quicker and—as he thought—safer route, one that would guarantee evasion of the *Swallow* and the *Weymouth*. First he sailed due west into the open ocean. Then he changed course and sailed directly north to what is now the Ivory Coast. He arrived there in the New Year of 1722.

Here Roberts and his men rested for a few days, secure in the belief that the two Royal Navy ships were by now snug in their berths eight hundred miles away. But Roberts soon became restless again. He set off on another raid. Again he followed the coast to the east and to the south. This route, he thought, would widen even farther the already considerable distance between himself and the Royal Navy men-of-war.

What Roberts did not know, however, was that the two Royal Navy ships had *not* returned to their base. They were, in fact, at Cape Coast Castle in what is now Ghana—only three hundred miles to the *east*—and right in the path that Roberts was now traveling.

The *Swallow* and the *Weymouth* had had a horrendous cruise. Sickness, shortages of water, and mishaps of various kinds had plagued the two ships throughout their fruitless chase after Black Bart. Consequently, they had not been able to return to their base by Christmas as planned.

One half-comic incident during their cruise seemed to symbolize all the frustration and bad luck the two ships had encountered during their hunt for Roberts. They had put in to a large slaving station on the coast to obtain water. The local king had thereupon demanded a bribe from the masters of the two vessels. When it was explained that the ships belonged to the king of England and were not ordinary cargo vessels subject to local "duties," the angry monarch swore: "By God, *me* King here!" He had then seized some sailors from the *Weymouth*, who had come ashore to get water, and demanded ransom for them. Eventually the ransom was paid and the water obtained, but much time had as usual been squandered.

Time was not the only thing the navy ships had lost. They had also lost more than one hundred crewmen to malaria and other illnesses. As a result, Captain Chaloner Ogle, commander of the two-ship patrol, had decided that before returning to Sierra Leone as planned, the *Swallow* and *Weymouth* would put in to Cape Coast Castle in order to press-gang crew replacements from merchant ships anchored in the roadstead.

Roberts, sailing eastward to raid the bustling slave port of Whydah on the Nigerian coast, was then, without knowing it, heading directly for the warships who had spent six maddening months fruitlessly pursuing him.

Now Roberts had another piece of bad luck.

Although he sailed right past Cape Coast Castle where *Swallow* and *Weymouth* lay at anchor, he never saw the two warships. He was too far out to sea to make them out in the roadstead. He continued on eastward toward Whydah, secure in the belief that the Royal Navy warships were many leagues away to the north.

But the men-of-war soon learned of Roberts's presence in the neighborhood. A fishing boat had recognized *Royal Fortune* and her consorts out at sea and had brought the news to Captain Ogle aboard *Swallow*. Without waiting for *Weymouth*, which was still short of crewmen, Ogle had *Swallow* prepared for sea duty. He went in pursuit of Roberts as soon as she was ready.

On January 11, 1722—still unaware of the danger now closely pursuing him—Roberts reached Whydah, where he captured eleven slave ships without firing a shot. In accordance with custom, he allowed the captains of these vessels buy them back for a ransom of £500 each. (One captain, however, refused to pay. The infuriated House of Lords then set the ship on fire—against Roberts's specific orders—forcing the chained slaves on board to leap over the side and risk the sharks or remain aboard and be burned to death.)

On January 13, still at Whydah, Roberts intercepted an over-land message from Cape Coast Castle to the Royal African com-pany's agent in Whydah. The message said H.M.S. *Swallow* was in pursuit of the pirates and would soon be at Whydah.

Roberts immediately put to sea.

Roberts's crew had a pretty good idea where their pistol-proof captain was taking them: the tiny island of Annobón, whose im-

AFTER A PORTRAIT IN THE NATIONAL MARITIME MUSEUM, LONDON

penetrable swamps would afford them shelter and camouflage that even the Royal Navy could not pierce.

But now, it seemed, Nemesis—or was it Roberts's own demon

at work?—was beginning to catch up with Black Bart. Perverse winds prevented his pirate fleet from reaching Annobón. Instead they had to take shelter in a vast region of swamp and lagoons near an area called Cape Lopez. Here Roberts anchored his ships—and waited.

Meanwhile Captain Ogle in *Swallow* had reached Whydah two days after Roberts had left. But this time Ogle was determined to chase the elusive Roberts down. Guessing correctly that the pirate captain had sought safety in the maze of inlets in the Cape Lopez region, Ogle ordered *Swallow* to the south. On February 5, 1722, he arrived off Cape Lopez and began a careful search of the silent swamps and inlets.

Now, as the pirate fleet lay anchored in the hidden marsh channels of Cape Lopez, Roberts and his men began to commit a series of inexplicable errors and misjudgments that in retrospect seemed designed, like the steady progression of a Greek tragedy, to bring about a confrontation between *Swallow* and the pirates.

As Ogle glided past this boggy land, searching its maze of silent jungle and waterways for his quarry, someone aboard one of Roberts's anchored vessels fired a gun that boomed across the vast swamps and set thousands of marsh birds flying and cackling. Now Ogle could be sure that he had guessed right: Roberts had indeed taken refuge in these bogs.

Directing his search toward the source of the noise, Ogle, whose ship was still standing well off the cape, at last made out his quarry in his spyglass: Roberts's own ship, *Royal Fortune*, and her two consorts, the *Great Ranger*, and the *Little Ranger*, half hidden within the swamps of the cape. Now Ogle could mull over his next move. Time, he knew, was at last on *his* side.

Ironically, it may have been Roberts himself who had ordered the firing of the gun that had attracted *Swallow* to his location, for it appears that Roberts had sighted *Swallow* long before she had spotted him. But for some reason—was it a mistake or some deliberate act of self-destruction?—Roberts had identified the man-of-war as a large merchantman and may have ordered the gun fired to gain her attention. (Interloping traders and black kings often used a cannon shot as a signal to merchants that they had goods available for trade.) Perhaps he hoped to lure her closer so he could capture her. But why would Roberts, knowing that a warship was in the area seeking him, resort to such a dangerous stratagem? Was he now set upon some private ritual of expiation? Had he decided that it was time for Black Bart to meet his end and release Bartholomew Roberts? Or was it simply a mistake born of arrogance?

Whatever his state of mind, Roberts acted as if he were sure that the vessel now standing offshore was, in fact, a merchant—possible prey—for he sent the *Great Ranger* out to take her. This, too, was an inexplicable deviation from Roberts's usual procedure. Normally he commanded in an action of this kind.

Meanwhile, aboard *Swallow*, Captain Ogle saw with satisfaction that the pirate ship *Great Ranger* was coming out to meet him. Now he would have an opportunity to employ a stratagem he had been contemplating for picking the pirates off one at a time. Ogle brought *Swallow* about and made for the open sea as if fleeing the pirate. In fact, it was his design to lure *Great Ranger* away from sight and sound of her companions—and then to engage her far out at sea.

Toward this end, Ogle piled on sail and drove *Swallow* out of sight of land. Gradually, however, he allowed the pirate vessel to close the gap. After a chase that lasted for hours, *Great Ranger* had closed within musket range of *Swallow*. Now, for the first time, the *Great Ranger's* captain, James Skyrme, who had been flying a variety of flags, apparently in the hope of disguising his purpose, finally ran up his Jolly Roger. He ordered his men to combat stations. Then he let fly at *Swallow* with his bow cannon.

Suddenly *Swallow* turned to starboard and delivered a shattering broadside at her pursuer. The pirates for the first time realized, to their horror, that they faced a powerful warship rather than a fat merchant.

Captain Skyrme hesitated. He did not immediately reply to *Swallow's* broadside. He seemed unsure what to do. He hauled his Jolly Roger down as if about to fly. But then he seemed to change his mind. The Jolly Roger fluttered up the mast again. The pirate had decided to fight. *Great Ranger* delivered a broadside of her own at *Swallow*. Now the pirate crew, cheering wildly and brandishing their cutlasses, crowded to the deck, shouting curses at the men of *Swallow*—while their captain maneuvered to bring *Great Ranger* alongside the navy ship so that his cutthroats could board her.

But the well-trained gun crews aboard the *Swallow* were not daunted. They kept up a rapid cannon and small-arms barrage that the pirates could not match. *Great Ranger's* main topmast was shot away. Many pirates were wounded. Skyrme himself had one of his legs shot off. But there was no sign of surrender by either ship. They pounded each other for hours on the rolling Atlantic swell under the burning tropical sun.

Skyrme, despite his terrible wound, continued to direct the battle for the *Great Ranger*. His aim was to position his ship so that his men could board *Swallow*. More than once as the ships maneuvered close in to each other, the pirates had an opportunity to do this, but they could not bring themselves to face the tremendous fire from the navy ship.

By three o'clock in the afternoon the *Great Ranger* was so badly battered, and her crew so badly mauled, that she could no longer fight effectively. Nor could she escape. Skyrme saw that the game was up. He surrendered. But before he did so, he ordered his Jolly Roger thrown into the ocean, thinking it might be used as evidence against him in a future Admiralty court.

Not all Skyrme's men agreed with his decision to surrender. One of them, a member of the House of Lords named John Morris, fired his pistol into a barrel of gunpowder in the ship's maga-zine with the aim of blowing the *Great Ranger* to Hell. But the gunpowder barrel was more than half empty. The explosion that Morris achieved did little damage to the ship, although Morris himself was burned to death, and its flash inflicted severe burns on several others who had been with Morris in the magazine.

The boarding party from *Swallow* found that ten pirates had been killed and twenty had been wounded—many of them as se-verely as Skyrme himself. The rest, approximately one hundred, were exhausted, unable to fight anymore. Blackened with powder and smoke, they lay unmoving on the debris-strewn decks.

The *Swallow*'s surgeon, Dr. John Atkins, patched up the wounded pirates as best he could, while the navy boarding party took the unwounded prisoners back to *Swallow* and chained them below. The navy men searched every corner of the *Great Ranger* looking for the pirate booty they had expected to find in abun-dance. Disappointed, they had to settle for whatever they could strip from their prisoners, including such petty items as shoes and clothing.

Amazingly enough, *Swallow*'s crew had suffered no casualties during the battle, although the ship had received some damage that would have to be repaired before she returned to action.

After chaining his one hundred unwounded pirate prisoners—fifty-nine Englishmen, twenty-three blacks, and eighteen Frenchmen, according to Dr. Atkins—in the hold of *Swallow*, Captain Ogle sent the heavily damaged *Great Ranger*, with the wounded prisoners under guard, to Principe Island, two hundred or so miles to the north. He then set about repairing his own damage and refreshing his crew, which took some time. Several days passed before Ogle set off once more for Cape Lopez where Roberts still lay in hiding with *Royal Fortune* and the *Little Ranger*.

On the morning of February 10, *Swallow* arrived off the inlet where Roberts was anchored. Although it had been five days since Roberts had sent the *Great Ranger* after a supposed mer-chantman—and the ship had not returned—Roberts had pro-fessed to be unconcerned. He had made no move to find out what might have happened to the *Great Ranger*, nor had he changed his own anchorage. It was as if he had long expected what was now at hand, and was resolved to remain in this African coastal swamp to meet it.

When word was brought to Roberts that a strange sail had appeared, he calmly continued his breakfast of salmagundi in his cabin aboard the *Royal Fortune*.

Taking their cue from their captain, Roberts's men seemed equally unconcerned about the approaching stranger. Many of them, according to later testimony, were still hung over from their usual drinking bout the night before—and they idly watched the oncoming vessel and speculated about her nationality and possible mission. Suddenly one of the crewmen—by coincidence a Royal Navy deserter who had once served on the *Swallow*—recognized the ship that was advancing toward them as the sixty-gun man-of-war he knew so well. He cried out his identification of the onrushing *Swallow*.

Immediately Roberts was up on deck.

Deadly calm, he issued orders for the men aboard the *Little Ranger*, anchored nearby, to come aboard *Royal Fortune*. He also ordered his men to arm themselves and to take up battle stations. He then slipped his cable. *Royal Fortune* slid away from her anchorage. It was 10:30 A.M.

Roberts ordered full sail crowded on. He indicated that, with full sail set, he would try to run before the wind in an effort to escape the oncoming *Swallow*. If *Swallow* managed to cut him off before he could make the open sea, he said, he would try to run *Royal Fortune* aground so that they could all escape into the jungle. And if *that* strategy miscarried, he would try to board the warship and then blow up both *Royal Fortune* and *Swallow*. He did not intend to hang.

Now Roberts did something that probably reveals his state of mind at this moment better than anything he said aloud: He went below and dressed himself in his best finery. He donned a crimson waistcoat, silk breeches, the hat festooned with the red ostrich feather, a gold chain, and a silk sling into which he jammed two ornate pistols. He then returned to the deck. His gaudy attire seemed to celebrate a destiny he saw rushing toward him in the shape of the hard-driving *Swallow*.

Now Roberts took an action that was wholly inexplicable—unless he *was*, in fact, deliberately seeking his own destruction.

Instead of trying to escape, as he had proposed, he directed his ship *toward*, rather than away from, the powerful *Swallow*. His amazed crew obeyed his orders, doubtless certain that their captain—the brazen pistol-proof Black Bart—had some method even to this madness.

At about 11:00 A.M. *Royal Fortune* and *Swallow* came within cannon range of each other. Suddenly Roberts ran from his station on the quarterdeck to the railing where the *Royal Fortune's* guns were now ready to fire. He jumped onto one of the gun carriages the better to direct his ship's fire. *Royal Fortune* and *Swallow* delivered almost-simultaneous broadsides. Both vessels shuddered beneath the blast of the cannon. Clouds of dense smoke rolled across their decks. *Royal Fortune's* mizzen-topmast came crashing down.

When the smoke of the broadside cleared, the men of *Royal Fortune* saw that their captain seemed to be slumping over one of the guns. When the helmsman went to his aid, he saw that Black Bart was dead. A blast of grapeshot had torn away his throat. The helmsman, and many others among the hardened pirates in the House of Lords, burst into tears.

They knew that they were finished. Without their bold and brilliant leader, they were no match for a Royal Navy man-of-war. Roberts had not only been their captain, he had been the heart and brains of their whole enterprise. But they did not surrender.

With *Swallow* pouring fire into *Royal Fortune*, some members of the House of Lords took Roberts's body, decked out in all its finery, and threw it overboard—in accordance with Roberts's own longstanding and strict instructions.

Now the leaderless crew of the *Royal Fortune* (there was no second-in-command) tried to sail their ship out to the open sea to escape. It was a forlorn hope, but it was the only one they had. When one of the crewmen—a forced man—tried to persuade his fellows to surrender, the House of Lords, many of whom had served with Howell Davis as well as Roberts, rejected the idea. For them, as they well knew, surrender meant the noose.

But it soon became clear that the *Royal Fortune*, poorly handled, could not escape. Slowly *Swallow* closed on her. Although the pirates kept up a desultory fire, they made no wholehearted attempt to stand and fight. Nor did they try to run *Royal Fortune* aground, an alternative that Roberts himself had been considering. Instead, the House of Lords, having lost its brain, now lost its heart as well. As *Swallow* neared, Roberts's crew began to drink. At 2:00 P.M.—three hours after Roberts's death—the

House of Lords, many of them too drunk to care any longer, surrendered.

A navy boarding party swung aboard the *Royal Fortune* to take possession of their prize and to take the pirates into custody. A search of the ship turned up a considerable quantity of gold dust and plunder stored in the ship's hold. The navy men also retrieved Roberts's papers—and his personal pirate flag.

By 7:00 P.M. all the prisoners had been taken aboard the *Swallow* and chained belowdecks with the prisoners captured earlier from the *Great Ranger*.

Captain Ogle now sailed off with his prisoners—254 of them in all—to Cape Coast Castle.

There Black Bart's crew would be kept in irons in the underground slave dungeons beneath the castle until they could be put on trial for their crimes—not the least of which was their contempt and hatred for the Authority that would try them.

20

Saga's End

So died Black Bart, not yet forty years old.

In a career that spanned not quite three years, he had captured more than four hundred ships—and he had, with audacity, demonic energy, and masterly seamanship, made his name a terror from Newfoundland to Brazil and the swampy Guinea Coast of Africa.

If he had sought vengeance against the world that rejected him, he had achieved his aim. And if he had also sought the punishment of God for sins committed in defiance of his own creed, then Black Bart had achieved this too.

In the aftermath of Roberts's extinction, there were accolades and rewards for the victorious forces of law and order—and swift and certain punishment for the defeated followers of Black Bart.

Captain Chaloner Ogle of H.M.S. *Swallow*, the man who had finally put an end to Roberts, was knighted for his feat—the only man ever to receive such an honor for action against pirates.

Ogle's career flowered after his victory over Roberts. He was offered important commands and eventually rose to the rank of admiral.

Ogle's officers and men also profited from their victory. The loot taken from the captured *Royal Fortune*, although less than had been expected, still amounted to a considerable sum when it was distributed as prize money among the crew and officers of *Swallow*. (It was said that Captain Ogle profited most of all, having appropriated for himself a significant quantity of gold dust that had been found in Roberts's cabin.)

For Roberts's crew—those who had survived both the battles with H.M.S. *Swallow* and their subsequent confinement in the dungeon of Cape Coast Castle—the day of reckoning came on March 28, 1722, when they were taken to the great hall of the castle to be tried for their crimes before a vice-admiralty court.

In the end, a total of 169 members of Roberts's crew were brought to trial. Of the rest, some had died of wounds received in the battles. Others had perished under the harsh conditions of their captivity. A number were set free without trial. Among these were musicians, surgeons, and "sea artists" (such as sailing masters and blacksmiths) whom the court determined had been forced into service with Roberts. Also freed were the 18 Frenchmen who had served with Roberts. The court decided that it had no jurisdiction over these "foreigners"—and it set them at liberty. The remaining prisoners—including the 50 or so members of the House of Lords—went to trial.

Rattling in their chains and blinking like owls in daylight after their confinement in the underground cells of the castle, these defendants were brought before the tribunal and pleaded, to a man, that they had been forced into piracy. For many of them, especially the hard-bitten House of Lords, this was a defense that would not stand up to scrutiny and they knew it. Still, it was the only plea they could make under the circumstances. Doubtless they hoped that if they exhibited sufficient contrition during their trial, the court just *might* believe that they had been forced aboard Roberts's ship.

For this reason even the House of Lords muted their customary blasphemy and sarcastic banter during the trial.

The trial itself was fair by the standards of the day. Sitting as judges on the court were four officials of the Royal African Company, including its director general, James Phipps, and the skipper of the H.M.S. *Weymouth*, Captain Mungo Herdman. The court allowed all the accused to speak if they wished, and allowed the defendants to tell their stories in their own words. Unlike the magistrates who would have tried the defendants in England, these court officers were knowledgeable about pirates. They were well aware of conditions that sometimes caused seamen to end up in pirate crews. They were sympathetic—but they could not be fooled, either, by invented excuses for piracy. Thus they made it clear that they were prepared to acquit any of the defendants who could verify, by testimony of witnesses or documentation, that they had indeed been forced into piracy—as all of them claimed—but would grant no leniency to those who had chosen the outlaw life of their own free will.

In the end 74 of the 169 accused men were able to satisfy the court that they were truly "forced men." These defendants were set free. The rest—95 of them—were convicted. The punishments handed out by the court varied widely.

Twenty of those convicted were sentenced to seven years' hard labor in the Royal Africa Company mines—a sentence none of them survived.

A total of seventeen other men were sentenced to varying prison terms in England. (But thirteen of these men never served their sentences, having died on the journey back.)

The court condemned fifty-four men to death. Most of these were the hardcore elite House of Lords. Among those sentenced to death was Captain Skyrme of the *Great Ranger*, who, despite the loss of his leg in the battle with *Swallow*, had survived to keep his date with the hangman. (Two of those originally condemned to hang were later reprieved and given long prison terms instead.)

With their trial over, the House of Lords—all of them now condemned to death—reverted to their true selves. Reclaiming their self-appointed titles, they affected unconcern with their fate. They would go to the gallows jauntily, figuratively thumbing their noses at the Authority that would hang them, as if by mocking the law, they were asserting their free status as members of the pirate brotherhood. Despite their chains, their actions implied, they were still free men in their hearts.

This attitude had been demonstrated most trenchantly in a sar-

donic little exchange that took place between one tough, unrepentant pirate, Lord Sutton, and another prisoner who had been
loudly expressing his contrition for his crimes. Lord Sutton protested vehemently when the contrite man, who was chained next
to Sutton, began to intone prayers for forgiveness from a devo-
tional book.

"What," Lord Sutton demanded, "do you propose by so much
noise and devotion?"

"Heaven, I hope," the contrite prisoner responded.

"Heaven, you fool?" exclaimed Lord Sutton. "Did you ever
hear of any pirate going there? Give me Hell, it's a merrier place.
I'll give Roberts a salute of 13 guns at entrance." Lord Sutton
then asked the guard to take either the prisoner or his prayer
book away. "Because he is disturbing the peace."

The executions of those sentenced to hang were carried out
over a period of approximately two weeks. Beginning on April 4
or 5, small groups of the condemned men were taken every other
day or so from their dungeon prisons beneath Cape Coast Castle
to the scaffold that had been erected outside the castle walls. Pro-
ceeding on foot, with their hands tied behind their backs, the
condemned men, guarded by Royal African Company soldiers,
had to make their way to the gallows through a crowd of Royal
African Company employees, slave dealers, sailors, and curiosity
seekers, both men and women.

The members of the House of Lords made this last journey
with no outward diminution of their cockiness. According to the
Swallow's surgeon, Dr. Atkins, who was a close observer of the
executions, the condemned men—even in their last moments—
showed no repentance for their crimes. Said one of them, according to the doctor: "We are poor rogues, and so must be hanged,
while others, no less guilty in another way, escaped."

One of the "poor rogues," Lord Hardy, complained bitterly
about the "irregularity" of being hanged with his hands tied behind his back.

Another, Lord Sympson, on his way to the rope, spotted a
woman in the watching crowd who had been a passenger on a
ship captured by Roberts. "By God," cried Lord Sympson, pointing with his chin toward the lady in question, "I have lain with
that bitch three times—and now she comes to see me hanged!"
The crowd laughed.

Dr. Atkins recorded the names, birthplaces, and ages of the executed men. The oldest pirate hanged was forty-five, the youngest nineteen. Only four of those hanged were over forty—and only four were twenty or under. The veteran pirates of the House of Lords, despite their long years of pirating, averaged only thirty years of age.

The last batch of the condemned—fourteen of them—went to the gallows on April 20, 1722.

The bodies of eighteen of the executed men—those considered the most outrageous wrongdoers—were preserved by dipping them in tar. Then they were hung from gibbets visible to all approaching ships. It was the same fate that Captain Kidd had suffered a generation earlier.

With the death of Black Bart, and the execution of the House of Lords, the final defeat of piracy was sealed.

But even now a handful of pirate captains carried on a last-ditch combat on the sea-lanes against the forces of law and order.

As happens with most lost causes, these last adherents of the defeated outlaw nation fought with special fury and cruelty.

George Lowther was one who made his career in these last days. Little is known of Lowther's history until June 1721 when he was serving as mate aboard the Royal African Company ship *Gambia Castle*. While the ship was operating off the Guinea Coast, Lowther seized control of her, set her captain adrift, and ran up the Jolly Roger on her mainmast. Renaming the ship *Happy Delivery*, Lowther—with fifty men who had joined his mutiny—set sail for the West Indies.

After taking a number of prizes in the Caribbean, Lowther and *Happy Delivery* became the object of a Royal Navy hunt. To escape the navy's pursuit, Lowther made for the North American coast. He soon captured a number of prizes off New York and New England.

For Lowther, mistreatment of prisoners became common practice. He claimed he tortured captives only to make them reveal where they had hidden their gold. But stories of his cruelty indicate a strong streak of sadism in his makeup. For example, one of his favorite tortures was to place burning hempen matches between the fingers of his captives and to allow them to sear the flesh to the bone. It is said that he would smile throughout this grisly procedure, enjoying the smell of burning flesh and the screams of his victims.

Because he was operating in the twilight of the pirate brotherhood when pirate-hunting men-of-war actually outnumbered outlaw vessels, Lowther could not remain long in any one location without attracting the attention of warships. It was his custom, therefore, to keep constantly on the move. Thus, he had left New England waters and was sailing off the coast of South Carolina in the autumn of 1722 when he attacked a merchant vessel that resisted so fiercely that *Happy Delivery,* her rigging and rudder badly damaged, ran aground on the beach.

Although Lowther managed to refloat *Happy Delivery* before any warships came upon her, his pirating was at an end—at least temporarily. He and his men sailed their badly wounded ship to an isolated inlet on the coast of North Carolina. Here they had to spend the bitter winter of 1722–23, living in makeshift tents on shore while they worked to repair their ship.

By the following summer, however, Lowther and *Happy Delivery* were back in business, operating off Newfoundland with some success. But when the weather turned cool again, Lowther steered south. This time he was heading for the Caribbean to hunt Spanish prey.

After arriving in the West Indies, Lowther careened *Happy Delivery* on the little-known island of Blanquilla, northeast of Tortuga. While his ship was careened, she was spotted and recognized as a pirate by an English sloop out of Barbados, the *Eagle.* The *Eagle* immediately attacked the vulnerable pirates. Caught by surprise, Lowther and his men resisted fiercely. But they were overwhelmed. About thirty-five of the outlaws were killed. The rest were taken as prisoners aboard the *Eagle,* but Lowther was not among them.

As soon as he had realized that the battle with the men of the *Eagle* was lost, Lowther, with three of his men and a cabin boy, had fled the combat and had tried to find someplace to hide on the little island. But Blanquilla offered little refuge. A search party was sent ashore to hunt down the cruel captain of the *Happy Delivery.* Lowther must have realized that for him the war was over. He blew his brains out with a pistol rather than face the hangman. The searchers from the *Eagle* found his body on the beach of Blanquilla, a burst pistol at his side.

*   *   *

Perhaps the deadliest of the last pirate captains, however, was the sinister Edward Low.

Born in Westminster, England, Low was known, even in boyhood, as a bully and a thief. Unable to hold a job for any length of time, Low had worked as an ordinary seaman, a shipyard worker in Boston, and a log cutter in the Bay of Honduras. Time after time he had lost jobs when his evil temper landed him in trouble with the law. His final break with honest society, however, came sometime in 1721 in Honduras. During an argument with his employer, Low fired a musket and killed a bystander by mistake. He then fled to sea in a small boat with a dozen companions whom he talked into going pirating with him.

Somehow Low and the others, operating in an open boat far out at sea, managed to overhaul a small merchant vessel, which they took for their own.

According to Defoe, Low now made a black flag for himself and "declared War against the World."

But despite his grandiose declaration, Low was less than a rousing success as a pirate captain. Then he met Captain George Lowther of the *Happy Delivery* in the Grand Caymans sometime in the autumn of 1721. For the next nine months Low sailed in company with Lowther, acting as his lieutenant and learning his trade.

In May 1722, Low—with forty-four men—went off on his own account in a ship taken off the coast of Virginia.

Now, as captain of a formidable ship, which he named the *Fancy*, Low showed that he had learned his craft well from his mentor. Over the next year or more he ranged widely over the sea-lanes from New England to the West Indies, and as far eastward as the African coastal islands, taking at least ninety-three prizes and making a specialty of boldly charging into protected harbors and plundering anchored prizes. Eventually he gathered several ships under his command—and earned an unsurpassed reputation for cruelty.

Low's cruelty was strangely deliberate and cold in nature. This was apparent, for example, in his treatment of blacks. Unlike most other pirate captains, Low did not welcome blacks aboard his ships. But at the same time he did not make this policy widely known. Instead, he often allowed free blacks to voluntarily sign ship's articles. Then, when they were aboard and thought them-

selves full members of the crew, Low would clap them in irons to be sold into slavery when convenient.

For some reason Low also had a particular hatred for New Englanders and Portuguese. Whenever he took a ship from New England, his practice was to strip the ship's captain naked and to whip him around the deck, all the while nicking him with a cutlass in various parts of his body, often slitting the unfortunate's nose. Sometimes when Low wearied of such sport, he simply put a pistol ball through his victim's head "to put him out of his misery."

The atrocities he committed against Portuguese captives were even worse. Decapitation and disemboweling were among the milder treatments meted out to unfortunate Portuguese prisoners. One Portuguese captain had enraged Low by dropping a sack containing eleven thousand gold coins out of his cabin into the sea before Low could take them as booty. Screaming with rage, Low lashed the Portuguese captain to the mast of his own ship and then he had the man's lips sliced off and broiled in a pan before his eyes.

Low's barbarous behavior inevitably rubbed off on his crew—who did not limit themselves to torturing only New Englanders and Portuguese. In one instance Low captured a French prize and took her crew prisoners aboard his ship. But his crewmen—apparently for sport—took the cook of the captured ship and bound him to the mast of the prize vessel, which they then set afire. The cook, they joked among themselves, "being a greasy Fellow, would fry well in the Fire."

It is said that a bizarre accident that occurred at the height of Low's piratical career made his appearance as hideous as his character. According to the story, during a battle a member of Low's crew slashed at a victim with his cutlass and missed, slicing open his captain's jaw instead. Low's surgeon, drunk and incompetent, did his best to repair his captain's face by stitching up the jagged wound that gaped from Low's lower lip to his ears, like some gigantic bloody grin. After the job was done, however, Low complained of the doctor's poor stitchwork, whereupon the drunken medical man punched Low so hard in the face that all the stitches came loose again. The surgeon, according to Defoe, "then bid him sew up his Chops himself and be damned." The result was that ever after Low carried a scar on his face in the shape of a perpetual evil grin.

Whether the tale of Low's horrible face is true or not, it reflects the general belief that he was a monster. Even other pirates wondered at his heedless, maniacal cruelty—and expressed the fear that it would ensure the final demise of the sweet trade by stiffening the forces of law in their determination to put an end to piracy once and for all.

In June 1723, however, Low met his match. Cruising in the *Fancy*, with a consort, the *Ranger*, under the command of one of his lieutenants, Charles Harris, Low encountered a guard ship from New York, H.M.S. *Greyhound*.

Thinking her a potential prize, the two pirate vessels bore down on *Greyhound*. The man-of-war, a formidable vessel with sixty cannon and a well-trained crew, adopted the tactic that H.M.S. *Swallow* had used so effectively two years earlier against Bartholomew Roberts's lieutenant, James Skyrme, in the *Great Ranger*: She pretended to flee from the chasing pirates, but allowed them to close within cannon range.

Then, just as *Swallow* had done, *Greyhound* came about and loosed a series of broadsides at the pirates. *Ranger*'s main yardarm was soon shot away, leaving her crippled. Now Low, so terrible when torturing defenseless merchants, left his damaged consort to the mercies of the warship. Turning tail, he ran before the wind and fled from the scene as soon as possible. H.M.S. *Greyhound* took the officers and crew of *Ranger* into custody. Charles Harris and twenty-seven members of his crew went to the gallows.

As for Low himself, there is no positive evidence of his fate after his escape from *Greyhound*. One story says that he went to Brazil and continued pirating until he retired. Other stories say that he lost *Fancy* in battle but took another ship, which he called, with characteristic sarcasm, *Merry Christmas*—and that this ship sank in a storm with all hands. Other stories say that Low was finally the victim of a mutiny and was set adrift in a small open boat, and that he was rescued by a French warship and subsequently hanged in Martinique.

Whatever his final end may have been, it is certain that his cruel career came to a halt sometime after 1723. For he was never heard of again. It is also certain that if it was death that put an end to his career, no one wept at his demise, or offered a prayer for the repose of his savage soul.

---

*   *   *

But even the closing out of Edward Low's career did not mark the final end of the once-proud pirate brotherhood that had terrorized the maritime world for more than thirty years.

In far-off Madagascar—once fearfully looked upon as the embryo homeland of an emergent pirate nation—King John Plantain had achieved his ambition to make himself sovereign over all of the great island.

Although pirate ships had been chased from eastern waters, Plantain had continued to flourish during the 1720s. After defeating his archenemy, King Dick, and consolidating his power as king of the northern half of Madagascar, Plantain had—probably in 1723 or 1724—launched a war against the native chieftain of Port Dauphin, whose name is now unknown but who was then Plantain's only rival for the overlordship of Madagascar. For eighteen months Plantain had beseiged Port Dauphin. Finally the place had fallen to him—and he had proclaimed himself truly "King of Madagascar."

As sole ruler of his domain, however, Plantain had then fallen into the trap that awaits all who wield absolute power: He became corrupt, capricious, and cruel. Although his half-caste wife, Holy Eleanora, remained at his side, she had been unable to curb his excesses. Blind like any tyrant to his own vulnerability, and convinced, like most white Europeans of this time, that darker-skinned people were necessarily inferior creatures, Plantain had set himself up as a slave trader, selling native captives and offenders against his realm to the slave ships that called from time to time at his kingdom.

In time King John Plantain's subjects had begun to mutter against their sovereign's cruel practices. Plantain, with his native canniness, had sensed a serious rebellion being prepared against him.

Perhaps he had wearied of war. Perhaps power over his benighted subjects no longer seemed so heady. Perhaps, having conquered one kingdom, he now began to yearn for another. Perhaps he merely decided that he was no longer willing to risk his life, or the lives of his beloved Holy Eleanora and their children, to maintain his throne.

Whatever the case, King John Plantain, sometime toward the end of the 1720s, made up his mind to forsake his hard-won kingdom.

He ordered a sloop built for his use. Then, with Holy Eleanora and his children and all the ill-gotten riches he could cram aboard his boat, he departed his realm. He first made for Johanna Island off Madagascar's northwest coast. Here he reverted to his earlier career as a pirate and looted an Indian ship in the harbor. Plantain then set sail eastward into the vast Indian Ocean.

Some say he fetched up on the Malabar Coast and ended his days peacefully. Others say he served a prince in India. But there is no solid evidence of his eventual destiny. Whatever the truth, the pirate king of Madagascar disappeared from the world into fable, where he probably belonged anyway.

After the departure of its pirate king, Madagascar declined into a squalid pesthole where native tribes fought each other for possession of the ruins. Within a decade, all trace of Plantain's kingdom had vanished. Vestiges of the outlaw nation, however, lingered on. English names and the use of English words persisted among the natives for another thirty to forty years. The half-caste progeny of the pirate lords who had once ruled the great island were also present in Madagascar past 1750. But when the last of these light-skinned speakers of pidgin English died, the final traces of the pirate nation died also.

Meanwhile, as John Plantain fled his island, another island—halfway across the world—welcomed back the man who had wrested it from its pirate conquerers: the indomitable Woodes Rogers.

Since Rogers had departed his Bahamas colony to return to England in 1721, the island of New Providence, once called the Republic of Rogues, had become a peaceful plantation colony. The shantytown of Nassau, where Blackbeard had plied his trade and Calico Jack Rackam had wooed and won the tempestuous Anne Bonny, had turned into a thriving port city where respectable merchants conducted honest business and cargo vessels anchored unmolested under the guns of the formidable fort that Governor Rogers had built.

Although Nassau was a real town now, its waterfront was still crowded with taverns where reformed veterans of the sweet trade talked nostalgically of the good old days before Woodes Rogers had tamed the lords of Nassau.

If the years had changed Nassau, however, they had not much altered Woodes Rogers.

After returning to England and finding that his efforts in the Bahamas had earned him only a pile of debts and the ingratitude of both his nation and his partners in the Bahamas colony scheme, Rogers had set out to restore his honor and his fortune. Although thrown into debtors' prison because he had been unable to pay the bills he had incurred as governor of the Bahamas, Rogers had remained as undaunted by poverty as he had been by the threats of the pirate captain Charles Vane.

Relentlessly he had pleaded his case in high places. With the help of friends and—apparently—by selling family properties, he had managed to extricate himself from the worst of his poverty.

Then in 1726, after the Admiralty had turned an unsympathetic ear to his plea for a just recompense for his labors in the Bahamas, the army had come forward to do him justice. He had been granted the rank of an infantry captain and placed on half pay. The king had also come forward to grant him a pension for his work on behalf of the nation. In 1728, with his honor intact and his purse revived, Rogers had been reappointed governor of the Bahamas, where pirates had not been seen for years.

In 1729 he returned to Nassau again, this time accompanied by his family and at an annual salary of £400. When he resumed his labors as governor, he was presented with the official seal of the colony, which bore this motto in Latin: "The Pirates Expelled, Trade Restored." The seal pictured a pirate fleet retreating. It was a truthful representation.[1]

The pirate war against the world was over.

There would never be another Black Bart.

Epilogue

Of course piracy, as a crime at sea, continued long after Bartholomew Roberts, Blackbeard, and Kidd had become the stuff of legend and fiction. But after the great outbreak of 1692–1725, piracy steadily diminished as a factor affecting the commerce of nations.

Pirates themselves also seemed to diminish after the great outbreak, becoming steadily meaner in spirit until they were mere caricatures of the men who sailed the Pirate Round.

But if piracy—after 1725—became the shabby trade of a relatively few petty thieves and psychotics, privateering remained a respectable pursuit for enterprising seamen for many decades.

For example, French privateers based in Guadaloupe and Martinique preyed so effectively on slave ships bound for the British colonies in the mid-eighteenth century that they almost put an end to the slave trade.

During the American Revolution, the Continental Congress

commissioned almost anything that would float—whalers, traders, fishing smacks, and even yachts—as privateers against the British fleet. In all, Congress and its constituent states commissioned more than 2,500 privateers, and the Americans captured 2,300 prizes from the British, losing fewer than half that number to the enemy. Yet as effective as the privateers may have been against commerce, they were all but useless against the Royal Navy. As a consequence, the British had no trouble controlling major colonial ports such as New York, Boston, and Charleston. Control of the ports by the Royal Navy meant that the British could move troops as they chose, could resupply easily, and could bring military pressure to bear where and when they chose. It was only when a French fleet blocked the British from relieving Cornwallis's army at Yorktown that the Americans won their war for independence.

The French also utilized privateers during *their* revolution. Between 1793 and 1796, French privateers seized some 2,100 English vessels. But French privateering came to an end during the long struggle known as the Napoleonic Wars. During this era the Royal Navy developed effective convoy tactics, fast frigate escorts, and matchless gunnery skills—all of which made the lone-wolf privateer all but obsolete.

The fledgling United States, however, continued to rely on privateers during the War of 1812—and for several decades thereafter. The U.S. brig *Yankee*, for example, was credited with destroying or capturing some $5 million worth of English shipping and cargo during that time.

By the 1840s the navies of the world had become permanent, professional forces possessed of advanced technologies in the hands of highly trained crews. Privateers no longer had a place in the strategic dispositions of such armed fleets. In 1856, by the Declaration of Paris, Britain and most other European countries agreed to ban the use of privateers in their navies. (The United States, however, did not formally agree to the ban until 1890, although for all practical purposes privateering had ceased long before then.)

Although the pirates of the nineteenth century (as differentiated from the privateers of the time) were as a rule nasty, unglamorous figures, a few of them *did* attain some notoriety. One of these was Jean Laffite.

Born in France in 1779, Laffite made a business of capturing slave ships in the West Indies during the first decade of the nineteenth century, and then auctioning their human cargoes to the highest bidders at his island base in Barataria Bay south of New Orleans. Laffite's racket came to an end in 1814, however, when an American expeditionary force destroyed his operation. But it was only a year later that Laffite became a hero of sorts when his ships helped General Andrew Jackson defeat a British invasion force at the Battle of New Orleans. Laffite received a presidential pardon as a reward for his services during the battle.

But Laffite was far less a hero than he was a crook. He was soon back at his old racket of stealing slave ships and selling their cargo. This time, instead of operating out of an offshore island, he set up his business at Galveston, then part of Mexico. James Bowie, inventor of the Bowie knife, was one of Laffite's valued customers. Bowie would buy stolen slaves from the French pirate at a dollar a pound and then smuggle them to American cotton states where he was paid from $500 to $1,000 for each slave delivered. In 1821, Laffite's Galveston market was captured and shut down by an American warship, notwithstanding that it was in Mexican territory. Laffite then sailed off into the Caribbean—and was not heard from again.

In the 1820s the U.S. Congress sent a special West India squadron under the command of Commodore David Porter to put an end to a plague of petty pirates who were attacking shipping in the Caribbean. Porter sailed from Norfolk, Virginia, with a force of eight fast-sailing schooners of shallow draft, a paddle-wheel steamer, and five flat-bottomed barges designed to navigate the shallow reefs and banks of the Caribbean islands. Porter's squadron worked in cooperation with six American warships already in the area.

In April 1823 Porter caught one of the most notorious of the pirates at large in the islands. He was the Cuban brigand known as Diabolito, whom Porter took after a bloody battle in which seventy of the Cuban's men were killed. Over the next two years, Porter's squadron captured hundreds of the minor villains who operated in the West Indies—and swept the Caribbean clean of pirates.

Even before Porter's successful sweep, the U.S. Navy had put an end to the career of one Charles Gibbs—an American ex-privateer who had put together a fleet of four pirate schooners and had been harrying commerce in the Gulf of Mexico and off Cuba. In October 1821 the Navy brig *Enterprise*, commanded by Lieutenant Commander Lawrence Kearney, had encountered Gibbs and his flotilla in the act of looting three merchant vessels in Cuban waters. Kearney had immediately engaged Gibbs's little fleet and, after a ferocious fight, had captured not only the pirate vessels but forty of the pirates. But Gibbs, with a number of his men, had managed to take refuge ashore. He remained a fugitive for the next ten years. He was finally caught in 1831—and hanged.

These actions of the U.S. Navy in the Gulf of Mexico and in the Caribbean sounded the death knell of piracy in the region, although petty and intermittent piracy has never been fully eradicated in those waters.

Pirates also continued to flourish in the China Sea long after piracy had all but ceased elsewhere in the world. Throughout the nineteenth century, and even into the early twentieth century, fleets of pirate junks, many of them based on Macao, disrupted commerce from Shanghai to Singapore. At one point during the middle of the nineteenth century, Chinese pirates were so numerous and well organized they fought battles on equal terms with gunboats of the Chinese government and even, on occasion, with the Royal Navy. There are still pirates in the South China Sea. But today they prey on helpless refugees from Vietnam, the sorrow-laden Boat People.

There are also piratical drug smugglers who operate in the waters around the Bahamas.

But such modern pirates are small-scale, mean creatures—unworthy descendants of Henry Every.

Despite the fact that piracy as a crime has never been completely suppressed in the world, the record makes it clear that after 1725 the maritime nations never again confronted a pirate captain of stature, or style, to equal the men of the outlaw nation.

But *why* did the great pirate outbreak of 1692–1725 come to an end when, and as, it did?

Some answers to that question come immediately to mind, along with some corresponding reservations.

First, the death of Bartholomew Roberts and the mass hangings of his crew at Cape Coast Castle no doubt dampened enthusiasm for piracy by underlining the determination of the maritime nations, especially England, to punish pirates to the full extent of the law instead of bribing them with pardons as had been done so often in the past. (Yet pirates had been hanged before without stopping piracy. There were, for example, Kidd, Vane, Rackam, Bonnet, and Every's crew—to name just a few.)

Second, the loss of Madagascar and the Caribbean as bases of operation badly crippled the pirate brotherhood—as did the closing of American markets for pirate contraband. (Yet there were other havens that *could* have been used as bases: Zanzibar, South Africa, the Gulf of Mexico coast, and Brazil, to name just a few. But no serious attempt was made to reestablish a Republic of Rogues in any of those places. And there were certainly ports in South America, as well as enclaves of illegal merchants on the Guinea Coast, where pirates *could* have exchanged booty for rum, women, food, medicine, or any other commodity. But no effort was made to use these potential markets.)

Third, the determination of the Royal Navy from about 1720 onward to protect England's mercantile fleet from pirates made it much more dangerous to locate and attack prey. (But pirate captains had evaded the Royal Navy in the past, and even the Royal Navy lacked the resources to guard *all* the sea-lanes *all* the time. Rich cargoes were still moving, virtually unguarded, over the sea-lanes of the world after 1725—and there would have been plenty of rich prizes for resolute pirate captains despite the Royal Navy. But no such resolute captains appeared.)

Fourth, laws were passed early in the eighteenth century that improved the outlook for ordinary seamen by furnishing them with pensions and medical care. The new laws also provided rewards to sailors who resisted pirate attacks. These changes in the sailor's lot greatly reduced the incentives for the average sailor to become a pirate. (But despite such improvements, a sailor's lot still remained pretty awful—and life aboard a ship, for many long decades after 1725, could still be a hell.)

Each of the causes cited here no doubt contributed—to a greater or lesser degree—to the cessation of the pirate war on the world.

But there was another, far more powerful, factor that contributed to the demise of the outlaw nation—and it had nothing to do with hangings, or loss of bases, or the Royal Navy, or even with improvements in the sailor's life. It had to do with freedom.

As the first quarter of the eighteenth century came to an end, the western world was astir with new ideas about individual rights, social justice, and the worth of every human being. The Rights of Man idea was taking root. Already it was beginning to give impetus to invisible psychological shifts that would, later in the century, result in both the American and the French revolutions. But long before those climactic events occurred, the powerful new notion that all human beings, regardless of station, possessed "certain unalienable rights," initiated social and legal changes that began to liberate the ordinary folk of the western world from the worst of the longstanding tyrannies imposed upon them by custom and by history.

Major revisions in the laws reflected these new attitudes and new social ideas. For example, torture was abolished as an approved method of extracting information. Capital punishment was reserved for heinous crimes. No longer could a man hang for stealing a loaf of bread. So-called "poor laws" were enacted to provide relief to the indigent. More humane treatment became the rule in workhouses and in prisons.

Such measures, while exceedingly limited by current standards, nevertheless resulted in a sudden improvement in the lives of most ordinary people. The oppressive weight of Authority, which so limited and burdened the lives of the great majority in the seventeenth century—and against which the pirates had rebelled—began to lighten perceptively as the eighteenth century ripened.

Furthermore, as the American colonists began in the eighteenth century to push inland from the Atlantic Coast and discovered that more people were needed to work the new lands, immigration to the New World—and escape from the Old—was encouraged.

Freedom was no longer reserved to the rich and to the rebellious.

And so the wellsprings of piracy began to dry up. Reforms were beginning to create reasonable hope for tolerable liberty at home, and there were new opportunities to live free in the colonies. The sea was no longer the only refuge open to the oppressed. Nor was the desperate act of nautical rebellion known as piracy any longer the sovereign route to liberty for seafarers.

And so the pirate brotherhood—the piracy of the great out-break, fueled by the hunger for freedom—withered away.

It had lasted just thirty-three years. Yet the outlaw fraternity of that era has left an ineradicable imprint on the world. The pirates of the great outbreak remain alive for us in our novels, plays, movies, and stories. Although the swashbuckling outlaw, with his buried treasure and eye patch, is largely a myth that obscures the *real* pirate rebel at war with his society, the fictional pirate *does* express—even if inadvertently—some of the genuine flavor of piracy.

There is still, even after two and a half centuries, something so fundamental and compelling in the way the brigands of the outlaw nation lived that it continues to come through to us today. Tales of pirate life call forth in most of us a yearning for a life of adventure under sail, upon a boundless ocean, where the horizon changes every day and there are no responsibilities to hinder us.

Clearly the brigands of Madagascar and New Providence still speak to us. They tell us, even across the centuries, that if men are denied the chance to live in freedom, they will make their own freedom, even if the specific shape of that freedom may not be beautiful or idealistic. For to be free is also to be free to commit sin, to do wrong, to indulge in excesses, and the free pirates of the outlaw brotherhood, most of them simple sailing men, committed the sins of sailors: drunkenness, whoring, thievery, and—too often—cruelty and murder. Yet, for all that, it was the yearning for freedom that lay at the heart of pirate life and *that* is what still calls to us.

But the sea rebels of 250 years ago affected more than our literature and our psyches. They also profoundly affected our history.

Because the pirate raiders of 1692–1725 severely damaged the national wealth of maritime countries, the governments of those countries undertook to back private merchants with military and naval strength—as, for example, the British government did with the East India Company and the Royal African Company. Soon protection of trade by armed fleets became national policy not only for England but for every maritime state. Sea commerce was seen as fundamental to national power.

The pirates also forced the trading nations to cooperate with each other against sea brigands. From this essential collaboration the maritime countries learned to forge rules among themselves for civilized behavior at sea. Laws were formulated to regulate international commerce. By degrees governments came to regard international agreements as the proper method for safeguarding the freedom of the seas. Such international cooperation, initiated first in response to the threat of piracy, did much to advance maritime intercourse on all levels. Thus, in an irony of history, the pirate nation, by the very success of its predatory war against the world, helped to further the establishment of international laws that made another pirate war impossible.

One of the most important consequences of the pirate outbreak of 1692–1725 was the redefinition of the Royal Navy's role in the world. Prior to the pirate war, the Royal Navy had been, for the most part, a small, defense-oriented force. Although England in the seventeenth century disposed of a vast oceangoing fleet, this fleet was not an armed professional fleet of a nation. It was rather a conglomeration of individually owned ships. The Royal Navy, the maritime force of the state, was not only small, it was usually confined to home waters in time of war and allowed to rot at anchor in time of peace.

But all that began to change during the pirate war as the British government came to understand that national interest and overseas trade were synonymous. Called upon not only to fight the king's enemies but also to protect British mercantile interests, the Royal Navy in the eighteenth century became the most professional naval force in the world, as well as the largest, on perpetual patrol in every sea and ocean.

And so, paradoxically, the pirate rebellion against Authority helped convert the Royal Navy into the instrument that created the British Empire—an Authority that ultimately came to embrace much of the globe and to exercise dominion over all its seas.

Black Bart would have honored the irony in *that* with his bitter laughter.

Notes

Our Lady of the Cape

1. It is always extremely difficult to assess with accuracy the value of money used in a past age. It is even more difficult to express the value of past currencies in terms of money circulating today. However, since much of the story of the pirate war involves the plundering of rich cargoes, it is important that the reader obtain at least some *general* idea of the worth of pirate 1booty, based on the purchasing power of modern currencies. For this reason I have worked out an admittedly makeshift method for estimating the worth of the English pound—the currency in which the value of booty was most often expressed—during the era covered by this story. Based on contemporary prices, a worker in the London of 1720 would seem to have required about 15 shillings a week to provide the bare minimum of food, shelter, clothing, and other necessities for his family. To provide the same today would require at least

$150 per week. This would mean that the shilling of 1720 was probably worth at least $10 in today's purchasing power—and the pound worth something like $200.

By this rough reckoning, then, the loot from the *Cabo* could have exceeded $160 million in today's purchasing power. Throughout this story I have valued the English pound of the era at approximately $200, but the reader is earnestly cautioned to regard that figure as far more indicative than real.

2. After sharing out their plunder, Taylor and his men remained active in the Indian Ocean. However, as wanted men, they eventually departed eastern waters and made for Panama. In July 1723 they arrived at Portobelo. After discreet negotiations with the Spanish governor, which very likely included a substantial bribe, the rich pirates found themselves welcomed to Panama as free men, recipients of the Spanish king's clemency. Taylor himself, although now a wealthy man, remained wedded to the sea. He spent the rest of his life as an obscure, but very well-to-do, captain of a patrol vessel in Spanish service. None of Taylor's crew ever faced charges for the rape of the *Cabo*.

One: The Opening Gun

1. What we know about the pirates of this age is derived from relatively few sources. Pirates, for obvious reasons, did not seek notoriety. If a pirate made a big strike, as John Taylor did, and managed to avoid the hangman's rope, he was more likely to take his swag and seek obscurity than he was to write his memoirs. Furthermore, most pirates, like most seafaring men of the age, were illiterate. Nor did pirate vessels sail with recording secretaries aboard.

Nevertheless, historians have been able to dig up a fair amount of significant, reliable information about pirates from such sources as the records of Admiralty trials, accounts of pardoned pirates, the testimony of ship's officers who escaped from pirate captivity, reports by naval officers, and—most notably—from a remarkable book first published in London in 1724. This book was *A General History of the Robberies and Murders of the Most Notorious Pyrates*, by a writer who signed himself "Captain Charles Johnson." The book, clearly based on personal knowledge of, and contact with, the pirates of the age, as well as with pirate victims and prosecuting authorities, was tremendously successful. It went through at least four editions before 1730, and has gone through more than sixty editions since it first appeared. The *General History* rings with the authentic sound of the speech of eighteenth-century sailing men. Its narrative is filled with detail that could only have come from a man who made it his business to obtain firsthand knowledge of his subject. It is now generally acknowledged that the author of the *General History* was really the stupendously energetic novelist and chronicler of his times Daniel Defoe, the creator of *Robinson Crusoe* and a man who utilized many pseudonyms, among them Captain Charles Johnson. Defoe is plainly fascinated by the pirates whose careers he chronicles. While he does not condone their actions, he does try to understand their motives. His narrative, spikey with telling detail, is also liberally studden with observations regarding the characters of specific pirates and the significance of the pirate phenomenon for the world of his time. Throughout this telling of the pirate story, we will be quoting descriptions, observations, and conversations from Defoe's engrossing and rich narrative.

Although Defoe's *General History* of the pirates was published with woodcut illustrations that purported to show what the pirates described in the narrative looked like, the fact is that there are *no* reliable portraits of the pirates of the years of the great outbreak. The reason is very simple: All the pirates were either dead or in hiding. They were not available for sketch artists, so the drawings in Defoe's book are not actual portraiture. Instead they attempt to portray the "character traits" of the pirates—peculiarities that set them apart from each other and from honest seafarers. Thus, for example, the great pirate Captain Bartholomew Roberts, who thought himself as good as any "gentleman," is depicted as a dandy in a plumed hat, while the "Arch-Pirate" Henry Every, who reportedly "gave himself the airs of a monarch," is shown with a servant or a slave holding a parasol over his head to shield him from the sun—a royal affectation. Nevertheless, even though we have no faithful depiction of their features, we *are* able to infer what the chief actors in this story probably looked like, and what was most likely in their minds as they went about their careers, thanks to the *written* descriptions of them and the pungent assessments of their careers and characters found in Defoe and other sources.

2. Careening was an essential activity in the age of sail and wooden ships. The hulls of wooden vessels—especially those that sailed in warm, tropical seas—became quickly fouled with marine growth, which checked speed. In addition, a tropical pest called the teredo worm could bore through the bottom, causing serious leaks, if the ship was not properly cared for. To resist the teredo worm, ships of this period were usually sheathed with double timbers on their bottoms. But even so, this sheathing had to be repaired periodically where worm damage had occurred. To repair the sheathing and to scrape clean the bottom of the ship, mariners resorted to an operation they called "careening." The ship was run up on a sandy shore and emptied of cargo and heavy equipment, such as cannon. She was then pulled over on her side for cleaning and sheathing. The scraped bottom was often smeared with a noxious, oily paste of tar, tallow, and sulfur. This mixture kept the worm and marine growths off for a time—and added to speed. Pirates—and privateers, too—depended greatly on speed not only in the attack but also to get away quickly with their loot. For this reason they were even more conscientious than their enemies—merchants and naval vessels—in keeping their hulls clean. However, pirates were never more vulnerable than when careened. It was for this reason that they sought out little-frequented coves, hidden inlets, and guarded harbors to lay up. Many such places became known as "pirate lairs"—and the largest of them were sometimes so popular among sea brigands that they became veritable pirate bases.

When Captain Tew put into St. Mary's he knew exactly what he was doing. This little island had long been used by merchant vessels, bound to and from India, as a safe haven, a place where fresh water could be found, and where ship traffic was so light that careening could usually be accomplished without fear of interruption by another vessel—friend or foe.

3. What happened to *Amity* and her crew after the death of Captain Tew is unclear. It appears, however, that the surviving crewmen participated later in a prearranged rendezvous with the other sea raiders with whom they had been operating, and took a share of the loot that these others had taken from Mogul

prizes. It is said that some of *Amity's* men returned home, while others went pirating on their own. As for *Amity*, it appears that she ended up as a pirate vessel, passing through many hands and eventually being wrecked or abandoned in Madagascar.

Two: A Brilliant Time, a Brutal Time

1. The Holy Roman Empire was the rather anomalous designation applied to a shifting, amorphous, political entity of Europe created by Pope Leo III in A.D. 800 as an attempt to re-create the Western Roman Empire, which had collapsed in A.D. 476—an event that led to the so-called Dark Ages.

   The first emperor of the Holy Roman Empire was Charlemagne. Although it persisted—at least in name—until 1806, the empire was always an unstable entity since it did not rest on any national foundation. Generally speaking, the Holy Roman Empire was a political union of many German-speaking states, including Austria, parts of Italy, and a number of principalities of central Europe. Although the empire was politically important for approximately four hundred years after its establishment, its influence in European political and religious development declined during and after the thirteenth century. In the middle of the seventeenth century, after the conclusion of the Thirty Years' War with its divisive religious conflicts between Catholics and Protestants, the Holy Roman Empire, for all practical purposes, ceased to exist in all but name. Its constituent states became virtually independent duchies, principalities, and "free cities." The Hapsburg rulers of Austria, however, who had since the thirteenth century held the title Holy Roman Emperor, continued the fiction of the empire's existence until Francis II, the last of the emperors, formally dissolved it on August 6, 1806, and instead proclaimed the Empire of Austria. Voltaire delivered what was probably the most telling assessment of the Holy Roman Empire when he declared that it was "neither Holy, nor Roman, nor an Empire."

2. Even the offspring of royalty died young. England's Queen Anne, who succeeded William III, gave birth sixteen times, but none of these potential heirs to the throne even lived to puberty.

Three: A Seaman's Lot

1. It was common practice in the days of sail for warships to take prizes and to sell the captured vessel and its cargo to interested merchants, and then divide the proceeds among the officers and men of the ship that had made the capture. In the Royal Navy, prize money was usually divided according to the following formula: The captain took three eighths of the total, with the officers dividing one eighth and the Admiralty receiving one eighth. The remaining three eighths would be shared among the crew members. Thus, unless a prize realized a great sum at sale, which happened very seldom since merchants were usually buying damaged goods at bargain prices, the share of each individual crewman would amount to relatively little, usually only a few pounds, but often only a handful of shillings. For example, if a prize fetched £1,600, which would be a relatively good price, the crew's share would amount to some £600 and would, depending on the size of the crew, fetch each sailor £2 or £3. It was a tidy sum, probably the equivalent of $400 to $600, but it was hardly equitable. Moreover, of such worth were rare. Only a few warships took prizes, and even when they did, prize money usually had to be shared among several ships, since men-of-war seldom acted alone.

   The Royal Navy formula for sharing prize money was also the formula generally followed by merchant vessels, including the vessels of the East India Company. Privateers, on the other hand, generally divided prize money into equal shares, with the captain or other officers receiving an additional amount, depending upon the agreement stipulated for the privateering voyage. Almost without exception, prize money realized by privateers was shared out in a generally fair manner, which was one of the circumstances that made privateering so attractive to the ordinary sailor.

2. Much of what we know about the buccaneers comes from a memoir written by one John Esquemeling who was probably a Fleming or a Hollander and who published a history of the buccaneers of America in Amsterdam in 1678. Esquemeling apparently arrived at the island of Tortuga in 1666 as an indentured servant and, after a number of misadventures, joined the buccaneers, remaining with them until 1672. Apparently Esquemeling served the buccaneers as a barber-surgeon and

was present at many of their exploits. His firsthand observations are generally considered the only truly authentic history of the buccaneers of the Spanish Main.

3. Although the buccaneer brotherhood was already past its glory days on the Spanish Main when King William's War broke out, French buccaneers continued to play an important part fighting for France during the war. Although described by French officials in the Caribbean as "refuse" and as "men without honor and without virtue," the French buccaneers were accorded special privileges by France and utilized in devastating raids against the old English buccaneer island of Jamaica. Although they never managed to take Jamaica for France, they caused immense damage and took much booty. The French buccaneers also participated in the capture and sack by a powerful French fleet of the heavily fortified Spanish port of Cartagena. Located on the coast of South America in what is now Colombia, Cartagena fell to the French and their buccaneer allies in June 1697. It was the last major victory of the buccaneers. In succeeding decades the French joined with the Spanish and the English in suppressing them.

English buccaneers, centered mainly in Jamaica during King William's War, played little part in the war, unlike their French counterparts. Some turned to outright piracy. A few settled down as planters on Jamaica, fiercely resisting French efforts to take Jamaica for France. Henry Morgan, the quintessential English buccaneer, had died in 1688 at the age of fifty-three, so bloated from drink that he could not move from his hammock. Perhaps, if he had lived, the English buccaneers of Jamaica would have played a more important role in King William's War. But this is doubtful, given the fact that Morgan's incessant drunkenness had caused him to be ousted not only as lieutenant governor but also from the governing council of Jamaica.

Another event that did much to cripple the fighting capacities of the English buccaneers was the catastrophic earthquake that struck Port Royal, Jamaica's main town, in June 1692. The quake leveled a third of Port Royal and dumped it into the sea. More than two thousand of the town's inhabitants were killed. Some said the quake was God's judgment upon the wicked buccaneers.

Four: The Very Model of a Pirate Villain

1. Bristol, England's second-largest city at the time, was the home port for most of Britain's slave ships. In the late seventeenth century it was also the prime territory for recruiting sailors for privateer missions. The thinking was that men hardened by the slave trade would make excellent privateers. Many of the toughest pirates ever to sail under the black flag called Bristol their home.

Five: The Outlaw Nation

1. The origin of the term "Jolly Roger" as the name for the pirate flag is obscure, although there are at least two possibilities. The first holds that French buccaneers, with Gallic irony, called their blood-red flag *joli rouge,* meaning, roughly, "pretty red." Untutored English sailors corrupted this to "Jolly Roger," and the name was later applied to the black flag. This seems a very likely explanation, since English sailors were responsible for other similar corruptions, such as turning the Dutch word *vrijbuiter,* meaning "plunderer," into "freebooter."

   A second theory about the origin of the Jolly Roger also involves the English sailors' propensity for mispronouncing foreign words. According to this version, Muslim pirates operating in the area of Indonesia often gave themselves the Tamil title Ali Raja meaning "King of the Sea." These eastern pirates also flew a red flag, and it is easy to imagine English sailors supposing, in error, that the term "Ali Raja" referred to the flag—and then further corrupting the term to something like "Olly Roger," which then easily becomes "Jolly Roger."

   Another explanation begins with the fact that in the late seventeenth and early eighteenth centuries, the Devil was often called by the slang term "Old Roger." According to this explanation, pirates simply adopted the slang term for their flag.

Six: The Rage of Rich Men Balked

1. In fact, the competition between the two companies proved ruinous to both of them, and after only four years of head-to-head competition, the two companies began to cooperate in

1694—in effect restoring the monopoly that had existed for almost one hundred years. Although for an additional fifteen years the two companies continued to maintain the fiction that they were separate competitors, in reality they were one enterprise. But it was not until 1709 that they formally amalgamated under the name The United Company of Merchants of England Trading to the East Indies.

2. Oddly enough, one of the most important figures in the company's history was an American who entered the company's employ about this time. He later became governor of Madras and amassed an immense fortune in India, returning to his home in Connecticut to endow the university named after him. He was Elihu Yale.

3. These native pirates, called the Malabar Coast pirates, were every bit as vicious and in many ways even more successful than the European pirates who came to Indian waters in these years. Under the leadership of one Kanhoji Angria, the Malabar Coast pirates terrorized the waters off India, taking not only Mogul ships but East India Company ships as well. Aurangzeb and his successors failed completely to root out Angria and his cohorts. By 1715 Angria had under his command a total of twenty-six coastal forts in the area south of Bombay. Under the guns of these sanctuaries, Angria's fleets could find protection after pirating voyages far out into the Indian Ocean. Angria died in 1729 and his five sons quarreled among themselves for leadership of his pirate kingdom. In 1743 one of the sons, Tulaji, finally gained control of the pirate dominion established by his father. Under Tulaji's leadership the Malabar Coast pirates grew stronger than ever. Then the British government, finally fed up with the depredations of these native brigands, sent a Royal Navy squadron to put an end to them. In April 1755 four British warships under Commodore William James began a two-day bombardment of the pirates' main stronghold. The pirates held out until a powder magazine inside the fortress blew up; then Tulaji and his men abandoned it. Subsequently Commodore James bombarded other pirate forts into submission. Tulaji himself was captured in February 1756 by a second English squadron operating in the area, and with him the reign of the Malabar Coast pirates came to an end.

---

4. Before the East India Company is blamed too much for a shortsighted niggardly attitude in arming and crewing its ships, it should be remembered that the company was caught in a double bind. If it made no profit, it would soon cease to exist. In order to maintain profits in the face of competition from rivals, it had to keep costs down and tonnage of cargoes up. Company officials certainly knew that they were risking both ship and cargo by underarming and undercrewing their vessels. But they also knew that the chances were better than fifty-fifty that an underarmed and undercrewed East Indiaman would get through and make a big profit, while the chances were absolutely 100 percent that a properly armed and properly crewed vessel would *lose* money. The only sensible course open to the company was to take the fifty-fifty bet and continue to operate its ships with too little armament and too few crewmen.

5. Not *all* stories of pirate cruelty and punishments were true, however. For example, there is absolutely no record of pirates forcing anyone to "walk the plank." This pirate punishment, like such pirate lore as the "black spot" and buried treasure, is largely the invention of fiction writers of the nineteenth century.

6. Another peculiar tactic employed by pirates to create terror was the creation of a cacophony, by beating on drums and cymbals, when a pirate ship neared its victim. Apparently many pirates believed that by setting up a horrible din, they would make themselves seem like madmen to their victims, who would then more readily surrender. It is not clear whether this tactic actually struck terror into pirate victims or merely confused them. It seems highly unlikely that sensible people would more *readily* surrender themselves to madmen than to rational beings.

7. Perhaps it was no more than the bitter gossip of men who feared for their fortunes, but a number of investors in the East India Company believed that the *real* reason a Royal Navy force was not sent to Madagascar was because William of Orange, now King William III of England, had no love for the East India Company. As a Dutchman, William, prior to his becoming king, must have resented the East India Company's private wars with Dutch merchant companies. As the Parlia-

ment's chosen ruler, William must also have harbored suspicions about the company's close ties with the deposed Stuarts. Further, it was William who had affixed his royal signature to the license of the competitive English East India Company voted into existence by Parliament in 1688. Whatever the reality may have been, the Royal Navy was not sent eastward to Madagascar.

Seven: On the Account

1. The term "on the account" as a euphemism for piracy traces back to the early seventeenth century when crewmen aboard merchant ships were sometimes allowed to bring small amounts of freight or cargo on a voyage to trade "on their own account" at the ports visited by the vessel. The custom was not apparently very widespread since only a few seamen could afford to do this. It was, however, often a poor sailor's ambition to accumulate enough cash to buy trade goods for his own account. Later in the century, when every inch of cargo space was extremely valuable, the custom of allowing individual sailors to trade privately was gradually discontinued. But the term "on the account" remained in usage, transformed by the rough humor of sailors into a euphemism for piracy.

2. The chances of a pirate's being caught were probably about as great as the chances of any other criminal's being caught; that is, the longer a pirate kept at it, the more likely the law was to catch up with him. There are instances of pirates "retiring" after making a big score, but most of them—even if they did score big—stayed in the life or around its fringes because the life itself was what attracted them. Many, when they grew too old for the life, or too infirm, retired by accepting pardons that were periodically offered by governments more intent on halting the sweet trade than on hanging sailors. Nevertheless, the record is clear that pirates who went pirating too long, or who—like Henry Every's men—tried to return to a society where the law was strong and vindictive, usually ended up paying the price for their crimes. It is also important in this connection to make the point that although the noble concept of individual liberty was the lure that drew men to piracy, the desire for freedom does not by itself make men noble, nor does it excuse crimes. Pirates wanted to live free, but they also

often behaved abominably, and they frequently committed terrible crimes to maintain their freedom. To be motivated by a noble concept is not necessarily ennobling, as history makes plain over and over again.

3. It is interesting to note that although boys were common aboard pirate ships, some ships—most notably Bartholomew Roberts's vessels—specifically excluded them, as they did women. It is possible to infer from this fact that for the strait-laced Roberts at least, boys aboard ship could cause as much trouble as women—and perhaps for the same reason.

4. For all their barbaric cruelty, however, pirates could be capriciously generous to those they liked. They often made magnificent gifts to the whores who eased their nights. Old shipmates and comrades, especially if they had fallen upon hard days, were often the objects of their generosity. Many pirate ships included in their crews men who had lost an eye or a limb in previous service, whose usefulness to the ship was now doubtful at best but who were kept on at a full or half share out of affection and remembrance of past services.

5. Loss of an arm was always worth more in compensation than the loss of a leg—and the loss of the *right* arm or leg was worth more than the loss of either left limb. Curiously, the loss of an eye ranked only with the loss of a finger. Generally speaking, pirates compensated the loss of a left leg with 400 pieces of eight, while a right leg was worth 500. The loss of a left arm was worth 500 pieces of eight, while a right arm was worth 600. The loss of an eye earned the wounded man only 100 pieces of eight. Compensation for total loss of sight was usually decided by a special vote. The amounts paid for wounds of all kinds, however, varied greatly from crew to crew.

Eight: The Trusty and Well-beloved Captain

1. There were a number of reasons why Bellomont's backers might have wanted to keep their names out of the business. First, as parliamentary grandees not particularly friendly to the East India Company, they might have been reluctant to have their names associated with an effort that could be construed as bailing out the company. Second, and far more likely,

as close associates of the king, they might have wished to shield the sovereign from any embarrassment should the enterprise go wrong in any way. Third, and the most likely of all, there was a whiff of "something not quite right" about the whole idea of profiting by plundering the plunder of pirates. Seizing pirate loot might be judged in some quarters as just another form of piracy or, at the very least, an unsavory game for lords of the realm to be playing. It is worth noting in this regard that although the king had originally stated his willingness to buy a share in a pirate-killer privateering venture, in the end he did not participate. Perhaps, upon reflection, he did not consider it suitable. More probably he was away in Flanders prosecuting his war at the time Bellomont was forming his syndicate.

2. According to tradition, Kidd was the son of a Calvinist minister, the Reverend John Kidd, of Greenock, Scotland. Yet there is no record of a minister by that name serving in Greenock around the year 1645 when, according to informed conjecture, William Kidd was born. In reality, the records tell nothing about Kidd's birth or his parents. The only incontrovertible fact about Kidd's origin is that he was a Scot, a fact no doubt deduced from his accent. Even Kidd's birth date is open to some question, although the year 1645 seems about right since, at the time of his death in 1701, the chaplain of Newgate Prison, where Kidd spent his last days, reported his age as "about 56 years."

3. Kidd himself also owned some real estate that would now be among the most valuable in the world. He owned several lots on what is now Wall Street in the heart of the New York financial district. He also owned property on Water Street and on Pine Street, all occupied today by Manhattan skyscrapers.

4. One of these honest men was Kidd's brother-in-law, Samuel Bradley, who had been with him throughout the cruise. Unfortunately, Bradley had not been of much help to Kidd since he had been ill for more than fifteen months—of the mysterious malady that had killed fifty of Kidd's crew at Mohéli in the Comoros during *Adventure Galley*'s initial foray into Indian Ocean waters.

Nine: A Voyage to Wapping

1. Although not yet formal parties, the terms *Whig* and *Tory* described divisions that already existed in Parliament—and which would lead to the emergence of party government. Basically the Whigs were regarded as liberal, tolerant of religions other than the established Church of England, committed to parliamentary government, and—usually—supporters of King William and his war against Louis XIV. Tories, on the other hand, were generally considered more conservative, more likely to defend "Divine Right" and royal prerogatives. Generally speaking, if they did not openly oppose William and his war, they were not enthusiastic—and they hated the Dutch courtiers William had brought with him from Holland to serve as his aides in his strange new realm of England. Tories were also strong supporters of the established Church of England. The actual names Whig and Tory were unflattering terms that each emergent party had pinned on the other. *Whig* was a term meaning a Scottish outlaw, while *Tory* meant an Irish robber. King William tried to stand apart from the parliamentary wrangling between Whigs and Tories, saying that the only difference he could discern between the two parties was that "the Tories would cut your throat in the morning, the Whigs in the afternoon." Kidd, unfortunately for him, was victimized by a particularly ugly eruption of the new party feeling in Parliament. It is interesting to speculate whether Kidd's cruise would have become a political scandal, and Kidd himself a wanted man, if King William had invested in the enterprise—as he had originally intended.

2. All the Whig grandees impeached by Parliament were acquitted. Under the parliamentary procedure of the time, the House of Commons had the task of bringing charges of impeachment, while the Lords later passed on their validity. In this case the impeachment charges were judged by many to be merely political, and the charges were not even placed before the House of Lords.

3. The judge was alluding to an incident that took place after the battle that Kidd and *Adventure Galley* had with the Portuguese warship. As a result of that gun duel, *Adventure Galley* had suffered some serious damage and eleven of Kidd's

men had been wounded. Kidd had then taken his ship south to the Maldives for repair. While he was refitting, unfriendly natives had attacked him and his crew, killing the ship's cooper. Kidd had retaliated by shooting one of the natives and by burning their huts.

4. Only one of the six men convicted with Kidd actually went to the hangman. The others were reprieved, and eventually released.

The Crown's star witnesses, Bradinham and Palmer, received what they had been promised in exchange for their testimony against Kidd: full pardons. Kidd's little family felt the shame of his fate deeply. They hid away in their New York home for months after the captain's execution. But the lively and beautiful Sarah was not one to sit for long alone in a room. Approximately eighteen months after Kidd was hanged at Wapping, Sarah plighted her troth to a New Jersey politician and lived many more years of comfortable and productive life. She died in 1746. Kidd's two daughters also recovered soon enough from their shame, and both of them made good marriages and raised families of their own.

5. It is not likely that Kidd's fate would have been very different even if he had managed to find the French passes and to have them introduced into evidence. There were too many other circumstances against him, from the testimony of Palmer and Bradinham to his own admission that he had violated Admiralty codes by distributing booty among his men and by taking Moorish and Portuguese ships—which were not, after all, covered by French passes. There is absolutely no reason to suspect deliberate attempt to deprive Kidd of this "evidence," which he was so sure would save him. The French passes simply got lost in the bureaucratic shuffle, for—much too late to do Kidd any good—they were eventually located in the Public Records Office. As for Kidd's treasure, it seems beyond question that Lord Bellomont recovered all that was recoverable and shipped it off to London while Kidd was still in colonial custody. Despite all the later stories about Kidd's having buried treasure in various places, the reality seems to be that any goods that might have been left aboard the *Quedah Merchant* were sold by her "guards" and that the rest of Kidd's treasure was quickly found and confiscated. Following Kidd's death, his

booty—gold, silver, jewels, and silks, forwarded to London by Bellomont—was sold at auction for approximately £6,500. The proceeds were turned over to the Crown. Part of the money was used to buy a house that is now part of the National Maritime Museum at Greenwich.

6. One of the most ironic sidelights to Kidd's story is the career of Robert Culliford, the pirate captain with whom Kidd had sworn a pact of friendship in Madagascar. After Culliford sailed away from St. Mary's harbor in *Mocha Frigate,* taking with him most of Kidd's crew and the guns from *Adventure Galley,* he resumed his piratical career, sailing in company with other pirate vessels off the coast of India. Concentrating his attentions on Moorish ships, Culliford gained a reputation for cruelty and barbarity in the treatment of captives. He eventually returned to St. Mary's and was there in 1699 when he accepted one of the pardons periodically offered to pirates by the Admiralty. This turned out to be a serious mistake on his part, for the act of grace had already expired when he accepted it.

Eventually Culliford and a number of others who had also mistakenly accepted the pardons were brought to London for trial. Though they argued that they had only surrendered in the belief that they would be pardoned, the court found them all guilty. In a supreme irony, Culliford was tried and convicted at the Old Bailey on the same day that Kidd was. But Culliford, unlike Kidd, never made the journey to Wapping. The wily pirate had apparently convinced a high-ranking churchman that he was worth saving, and he was released after a year's imprisonment. Apparently he learned from his experience and did not return to piracy.

Ten: Counterstroke and Intermission

1. By the time Bellomont initiated his campaign against colonial pirate brokers, Baldridge had already left Madagascar, toppled from his throne by a native revolt. His fall from power was precipitated, apparently, when Baldridge attempted to pull one slick slave trade too many. Although the details are not clear, it appears that Baldridge had unwisely attempted to sell to slave traders some young native women and men who happened to be related to a powerful local chief. The chief took umbrage at Baldridge's unfriendly act and attacked him in suf-

ficient numbers to force the canny trader to flee forever from his palatial home on St. Mary's. Baldridge, however, always knew where his bread would be buttered. He therefore made his way to New York where, in 1698, he was able to witness Bellomont's suppression of the trade from which he had profited so handsomely and for so long. It is said that Baldridge became a successful merchant in New York, lived well into his seventies, and died comfortably in bed.

As for Philipse, despite the loss of his ships to Bellomont's coast guards, he remained one of New York's wealthiest men. He also remained a pillar of the community. When he died in 1702 on his 90,000-acre estate overlooking the Hudson River, he still refused to admit that there was anything immoral or unlawful about his role in the sweet trade.

2. Lord Bellomont himself did not live to enjoy the triumph of his policies. He died in February 1701. Wrote his widow of his death: "He wore out his spirits, and put an end to his life by the fatigue he underwent to serve his Majesty." Bellomont's death came five years and six months after his first meeting with Kidd in London—and three months *before* Kidd himself went to the gallows in Wapping. It is not known whether the captain knew of his aristocratic backer's passing.

Twelve: Nemesis of Pirates

1. Dampier was one of the most improbable seafaring figures of the late seventeenth and early eighteenth centuries. According to his own account, he had served with the buccaneers of Jamaica in the late 1670s, after which he crossed the Isthmus of Panama (on foot, of course) to the Pacific. From there his adventures had taken him on a twelve-year odyssey around the world. He kept extensive notes of his journeys, bringing them home safely in bamboo cases that had been waxed to seal them against rain and humidity. He wrote two books about his adventures: *A New Voyage Round the World*, which appeared in 1697, and *Voyages and Discoveries*, which appeared in 1699. Both books were much admired. Later Dampier explored the west coast of Australia. In 1703, after the outbreak of the War of the Spanish Succession, he joined a privateering expedition and circumnavigated the world for a second time—the only man of his time ever to have done so. In the first decade of the

eighteenth century no man in the English-speaking world knew as much about the Pacific, its winds and its currents, as Dampier did. So valuable was his knowledge that the Royal Navy had given him a command, despite the fact that he was not, strictly speaking, a "gentleman." He was later relieved by the Admiralty for quarreling with his officers. This was hardly surprising. Dampier, who could be infuriatingly sulky at one moment and explosively wrathful at the next, was not a man to get along in the bureaucratic and snobbish Royal Navy of the day. But he seems to have gotten along well with Woodes Rogers—or at least well enough to avoid any overt break in their relationship. Rogers, in fact, may have been the perfect complement to Dampier: calm where Dampier was choleric, determined where Dampier was sometimes despairing. In any case, they worked well together and Dampier's knowledge of the Pacific proved invaluable on the voyage.

2. Although there is no doubt that Alexander Selkirk was the model for Defoe's "Robinson Crusoe," Selkirk himself profited little from the book. According to William Mavor's *Historical Account of the Most Celebrated Voyages, Travels, and Discoveries,* published in 1796, Selkirk was advised, upon his return to England, to consult Daniel Defoe in order to arrange for publication of his story. This Selkirk did, turning over to Defoe written notes of his years as a castaway. But instead of writing a book about Selkirk, Defoe converted Selkirk's rough material into the fictional *Robinson Crusoe,* published in 1720 and a great success. Selkirk was thus deprived of the remuneration he might have realized if his story had been published as his memoirs.

Selkirk's life in England, after so many years as a castaway, took several odd turns. He went back to his home village of Largo and dug a cave in the garden in back of his father's little house. Here he sat for long hours and even for days, deep in solitude and meditation. If the people of Largo thought Selkirk mad, at least one young woman did not share their opinion. She was Sophia Bonce and *she* found Selkirk fascinating. She often visited him in his cave where the two would spend long hours together in conversation and, apparently, in other even more pleasant activities. Eventually Selkirk and Sophia eloped to Bristol, where they lived together, although—to the scandal of Largo—they were not married. In time Selkirk abandoned Sophia and married a widow, a certain Mrs. Frances Candis. But he apparently found life ashore, even with the willing widow, too busy, or too boring, or perhaps just too civilized, after the quiet of Juan Fernandez. In any case, Selkirk returned to the sea in 1720—the year of *Robinson Crusoe*'s publication—and served as mate aboard the Royal Navy man-of-war *Weymouth*.

He died aboard the *Weymouth* in 1721. He was only forty-five.

Thirteen: Blackbeard Himself

1. Blackbeard's relationship with Stede Bonnet remains a curious puzzle. The flamboyant Teach seems to have harbored a peculiarly ambivalent feeling for the gentleman pirate. Although it is clear that he despised the ex-major, he treated him with a civility that was far from characteristic. Instead of disposing of Bonnet at their first meeting, Blackbeard carried him with him for months, and even propounded the fiction that Bonnet was a colleague, not a prisoner. Blackbeard also seems to have been in the habit of addressing Bonnet with an odd mixture of rough courtesy and sarcasm. There are, perhaps, several explanations for Blackbeard's atypical behavior with Bonnet. It may be that the bumbling major simply tickled Blackbeard's unsubtle sense of humor, and that it amused the evil giant to treat Bonnet with exaggerated courtesy. It is also possible that in Blackbeard's devious mind, Bonnet, as a gentleman, represented a potential payday, that Blackbeard kept him alive and relatively happy in the expectation that one day he might offer Bonnet for ransom to Bonnet's wealthy Barbadian family. If so, Blackbeard gave up on that scheme when he severed his relationship with Bonnet. It is also possible that, as a gentleman, Bonnet elicited some residual respect from Blackbeard, or by his presence in Blackbeard's fleet, imparted some respectability to the giant's piratical enterprise. Whatever the explanation, Blackbeard kept it to himself. Perhaps he was not quite clear in his own mind why he showed such consideration for the major. It was, however, as much a puzzle then as it is now.

2. Because of his lameness, Hands left Blackbeard's employ, eventually getting back to London where, according to Defoe,

he became a well-known beggar and, of course, the model for the evil gunner in *Treasure Island*.

3. Unlike most colonial governors of this era, Spotswood did not return to England when his term ended in September 1722. Instead, he remained in Virginia, making his home in Germanna, a settlement of Germans. He also established an ironworks in the area. From 1730 to 1739, Spotswood served as deputy postmaster general of the colony. Spotsylvania County is named in his honor and was later the scene of a bloody battle during the Civil War. Spotswood died in 1740 at the age of sixty-four.

4. All the pirates captured by Maynard aboard the *Adventure* were hanged, including Caesar. Although Maynard found an incriminating letter from Tobias Knight among Blackbeard's papers, and although Governor Spotswood reported the details of Blackbeard's capture and his relationship with the officials of North Carolina to the Board of Trade in London, neither Governor Eden nor Tobias Knight was ever convicted of collusion with the pirate. Both remained in office. Governor Eden, however, died of yellow fever three years after his friend Blackbeard was killed in battle. The reward money for the capture of Blackbeard and his men was a source of disagreement for years. The captains of the two Royal Navy men-of-war, H.M.S. *Pearl* and H.M.S. *Lyme,* argued that the reward should be shared out equally among all the crewmen of both ships. Lieutenant Maynard, on the other hand, maintained that only those who had actually participated in the battle should share in the reward. In the end a reduced reward (reduced because Blackbeard and many of his men had not been taken alive) was shared out among all the navy personnel with those who had actually fought getting a slightly larger share than those to who had remained behind. As finally determined, each combat share came to something less than £2 per man. There is some strong evidence that Lieutenant Maynard either resigned or retired from the Royal Navy in order to settle down in Prince George County, Virginia. The records there indicate that a *Captain* Maynard was murdered in that county by two black slaves in the late 1720s.

Fourteen: Rogers at Bay

1. The eight backsliders were not the only men Rogers hanged in that December of 1718. He also tried and condemned a man, apparently an ex-pirate, for "robbing and burning a house." In reporting *this* capital action to London, Rogers wrote: "If for want of lawyers our forms are something deficient, I am fully satisfied we have not erred in justice." It was a most characteristic remark.

Sixteen: King of Madagascar

1. John Plantain was undoubtedly the most successful pirate "king" in Madagascar. But he was not the *first*. There was, of course, the trader prince Adam Baldridge, who built a fort and settlement in St. Mary's, and who had made himself the virtual ruler of his island in the 1690s. There had also been successful leaders of settlements of ex-pirates who had used their European knowledge and their European weapons to establish rough sovereignty over the natives in their neighborhoods. Many of these leaders gave themselves the title of king.

   One of the most successful of these pirate kings of Madagascar—prior to Plantain—had been one Abraham Samuells, a Jamaican mulatto. Samuell's story began when the pirate ship he was serving on was wrecked off Port Dauphin and he was washed ashore. He was taken in and well treated by the natives. Then the old chieftainess of the tribe became convinced that Samuells was her long-lost son whom she had borne twenty-five years earlier as a result of a love affair with an English sea captain stranded on Madagascar. When the captain was rescued, he had taken the mulatto boy child with him. Now, in Abraham Samuells, the chieftainess "recognized" her son, providentially restored to her by God. She immediately abdicated her throne, and the shipwrecked Abraham Samuells became king of the tribe. For the next ten or twelve years, Samuells led his tribe in a gruesome business: Sighting ships out at sea, they would lure them onto the rocks and then loot the wreckage. Samuells's fate is unknown but it is thought that he was killed in a revolt by members of his tribe, or by European pirates whom he had befriended and made colleagues in his enterprise.

Most ex-pirate settlers on Madagascar, however, did not seek to rule, but only to live in ease and in peace among the natives. Most of them found contentment.

But not all white men who lived in Madagascar during these years were either powerful or at peace. A few apparently lived in misery. One of these unfortunates was an Englishman named Robert Drury who was wrecked off the southern coast of Madagascar in April 1703, when he was only fourteen, and spent the next thirteen years as a slave to native princes. According to a journal that he published after he finally returned to England in 1717, Drury was sold from one black ruler to another, and he learned to speak the language of the Madagascar natives. He recounts how he was made to go on war parties and cattle raids with his native owners, and forced to follow such Madagascar slave practices as licking the soles of his masters' feet. Drury also paints a vivid picture of the lives of European pirates who had settled on Madagascar. One of them, a Dutchman, John Pro, he says lived in "a very handsome manner. . . and owned many cattle and slaves." Drury was finally rescued when—according to his story—his father in London learned from a slaver who had just returned from Madagascar that his son was still alive on the island. The father then sent the captain of a slaving ship, the *Drake*, to rescue young Drury. Before returning home, Drury helped his benefactor—the captain of the *Drake*—to obtain slaves from the local chieftain.

Drury did not tarry long in England. He was soon back in Madagascar, this time as a respected slave trader. Although he claims he became wealthy in the slave trade, he ended up a poor man, cadging drinks in taverns in exchange for stories of his life and adventures as a captive in Madagascar.

But Drury's experience on Madagascar—if his story is true—was exceptional. Most white men flourished on the island.

Seventeen: Where White Men Die

1. The reports, of course, proved to be true. In fact, so pure and so distinctive was the gold obtained along the Guinea Coast that when the English made a coin from it, the coin was called a "guinea."

Eighteen: The Black Captain

1. There is some indication that the idea of referring to themselves as the House of Lords actually began when the crew was still under the command of Howell Davis. If so, however, it was then only a desultory practice. Under Roberts the practice of referring to the crew as the House of Lords and of each crew member prefacing his name with the title Lord—as in Lord Sympson and Lord Ashplant, to name just two—became a regular practice, an integral part of the ship's life. Later, as Roberts's crew grew more numerous, the original members of the House of Lords seem to have jealously limited membership in their club.

2. Roberts designed his own personal black flag apparently to express his special hatred for the people of Barbados and Martinique. It showed a figure, seemingly intended to represent Roberts himself, carrying a cutlass in his right hand and standing with each foot on a skull. Beneath one skull were the initials "A B H," meaning "A Barbadian's Head." Under the other skull were the initials "A M H," standing for "A Martinican's Head." It may be that Roberts's flag was not meant to express hatred of the people of those islands so much as contempt for the efforts of their governors to catch him. It is true, however, that Roberts was often more cruel to prisoners from Martinique than any others. The governor of Bermuda wrote home that Martinican prisoners taken by Roberts were "barbarously abused, some were almost whipped to death, others had their ears cut off." It is entirely possible, too, that Roberts was by now half mad with self-hatred.

Twenty: Saga's End

1. As governor of a peaceful Bahamas colony, Rogers never did succeed in turning his island into the self-sufficient concern he had always envisioned. Although he worked hard to found a "plantation colony" that would produce cotton and sugar for export, the poor soil never yielded crops sufficient to create such an economy. Rogers died in 1732. He was fifty-four years old.

Bibliography

Allen, Gardner W. *Our Navy and the West Indian Pirates*. Salem, Mass.: The Essex Institute, 1929.

Ashley, Maurice. *The Golden Century*. New York: Praeger, 1969.

Baldwin, Robert. *The Tryals of Captain John Rackam, and Other Pirates*. Robert Baldwin, 1721.

Botting, Douglas. *The Pirates*. Alexandria, Va.: Time-Life Books, 1978.

Bradlee, Francis B. C. *Piracy in the West Indies and Its Suppression*. Salem, Mass.: The Essex Institute, 1923.

Braudel, Fernand. *The Structures of Everyday Life*. New York: Harper & Row, 1982.

Brooks, Graham, ed. *Trial of Captain Kidd*. London: William Hodge and Company, Ltd., 1930.

Brown, Henry Collins. *The Story of Old New York*. New York: E. P. Dutton, 1934.

Carse, Robert. *The Age of Piracy*. New York: Rinehart & Company, 1957.

Craton, Michael. *A History of the Bahamas*. New York: Collins, 1962.

Davis, Ralph. *The Rise of the English Shipping Industry in the Seventeenth and Eighteenth Centuries*. New York: St. Martin's Press, 1963.

Defoe, Daniel. *A General History of the Pyrates*. Edited by Manuel Schonhorn. Columbia, S.C.: University of South Carolina Press, 1972.

Drury, Robert. *Madagascar; Or, Robert Drury's Journal*. Westport, Conn.: Negro Universities Press, 1969 (reprint of 1890 edition).

Esquemeling, John. *The Pirates of Panama*. New York: Dover, 1967.

Gardner, Brian. *The East India Company: A History*. New York: Saturday Review Press, 1972.

Gosse, Philip. *The History of Piracy*. New York: Burt Franklin, 1968.

———— *The Pirates Who's Who*. New York: Burt Franklin, 1968.

Green, John Richard . *Short History of the English People*. 2 vol. New York: Dutton, 1951.

Grey, Charles. *Pirates of the Eastern Seas*. London: Kennikat Press, 1933.

Hurd, Archibald. *The Reign of the Pirates*. New York: Alfred A. Knopf, 1925.

Karraker, Cyrus H. *Piracy Was a Business*. Peterborough, N.H.: Bauhan, 1953.

Mahan, Alfred Thayer. *The Influence of Sea Power Upon History—1660–1783*. New York: Hill & Wang, 1968.

Mannix, Daniel P., and Crowley, Malcolm. *Black Cargoes: A History of the Atlantic Slave Trade*, 1518–1865. New York: Viking Press, 1962.

Massie, Robert K. *Peter the Great*. New York: Ballantine Books, 1981.

Mitchell, David. *Pirates*. New York: Dial Press, 1976.

Newark, Peter. *The Crimson Book of Pirates*. London: Jupiter Books, 1978.

Pringle, Patrick. *Jolly Roger*. New York: Norton, 1953.

Rankin, Hugh F. *The Golden Age of Piracy*. New York: Holt, Rinehart & Winston, 1969.

Rogers, Woodes. *A Cruising Voyage Round the World*. Magnolia, Mass.: Peter Smith (reprint of 1712 edition).

Snelgrave, Captain William. *A New Account of Some Parts of Guinea and the Slave-Trade*. Portland, Ore.: International Scholarly Book Service, 1972 (reprint of 1734 edition).

Wells, H. G. *The Outline of History*. New York: Doubleday, 1971.

Winston, Alexander. *No Man Knows My Grave*. New York: Houghton-Mifflin, 1969.

Woodbury, George. *The Great Days of Piracy in the West Indies*. New York: Norton, 1951.

Index